CW01370297

Facebook

Spotify

QUANTUM CAPITALIST

A special thanks to Shannon Conway, Shannan Sinclair, Chris Majeski, my ITI admins and moderators, Xavier Waterkeyn, Andrew Magic, Matthew McMillion, Katelyn Cyfers, Amber LaValley and everyone who has believed in me throughout this journey.

An extra special, magical thanks to Suzy Rowlands and Vadim Zeland.

This book is dedicated to my grandma and the generations before me. May our souls now fly in tandem as I venture through The Quantum Field.

Contents

Introduction VIII
Foreword by Chris Majeski XII
How to Engage with This Revolutionary Guide XXIV
About Me XXVII

PHASE I: MATRIX OBSERVANT

Lesson 1: The Matrix 31
Lesson 2: Playing vs. Being Played 39
Lesson 3: The Quantum Field 46
Lesson 4: Reclaiming Your Magic 51
Lesson 5: What Is a Quantum Capitalist? 55
Lesson 6: Conformity Can Go Suck It 61
Lesson 7: Sectors of Reality 66
Lesson 8: Game-Changer 72
Lesson 9: Designing A New Guiding Theory 78
Lesson 10: Supercharging with the 4 Qualifiers 85
Lesson 11: Blackholes 91
Lesson 12: Cutting Matrix Puppet Strings 99
Lesson 13: Importance - Sector Super Poison 105
Lesson 14: Why We Generate Importance 115
Lesson 15: Creating Chaos With Disproportionate Energy 125
Lesson 16: The Energetic Nosedive 132
Lesson 17: Importance Pandemic 139
Lesson 18: A Band-Aid for Now 143
Lesson 19: The Downward Spiral 149
Lesson 20: Trauma Triggers 155
Lesson 21: The Upward Spiral 160

Lesson 22: The Cosmic Comet of Fortune 166
Lesson 23: The Quantum Flow 172
Lesson 24: The Anti-Flow 179
Lesson 25: Guiding Signs 185
Lesson 26: Internal Guiding Signs 189
Lesson 27: The Recalibration 194

PHASE II: QUANTUM YOU

Lesson 28: Mirror | rorriM 200
Lesson 29: Your Algorithm 206
Lesson 30: Boomerang 212
Lesson 31: Blackhole Slingshot 218
Lesson 32: Inner Force 225
Lesson 33: Outer Power 230
Lesson 34: Harnessing and Leveraging 235
Lesson 35: Quantum Dance 241
Lesson 36: Face-Off 246
Lesson 37: The Purge 256
Lesson 38: Your Real Dream 262
Lesson 39: Soul Code 268
Lesson 40: Unleashing 277
Lesson 41: Heart and Mind Synchronization 282
Lesson 42: Quantum GPS 290
Lesson 43: There's a Better Way 296
Lesson 44: Spotlight 303
Lesson 45: Raiding the Vault 309
Lesson 46: Hard Money Truths 314
Lesson 47: Dreams Are Your Unlived Realities 322
Lesson 48: Sleep Spell 328
Lesson 49: Waking Up 332
Lesson 50: Reality Flip 341
Lesson 51: Turbo Allowing 346
Lesson 52: Cognitive Dissonance 352

Contents

Lesson 53: Hyperspace Odyssey 357

PHASE III: THE EXPLORER

Lesson 54: YOUR Project 361
Lesson 55: Leveling Up 367
Lesson 56: Mindfilm Mastery 373
Lesson 57: SectorSyncing 378
Lesson 58: The Negative Mindfilm 384
Lesson 59: Transport Links 391
Lesson 60: Triple-Threat You 397
Lesson 61: The Labyrinth 403
Lesson 62: Navigating NPCs (Non-Playing Characters) & Narcissists 409
Lesson 63: Stealth Mode 414
Lesson 64: Cracks in The Matrix 420
Lesson 65: Candy Bridges 427
Lesson 66: Magic and Miracles 432
Lesson 67: Turning Lead Into Gold 436
Lesson 68: Chaos Theory & Quantum Disturbances 443
Lesson 69: Magical Middle World 449
Lesson 70: Superskill 457
Lesson 71: Ending the Battle 464
Lesson 72: Dividing Your Time 469
Lesson 73: Anomalous Action Ascension 476
Lesson 74: Human Ego Sacrifice 483
Lesson 75: Monkey Brain, Rice Desires & Coconut Conundrums 488
Lesson 76: Trust 494
Lesson 77: Sovereign Self 499
I Decree the Quantum Me 503

The Extras 507
Glossary 532

Introduction

Reality often seems cruel, doesn't it? All too frequently, we find ourselves at a crossroads, compelled to exchange something invaluable—our time, our integrity—for the allure of power or the necessity of money.

You sense it, right? That unsettling discord when the world demands you prioritize profit above all else. That internal whisper questioning if this is all life has to offer—a deep yearning for more, for a balance between wealth and enlightenment.

Welcome to Quantum Capitalism. It's not just a theory, but a promise—a conduit between material accomplishment and spiritual awakening. It respects the essence of our conventional systems but also dares to imagine beyond them. Quantum Capitalism awaits those prepared to confront some uncomfortable truths and adopt a radically new viewpoint. Are you among the chosen?

Let's unpack this:

Quantum Mechanics: at its heart, quantum mechanics delves into the intriguing, often paradoxical, world of the subatomic. It suggests that particles, such as electrons and photons, linger in a probabilistic state—simultaneously existing in various locations—until directly observed. This intricate dance between potentiality and reality upends our customary perceptions. While our physical world adheres to classical physics, the quantum realm narrates a different story—one where particles exhibit mysterious entanglements across vast expanses, reality can shift almost magically, and the mere act of observation influences the narrative. Essentially, quantum mechanics portrays a Universe that's profoundly interconnected, and more pliable than our day-to-day experiences indicate.

Classical Capitalism: this is the well-known framework wherein trade and industry pivot to private ambitions, predominantly for profit. While capitalism has undeniably catalyzed societal advancement and ignited dreams, it's not without its shadows. Despite its merits, capitalism can evolve into a voracious entity, spawning passive, zombified followers, imposing stifling conventions, and endorsing exploitation. The aftermath? A pervasive culture of scarcity, unbridled ego-driven objectives, and an ever-widening chasm from our spiritual roots.

Ever watched "The Matrix"? It portrayed reality as a contrived illusion, with only a chosen few breaking free to perceive the vastness beyond. This reality, as insinuated by the movie, stretches beyond the confines of our conditioned mindsets. Quantum mechanics supports this view, shedding light on the deeper layers of our existence.

Anchored in quantum tenets, the knowledge in front of you presents a daring promise: you can achieve prosperity, indulge in comfort, and guarantee security without falling prey to the intrinsic drawbacks of classical capitalism. Marrying material prosperity with spiritual growth is not just a dream—it's achievable. Picture this: harnessing the insights from quantum mechanics while capitalizing on the world's opportunities, all while transcending societal constraints and emerging as a version of yourself that not only sidesteps entrenched inadequacies but also facilitates global rejuvenation.

Should these words resonate, understand that you're poised at the brink of a revolutionary paradigm—a system that revamps your worldly rapport and reimagines affluence. It's an opportunity to prosper without forsaking your soul.

Tired of the ceaseless rat race? Tormented by perpetual inadequacy or seeking refuge from relentless stress? This enlightenment might be your guiding star.

If you desire a life replete with financial freedom, comfort, and security, all while pursuing your passions; if you yearn to transform life's mundane elements into gold, or if you seek a perspective that discerns positivity, advantage, and growth in every scenario, then Quantum Capitalism might just be the beacon you've been searching for.

This is your call to action. A beacon in the haze of conventional thinking. Through these pages, we will venture into uncharted territories, seeking a future where wealth and wisdom are two sides of the same coin.

The question now is: are you prepared to take this leap? To explore a realm where your true potential, both material and spiritual, awaits? Because the future of capitalism is not just about accumulation—it's about awakening.

Before we dive headfirst into the realms of Quantum Capitalism, let's set the stage for what lies ahead. You see, while quantum mechanics is often the star of the show, our references might occasionally take a detour into the intriguing domain of astrophysics. The beauty of this journey lies in its diversity, much like the cosmos itself. Quantum mechanics, with its subatomic enigmas and probabilistic dance, undoubtedly forms the bedrock of our exploration. But don't be surprised if we wander into the awe-inspiring expanses of astrophysics, where galaxies collide, black holes devour light, and cosmic threads weave the fabric of The Universe. These are not opposing forces but complementary facets of our cosmic understanding. So, dear reader, I urge you to wear a flexible lens, for we are traversing a multidimensional tapestry where quantum mechanics and astrophysics coalesce, transcending boundaries and expanding our horizons in tandem.

Foreword by Chris Majeski

"Everybody, everybody everywhere, has his own movie going, his own scenario, and everybody is acting his movie out like mad, only most people don't know that is what they're trapped by, their little script. "

-Tom Wolfe

What's "real" to you?

What are you capable of achieving?

And where are your perceived limits that keep you from living the life you've always dreamed of?

Big questions, indeed.

We now live in a time where facts and previously held beliefs seem more flexible than ever. Science is continually proving how weird The Universe is at the most galactic and microscopic levels.

Given the phenomena of "fake news", reality TV, social media, A.I., the metaverse…

It's hard to now argue against the fact that there are almost 8 billion people on Earth, all living in their own reality. Some are very similar; others are worlds apart.

An easy way to illustrate this is to head over to Amazon and read some of the 1 and 2-star reviews for a book or item that you personally LOVE. You'll find it hard to understand how someone's perspective can contradict yours. We often view these people as "stupid" or "out of touch".

But that's probably the same way they feel about you.

We're all watching the same screen but projecting different movies. Most of our movies are like small, lower-budget, independent films, which few others ever see.

But then there are the movies that win awards, global recognition, and make an impact for generations.

Ok, with that rant over, you may be wondering:

"That's all great. But what the hell is a 'Quantum Capitalist?'"

Capitalism and Quantum Physics are two of the most exciting, grand-scale reality movies ever projected onto the screen. They revolutionized systems that were in place before them. Similarly, with Quantum Capitalist, Renee Garcia has made a massive innovation to the world of personal reality creation (more popularly known as the Law of Attraction).

More specifically, she's taken the power of a school of thought known as Reality Transurfing and made it more digestible, impactful, and actionable.

More on that in a minute. But to set the stage, it's essential to introduce some of the themes Renee uses to achieve her aim.

Is "The Matrix" Just A Movie? Or Something More…?

Renee begins Quantum Capitalist with a sobering wake-up call: We all exist in an artificial simulation of reality that few of us have (up to this point) had a say in.

For the more skeptical reader, I refer you to the words of one of the O.G.s of advertising and public relations:

> "The conscious and intelligent manipulation of the organized habits and opinions of the masses is an important element in democratic society. Those who manipulate this unseen mechanism of society constitute an invisible government which is the true ruling power of our country.
> ...We are governed, our minds are molded, our tastes formed, our ideas suggested, largely by men we have never heard of."
>
> -Edward Bernays, Propaganda, 1928

The nephew of Sigmund Freud, Bernays was employed by both the U.S. government as well as major corporations to help mold ideas, tastes, and minds. He created a reality where getting involved in World War I was "the right thing" (despite an overwhelming majority of Americans' opinions opposing getting involved).

He also created a reality where smoking cigarettes symbolized women's liberation and independence (while making his tobacco company clients— and himself—rich as hell).

Fast forward to today.

The manufactured Matrix has grown and evolved as if it were on technological steroids.

Advertisers, politicians, cognitive scientists, social media platforms, and intelligence agencies have used tech and the internet to build skyscrapers on the psychological foundations laid by Bernays. The Information Revolution has shifted the global paradigm to the same degree as the Industrial Revolution.

Foreword by Chris Majeski XV

The point of all of this is that reality is constantly shifting; movies are quickly followed up by sequels. And this is evident when we try to understand just what The Universe is made of in the first place.

The Quantum Revolution

Around the same time Ed Bernays was blacksmithing new social realities, some physicists were making shocking discoveries that upended everything we knew about what the world is actually made of.

I won't pretend to claim any significant understanding of quantum physics. However, even the most rudimentary awareness of its discoveries is nothing short of mind-blowing. The "stuff" The Universe is made out of (including me and you) doesn't act like the stuff we can see.

Particles exist as both individual "things" as well as waves of probability that are everywhere until observed.

Quantum theory shows that reality isn't fixed like a game of billiards where everything that exists can be accurately calculated. We are direct participants in its creation. Your consciousness plays a role in establishing the world you live in.

Consider the following quote:

> "I regard consciousness as fundamental. I regard matter as derivative from consciousness. We cannot get behind consciousness. Everything that we talk about, everything that we regard as existing, postulates consciousness."

As much as that sounds like a quote from the Dalai Lama, it's actually from Nobel Prize Award winner Max Plank, physicist and one of the pioneers of quantum theory. The implications of what Plank said are enormous.

Fifty years after Plank, a physicist at Princeton University named Hugh Everett projected the "Many-Worlds Interpretation" (MWI) of quantum mechanics.

Before Everett, the most widely taught interpretation of quantum mechanics was known as the Copenhagen interpretation. This interpretation says that when a quantum system is observed, its wave function "collapses" to a single outcome. For instance, when you measure the spin of an electron, it's either up or down. However, the wave function before measurement describes the electron as being in a superposition of both states.

Everett's MWI says things are a lot freakier than that.

Instead of wave function collapse, he suggested that all possible outcomes of a quantum measurement actually occur but in different "branches" of The Universe. So, if you measure an electron's spin, there is one Universe where it's up and another where it's down. Each time a quantum event has multiple possible outcomes, The Universe "splits" into multiple branches.

The most striking implication of MWI is the existence of a vast multiverse of parallel Universes. Every quantum event creates a multitude of Universes that are all equally real.

In a nutshell, in some parallel Universe, you are already living the life of your dreams. And Everett's theories, in modern times, are gaining wider acceptance among scientists.

Capitalism: Beyond Good & Evil?

Let's shift gears now:

What comes to your mind when you hear the word "Capitalism"?

Greed?

Success?

The American Dream?

At its best, Capitalism can drive innovation, generate wealth, and improve living standards. Ideally, anyone can enter the competitive market and create improved products, services, and living conditions through innovation and hard work.

However...

Capitalism can lead to inequality, with wealth concentrated in the hands of a few while perpetuating socioeconomic disparities. Additionally, we've seen profits be prioritized over people on too many occasions.

While Ed Bernays and Max Plank were forging their respective new realities, Russia was producing a massive reality-movie called Communism, which featured Capitalism as the evil anti-hero. We all know how that movie ended.

Coincidentally, it was out of the failed Russian reality of Communism that a new reality creation methodology emerged.

Former Russian quantum physicist Vadim Zeland created Reality Transurfing. This modality incorporated elements of the Law of Attraction, Taoism, Buddhism, Quantum Theory, and Shamanism (among others) into a new psycho-spiritual war of choosing the life one wants. When I first came across it around 2015, it blew me away.

But there were some obstacles.

For one, the book Reality Transurfing Steps I-V is encyclopedic in length. Some of the translations from Russian to English made for a sometimes-clunky understanding of the concepts. Also, there needed to be more specific instructions or action steps.

Becoming a Quantum Capitalist

Renee Garcia has drawn from all of the ideologies mentioned above to forge a concept of Quantum Capitalism.

One might argue:

"There's nothing spiritual about Capitalism! This is purely a pursuit of the ego, an illusion."

That may be true. Sitting somewhere in meditation and dissolving the ego might be an option for those who don't have bills to pay or other societal obligations. For the rest of us, the ego is a necessary aspect of our being, helping us navigate modern culture and provide for ourselves and our families.

The ego is simply another tool you can use to create your own reality. Humans are generative beings. We are creators. The ego can be an asset. In Quantum Capitalist, you'll learn how to reduce its importance and leverage it to new states or personal power.

Renee invites you to consider Capitalism as not merely a system of external trade and profit...but a living, breathing entity that reflects our collective consciousness. Each thought you harbor, each feeling you nurse, and each intention you nurture are akin to the currency being traded in a vast, unseen market—a market where reality itself is the commodity on offer.

Your "capital" refers to much more than just money; it's your energy, time, and vibration. These are the resources you "invest" into creating a life worth living as defined by YOU. But, like in the stock market, progress isn't linear: there will be ups and downs. If you've ever seen a stock price chart, your personal "lifeline price chart" could look similar.

Sometimes you're up, sometimes you're down.

Investing some of your capital into working with this book's material will teach you how to keep the falls less dramatic and the rises more regular and inspiring.

And like the Many Worlds Interpretation of Quantum Mechanics, little changes or actions can switch you to a chain of events that carries you to a reality you LOVE. Life can be easy, enjoyable, and fun!

Becoming a Quantum Capitalist isn't about manifesting a million dollars next week. It's about FEELING like a million bucks, which, ironically, is when financial abundance seems to appear as a byproduct. You'll understand why as you read the book.

The tricky part about any manifestation ideology/Law of Attraction is best summed up by a legendary Quantum Capitalist, Henry Ford:

"Whether you think you can or you think you can't – you're right." When one refers to metaphysical sciences like Quantum Capitalism as, "This stuff is a bunch of bullshit."

Guess what? They're right!

At least, they're correct in how they've limited their capacity as creative beings. Unfortunately, this applies to the overwhelming percentage of the population. After all, piercing holes in The Matrix is no easy task. But like the Capitalism and Quantum Theory revolutions, the tide is slowly turning. Quantum Capitalist is a manifesto of embracing and thriving with ideas still hard for most to grasp. The phrase "investing in yourself" was never so poignant.

Quantum Capitalists are the ones who thrive amid the naysayers through solid investments in themselves. And they're the ones that go on to change the world.

So, I urge you to keep your mind open and believe in your natural ability as a reality creator. Don't just read this book. ABSORB it.

Prove It To Yourself

One of the aspects of the Reality Transurfing modality that appealed to me was that it asked you to accept nothing based on blind faith or authority. Instead, the reader was instructed to experiment with the concepts themselves and see if the proof was in the proverbial pudding, so to speak. Unfortunately, this also led to a significant amount of confusion.

As I mentioned, the original body of work comprising Reality Transurfing is exceptionally long. And while it makes for inspiring and thought-provoking reading, there is a noticeable lack of brass tacks instructions to put the rubber to the road regarding implementing the concepts into daily life. At the time, virtually nobody in North America had heard of this book, and one was left alone to figure it all out.

Then, I stumbled across Renee Garcia.

Renee had become the only English-speaking Transurfing instructor certified by the author, Vadim Zeland himself. She saw the same paradigm-shifting potential in this work, and realized that people in the West could greatly benefit from it. So, she undertook the formidable task of bringing this knowledge to the North American audience in more easily digestible ways.

In all honesty, I was about ready to set Transurfing aside. I was suffering from paralysis by over-analysis, stuck reading and re-reading through the hundreds of pages of the original work, and getting lost in theory. I was in a rut, stuck in a dead - end job and numbing myself with alcohol on the weekends.

When I found Renee online, I reached out with questions that were keeping me chained to a lower version of myself. With one email, her response altered my perspective on my challenges. She shed light on how I was putting way too much strain and importance into trying to "do Reality Transurfing." I immediately recognized her ability to make this stuff "make sense" to those who needed clarity.

With a re-ignited passion, I began following Renee's work as she began teaching Reality Transurfing in ways I could relate to. I FINALLY started to loosen my reins on the victim mentality that I didn't even realize I had adopted...

"My job sucks. How do I always get stuck in these dead-end positions?"

"I can never catch any lucky breaks."

"Why do I keep repeating the same mistakes in life?" Renee's interpretation of the principles of Reality Transurfing (so masterfully broken down into action steps in this book) cleared something that was blocked in my heart and mind. Now, I had a game plan. Now, I had explicit tools to deal with the ebbs and flows of life. Now, I could surf the waves of reality that had previously almost drowned me.

Through Renee's own methodology of Anomolous Action, I began seeking means of self-employment that were more in line with my interests but which I had abandoned due to their being "unrealistic."

Fast forward to today...

I'm happily self-employed as a marketing consultant and financial derivatives trader. At 43, I'm in the best shape of my life. I live each day as a mini-adventure instead of dreading dragging myself out of bed in the morning.

Had Quantum Capitalist been around all those years ago, it would have saved me a ton of frustration in working with these esoteric concepts on my own. But I do believe that things happen for a reason. The killer news is that you can benefit from Renee's superhuman work ethic and expertise in this field, and not have to sink enormous amounts of time into deciphering the original teachings for yourself.

And you sure as hell don't need to take my word for it. Just begin reading this book and applying what you learn. Be patient with yourself. Don't underestimate the programming that we've all been subjected to; it may take time to re-write your spiritual software. When you see your life begin to shift in new and beneficial ways, that momentum then builds fast as you further refine your ability to star in a reality movie more to your desires.

This ability to choose where you want to go is what Quantum Capitalism can offer you, too, no matter what your ideal reality looks like. This book is a manual on how to get there.

The references I made in this introduction should, at the very least, let you consider that reality is malleable. New movies are continually being released.

The Matrix is real. Most will never even become aware of it. But participation in it isn't obligatory.

The only question is…

Will you be sitting in the seats watching someone else's movie with the precious time you have left in this life…

Or will you be directing one?

How to Engage with This Revolutionary Guide

This isn't just a book; it's a cerebral revolution, dynamically rewiring your belief systems. Prepare to embark on an intellectual odyssey that will challenge the very foundations of your understanding.

You might be asking, "Why all the fuss?" This tome is more than mere words on paper; it's your gateway to pioneering insights, a portal to concepts that challenge the status quo. Navigating this wisdom is akin to piecing together a complex, beautiful puzzle. Each concept, each fragment you connect, gradually reveals a stunning, paradigm-altering vista. You'll soon be asking yourself, "How did I ever see the world in just black and white?"

Here's the raw truth: your current reality is but a shadow of the potential that awaits. This book is your lens to view life in its pure, unfiltered form.

Picture your life as it is now—an Instagram snapshot, edited and angled for effect. Now, imagine the Quantum You—unbounded, real, the essence of potential. This book is where quantum mechanics shakes hands with self-development, a fusion that will challenge and invigorate you. Even if just a fraction resonates, it will send ripples through your existence. For those brave enough to turn the volume up on life, this is your anthem.

How to Engage with This Revolutionary Guide

Most books are fleeting distractions—enjoyable but transient. This one? It's a feast for the mind. Savor it. As you step into this electrifying journey, your former self may resist. It's the moment of truth: do you heed the call of the familiar, or do you step boldly into a new realm of understanding? Embrace each breakthrough, seek deeper understanding, and celebrate the transformation. In time, you'll look back at this decision as the moment your life transformed.

Fast forward to a future moment, when you'll reflect on this decision and recognize it as the turning point. This isn't hyperbole; it's a commitment to your journey.

So, intrepid explorer, are you ready to dive deep into the unknown and discover your true essence? Will you take the red pill and see just how deep the rabbit hole goes?

Before we launch into this unparalleled adventure, ensure you're fully equipped:

Pre-Launch Checklist: Gear Up for Your Metaphysical Voyage!

1. Join our dynamic Quantum Capitalists Facebook Group for an extra layer of support, guidance, and vibrant discussions that complement your journey through these pages.
2. Dive into the digital sphere, where Renee Garcia brings these concepts to life on YouTube, making the complex beautifully simple.
3. The Juggernaut Journal: this isn't just a diary; it's your mental sanctuary. Here, you'll document every insight, every epiphany, every challenge. It's a haven if you're dedicated to transformation. Select a journal that echoes your spirit, one that feels like an extension of yourself.

Then, pay special attention to the "Your Next Power Move" sections. They're not just crucial; they're transformative. Without engaging in these activities, true progress remains elusive. These exercises are fundamental to your initiation into Quantum Capitalism. To manifest a reality beyond the ordinary, you must actively break free from the mundane and commit to the action steps provided.

Got your gear sorted? Fantastic! Strap in and let the introspection begin!

About Me

I shouldn't be here. Not by any stretch of the imagination. Born into the farthest thing from an idyllic life, I was the oldest of five kids in a household that hovered around the poverty line. To my family, I was less of a cherished child and more of an inconvenient burden. Feeling undernourished and unloved, I set out into the world prematurely, armed with a ninth-grade education and a backpack full of limiting beliefs.

As a young adult, I dove headfirst into the depths of life's lower levels: abusive relationships, minimum wage jobs and strip dancing, crushing debt, low self-worth, drug and alcohol addiction—you name it. By my mid-20s, life had beaten me down, left me with nothing to show for it, and was crushing me under its weight.

But then, a miracle. A small, unexpected spark that ignited my evolution out of debt and poverty and propelled me to unexplainable heights. Eventually, I was living a life of luxury, sailing single-handedly on my own yacht, jet-setting with the elite, and living the lifestyle of the rich and famous. And yet, I was absolutely miserable. I had lost touch with myself trying to prove something to the world. I was in a death spiral with poverty mentality that only seemed to intensify as my bank account grew.

Cue epic nervous breakdown.

I released myself from the life I had created and retreated into the woods in the Pacific Northwest to lick my wounds. It was there that I stumbled upon a body of mystic knowledge that transformed me and my reality before my very eyes. Incredible things happened during that time, things so profound that I knew I had to share this knowledge with the world. Today, I lead a thriving community of others who are sharing in the knowledge I extend within this book. I have found my purpose, my reason to leap out of bed in the morning, and life looks entirely different than I ever could have imagined.

Today, I live the life of my absolute dreams. Zero debt, financial accomplishments, and most importantly, recovery from debilitating poverty mentality, trauma, learned helplessness, and succumbing to lower programming. Life has taken on a dream-like hue, and I'm here to shout from the rooftops that this is available for you too.

Join me on this journey. Let's transform our realities together.

"Tension without cosmic pulsation to animate it is the transition to nothingness."
—Oswald Spengler

PHASE I

MATRIX OBSERVANT

Lesson 1
The Matrix

Alright, prepare yourself, because we're about to free-fall straight down the most paradoxical rabbit hole of all—The Matrix. You know what I'm talking about: that ambiguous shadow gnawing at your subconscious, those ever-tempting external distractors engulfing your every waking thought, urging you to submit, to resign your attention to a fleeting image on a screen, grooming you for complacency, combat, or competition.

Yeah, that's right; we're pulling back the curtain on the great and powerful Oz here. Picture it—a voracious entity, evolving at breakneck speed, advancing civilization while simultaneously steering it towards ultimate slavery. Systems of impeccable design, crafted to keep you locked in and dependent on that next dopamine hit.

The Matrix resembles an enormous worldly structure, brimming with society's cunning brainwashing tactics and illusions, confusing you like staircases in eerie old mansions leading to nowhere. The Matrix infuses limiting beliefs, societal norms, and cookie-cutter plans, all pitched as standards that you would do well to follow. Why do they do this? Because The Matrix benefits from keeping you trapped within the labyrinth it has meticulously crafted for you and the masses. Media, social media, mind-numbing series, movies, porn sites, and dating sites are all part of this system. Sure, they entertain you and momentarily distract you from your perceived powerlessness and the monotony of your day-to-day reality, but stop and think, do they truly add value to your life? Not really.

The Matrix, playing puppeteer with your life, poses as your buddy, helping you cut through boredom with infinite options to occupy your time. Come on, be honest with yourself. You feel it, right? The whispers that convince you to stay in the mundane, to accept what you are given, to choose sides, to be angry, and ultimately to dislike yourself and feel inadequate by comparison.

Oh yes, The Matrix, that crafty maestro conducting a symphony of mind games from your periphery, ensnares you in a relentless cycle of work, binge, sleep, repeat, all while masquerading as the "real world." News flash: this isn't reality; it's a carnival of illusions designed to keep you in line, to keep you clicking the next episode, to keep you angrily typing away in comment sections over the latest political puppet show, to buy things you can't afford. It's a theatrical masterpiece where you're not just the audience; you're the puppet. Then this rigid structure urges you to believe that this is the only way, that any perspective outside of the one it has crafted for you is delusional.

Think about it. If you don't take a political stance, you're "not doing your part." If you don't adhere to the exact ideology of the group you have chosen to align with socially, you fear being ostracized. If you put yourself first above all else, "you're selfish or a narcissist."

You are urged to stay informed, to feel the pain of others in lower circumstances, to vote, to get fired up by injustices, to care about wars and conflicts that would cease to exist in your day-to-day life unless you actively tuned into them. And for what? Would you not agree that it all seems to be reaching a feverish boiling point regardless of the attention it is all given? Yet everyone tunes in more and more, and the chasm between what society wants from you and a healthy, thriving version of yourself widens.

The bottom line: if you're struggling, don't have what it is you want in this world, or are not living the life you want, The Matrix has taken you on a ride. Now it's time to cast these illusions aside and break free from this mental lockdown.

The red pill is available to us all. There is another way, if we choose it.

Maybe you are nodding along, a smirk of recognition playing on your lips because deep down in places you don't talk about at parties, you glimpse something beyond, you want to break free from the hypnotic rhythms of the daily grind, a force that doesn't give a damn about you.

So, what's it going to be? Are you going to keep playing the NPC in this tired old show, or are you ready to step up to the helm and steer your own ship through the chaotic sea of fabricated reality?

Wake the fuck up. It's time to see the world for what it really is—a playground for your unique creativity, not a factory line where you sell your non-renewable resources for a wage, or submit to contributing these resources to The Matrix without receiving anything in return.

The Money Shot: Break Free & Bank Big

The Matrix has been dishing out some stale-ass money recipes, and it's time to toss them in the trash like yesterday's Chinese take-out. From an early age, The Matrix dictates what success looks like, how to achieve it, and what holds meaning and value. The Matrix convinces you how you should make money, and yet, you may find yourself broke, in debt, or struggling to obtain what you desire. So, what the hell is going on? You were told, "Go to school, get a job, work until you're old and retire"—that's The Matrix's blueprint for your life.

Perhaps you don't know another way. But I assure you, from my own experience, another way does exist. We've got everything you need right here, presented in an easy-to-follow system that empowers you to exit The Matrix and reclaim your power. You possess all the ingredients to be the master chef of your financial feast right now, so let's whip up a banquet of freedom, adventure, and security.

Did you just think, "Sure, that would be real nice, maybe for someone other than me"? Well, The Matrix really does have you by the nuts or ovaries then.

Here's a little secret—financial freedom isn't solely reserved for the lucky few or silver-spoon-fed trust fund kids or those hustling and grinding until the breaking point. Financial freedom is for those of us willing to defy The Matrix. We're talking about becoming a real-life maverick who takes calculated risks, challenges the norm, and turns away from the soul-numbing lullabies The Matrix sings to us every day.

I invite you to step out of the "safe" zone and embrace options you may not have believed were available to you. Beyond the "safe" zone is where magic truly happens. Certainly, you might stumble and fall along the way, but don't let that deter you. The Matrix encourages you to play it safe and adhere to its conventional narrative. However, you have the potential to transcend it all—if you choose to. How? I'll show you just that.

A word of caution for those seeking shortcuts, for the doubters, and for those unwilling to give their best: this is NOT a quick fix. It's not about "manifesting" from the couch or merely wishing things into existence. The Quantum Capitalist system you're about to discover truly works.

THIS. SYSTEM. WORKS.

But it demands your commitment. You need to invest time, challenge your beliefs, and begin to perceive reality differently. Staying rooted in the "same old, same old" is precisely why you find yourself where you are now, in your current place in space and time. So, a warning to the complacent, the know-it-alls, and the skeptics unwilling to let your old ways go: you might simply be wasting your time reading this.

Meet Alice

Alice's life was a never-ending loop of mundane tasks. Wake up, eat, go to work, eat, Netflix binge, sleep, repeat. Excitement for her was a weekend away at an overpriced seaside resort that she slapped onto an almost maxed out credit card. One morning, however, Alice woke up with an unsettling feeling. Is this all there is, she wondered?

Alice had an epiphany—but still so many questions. She suddenly felt as though her life wasn't her own. She felt lost in a way that she couldn't quite put her finger on. She wasn't the person she wanted to be. She felt bored, understimulated, and controlled by something, but what? It all felt vague and foggy, yet she didn't dismiss this gentle nudge that seemed to come out of nowhere. As she sat with these thoughts and sensations, she caught a fleeting glimpse of something as she sipped her morning coffee—a complex system of societal norms and expectations as suffocating as a pair of skinny jeans after a Thanksgiving dinner. Had life been convincing her that her soul-crushing job, mounting debt, and addiction to mind-numbing TV and doom-scrolling were all part of the "real world"?

The "real world" suddenly seemed like a bad joke. Was it all just an illusion, a mirage erected by the powers that be to keep the masses, herself included, blissfully ignorant? Politics, media, social media—all just smoke and mirrors meticulously crafted to keep her docile, "satisfied," and most importantly, compliant, she wondered.

After arriving at work, Alice jumped on the internet and stumbled upon a book called "Quantum Capitalist." As she was reading the description, a bell seemed to ring in Alice's head. She anticipated the arrival of the book. The next day, as she flipped through it, she realized the book mirrored that exact moment she felt while drinking her coffee. It was a manifesto for breaking free from The Matrix and taking control back. Alice quickly realized that the stale, regurgitated money advice she had been swallowing was getting her nowhere. In fact, it was actually keeping her broke, miserable, and stuck in a rut deeper than the butt groove she had carved out for herself on her couch.

Alice decided it was time for a change. She realized that she had been on autopilot for too long and it seemed to be getting worse with time. She felt a queasiness within and knew her morning epiphany and the knowledge she was reading meant she was getting ready for a real shakeup of her life. She was ready.

The Recap

Hundreds of thousands of people have found success with this knowledge, but this knowledge will only take you as far as you are willing to go with it. YOU have to make the journey, and it all begins right here, today, right now.

Poke The Brain

Are you where you want to be today? If not, are you ready to wake up from The Matrix?

Your Next Power Move

Juggernaut Journal Exercise: Matrix Detox.

Find a quiet space with your Juggernaut Journal. Let's do a real-life audit. Divide a page into two columns. Label one "Matrix Influences" and the other "My True Desires."

Matrix Influences: in this column, jot down all the societal norms or influences you feel pressured by. For instance, having a stable 9-to-5 job, buying a house by a certain age, or even watching a particular popular TV show because "everyone else is." Here's a hint—if you don't know why you do it but you have a compulsion to do so, it probably belongs in this category. Especially if it leaves you feeling bloated but empty like binge-ing a whole bag of cheesy puffs.

My True Desires: now, without overthinking, list out all the things you truly desire in life, independent of any external influences. What kind of job excites you? Where do you want to live? What experiences do you yearn for?

Once you've filled out both columns, look at the "Matrix Influences" side. Ask yourself how many of these things have seeped into the "My True Desires" side without you consciously choosing them. Are there any patterns or particular influences that have overpowered your genuine desires?

This exercise is meant to give you clarity on how The Matrix might be subtly dictating your choices and to empower you to realign with your authentic desires.

By identifying these Matrix influences, you'll be better equipped to challenge them and design a life path more attuned to your true self. Remember, it's about choosing your narrative, not letting The Matrix choose for you.

Create your own reality, or one will be created for you.

—Deepak Chopra

Lesson 2

Playing vs. Being Played

Did you just glimpse The Matrix's stranglehold on your reality? That red pill you swallowed in the first Power Move—it was your wake-up call. Now, brace yourself as we venture further, delving into the intricate dance between perception and control. The curtain rises on Lesson 2, where the spotlight's on you as a player, not a bystander. Are you ready to transition from mere passive participant to becoming the lead character in the captivating drama of life, scripting your own narrative? Is it time to embrace the challenge to unveil hidden strings, decode The Matrix's manipulations, and seize your role in this cosmic stagecraft? Do you want to learn to rewrite the rules or continue to allow them to be dictated? Welcome to the next lesson—where you either begin to direct the play or risk remaining its unwitting extra.

Now is the time to face the truth: until this moment, your life may have been nothing but a game imposed upon you. When you're deeply immersed in this game, it's hard to see the game objectively or have any influence over the game. But this doesn't have to be true any longer: it's time now for you to step back and take a good look around with a clear mind. Ask yourself, "What's going on, and why am I doing what I'm doing? Am I truly in control, or is The Matrix taking advantage of me?"

When you're snoozing away, and not tapping into your awareness, you're at the mercy of circumstances. Your mind is in slumber mode, accepting everything as is without questioning a thing. Have you felt like reality exists independently of you, and you're helpless, with no ability to make an impact? Have you resigned yourself to the hand you've been dealt? Probably a combination of feeling inadequate and helpless and accepting your environment for what it is? Have you felt as though you are floating downstream, only making futile attempts to assert yourself every now and then, with unpredictable or lackluster results?

Well, guess what? Something is stirring—CHANGE! And you're the only one who can make this change happen. In the past, you've probably bought into reality as it is presented to you by The Matrix. Now it's time to see it for what it really is—an illusion—a game. Only in a conscious state can you truly take control of your situation.

I'm going to give it to you straight. When you are not experiencing the life you want and continue to struggle to obtain the things you desire, you are absolutely being taken advantage of by The Matrix. Will you decide to disconnect and regain control? You might already feel deep inside yourself that you are more powerful than The Matrix has led you to believe, and here's where it gets real. You've got a massive advantage now—the awareness of the game The Matrix is playing. And the more you tap into your awareness, nurture it, and seize the power this awareness holds, the easier you can harness your ability to shatter The Matrix's game to pieces.

Here is a fun fact: everyone around you has a role to play in your game of life, and they're all interacting with you in some way: expecting, imposing, asking, helping, hindering, loving, hating... It's a whole dramatic production!

Embrace your role as someone who simply observes what's going on. Watch this game consciously, from the vantage point of an observer just watching someone else playing a video game. Soon you'll realize you've begun cracking the riddles of The Matrix for yourself, including your role in the game. Get ready to level up.

Meet George

George is a modern-day hero in the epic battles of consumerism. He's the kind of guy who can't resist the siren call of the latest and greatest, ultimately luring him to shipwreck on the rocks of debt and buyer's remorse.

Yeah, George marked his calendar, a red circle highlighting the anticipated "iPhone day," a festival of credit cards, long queues, and tantalizing tech dreams coming true. Not even morning gridlock could dampen his spirits.

"Step right up, ladies and gentlemen!" No one actually said, but it could be felt in the air as George lined up outside the tech temple—the Apple store. The store was a beacon of modernity, with its sleek lines and futuristic design practically oozing sophistication. You see, it wasn't just a store; oh no, it was the future, a haven where all your productivity dreams stood ready to be fulfilled—oh, never mind the cost.

There George stood, wallet shaking slightly in his hand, as if the small piece of plastic within was saying, "Are you sure about this, George? I'm almost maxed out." But who was he to listen to a piece of plastic?

As George finally entered the store, he felt as though he had arrived. He was "in," a member of the hip tech crowd. He couldn't wait for his friends to see it. The biggest model, the best camera, maxed out memory, leather case, and a screen protector—George threw down.

A rushed drive home, George ripped off the packaging as if his life depended on it. The touch of the cool, pristine surface, the smell of fresh off-gassing; he cradled his new treasure. A new beginning, a fresh chance to be cool, ahead, modern, up-to-date.

As George transferred his life, from old to new, a nagging realization crept in. A realization so blatant yet it completely caught him off guard—his old phone was a champion, a reliable steed that had carried him through nearly infinite tasks. All his apps were neatly organized, it was set up exactly the way he needed it to be and functioned exactly as it should, a testament to the fact that "old" was not synonymous with "obsolete."

The revelation hung in the air, a tragic comedy unveiling before his eyes as he held the two phones, like a man caught between two lovers, realizing too late that his chase for the new was just a farce, a scripted drama by the maestros of marketing, leading him to believe that love, or in this case, tech, was always greener on the other side. For the first time, George felt utterly played.

And so, with a laugh that carried a tinge of self-mockery and wisdom, George embraced the ludicrousness of the situation. He sat there, a new resolve burgeoning within him, an understanding that sometimes the "new" is just a glittery version of the "old," a repackaged dream sold with a higher price tag. A lesson not just for George but for you, dear reader, to navigate this world that constantly shouts, "Buy me, upgrade to me, you need me!"

Oh, George would tread this path with a wiser heart and a keen eye, a beacon of light ready to challenge the ostentatious parade of the "next big thing." Because deep down, nestled between humor and irony, George found a nugget of truth—the real upgrade might just be realizing you had what you needed all along.

The Money Shot: Taking Control of Your Cash Game

Face it. We are like cattle being herded in a single direction. The Matrix offers only a couple of models to choose from: the overworked capitalist or the starving artist. Yet, we are all programmed to pursue the same material gains, regardless of our ilk.

The essence of Quantum Capitalism involves extracting yourself from The Matrix in ways that don't serve you, while still capitalizing on it from a place of authenticity and integrity for your benefit. This begins with acknowledging and reconciling the ways in which you are being used and manipulated, and reclaiming control.

If you feel overworked and underpaid, you are being played. If you feel lethargic and uninterested in taking action, you are being played. If your lifestyle exceeds your budget, you are being played.

When you feel confused by the game of life and your place within it, you fall into roles that do not serve you, such as "victim," "helpless bystander," and "the unlucky one." But now that you know it's a game, you can choose a new role in it.

Prepare to confront The Matrix's crafty arsenal of poverty tricks! The Matrix plays a clever game, trapping you in the never-ending pursuit of the standards it sets for you. Through incessant consumerism and reckless spending, you trade your freedom for fleeting pleasures, unaware of the chains tightening around you.

The Matrix's most powerful weapon is the instillation of learned helplessness. It sows seeds of doubt in your abilities, making you believe that your financial circumstances are beyond your control. But the truth is, you possess the keys to unlock the vaults of prosperity within you.

The Recap

Ever felt like a puppet with The Matrix as your puppeteer? Well, it's time to snip those strings! Dive deep, realize life's a game, and guess what? You've been dealt a winning hand and just haven't realized it yet. Embrace the neon lights of reality, shift from the background to center stage, and redefine your starring role in this cosmic cabaret. Ready to steal the show?

Poke The Brain

How has The Matrix scripted your role? Are you playing the lead, or just an extra in your own story?

Your Next Power Move

Juggernaut Journal Exercise: Breaking The Matrix Code.

Arm yourself with your Juggernaut Journal and a pen. Now, think about a situation from the past week where you felt you were being played by The Matrix. Maybe it was a purchase you didn't really need but felt compelled to buy, or perhaps it was a decision made out of fear rather than what you truly desired.

- **Describe the Situation:** detail the situation as if you're writing a scene for a movie. What happened, who was involved, where did it take place, and what emotions were you feeling?
- **Matrix Influence:** pinpoint how The Matrix may have influenced this scene. Was there societal pressure? Maybe it was an ad on TV or social media? Or perhaps a comment from a friend or family member that made you second guess yourself?
- **Your True Desire:** reflect on what you would have genuinely wanted in that scenario, minus The Matrix influence. How would your character (you) have acted if fully aligned with your true self?
- **Re-scripting the Scene:** rewrite the scene, this time with you taking charge, free from the Matrix's influence. How does the scene change? What decisions are made differently? Review what you've written. Realize that each time you identify The Matrix's influence and re-script the scene to fit your authentic desires, you're taking back control of your narrative.

This exercise will help you become more conscious of your decisions, differentiating between what The Matrix dictates and what you truly want. As you practice this more frequently, you will become better equipped to identify and reject The Matrix's subtle manipulations in real-time.

Lesson 3
The Quantum Field

Welcome to The Quantum Field, the grand stage where reality bows to your whims. Did you peek behind The Matrix's curtain last time? Forget being a mere spectator; this is your show, your extravaganza. Imagine The Universe as your playground, a wonderland where every slide and swing is a potential reality. It's time to ditch those old, dusty rules and waltz with your thoughts and perspectives. Are you ready to bid adieu to limitations and flirt with the realm where your mind is the ultimate sculptor of your world? Buckle up, because you're about to unlock a treasure trove of metaphysical marvels.

The Quantum Field isn't your average mystical mumbo-jumbo; think of it as the superhighway of energy, and darling, you've got the keys to the sports car. Picture this field as a cosmic cloud, brimming with every possible idea, outcome, and variation of reality. Every melody you've hummed in the shower, every gadget that's graced your palm, and every stroke of art that's caught your eye—they've all pirouetted through The Quantum Field before sashaying into your reality. Craving a VIP pass to this realm of endless possibilities? Honey, you're already holding it.

Now, let's get spicy: those thoughts of yours aren't just whimsical daydreams. Imagine them as dynamic radio waves, each frequency connecting you to a different reality tangoing within The Quantum Field. The stronger and more passionate your belief in a certain outcome, the clearer and more tantalizing that connection gets. And when it's crystal clear? That's when the magic happens. Your beliefs light up The Quantum Field like the Vegas Strip on a hot Saturday night, setting the stage for a spectacular show.

Think of life as a kaleidoscopic, multidimensional game, with you as the master player. Each choice is a key, unlocking realms and experiences beyond your wildest fantasies. Picture yourself cruising down a familiar path, and then—wham!—you play a wildcard. Instantly, you're whisked away to an exotic new level, taking on thrilling roles, acquiring new treasures, and embarking on adventures that leave you breathless. That, my friend, is you playing tag with The Quantum Field.

Wondering why this cosmic carnival isn't already unfurling in your life? Plot twist: it's been happening all along. Every moment, every day you've lived, has been meticulously crafted by your choices and beliefs. No fluff, no frills. You've been the architect of your own reality, even if you didn't realize it. The upcoming lessons? They're simply here to fine-tune your skills, raise the stakes, and help you see that you've been writing, directing, and starring in this blockbuster called life, every single second.

The Money Shot: Quantum Cash Remix

Feeling short-changed by life? Thirsty for more wealth, comfort, and security? Here's the hard-hitting truth: you've been spinning your own financial records in The Quantum Field's DJ booth all this time. Each twist and turn in your money saga? They're your selections from the Field's endless jukebox. But now, with this knowledge in your arsenal, you're free to change the track. Dreaming of opulence, lavish comfort, unbreakable security? They're all seductive rhythms waiting for you on the dance floor. And making that shift to a richer reality? It's not rocket science. It's just about choosing a new beat to groove to.

The Recap

The Quantum Field is your limitless playground, packed with every imaginable version of reality. Envision it as an infinite sea of potentialities. The catch? Your beliefs and choices sculpt these possible variations. Ready for something different? Dive into The Quantum Field wielding the tools to come and you're on your way to a reality upgrade. Embrace the limitless avenues of possibilities. Because in this game, there is no end—only new beginnings.

Poke The Brain

Do you believe a higher version of reality exists for you? Congratulations! This is the first step in connecting with one of the infinite potentialities available.

Your Next Power Move

Quantum Field Visualization Exercise

Imagine stepping into a world where The Quantum Field is vividly alive, waiting for you to explore and interact with it. This exercise invites you to visualize The Quantum Field in a way that resonates deeply with you, using imagery that sparks your imagination and helps you connect with the concept of infinite possibilities.

Picture yourself in an environment that symbolizes endless potential. Maybe it's a sprawling, cosmic diner where the menu lists infinite delicacies and experiences, each dish representing a different life path or outcome. Envision the aroma of possibilities, the ambiance of adventure. What dish catches your eye first? How does it feel to know you can order anything, from the mundane to the extraordinary?

Alternatively, you could find yourself in a vast, interstellar supermarket. The aisles stretch endlessly, each one stocked with a dazzling array of potential realities. These aren't just products on a shelf; they're snapshots of lives you could lead, experiences you could have. Walk down an aisle, pick up an item—what does it represent for you? Maybe it's a career change, a new relationship, a skill you've always wanted to learn.

Or, embark on an intergalactic journey, where each planet in a sprawling galaxy represents a distinct reality. You're at the helm of your own rocket ship, free to navigate to any world you choose. What do these planets look like? Are they teeming with life, rich in color and texture? Each planet holds a story, a life you could live. Which one do you visit first?

Another vivid scene could be a garden where every plant or flower symbolizes a different path or choice. Each seed you plant, each bud you nurture, grows into a unique reality. What does your garden look like? Is it wild and untamed, or carefully curated? What realities are blooming there?

Lastly, imagine a tranquil backyard where a clothesline is strung up, each piece of clothing flapping gently in the breeze representing a different life variation. As you walk along the line, you see different outfits, each embodying a unique erience or aspect of life. What do you choose to try on? How does it feel to "wear" that reality?

Through this exercise, allow yourself to play, explore, and connect with The Quantum Field's vastness. As you visualize, remember that each image, each scene, is a gateway to understanding and engaging with the infinite potentialities of your life. Let your creativity flow, and feel the power and freedom that comes from knowing you have the ability to navigate these endless possibilities.

This exercise is designed to help you connect with The Quantum Field in a personal and imaginative way, encouraging a deeper understanding and engagement with the concept of endless potentialities.

Lesson 4

Reclaiming Your Magic

How does it feel to embrace your role as a creator with the insights from the last lesson? Feeling empowered to choose a new variation of reality? Now, as you stand poised at the threshold of the next lesson, get ready to delve even deeper. You are going to need to sharpen your tools and reconnect with magical powers that have been lost to you as you embark on the journey before you. Are you ready to reclaim your magic wand?

Dive into a quick flashback...

From the moment you opened your eyes in this world, you were handed The Matrix's rulebook. Your inherent knack for understanding and communicating with The Quantum Field hushed. The ability to communicate without words to animals, or feeling the unseen energies? All were silenced by the deafening noise of society's norms. You were seduced and distracted, pulled into a game with rules you didn't write. Your magical powers to craft reality were dulled. You shifted from magician to Matrix compliant.

When you made your grand entrance into this crazy thing called your life, it was like a fresh awakening after who knows how many previous lives you've lived. Back in these past lives, you had some seriously mind-blowing abilities. You could hear the whispers of the stars, see auras, and have deep, engaging conversations with animals and birds. The whole world was like this wild show of crackling energy, and guess what? You were the freakin' magician, pulling the strings.

But then, because of not knowing better and the influence of others, you dozed off. The influences around you deliberately directed your focus solely to the physical side of reality, The Matrix. And as a result, you lost contact with all those magical powers of yours. Well, my friend, is it time you reclaim that old magic you once possessed?

So, here's your mantra, if it suits you: "I am awakened. I see through The Matrix. I am a quantum magician." Let this echo in your mind, let it be your guidepost, rekindling the magic you've forgotten.

Today's mission, should you choose to accept: Stay. Wide. Awake. No drifting into autopilot. Keep those eyes open! Awareness is your way out of The Matrix.

The Money Shot: Money Magic Resurgence

Reconnecting with your inherent abilities might sound mystical, but it's genuinely actionable wisdom on your journey to greater wealth. At its core, Quantum Capitalism revolves around engaging with your surroundings in amplified ways, paving the way for impactful opportunities and unveiling pathways to loftier realities. The Matrix feeds you flawed beliefs, misguided paths, and offers ill-fated financial strategies that yield only meager returns in your present reality. Rekindling your connection to these powers signifies taking charge, dictating the terms, and learning to interact with your environment in more magical and rewarding ways. It's about leading the narrative, rather than letting The Matrix prescribe a financial script that no longer aligns with your prosperity goals.

The Recap

For too long, The Matrix has been playing puppeteer. Feeling out of sync with your true self? It's not a glitch. It's an invitation to tune into The Quantum Field as the magic wielding powerhouse you are. Recognize the puppet strings, cut them, and let your Quantum Self soar.

Poke The Brain

Ever felt like there's more to you than what meets the eye, but can't quite put your finger on it?

Your Next Power Move

Visualization Exercise: Introduction to the Past Incarnation

Embark on a journey through time and memory with this visualization exercise, designed to connect you with your past incarnations. Throughout history, it's believed that our souls have experienced various lives, each endowed with unique skills, knowledge, and experiences. This exercise invites you to tap into these past lives, uncovering abilities and wisdom that may have been forgotten over time. By visualizing yourself in different historical and mystical roles, you'll not only enrich your imagination but also awaken dormant powers within you. These past experiences, whether as a healer, innovator, or guardian of ancient lore, can offer insight, inspiration, and strength that you can harness in your current life. Let's dive into the realms of the past and reclaim the gifts that once were yours.

Visualize yourself in a mystical medieval era, where you were a magician known for your profound wisdom and spellcasting. The cobblestone streets, the enigmatic aura of the castle, and the magical artifacts in your possession speak of a time when you harnessed the arcane to shape destinies.

Imagine being a healer in a lush, green forest, intimately connected with the healing powers of nature. Your knowledge of herbs and plants made you a beacon of hope in your village, offering remedies and comfort to those in need. Feel the gratitude and respect of the community that relied on your expertise.

Think of yourself as an innovative craftsman in a bustling ancient market. Your hands, skilled and precise, created tools or techniques that transformed the way people lived. The pride in your work and the joy of creation filled your days with purpose and satisfaction.

Envision yourself as an explorer of unknown lands, navigating uncharted territories with courage and curiosity. The thrill of discovery and the awe of encountering new cultures and landscapes filled your soul with a sense of adventure and an unquenchable thirst for knowledge.

See yourself as a sage or a guardian of ancient wisdom in a lost civilization. Surrounded by manuscripts and sacred relics, you were the keeper of stories and traditions, ensuring that the knowledge of ages was passed down through generations.

Through these visualizations, you connect with the diverse and rich experiences of your past selves, drawing strength and inspiration from their lives. This exercise is not just a journey through imagination but a tool for personal empowerment, helping you to realize the vast potential that lies within you.

Lesson 5

What Is a Quantum Capitalist?

Time to slice through the haze and hit the heart of the matter. Our last dive unraveled The Matrix's masquerade and the critical call to reignite your dormant powers. What's on the horizon? Understanding the essence of being a Quantum Capitalist. Is this more than just a label? Let's decode.

You've caught the gist of it, right? That tantalizing murmur in the wind, a hint of micro-revolution—Quantum Capitalism. We're not here for a timid toe-dip; we're plunging into the deep end to unpack this powerhouse concept.

Quantum Capitalist—the term has a certain razzle-dazzle, doesn't it? At the heart, a Quantum Capitalist is someone who leverages The Quantum Field to their advantage. This isn't about chasing trends or slapping on a fashionable label. It's about casting off the dull, constrictive narrative of The Matrix and stepping out of the shadows of outdated ideologies. The Quantum Capitalist kicks off the clunky boots of outdated "isms" and "schisms" and ditches the heavy baggage of "shoulds" and "supposed tos." A Quantum Capitalist doesn't change who they are; they become their true self again, continuously unraveling the layers of indoctrination they've been wrapped in since birth.

A Quantum Capitalist sees through The Matrix's illusion, understanding that the prepackaged realities it sells are shallow and unfulfilling. They feel The Quantum Field's call, an urge to draw upon its dynamic energy for growth, healing, and a state of being far beyond what The Matrix can offer.

Think about it. Anyone who has achieved something truly innovative, progressive, or unique has harnessed The Quantum Field. They've tapped into their unique essence, blending it just right with The Quantum Field. You have this power, too. Yes, you. Right now, you're brimming with potential to be an inventor, artist, a visionary, or even simply happier than you've ever been. What's stopping you is a lost belief in your own capabilities. Those who have succeeded in these achievements have allowed the world to see them for who they truly are, embracing the limitless potential of The Quantum Field.

A Quantum Capitalist embodies a spirit of rebellion against convention. They use The Quantum Field as their secret passage out of The Matrix's labyrinth. Their tools? Thoughts, actions, and a deep connection to The Quantum Field. They're not just chasing wealth; they're architects of their reality, fixated not on money but on liberty, boundless opportunity, creativity, and a life that's a non-stop celebration. Sounds baller, right?

For those willing to take this ride, The Quantum Field is no mere concept; it's a treasure chest. They're not just following a fad; they're Quantum Capitalists, charting their destiny, claiming their space, and harnessing their innate powers.

A Quantum Capitalist sees the world with a childlike wonder. After shedding The Matrix's indoctrination, they experience a rebirth, a return to a time when life was vibrant, when simple pleasures were profound, and a day at the beach was pure joy. That magic? It's within your reach as a Quantum Capitalist.

Here's a nuanced and paradoxical nugget for you: while the essence of this knowledge empowers you to amplify your wealth, a Quantum Capitalist with merely $10 in his pocket could still be at the head of the class. How, you ask? Because Quantum Capitalism isn't purely about monetary riches; it's about the wealth of spirit. It's about exuding prosperity, evolving into the grandest version of oneself, and enriching one's surroundings in profound, lasting ways. For most, this will equate to a fatter wallet, but it doesn't necessarily have to.

But, fret not. We won't leave you hanging on the tangible wealth bit. Here's the twist: money isn't something you pursue or amass; it's an essence you embody. Financially challenged individuals often carry the weight of societal conditioning, money trauma, and a cascade of setbacks. And without insights like these, many find themselves vulnerable, as if lambs led to a fate they didn't choose. I've walked in those shoes, a testament to the transformative power of this knowledge.

So, are you ready to mend your fragmented self, rise as a Quantum Capitalist, and immerse in a life where prosperity flows, without obsessing over the financial scoreboard?

Now, Quantum Capitalists don't just do their own thing for the sake of rebelling; they play it smart. Free from The Matrix's chains, they still have the savvy to play in conventional markets, as long as they remain true to their moral compass. But it's up to you to decide how far you want to go with it.

This philosophy has its layers:

Matrix Observant: this is the primary stage of awakening, where one starts to understand the mechanics of The Matrix and its implications on personal freedom and prosperity. Matrix Observants are critical thinkers, beginning to question the standard narratives and societal norms. At this stage, you're peeking behind the curtain, becoming more aware of the constructed realities, and starting to develop a desire for something more authentic and aligned with your true nature.

Quantum Capitalist: at this juncture, you have not only recognized The Matrix but are actively seeking ways to harness The Quantum Field for personal gain. You've attuned to the boundless opportunities that exist beyond conventional realms. As you become a Quantum Capitalist, it's easy to comprehend that The Universe operates in energies and vibrations, and that by aligning yourself to these energies, you can manifest your desires and shape your reality. You are among the visionaries, the dreamers, and those who are brave enough to diverge from the herd, charting a course that is uniquely yours.

Quantumpreneur: this is the zenith of Quantum Capitalism. The Quantumpreneur not only understands and benefits from The Quantum Field, but they actively shape it, innovating and creating new paradigms for themselves and for others. They are the trailblazers, those who not only tread their own path but illuminate the way for others. As you rise to Quantumpreneur you don't just capitalize on The Quantum Field; you're co-creating with it, birthing new ventures, ideas, and realities that defy The Matrix's limitations. Far beyond the stifling anxieties once instilled by The Matrix, you place unwavering trust in The Quantum Field and your pivotal role within it. By surrendering to quantum energy and imbibing its infinite information, you masterfully capitalize on your innate creativity. And it's not just a solo act; these ventures ripple out, enriching the world and bestowing benefits upon others.

Consider it akin to choosing between a part-time gig, a full-time position, or taking the reins as the CEO.

Now, the real tea? No one genuinely thrives as The Matrix's marionette. Sure, the perks and bonuses might roll in, and you might become the talk of the cul-de-sac. But deep down? There's likely a hunger, a silent scream for purpose, spark, and unbridled freedom. Regardless of how deep you're willing to dive, even a minor step away from The Matrix can be transformative.

Everyone's ultimately seeking one thing: freedom. Did you think money? Nah, it's time to dig a bit deeper. How you interpret that freedom, whether you're the quiet strategist or the audacious game-changer, is entirely up to you.

The Recap: Bonus Round

Notice a glitch in this lesson? If you missed it, it's time to sharpen your awareness. Even Quantum Capital-ISM is an "ism." Don't just swallow everything you're fed. This journey is about tearing down those "isms" and paving your own golden path. No sheep, no herd mentality, and zero dogma here.

The Money Shot: Quantum Capitalist-ing

It's more than just the cash. It's about awakening your senses, reconnecting with your inner power, and claiming every slice of reality. As a Quantum Capitalist, you're not just playing the game; you're rewriting the rules. Every move is about more than scoring points; it's about defining freedom, igniting your imagination, and redefining success on your own terms.

Poke The Brain

Still cozy in your Matrix bubble? Think this is all woo-woo, overhyped, "too good to be true," new-age jargon? Head to the back of the class and just shut your brain off for a minute. The Quantum Field is trying to tell you something. Will you listen?

Your Next Power Move

Observation Exercise: A New Lens.

Observe the people around you, both in real life and online. Who's following The Matrix's script? Who's carving their own path? Who seems to be tapping into higher wisdom, fusing it with their energy to create something uniquely beneficial? Who's caught in The Matrix's hypnotic dance, blind to any other way?

There are shades of gray, but becoming a Quantum Capitalist is a two-fold mission: recognizing and detaching from The Matrix's shackles and merging with The Quantum Field in empowering ways.

For the next 24 hours, observe the people you encounter. What's their connection to The Quantum Field or The Matrix? What are their actions like? Are they slaves to addictions, creatively active, or commanding their reality?

Then turn the lens on yourself. What parts of you are still chained to The Matrix, and how can you strengthen your bond with The Quantum Field? If you're struggling to grasp what The Quantum Field is and how it can aid your personal evolution, don't trip. The rest of this book will unveil everything you need to know and more.

Lesson 6

Conformity Can Go Suck It

Alright, flashback moment: in our previous lesson, we unraveled the mystery that is the Quantum Capitalist and unveiled the myriad paths one can strut down, armed with this transformative knowledge. Now, gear up, because in this lesson, we're diving deep, plunging into the electric thread weaving through all the options before you. Prepare to grasp why this pulsating core is not just a detail, but the very heartbeat of this entire system. Ready to rock? Let's go!

Every level of Quantum Capitalism heralds a subtle battle cry from your soul, a call to defy the mundane and unveil your reinvigorated self. This defiance can manifest in a variety of ways: from halting the compulsive doom-scrolling—thereby harnessing your potent human energies—to a full-blown life makeover. It's your move.

The golden thread binding these stages together? A simple yet powerful command: Defy. Conformity.

In a world where conformity is king, the Quantum Capitalist is the shining star who sets a new standard of achievement. The Matrix may not like individuality, but it sure can't but help to latch onto a rising star and make it their favorite. Has the time come to tap into your superpower and break free from the collective formation?

Remember, you hold the power to grant or revoke your privileges to exit The Matrix and merge with The Quantum Field. This is accomplished as you embrace your authentic self and acknowledge the unique abilities and qualities The Matrix deliberately tries to convince you to hide. Individuality is The Matrix's worst nightmare, for it crumbles its control when followers reclaim their autonomy and uniqueness.

Here's the tricky part: stars are born in solitude, but it's The Matrix that ignites their brilliance. The Matrix crafts role models and success ideals to align others' aspirations in a singular direction. The Matrix also puts the individual going against the grain on blast. It's all about pushing and shoving everyone into conformity but at the same time showcasing those who defy the norms. Trippy right? The second option is how you break free. If you are not experiencing the life you desire, you're probably stuck in feeling inadequate, imperfect or just not up to snuff.

To frame it differently: success has two faces. The first wears the look of The Matrix's perfection—meticulously following its scripted path. That means scaling the career ladder, adhering to the rules, and epitomizing the quintessential Matrix player. If that resonates with you, sail on! The second face, however, turns away from all that jazz. It challenges norms, pushes against established boundaries, and compels The Matrix to spotlight your individuality.

Examples: social media stars like @sophiahadjipanteli the model with her overgrown eyebrows, @wackson_22 with his dorky super charm, and @fattiemcbaddie's graceful dancing are testimonials to people turning their quirks into their strengths and banking big.

Meet Lila

Rewind a few years, and you'd find her buried in corporate reports, her outfits meticulously color-coordinated with the drab gray walls of her office. Lila was the epitome of a Matrix poster child—ticking off boxes, chasing traditional success metrics, and spending her weekends doom-scrolling away. Yet, despite all outward appearances, she was consumed by a gnawing emptiness inside.

And then, everything changed.

Lila attended a street art exhibition one night. A spark ignited within her as she wandered amongst the vibrant murals, and she felt a sense of excitement that had long eluded her.

With a newfound determination, Lila shed her corporate cocoon and embraced her lifelong passion for urban art. Eyebrows were raised, of course. The Matrix's grip attempted to drag her back, labeling her "midlife crisis-ing." But Lila? She broke free from the external feedback.

As Lila handed in her notice at work, her boss, looking flabbergasted, said, "You are the last person I would have considered to do something like this." Lila just smiled and replied, "I know."

Fast forward to the present: Lila's colorful murals now adorn the city, transforming mundane alleys into portals to other dimensions. And here's the twist—those once-skeptical colleagues of hers? They've become her biggest patrons, commissioning pieces for their boardrooms and lobbies.

In breaking free, Lila didn't just redefine success on her own terms; she became a beacon for others to question The Matrix and follow their own calling. Like Lila, you hold the brush that can paint your destiny.

Are you ready to color outside the lines?

The Money Shot: Crushing Conformity

Here lies a key to your untapped wealth and financial freedom—crushing conformity! Breaking free from conformity's suffocating grip empowers you, granting yourself the freedom to be authentically you. Just watch as your distinctiveness ignites brilliance and blazes a trail towards higher opportunity.

The Matrix fears your true power, but it's also 100% willing to light your sh** up. You possess the potential, right now, to claim your rightful place as a truly unique individual, illuminated by your own spotlight. Dispel the notion that such radiance is reserved for only a select few. It's accessible to every single one of us—yes, including you. Are you ready to fearlessly embrace your individuality and unlock the hidden opportunities within The Quantum Field?

The Recap

It's a new dawn, a new perspective. Conformity is the past; Quantum Capitalism is the future. Bid farewell to societal molds. Embrace, showcase, and capitalize on your individuality. Your potential is vast, waiting to be unleashed in the vast expanse of The Quantum Field.

Poke The Brain

Can you identify one aspect of your life where you've suppressed your true self? How can you start flaunting that part of you, unapologetically, from today?

Your Next Power Move

Juggernaut Journal Exercise: Breaking the Chains of Conformity.

The Reconnect

Reflect on your past and present. What aspects of yourself have you tried to hide, suppress, or change because The Matrix told you they weren't "right" or "normal"? Write them down. Remember, these are your unique facets—traits that set you apart from the rest.

Shedding Traits Imposed by The Matrix

We often adopt behaviors, characteristics, or ideals that aren't truly aligned with our authentic selves but are rather encouraged or imposed by The Matrix. Identify such traits that you've felt pressured into embodying, even if they don't resonate with who you truly are. Write them down in a separate list.

Reflection

Now, looking at the two lists, contemplate how they've influenced your journey. How have they shaped your choices, your self-esteem, your life direction?

On a special page of the journal, maybe the very back page, write a commitment to yourself—a pledge to gently turn away from The Matrix's version of you and embrace your authentic self.

Remember, the Quantum Capitalist thrives on individuality, authenticity, and defying conformity that is unnatural to you. As you work through this exercise, envision yourself breaking free from the invisible chains that have held you back. Embrace your quirks, celebrate your uniqueness and allow yourself to be imperfect.

Lesson 7
Sectors of Reality

Now that you're shedding that heavy weight of societal norms and expectations, I bet you're feeling a touch lighter, right? Ready to truly soar? This upcoming concept might seem mind-bending at first, but bear with me. It just might reshape your entire understanding of reality as you've come to know it. Ready to dive in? Let's go.

Prepare to unveil the practical magic of turning focus into tangible reality. No hocus-pocus here; it's all about learning the process of shaping your layer of reality and it's actually quite a nifty trick. So, buckle up because we're about to explore the intriguing concept of the "Sectors of Reality"—a multi-level reality amusement park where you can tap into different Sectors in the blink of an eye. Don't believe me? Stay tuned for a powerful homework exercise that will display this concept in real time.

Think of reality as a series of levels stacked on top of each other. To visualize this, grab a plain white piece of paper and draw ten straight lines across it, each separated by about an inch. At the top is level #10—your happy place, where dreams soar and everything you desire exists: wealth, freedom, comfort, fulfilling relationships, and anything else you value. Level #1, at the very bottom, is filled with undesirable junk: scarcity mentality, depression, anxiety, feelings of meaning-

Sectors of Reality 67

lessness, debt, conflict-ridden relationships, low-paying jobs, and struggle. If you're feeling ambivalent, lazy, or hesitant to take action, you might find yourself in the middle, at level #5, which we'll term the "Suspended State." This is where mediocrity thrives and dreams are stifled by excuses.

A valuable insight: your position in this visual representation is never static. That's why the saying goes, "the rich get richer and the poor get poorer." You're either evolving or devolving, as matter is always in motion. Most people hover around the middle of the grid, however: a level up on a good day, a level down on a bad one. Notice how your thoughts and feelings often reflect the kind of day you're having? The reality is, your thoughts, feelings, and other attributes (we'll delve into those in future lessons) dictate your navigation through the Sectors. You're not experiencing your Sector. You're creating it.

For instance, think back to when you were having a bitchin' day. Everything was going well, no glitches, no drama. Then, suddenly, you received an unexpected bill, someone dented your car, or your recent fling ended things. Reality instantly looked grimmer, right? You descended to a lower Sector, and without tools to halt the downslide, you probably continued to fall. The art and science of Quantum Capitalism equips you with the necessary tools to not only stop your fall but also immediately propel you toward higher Sectors.

Alright, let's cut through the fluff and hit the core. You know how a bad moment can spiral out into an avalanche of crap, dragging you into life's dingy basement? Yeah, that. But here's the kicker: the positive stuff can do the same, shooting you up to the penthouse suites of life. Imagine life as this insane rollercoaster, not just random thrills, but a journey dictated by your focus. Up, down, sideways. Got that image? Good. Now, ask yourself: am I ascending towards the stars or nosediving into the abyss? Take a hard look at your current Sector. Ready to ditch the basement and go hard towards those higher Sectors?

Let's talk Law of Attraction. For some, it's like a dodgy Wi-Fi signal—hit or miss. Why's that? Because trying to "manifest" your dreams from the basement is like trying to grab a cloud from the ground. Inconsistent, right? Enter Quantum Capitalism. It's not about yanking your dreams down; it's about elevating yourself to where those dreams are just your everyday reality. It's about cruising up to those top-tier Sectors.

Now, let's get dark. Some folks are stuck in the basement, Sector #1, and it's pitch black. Ever felt like you're in a bottomless pit with no idea that just above you is a world bathed in light? It's like Sector #1 has you in a chokehold, whispering, "This is it. There's nothing more." But that's a lie. There's a way out.

If you're still breathing, you've got a ticket to change Sectors. Stuck in the lowlands, or worse, flatlining at Sector #1? Time to break out the party hats because hitting rock bottom is life's bizarre bounce house. Mental meltdowns, heart-wrenching breakups, bank accounts in the red—it's all part of the cosmic shakeup. These aren't just setbacks; they're wakeup calls, a siren blaring in your ear to snap out of the zombie march that got you here. Embrace the mess. Own it. And then, use it as your springboard. Bounce off that motherf***** like your life depends on it—because, guess what? It does.

The Money Shot: Quantum Catapulting Yourself

Don't have what you want in life? You're probably stuck in tired old Sectors. Is it time to break free and discover the untapped potential of a new Sector?

Your positive thoughts and actions serve as catalysts, propelling you higher, unearthing opportunities and encounters to elevate your life. But remember, negative thoughts and actions can pull you down just as easily. So, tune your spaceship (that's you! And more to come on this shortly!) to higher destinations and witness the magic unfold. Say goodbye to conventional money-making monotony and venture into uncharted territories brimming with opportunities. Blend creativity, strategy, and innovation to chart your cosmic treasure map. Remember, each Sector boasts its own unique riches; the power to choose lies with you.

The Recap

Your thoughts and actions serve as navigators in the journey through the Sectors of Reality. Understand how your thoughts, patterns, and actions shape different Sectors and you can smoothly navigate from the ground floor to the penthouse of reality.

Poke The Brain

Using this visual representation, in which numbered Sector of Reality do you mostly reside?

Your Next Power Move

Practical Exercise: Perspective Power Shift.

Objective

To deeply understand how your perspective can instantaneously navigate you to different Sectors of Reality, try this exercise out.

Dive into the Negative

Find a bustling public space where you can be an observant bystander.

Task: observe your surroundings, to start, focus solely on negative elements. Yep, you heard me right! Tune into the crying child, the arguing couple, the discomforts of urban life, trash piling up, the agitated driver looking unsuccessfully for a parking spot. Truly immerse yourself in this experience for a set time, say a couple of minutes. See it. Feel it. Live it.

Now, switch Sectors.

Embrace the Positive

Reset: close your eyes briefly, take a couple of breaths, and clear your mind.

With fresh eyes, search for all the joyous, serene, and loving moments around you. Watch the laughter shared between friends, the dog happily playing, the beauty of the natural world in the midst of the urban jungle, the couple in love, the child enjoying his toy. Engage with this perspective for another couple of minutes. See it. Feel it. Live it.

Reflect & Choose

Contemplate: realize you've just experienced two starkly different Sectors within the same setting, driven purely by your choice of focus.

Recognizing the power of perspective, consciously decide which Sector of Reality you wish to predominantly reside in. Remember, you have the autonomy to choose. Every time you feel swayed by the negatives of life, use this exercise as a reminder that the positives exist concurrently. It's simply a matter of where you place your focus.

Lesson 8
Game-Changer

Alright, the idea of "Sectors" is intriguing, right? It offers a fresh perspective on life's highs and lows. But what if I told you that you have the power to shift up a few Sectors with a single mind trick? And what if I revealed that so-called "poverty mentality" is merely a ruse orchestrated by The Matrix to keep you on those lower Sectors using the exact same trick? Not the most appealing thought, is it? But I've got insights to share, so let's dive in.

The truth is, the entire Universe, The Quantum Field, The Matrix, and your current Sector of Reality contain boundless information. There's so much data that every perspective a human can adopt, no matter how unusual, can find supporting evidence.

Think of it this way: if you're battling poverty mentality or scarcity thinking, you're subscribing to a singular theory among many: the belief in insufficiency, that others will always have more because they're somehow better, or that life's bounties are reserved for someone else. This is a single theory you've embraced, and your reality supplies the corresponding proof to support it. The beauty? You can adopt a new theory, and the world will furnish evidence for that theory, too.

Game-Changer

Now, armed with this knowledge, you can play the quantum scientist. Whether it's political leanings, your opinion of "how the world is," the state of global affairs, or your entire worldview, all are mere theories backed by respective evidence.

So, isn't it high time to ditch the desperate, Matrix suggested theory, step into the wizard's robe and create a new theory about your existence? If your current mindset feels as useless as a scratched CD from two decades ago, then toss it out. Recognize if you've been clinging to a mediocre, pre-packaged reality that has you seeing it all from a perspective of deficiency. Real recovery from poverty programming starts the moment you're willing to release outdated beliefs. There are superior alternatives available.

The brass tacks? You can choose any reality, and your world will show you all the ways in which you are correct in your thinking and support that version of reality materializing.

Heal traumas by saturating your thoughts with the wisdom that it's all for your greater good. Recover from the scarcity mindset and evolve your financial game by surrounding yourself with others who have done the same and adopt their theories about how it's possible. Believe The Universe, Quantum Field, and your Sector of Reality hold the absolute best for you, because they do. Proudly wear your rose-tinted glasses and ignore anyone suggesting that you take them off.

(In fact, why not order a pair from Amazon or your favorite store? Whenever The Matrix feels overwhelming, wear them and immerse yourself in your newfound Quantumy perspective.)

Recovering from poverty mentality is not achieved by wallowing in more of it. It's accomplished by shifting your theory to a self-serving one and absorbing all the information the world offers that aligns with that theory. You have current access to it all, so let the world be your buffet; it's all in front of you. Start to believe that, and you'll begin to see it. It's like discovering an endless ocean when you've been limited to a fishbowl.

Here's the thing: your attitude can color your world in vibrant hues or somber shades. If negative thoughts dominate your mind, your reality will reflect that negativity. But embracing a magical perspective, even amidst stormy weather, you fill your world with reasons to celebrate.

Start aligning with the theory that you have it all and more is headed in your direction, because it is, if you choose this option. Then, treat yourself to a special gift and luxuriate in thoughts of all you do have right now, even if it's just a roof over your head and $5 in your pocket. That's a lot! You will begin to notice those vibrant hues and all the reasons to celebrate. It's not wishful thinking; it's practical quantum mechanics.

The Money Shot: Hello BallerStatus

This knowledge equips you to paint your world with vibrant hues, no matter your origins. Flip the script and take control of your financial domain by acknowledging that you might be operating with a bogus theory. Riches are everywhere; elevate your mindset, soar above evidence supporting inferior theories, and chart new paths. Unchain your quantum spirit, embark on your ascension, and sculpt a financial legacy, tailored by you, from scratch. Believe, and your voyage to affluence, ease, and liberty will blow you away.

To cultivate wealth, immerse in affluent feelings now. When present circumstances try dragging you back, remember it's just The Matrix playing its yucky little tricks. Time to redirect your focus from absence to presence and shed constraining beliefs. It might sound clichéd, but adopting an affluent mindset works!

The Recap

Every belief or perspective a person holds finds supporting evidence in the world, whether it's about scarcity or abundance. Embracing a mindset of abundance and viewing challenges through a positive lens will allow the world to provide corresponding affirmations and experiences. Thus, by understanding and harnessing this principle, one can consciously curate a desired reality.

Poke The Brain

What gaps in your current perspective might be leading to a less-than-ideal life experience? Are you willing to embrace a new viewpoint?

Your Next Power Move

Juggernaut Journal Exercise: Dissecting Your Current Life Theory Self-Assessment.

Your Overall Life Theory

Reflect on your overall perspective on life. How do you view your journey, your experiences, and your potential? Write down the first thoughts that come to mind.

Your Money Theory

Delve deep into your thoughts about money. Do you view it as an ally or a constant challenge? How do you feel about your relationship with money, your ability to earn, save, and invest?

Your Place Within the System

Ponder on how you perceive your role within the broader societal system, The Matrix. Do you feel you have agency, or do you feel like one of the "have nots"? How do you feel about your capacity to navigate and find success within the system?

Identifying Patterns

Review what you've written and identify recurring themes or patterns in your beliefs. Are there common threads of doubt, fear, or feelings of unworthiness? Conversely, are there patterns of confidence, ambition, or optimism? Highlight or underline these patterns.

Pinpointing The Limiters

List down the beliefs that you feel might be holding you back or causing friction in your life's journey. These are crucial because even though we're not working on upgrading them right now, being aware of them sets the stage for our next lesson.

Reflection

Sit with the beliefs and patterns you've identified. Reflect on where they might have originated. Were they influenced by early life experiences, Matrix standards, or external voices? Understanding the origin can provide clarity on why they play such a significant role in your current theory.

End this exercise by acknowledging your willingness to dissect and understand these theories. Recognizing their presence and influence is the first step in growth and transformation.

Prepare yourself, because in the next lesson, you'll embark on the exciting journey of upgrading these theories. For now, sit with this newfound awareness and let it marinate.

Lesson 9

Designing A New Guiding Theory

Alright, in the last lesson we dropped the "evidence to support all theories" bomb. We also kicked the lid off that old crypt of crappy theories. Surprise, surprise—it's just dusty, old theories The Matrix is all too happy to jam to. I gave you a teaser about choosing a brand-new theory, and guess what? That's exactly our lesson this round.

This is where the journey truly begins. Fire up those spaceship engines, kids! We're going full-throttle into theory design! Woohoo!

Your theory is like the destination plugged into your GPS. Do your coordinates have you navigating in circles? We've established that if you aren't where you want to be in life, it's probably due to your janky theory. If your hopes and dreams don't adequately line up with your theory of life, well, you've got classic disappointment in your experience of reality. Mid-life crisis, anyone? Every scenic overlook and every dead end—it's all happening because of your theory. Think about it—the theory you've been using has led you to the exact position in life you are currently experiencing.

Let's call this concept your "Guiding Theory." It's your subconscious map, built from all the material we covered

Designing A New Guiding Theory

in the previous lesson: external programming, societal conditioning, and your influences throughout your entire life, just to name a few. However, many guiding theories now resemble an antiquated atlas. Personal evolution is hard to come by when the core theory stays intact.

So, you probably took this musty map, a Matrix party favor, and navigated your reality (perhaps unknowingly) gathering "evidence" to affirm that inferior theory. We do this with money, love, self-worth—you name it. Then, our world either extends its silver platter or hands us an empty potato sack, and voila, that's your life. It's not rocket science; it's straightforward cognitive science. Ever heard of "confirmation bias"? Precisely. Navigating reality with a defunct theory is confirmation bias in action, and sometimes the results aren't exactly ideal.

To put it another way, your personal Guiding Theory is like a self-fulfilling prophecy, whispering either meaningless jabber or declarations of grandeur into reality's ear. But now that you're aware you have the power to upgrade your theory, you have much greater control.

Here's the secret: it's as if you're strolling through a fair, and every game you play, you win exactly the prize you expect. Nothing more, nothing less. If your Guiding Theory is jacked, it's like you're showing up to the game with negative points, expecting to win nothing. You've got to level the quantum playing field.

The Matrix? It's cunning. It wants to keep you trapped, feeding you everything that supports subpar theories. Remember, it loves you stuck and doom-scrolling your days away.

But you? You're even sharper, bolder, and ready to break free. With a new Guiding Theory as robust as a diamond, you'll have your own luminous North Star, ensuring you don't get played anymore by The Matrix's mischief. Are you ready to install Guiding Theory 2.0?

A Personal Example

My theory used to be: "I'm worthless. No one loves me. I'm uneducated. My life has no meaning. I might as well settle for a minimum wage job." These thoughts either plagued my mind or simply remained a background narrative. As a result, I radiated this theory into my environment, emitting vibes that matched my beliefs, and projected them onto the world with the same intensity as the little girl in "The Exorcist" projectile-vomiting pea soup. And what happened? Reality served me exactly what I ordered, consistent with my theory. My world offered up infinite evidence, information, and experiences that perfectly fed into this dismal narrative and I ate it all. People told me I would never amount to anything, I faced rejection at every turn, and life seemed determined to pigeonhole me into a minimum wage grind. Any contradictory evidence supporting a different theory went unnoticed or was dismissed as nonsense. For instance, if someone tried to convince me I was worth more, they immediately needed to exit my reality because either something was wrong with them, or they had me all wrong.

Then I had my breakout moment. With audacity and nothing left to lose, I began to believe I had value. How did this happen exactly? Well, I somehow grasped that this was my only way out. After a traumatic series of incidents jolted me into a slightly different state of consciousness, I made a run for it. I was so low, things were so bleak and so hopeless that I declared to turn my situation around. Through my dire circumstances, I chose to remember I wasn't entirely worthless. I recalled a

9th-grade English teacher's encouragement, the time I won a poetry contest at school, and an uncle who believed in me. I clung to the collection of goodness I could muster, however small, and held on for dear life.

I began asking more from life and began elevating my theory to sound something like this: "I may have been born into poverty and have nothing but a pile of debt now, but I'm destined to be a success story. I'm determined to defy the odds. One day people will be shocked to learn I only have a 9th-grade education."

Fast forward to today: it's hard for people to fathom the heights I've reached with just a 9th-grade education. I'm wealthy by my own standards, debt-free, earning far more than minimum wage, and beholden to no one. My reality transformed to mirror my new Guiding Theory. Crazy, right? The kicker is, this transformation is within your grasp too, as you reshape and redefine your own theory.

The Money Shot: Solid Gold, Baby

Alright, here's your 24-carat advice: your Guiding Theory isn't just some fancy terminology—it's the alchemy that turns your ordinary into gold. When you align yourself right, The Quantum Field doesn't play hard-to-get. Every intention you throw, it catches. Every order, filled. Doubt? Toss it away; it's the monkey wrench you don't need.

And hey, since you're rewriting your Guiding Theory, why not be ambitious? You can choose anything you want. But hold up, be prepared to flex your adaptability muscles. Life isn't a straight highway to your chosen destination; it's filled with unexpected detours and challenges along the way. Embrace the reroutes, learn from the obstacles, and don't throw in the towel on your theory at the first sign of trouble. Evolve like a quantum chameleon. Change is constant, but so is your resilience. Took a fall? Learn to spin on a dime, adapt, and keep moving. Now a detour is a welcomed reroute to your destination. Who knows, you might find even more treasures along the way, because that's how Quantum Capitalists roll.

The Recap

Your Guiding Theory? Set it right, align it with action, and watch those dreams convert to reality.

Poke The Brain

How has your Guiding Theory evolved or regressed over the years? Are you ready for an upgrade?

Your Next Power Move

Juggernaut Journal Exercise: Crafting Your Upgraded Guiding Theory.

Building on our last lesson, where you put pen to paper to uncover your current Guiding Theory, let's further refine it. The beauty of this exercise lies in the power of written introspection. Let the words flow and see where they take you.

Step 1: Reflect & Revisit

Journal Entry: begin with the title, "My Current Guiding Theory." Write down the theory you identified in the last lesson. Allow yourself to then describe how this theory has shown up in your day-to-day life since our last session.

Pros and Cons: under a new subheading, "Impacts of My Theory," list the positive and negative influences this theory has had on your life.

Step 2: Envision Your Evolution

Free Write: under the title, "My Limitless Vision," allow yourself to dream. Write freely about where you see yourself if there were no bounds to your Guiding Theory.

Highlight & Extract: re-read what you have written. Highlight or underline phrases or sentences that resonate deeply with you. Extract these into a list titled "Key Pillars of My Upgraded Theory."

Step 3: Craft & Commit

Compose Your Theory: using a new page or a fresh section, begin with the title, "My Upgraded Guiding Theory." Craft a powerful statement or series of statements based on your reflections and pillars.

Affirmative Entry: create a short journal entry titled "Living My Upgraded Theory." Ponder on how you can reinforce and support this new theory into your daily life. Write down steps, commitments, or rituals that come to mind.

Note to Future Self: end this exercise by writing a short letter to your future self about your hopes and aspirations based on this new theory.

Remember, this writing journey is both a form of self-exploration and self-expression. Let your words be the bridge between your current self and the future self, guided by your newly crafted theory.

Conclusion

Your Guiding Theory isn't just words on paper; it's the heartbeat of your life. By evolving it, you're setting a new rhythm, one that's in harmony with a higher Sector. Shatter that old, cracked compass. Build your Guiding Theory from scratch. Challenge it, refine it, and then live it.

Lesson 10

Supercharging with the 4 Qualifiers

Let's get real for a moment. You've started crafting a new guiding theory, right? But here's the thing: it's not enough just to create a fancy theory and expect magic. This lesson? It's about turning that theory into a powerhouse. It's the difference between a bike and a Ferrari in mastering your reality. Ready to shift gears and zoom into a realm of endless possibilities? Let's dive into the "4 Qualifiers"—your reality's dashboard controls.

Think back to that time when you were stuck in a loop of negative self-talk. "I'm worthless. No one loves me. My life is a dead-end." Ring any bells? That's the kind of low-quality programming that keeps you chained to the ground floor of reality. But what if I told you that you can break free from that cycle with the right tools? The 4 Qualifiers are those tools.

Guiding Theory: this is your master plan. Without it, you're a ship without a compass. Define where you want to go and lock it in.

Thoughts: your thoughts are the fuel for your journey. Fill your mind with the good stuff. Negative thoughts? They're like pouring sugar in your gas tank.

Actions: dreaming big? Great. But dreams without action are just fantasies. Start small, gain momentum, and soon you'll be speeding towards your goals.

Frequency: this is the vibe you emit. It's the music you play to which The Universe dances. Want a better dance? Change the tune.

Here's where it gets serious. If your 4 Qualifiers aren't in sync, you're going nowhere fast. Want wealth but think you don't deserve it? That's like trying to drive with the handbrake on. Spending your days doom-scrolling yet hoping for peace and clarity? Good luck with that. It's time for a reality check. Are you really ready for what you're asking for? If not, it might be time to dig deeper.

Meet Alexandra

A Tale of Two Realities

Reality 1: The Misaligned Qualifiers

In the world where Alexandra's 4 Qualifiers are more jumbled than a crossword puzzle, her day unfolds like a comedy of errors.

Guiding Theory: Alexandra's blueprint for the day is more "oh god, not this again" than "let's conquer it." She starts her morning convinced that nothing ever goes her way. It's as if she's the lead in a sitcom titled "Ugh, Why Me?"

Thoughts: her thoughts are a merry-go-round of doom. As she scrolls through social media, she sighs at the success stories, thinking, "That'll never be me." Each negative thought scrambles her Quantum GPS, leading her further away from all the stuff she desperately longs for.

Supercharging with the 4 Qualifiers

Actions: in terms of action, Alexandra is a star performer in the grand play of procrastination. Rather than diving into the self-development course she's been putting off for a year, she's marathoning "Desperate Housekeepers." Her actions echo her belief: "Why bother trying when my couch is so comfy?"

Frequency: Alexandra's vibe is more Eeyore than Tigger. She's a walking raincloud, repelling opportunities and invitations to collaborate as if they're made of kryptonite.

Reality 2: The Aligned Qualifiers

Now, let's flip the script. In this reality, Alexandra's 4 Qualifiers are in perfect harmony, and her day is as smooth as a jazz ensemble.

Guiding Theory: her guiding theory is a well-drawn map to success. She wakes up with a mantra: "I am capable. I attract positive outcomes." She acknowledges her role as the creator of her own reality, one she holds on to and nourishes.

Thoughts: Alexandra's thoughts are her cheerleaders, not critics. Each positive thought plants a seed of potential. She looks at her Pinterest account, filled with all the stuff she's striving towards, and thinks, "I'm coming. Nothing can stop me now."

Actions: her actions are the steps of a winner. Instead of lounging in bed, she's working on her novel, networking with fellow creatives, and setting up the side hustle to her side hustle. Every step she takes feels like checking a box on the destiny ledger.

Frequency: Alexandra's frequency is so high people think she's on something, but she's not. She's a magnet, drawing in connections and chances like bees to nectar. It's like she's broadcasting "Who wants a piece of this?" on her personal radio frequency.

The Tale's Takeaway

Alexandra's two versions of reality are a stark contrast between a life led by misaligned Qualifiers and one driven by a harmonious set. It's the difference between sailing against the wind and having it at your back. So, can you relate with either tale? Where do you need an upgrade?

The Money Shot: Pimp My Ride

Tuning the 4 Qualifiers isn't just some spiritual hocus-pocus. It's a practical blueprint to real-world success. When you refine your Guiding Theory, you're not just changing how you see yourself; you're changing how The Universe responds to you. This is about attracting tangible wealth, unearthing golden opportunities, and climbing to those higher Sectors of security and comfort. Think of it as programming The Universe's algorithm. When your output (Guiding Theory, Thoughts, Actions, and Frequency) is on point, The Universe responds with customized success. It's a straightforward strategy to turn dreams into reality. So, want to see your fortunes rise and doors of opportunity fling wide open? Get those Qualifiers aligned and watch your world transform.

The Recap

Rise to higher Sectors with this formula: Guiding Theory, Thoughts, Actions, and Frequency. It's simple yet powerful, if you're committed to fine-tuning them.

Poke the Brain

Where are your 4 Qualifiers off balance? Is it time for a tune-up?

Your Next Power Move

Juggernaut Journal Exercise: A 4 Qualifiers Analysis

Objective: Examine your 4 Qualifiers in depth

1. Diving Deep into the Shadows

Thoughts: think back to the most challenging period in your life. What was a dominant thought you frequently held? Write it down: "During this time, I often thought..."

Actions: reflect on a defining action you took during that time. Write it down: "One thing I consistently did back then was..."

Frequency: capture the energy or emotion you most often felt during that period. Write it down: "During those days, I usually felt..."

Guiding Theory: what was your overarching belief or theory about life during this time? Write it down: "Back then, I believed that..."

2. Soaring Through the Peaks

Thoughts: now, reminisce about the best time in your life. What was a positive thought that empowered you? Write it down: "During this golden period, I often thought..."

Actions: remember a proactive step you took during this time that exemplified your growth. Write it down: "One impactful thing I did was..."

Frequency: reflect on the dominant emotion or energy that defined this happy phase. Write it down: "In those moments, I constantly felt..."

Guiding Theory: what was your uplifting belief or theory about life at that time? Write it down: "In those times, I strongly believed that..."

Now, with these reflections laid out before you, it's time for a crucial introspection. Are you consistently operating at your peak, or do you find yourself slipping into the shadows more often than you'd like? If your 4 Qualifiers were key drivers in both these phases, why would you ever choose to function beneath your potential? Isn't it time to elevate your Qualifiers and step into the best version of yourself? Reflect on these questions and decide what Sector you want to travel to going forward.

Now, with a primed and ready spaceship, you're all set to cruise through any junk storms and murky Sectors that come your way. Stay steady on your course, and soon, the clear, starlit skies will be yours to roam. Until next time, keep your eyes on the higher Sectors and your Qualifiers sharp!

Lesson 11

Blackholes

Alright, you've got those Qualifiers dialed in, all nice and sparkly, thanks to our previous lesson. You're soaring, engines humming, but... hold up, space cadet! Is that a Blackhole ahead, trying to suck you into its sneaky vortex? Wait, what?! But hey, don't hit the panic button yet. We've got the toolkit to steer you right out of that! Ready to navigate? Let's blast off!

We're diving into one of life's greatest disruptors: the "Blackhole." Picture it: pesky Matrix bullies, always lurking, eager to swipe your energetic lunch money! And who might these cosmic thieves be? The usual lineup: media, social platforms, the daily political circus, even the drama brewing in our very own homes. But keep your space boots on, because we're about to sidestep the Blackhole's greedy gravitational pull.

Blackholes? They're voracious energy vortexes. These culprits pull us in with promises of binge-worthy shows (hello, Netflix!), the latest gossip (celeb sites), staying in-the-loop (thank you, media), and even connecting with old pals (side-eye at Facebook). They're the family spats, workplace politics, trending sports, pop culture, and those ever-so-polarizing political parties. Essentially, anything that consumes your thoughts and urges you to pick a side—that's a Blackhole.

Here's the deal: you enter a sort of contract with these Blackholes, and don't even know it. It goes a little something like this: "Hey, give me some of your time and attention, and in return, I'll entertain you or keep you updated." But here's the catch: Blackholes have an insatiable appetite. They're not just content nibbling on bits of our energy—they want it all. The grander the spectacle—think high-stakes US presidential elections—the more engrossed we become. They swell and the more enchanting and triggering they become, the more human resources they can consume: time, money, attention. Their weapons? Our emotions, aspirations, and need to belong. They are cunning predators. They find our Achilles heel and exploit it.

From the booze biz to the latest TikTok craze, ensuing war, the media blasting the catastrophic event du jour, right up to the political debate of the decade—*all* Blackholes, every last one of them.

Remember the Deepak Chopra quote, "Create your own reality or one will be created for you"? Well, when a Blackhole has you in its suction, it starts molding your reality, feeding you stories, urging you to pick teams, and dictating your emotions. Blackholes are The Matrix's favorite tool to keep you compliant, perpetually chasing the next trend or fad, exhausted and/or tuned in. They set the rules, making you pine for what's "in" or hanging on to the edge of your seat.

All's not lost, however! It's all about Blackhole management. It's about assessing what the Blackhole is asking from you and weighing it against what you're genuinely getting back. Our human energy? It's gold, and if you're not living the dream, chances are, you're feeding these energy leeches more than they deserve. Recognizing these traps is your first defense. That draining romantic relationship? A BLACKHOLE. That soul-sucking job that keeps you up at night? BLACKHOLE. That ganja habit burning your time, brain cells, and pockets? Oh, you bet, BLACKHOLE. Is this a wake-up call? It's your chance to take stock and wisely audit your energetic resources to gauge what is benefitting from your energy and what you are receiving in turn.

Let's go deeper and identify more forms they take in your daily life. These are not just trivial aspects of life, but hold the potential to be insidious energy sappers embedded in your everyday existence.

Imagine the digital Universe of social media and mainstream media, the infamous scroll-hole, resembling a vast nebula of information and interaction. This nebula, while dazzling, is a deceptive Blackhole. It beckons with the allure of endless information and social connection, only to plunge you into a depth of distraction and lost time. This is the Blackhole that thrives on your curiosity and social urges, turning minutes into hours of unproductive scrolling.

Now, shift your gaze to the political cosmos, a domain rife with scandalous Blackholes. These are not just news stories or debates; they are bottomless energy traps, demanding your attention and emotional investment. However, it's crucial to navigate these spaces selectively, conserving your mental energy for issues that truly align with your values and contribute positively to your personal evolution.

In the professional sphere, beware of workplace Blackholes. These are not mere challenges or difficult colleagues; they are energy drains, capable of depleting your enthusiasm and creativity. Identifying these elements and recalibrating your approach can help preserve your professional zeal and prevent your job from becoming an energy void.

Family dynamics, much like a cluster of stars, can be both illuminating and consuming. While family ties offer support and love, they can also spiral into Blackholes of emotional chaos, especially during conflicts or high-drama situations. The art lies in balancing involvement with self-preservation, ensuring your energy isn't wholly absorbed by familial ordeals.

Parenthood, a journey filled with joy and challenges, can also manifest as an energy Blackhole. The demands of raising children, while rewarding, can be exhaustive. It's vital to balance this beautiful responsibility with self-care, ensuring that the parenting path enriches rather than drains your vital life force.

The consumerist culture, with its endless cycle of desire and acquisition, is another subtle Blackhole. This relentless pursuit often leaves you feeling unfulfilled, trapped in a cycle of temporary satisfaction and long-term emptiness. Recognizing this pattern helps break free from its gravitational pull, allowing you to find contentment beyond material possessions.

Substances, often sought for escape or relief, can transform into Blackholes of dependency, financial drain and escapism. They promise temporary solace but can lead to a cycle of reliance and detriment to your wellbeing. Awareness and caution are key in navigating this tricky terrain.

Entertainment, in its many forms, can be a delightful escape but also a dangerous Blackhole. When indulgence turns into overconsumption, it becomes a vortex that swallows time and energy, leaving you wondering where your precious moments have vanished.

In understanding and recognizing these varied Blackholes in your life's journey, you become equipped not only to identify them but also to navigate through them. This awareness allows you to chart a course that is enriching, fulfilling, and aligned with a worthy destination, free from the pull of these energy-sapping Blackholes.

Meet William

William was a typical millennial, lost in the world of social media, politics, and binge-watching TV series. One night, after diving deep into the never-ending scroll hole of Twitter, William fell asleep and dreamed of being sucked into a literal black hole. He felt the g-force pulling him into the vortex at high velocity. He felt the loss of control, the confusion, and the fall into vast nothingness. As William tumbled through the cosmic void at the speed of light, he felt his physical body dissolving into pure energy, and then he watched as all of that energy disappeared into the void.

He jolted awake, heart racing. "What the hell was that?" he thought. As he lay there trying to make sense of it all, something clicked within him. Memories of wasted time flashed before his eyes: endless hours doom-scrolling, arguing with internet trolls, being consumed by office drama, and spiraling down rabbit holes of conspiracy theories. It was in that moment of post interstellar free fall that William had an epiphany. His life was being sucked dry by metaphorical Blackholes!

Miraculously, William woke up from this experience and committed to not just shrugging it all off. He realized that it was a dream, but the lesson was very real. It was time for some better energetic management.

Gone were the days of being consumed by media, social platforms, and engaging negatively with others. William decided to take his energy back and redirect his mojo towards endeavors that genuinely pumped up his personal net worth.

He started by limiting his screen time, focusing on positive content, and engaging in activities that actually added value to his life. As he dodged the Blackholes, William found himself gravitating towards golden opportunities. He channeled his energy into creative projects, fitness, and meaningful relationships. With his newfound free time and energy, he began a side gig in the evenings designing and building pour over coffee stations in his garage, which were selling out on Etsy.

By recognizing and managing the energy drains in his life, he became the active creator of his journey rather than succumbing to the void.

The Money Shot: Unshackling Your Money Game

Alright, let's dive deep into The Matrix and decode this: grasping the whole Blackhole concept isn't just some fancy knowledge—it's your secret cheat code to amassing wealth and opportunities. When you dodge these sneaky energy thieves, you're not just saving your vibe—you're redirecting your mojo towards endeavors that genuinely pump up your net worth.

Bypass those time-sucking Blackholes, and watch how you naturally gravitate towards cash-making ventures and golden opportunities. By giving Blackholes the swerve, you're not just creating boundaries so you can thrive more energetically; you're channeling that energy into cash-making endeavors.

Look at it like this: it's the difference between Instagram consuming hours of your free time and mental bandwidth or you becoming a content creator and capitalizing on ad dollars. In the game of Blackholes, it's consume or be consumed.

The Recap

Blackholes—the insidious energy drains lurking in our daily lives. These voracious vortexes, from media to workplace drama, constantly vie for our attention, emotions, and time, subtly shaping our realities. By recognizing and managing these Blackholes, individuals can redirect their energy from being passively consumed to actively engaging in meaningful, fulfilling endeavors. Essentially, it's about taking back control and being the active creator of your life journey rather than a passive spectator.

Poke The Brain

Which Blackholes are you currently lost in?

Your Next Power Move

Juggernaut Journal Exercise: Blackhole Bypass Bootcamp.

This exercise is more than a simple task; it's an opportunity to delve deep into what you are engaging with energetically, understand your energy patterns, and reshape your daily life for optimal productivity and fulfillment.

Step 1: Blackhole Breakdown

Begin by introspectively examining your past week. Identify the top three activities or habits that have disproportionately consumed your time and energy. These are your personal Blackholes—be it endless doom-scrolling, engaging in political drama, or family disputes. Recognize that acknowledging these energy-drainers is the first step towards profound self-awareness and growth.

Step 2: Deep Dive Diagnosis

Now, engage in a deeper analysis. Write a sentence or two about the underlying reasons for each Blackhole's hold over you. Try to understand the "WHY." Are these habits a response to emotional needs, a result of conditioned behavior, or a means to fulfill a deeper psychological craving? Self-awareness is key, and by understanding your motivations, you're better positioned to alter them.

The Path Forward: Continual Growth and Self-Reflection

This exercise is not a one-time activity but a cornerstone of continuous self-development. Regularly revisiting and refining your approach ensures you're always moving towards a more fulfilled and energetically efficient life. Each step away from these Blackholes is a step closer to realizing your full potential. Remember, in the pursuit of personal growth, the energy you conserve and how you choose to redirect it, becomes the catalyst for profound transformation.

Lesson 12

Cutting Matrix Puppet Strings

Alright Blackholes, we are onto your sneaky little shenanigans. Do they really think they are gonna pull a fast one on us again? Wait, hold up... those pesky old habits are dying hard, huh? Dang it! Need the deets on taming these bad boy Blackholes? You got it! But brace yourself—combating Blackholes isn't about entering the boxing ring. Nah, they thrive on that drama. It's all about mastering the art of indifference and apathy. Let's deep dive into this madness, shall we?

Ready for a subject that's darker than dark matter itself? The Puppet Strings of Blackholes—those alluring distractors that will go to just about any lengths to keep you engaged. Gross, right? But here's the secret. You have the power to break free from these energy leeches and steer your own course.

These Blackholes are cunning. They toy with your sense of duty, emotions, and the innate need to belong. You see it every day in media and politics, roping you in with the charm of "staying informed" or "taking a stance." But the hard truth? These are energy vampires in disguise. Don't be fooled. Anything that consumes your attention, energy, money and time without contributing to your personal evolution is a destructive Blackhole.

Social media is the worst, it takes much more from you than just your time and energy. It's a well-known dopamine factory, isn't it? Every like, every share, every comment feeds this addiction, flooding your brain with the "feel-good" stuff. You think you're just scrolling away, but you're actually re-circuiting your synapses. Let's face it—you're not just losing time; you're messing with your mind, man, while also completely disregarding the masterplan blueprint for your life. Yuck!

Blackholes play a persuasive game, blending blatant coercion with covert manipulation to drain your thought energy and puppeteer your actions. But fear not! The curtain's about to be lifted on their deceitful performance!

Here's the Blackhole hack

Spot the Sleight of Hand: snap out of it and see through the Blackholes' ruses! Each nibble of fear, guilt, or anxiety they dangle is a dance step leading you away from your groove and straight into their twisted tango of dread and doubt. Geez, did I just crank the drama dial to 11 on that one? True though.

Say "No" to Manipulation: be the unyielding wall against those manipulative tactics. They tug at your emotions? You stand strong. Embrace your inner sovereignty and refuse to be an energy donor. Wrestling with a Blackhole gets you nowhere; indifference does. Draw that line in the sand and guard it. They say the opposite of love isn't hate. It's apathy. And apathy is exactly the antidote to the Blackhole's beckoning.

Unleash Positive Power: let positivity and empowerment be your new battle cry. Surround yourself with invigorating content, nurturing relationships, and wisdom that inspires.

Combat the Blackhole's negative influences with an armory of optimism.

Shatter the Habit Loop: break free from the chains of old habits that keep you circling the Blackholes in your Sector. Substitute those negative reactions with mindful, uplifting responses. Don't let the illusion of comfort fool you—break those familiar patterns!

The Money Shot: Cut Those Strings, Build Your Empire

Distracting Blackholes, like the allure of social media or the emotional tug of the news, are not just time-wasters; they're wealth-destroyers. Every moment spent being swayed by these distractions is a missed opportunity to create your product, learn a new high-value skill or invest in personal growth. Cutting ties with these energy leeches not only frees up your mental space but helps you discover optimal financial paths. As you focus on what truly matters, you open doors to prosperity, ensuring your energy and attention flow in the right direction.

Allowing Blackholes to dictate your thoughts and emotions can lead to uncalculated risks and impulsive decisions in your financial journey. This misstep can drain your financial resources quicker than a vortex. On the other hand, being in control of your energy can lead to clear, calculated decisions and a path of prosperity.

The Recap

Blackholes are out to consume your energy and hook you by twisting your thoughts and emotions. The path to freedom?

See through their deception, stand your ground, immerse in positivity, and break those old, binding habit loops.

Poke The Brain

What's your game plan? What decisive action will you take today to snip those puppet strings of Blackholes and reclaim your energy for your journey into the promising unknown?

Your Next Power Move

Juggernaut Journal Exercise: Plotting Your Energetic Landscape.

Objective: this exercise is your chance to visualize where you're operating in the multiverse and uncover which Blackholes are pulling at your strings. Let's chart out your energy landscape!

Step 1: Draw Your Sectors

Action: using a sheet of paper in landscape orientation, draw ten horizontal lines equally spaced from top to bottom. These represent the ten levels of reality, with the superior levels at the top and the inferior at the bottom.

Label each level, 1 through 10. Where do you perceive yourself to be right now? Put an "X" on that level.

Step 2: Identify Your Blackholes

Action: below your X representing where you currently stand, doodle a circle for each Blackhole in your life.

These are the drains tugging at your energy cords. Label each one—maybe it's "Instagram,"

"Friday Night Wine-athons," or "That Never-Ending Drama Relationship."

Step 3: Audit Your Energy Exchange

Action: within each Blackhole circle, split it in half.

On the left side, list out what these Blackholes are costing you. Is it your money? Your peace of mind? Your precious time? Your health?

On the right side, note what you perceive you're getting in return. A fleeting dopamine rush? A temporary distraction? A sense of social inclusion?

Step 4: Evaluate Your Bargains

Action: step back and review your diagram.

For each Blackhole, does the energy equation look balanced? Are you giving more than you're getting? Or does it look like you're on the losing end of these exchanges?

Step 5: Plot Your Escape Strategy

Action: think about strategies to pull back from these Blackholes.

How can you emotionally, energetically, and physically distance yourself? Do you need to set screen-time limits? Engage in healthier habits? Create stronger boundaries? List actionable steps beside each Blackhole circle.

Conclusion

By visually mapping out your energetic landscape, you've shed light on the shadowy Blackholes that have been clandestinely consuming your resources. Now, armed with awareness and a plan, you're all set to reclaim your energy and ascend to higher Sectors!

Lesson 13

Importance – Sector Super Poison

Alright, strap in for another revelation! We've delved into the clarifying world of Blackholes, but guess what? There's another layer to this cosmic onion. While we've established how Blackholes ensnare and drain, there's a secret ingredient that amplifies their gravitational pull on you: your Importance levels. Prepare for a dose of clarity and some genuine "aha" moments. This lesson is all about stabilizing the rollercoaster of emotions and energy. Ready to get to the heart of the matter? Let's unravel this!

One of reality's most potent disruptors—"Importance." It's the invisible force behind life's turbulence, creating chaos and tipping the scales of your emotional balance. Brace yourself for an eye-opening journey of freeing yourself from this powerful, self-concocted inner pressure that has most certainly disrupted your reality in the past.

Think of Importance as the super-glue, binding you to expectations and outcomes. You know the drill: "I just HAVE to nail this job interview," "I simply MUST get into that elite college program," or "The Universe will literally collapse if that Tinder date doesn't text back." But here's the twist: it's like telling The Quantum Field, "Hey, I demand the things I desire, MY way, and on MY timeline. Otherwise, meltdown central over here!" And guess what? The Quantum Field doesn't jive with that, turkey.

See, when you tag something with a high value or a "must-have" label, you're basically saying: "Quantum Field, if this doesn't pan out EXACTLY as I'm envisioning, *then expect drama.*" It's kinda like being a cosmic drama queen, telling The Quantum Field how it *ought* to unfold its grand design. And, oh boy, it doesn't like being told what to do.

It gets even juicier! There are two distinct flavors to this Importance game: Inner and Outer Importance. Inner is all about the "me, myself, and I"—it's the "Everyone better recognize how amazing I am!" and the "They better serve my meal pronto or else!" vibe. Outer Importance, on the other hand, zeroes in on external circumstances and events.

"Importance." Sounds like a VIP guest you'd welcome with open arms, right? But here's the twist: Importance isn't your BFF; it's the sneaky villain in the plot, staging all sorts of chaos for your storyline. It's the silent siren singing you into turbulent seas of emotional crisis, while you're just trying to get where you want to go.

When you slap that golden "Importance" sticker onto something, it's like rolling out the red carpet for Blackholes too. You're basically shouting, "Over here! I've got some juicy emotional vulnerability for you to feast on!"

Case in point: you've branded a political event as "mega important." Well, darling, prepare for a news binge that will suck the life out of you. Every twist, every turn, every tweet will have you glued because, well, "It's life and death!" Or so you think. The Blackholes? They're rubbing their greedy hands together, ready to feast on every ounce of your attention and energy.

But wait, there's a golden ticket out of this circus. And it's simpler than you think: lower the Importance, reduce the drama. It's like decluttering your cosmic closet, making space for a harmonious existence. Ready for some truth? The secret to mastering your reality isn't amping up the passion, it's chilling out.

The Matrix thrives on the illusion that by inflating the Importance you give to things, you'll achieve greatness. But let's strip it down: it's all about energy. Oversaturating your life with Importance drains your vital energy, and guess what? The Matrix feasts on that. Yet, in a stark twist, loading up on Importance doesn't propel you forward. Sky-high expectations, emotional turmoil, and frantic desperation? They don't pave the way to success. So, why the charade? Blame it on programming. The Matrix has us fooled into thinking this is the standard.

Take a gander at the entertainment industry. From blockbusters to binge-worthy series, what's the recurring theme? Characters steeped in exorbitant levels of Importance. Watch any movie or show through this lens, and it's glaringly obvious. The political stage? A veritable circus of Importance. Social media's cultural narratives? Skyrocketing Importance levels. "Feast your eyes on my gourmet dinner!" "Behold my brand-new car!" "Witness the wrath of a motorist's meltdown!" From cradle to grave, you're indoctrinated to operate on heightened Importance. Here's the real kicker: the higher one's Importance, the more they're ensnared in The Matrix's web.

We've all been there, chasing that next big paycheck or that nod of approval because we think it's the key to the elusive treasure chest of happiness. Spoiler alert: It's not. That promotion or shiny new toy? It's a sugar rush for the ego, not soul candy. Think about it. Expecting a swanky pair of shoes to elevate your spirit is like hoping a fancy hat can upgrade your IQ.

"But hold on," you object, "If I'm not living for those dopamine hits from my achievements, then what's the point?" Here's a thought bomb for you: how about some good ol' consistent joy?

From the get-go, we're trained to hunger, hanker, and haggle. But, aren't you fed up? Welcome to Quantum Capitalism, where the rules flip and where what we truly seek is that magical elixir of unwavering contentment.

Without that ego trap demanding a certain outcome, we stay in this breezy state, whether we're on cloud nine or navigating a storm. The truly free individual? They're vibing on a different frequency altogether, way above the mundane metrics of human wins and losses.

Now, don't twist my words. This isn't about being reckless or slothful. Quite the opposite. Detached, we're sharper, more dialed-in. Our head's clearer, and emotions? They're now our wingmen. Got a project that's your baby? Cool. Now, how'd you feel if you were at peace with whatever way it pans out? Aha! See the shift? Instant inner Zen, no matter the scoreboard.

Think of it this way: dive into the business venture, by all means, but do it to earn your living, never for ego-gratification. It's valuable to understand the difference. Do this, and those business migraines? History. You'll face challenges, sure. But while the board may be a maze, your mind's a clear sky.

Escaping the maze? It starts with emotional detachment. More detachment equals more liberty, a notion The Matrix detests. To truly master this game, you need to cut through the illusion.

CARE LESS TO CONQUER MORE.

Mind-blowing, right?

Now, to get a clearer picture, let's get down to the nitty-gritty:

Inner Importance—Think of this as your ego's rollercoaster, sometimes taking you to dizzying heights of arrogance or plummeting you into the depths of self-doubt. Both rides? Not fun, and way too extreme. Balance is the name of the game.

Outer Importance—Outer Importance is when you give excessive value or weight to external results, objects, events, people or perceptions of how things should play out, believing they hold the key to your happiness or self-worth.

In the grand dance of The Quantum Field, fluidity wins. So, loosen that grip, lighten that load, and let things flow. Trust The Quantum Field's choreography; it's got your back!

Meet Sarah

Sarah had earned a nickname among her colleagues: "The Promotion Mercenary." She invested all her hopes and dreams in the idea of climbing the corporate ladder, seeing it as the singular path to success and fulfillment. However, when one particularly coveted position slipped through her fingers, it felt like a high-speed roller coaster plummeting straight into the depths of Disappointment City! Cue the somber symphony and the soul-numbing "What's wrong with me?" moments.

But hold up! In an alternate reality, Sarah decided to unleash her inner give-no-f***s warrior and take back control. She realized that she was blowing things out of proportion and that her worth wasn't tied to a job title. With a newfound sense of perspective, she shook off her promotion anxieties, embraced her current role, and vowed to rock the opportunity with a detached attitude instead. That way, no matter what happened, Sarah wasn't going to jerk herself around emotionally, and most importantly, if the job didn't come to fruition, she wouldn't lose the high Sector of Reality she was on, thus having all the opportunities from that Sector still available at her own personal success buffet.

Now, Sarah's riding high on the freedom train, leaving behind the emotional Blackhole of "job promotion" that almost sucked her in. She's on her way to success, enjoying the dance floor of life without letting external stuff define her groove.

So, dear reader, is it time for you to drop the Importance and emotional baggage on something causing you distress?

Excessive Importance can be likened to unruly party crashers, but you possess the power to show them the door. Whether it's placing too much Importance on wanting a specific version of reality to unfold, expecting someone in your life to behave in a certain way, or obtaining something you deeply desire, it's essential to keep such tendencies in check. To truly embody your inner Quantum Capitalist and avoid complicating matters through heavily weighted expectations, it's crucial to address these levels of Importance.

Here's the deal: don't let things take over your dance floor anymore. It's not about suppressing emotions; instead, we're addressing the underlying problem. Too much emotional weight disrupts your groove, keeping you from the Sector where you excel.

View these problems as the illusions they genuinely are. They only appear significant because you shine a spotlight on them. But consider this: if you've deemed something important but then shift your focus to a completely different matter, the initial problem disappears. We're turning down that stage light and reclaiming our peace of mind!

However, don't mistake reducing the Importance of certain things with becoming emotionless. Far from it! Holding onto positive feelings regarding an outcome is beneficial. Yet, convincing yourself or your reality that you'll be utterly devastated if an anticipated result doesn't manifest? That's when complications arise in your life. By minimizing the undue Importance you assign to things, you pave the way to personal liberation.

3 Steps to Recognize Importance and Challenge Your Perspective:

1. **Observe Your Inner State:** monitor areas where you place undue Importance on yourself and your surroundings. Awareness is the first foot out of the maze.
2. **Check Your Attitude:** rather than fighting your emotions, check your attitude. Overwhelming feelings and emotions are born from the high Importance you assign to things.
3. **Remember You Hold the Freedom of Choice:** cherish the gift of being able to choose your perspective. If you decide, you can switch your viewpoint. Harness this ability. By doing so, you gain mastery over much of your life.

The Money Shot: Decoding Financial Instability

Let's discuss finances! You're familiar with the emotional highs and lows of money, right? The fear, the anxiety, the pride, and the greed—all contribute to a whirlwind of financial chaos.

But here's a revelation: your key to financial stability lies in recognizing and addressing the undue Importance you attach to money and financial matters. Begin to perceive financial challenges as magnified illusions, distorted by the lens of Importance. Cease allowing money to dictate your value and observe how your reality synchronizes with prosperity.

The Recap

Excessive Importance gives rise to unbalanced emotions and reactions. Lowering Importance means addressing your underlying attitude and perspective rather than suppressing your feelings. Problems are illusions, magnified by the lens of Importance. By reducing emotional weight and observing situations with clarity, you break free from the roller coaster of emotions that Importance creates.

The bottom line? Excessive Importance attributed to anything locks you in unhealthy to one specific reality only. It limits your access to infinite potentialities and therefore, higher Sectors. If you want to ascend, you must let go.

Poke The Brain

In your reality, where have you let Importance take the driver's seat?

Your Next Power Move

Meditation: Importance Awareness

Objective: a meditation to help you identify areas of excessive Importance in your life.

1. Setting the Scene:
   - Find a quiet and comfortable space where you won't be interrupted.
   - Sit or lie down in a relaxed position. If sitting, keep your spine straight.
   - Close your eyes and take a few deep breaths to center yourself.

2. Grounding:
   - Envision roots extending from your body, connecting you deep into the Earth.
   - Feel this grounding energy anchoring you in the present moment.

3. Journey to Your Inner Space:
   - Visualize yourself in a vast cosmic space, where stars, planets, and galaxies surround you. This is your inner Universe.
   - Notice in the distance, a scale, like the one Justice holds—perfectly balanced.

4. Identifying Importance:
   - As you approach the scale, you notice items or symbols on one side, representing areas of your life where you've placed excessive Importance.

- Take a moment to recognize these items without judgment. Maybe it's a work badge, a heart, or a pile of money. Recognize the emotional charge you feel when seeing these symbols.

5. Statement of awareness:

    - Silently repeat to yourself, "I recognize the Importance I place on various aspects of my life. I am aware of its existence."

Reflection

Spend a few minutes journaling or contemplating on what you discovered during the meditation. Did certain symbols surprise you? What areas of your life might need less attachment and emotional turbulence due to elevated Importance?

This meditation allows a gentle exploration into where we might be placing too much Importance in our lives. It encourages awareness in a peaceful, introspective manner. Practice regularly to keep your inner scales harmonized.

In conclusion, we've discussed the concept of Importance and how it can disrupt your realm of reality. What to do next? We got you. We'll delve deeper in the next lesson, offering clear guidance on why this all matters and its significance in shaping your reality. Onward and upward!

Lesson 14

Why We Generate Importance

Alright, in our previous lesson, we dived deep into the concept of Importance and began to clearly acknowledge the emotional traps we create in our paths by operating with elevated Importance. Let's take a deeper look at what Importance looks like and why exactly we invite this disruption into our lives. Ready to face this beast head-on?

There are two primary culprits behind the generation of elevated Importance levels. The first is your triggers. These are emotional hotspots linked to something you've overvalued, often due to a past experience, possibly trauma, or an intense, unchecked desire. It might also stem from a deep-seated need to prove something to yourself. The second culprit is the Blackholes in our reality. Yes, if your Importance levels are sky-high, you can bet your bottom dollar a Blackhole is likely involved. Blackholes engage us by convincing us to adopt certain standards, which we then deem crucial, effectively signing a contract with these imposed values.

In a world where every ping and buzz could be the next big political revelation, it's easy to get caught in the whirlpool of constant news updates. Picture someone, much like any of us, whose personal values deeply resonate with the unfolding dramas and triumphs of the political arena. This connection isn't just intellectual; it's visceral, tapping into their most profound convictions and fears.

Enter the Blackhole: the ever-spinning, never-sleeping cycle of political news. It doesn't just inform; it seduces, presenting each piece of news as a critical thread in the tapestry of global affairs. For our protagonist, checking the news isn't just a habit; it's a ritual. It's the first thing they do in the morning, their constant companion during the day, and the last voice they hear at night.

This engagement isn't casual; it's intense and emotional. Each headline, each breaking story, sends ripples through their day, stirring up a cocktail of worry, anger, or fleeting hope. The news cycle, with its pulse-quickening urgency and dramatic flair, has convinced them that tuning out is not an option, that being constantly connected is the only way to be a responsible member of society.

In this narrative, the individual's emotional triggers and the compelling allure of the news Blackhole merge into a relentless dance of information consumption. They find themselves trapped in a loop of heightened Importance, where staying perpetually plugged into the political saga feels not just necessary, but vital.

Those Blackholes? They're on overtime, constantly sucking you into an intense whirlwind of Importance. You end up teetering, off-balance, and exposed. And guess what? They are all about that life. Blackholes thrive on this chaos because they get to siphon off your energy faster than you can even generate it, again, a state the system loves to keep you in. In this state, you remain confused, complacent, and vulnerable, yet at times still desperately clinging to the things you want.

But, you've got such little energy, well, you might as well resign to another night of garbage content trying to "relax."

Before you can take back the wheel and steer your life, you must first discern where and then why your levels of Importance are skewed. Living with Importance isn't a leisurely stroll—it feels more like being ensnared in a relentless tug-of-war, torn in every direction. Do you ever feel like you've been duped into this eternal showdown with yourself, your environment, and this entire Matrix construct you're living in? Does it sometimes seem like you're stuck in a perpetual dance-off, and the tune playing has convinced you that this exhausting jig is just "how life is"? Yet, as the days roll on, more and more anxiety, depression, and self-doubt. At the same time, everyone else is seemingly too bothered by their Importance levels to question anything either.

But, here's where it gets dicey: instead of looking for a new tune, we double down, convinced that amplifying the volume will help. "Oh, if my political party wins, the sun will shine brighter." "That promotion? It's my ticket to happiness." "A flashier car, a bigger home, that designer bag? Must-haves for a "better" life." Seriously? It's almost like we attempt to mask the distress our Importance levels create by piling on more things to load up with Importance, instead of just trying to get to the root of the issue. Can we just hit pause and evaluate?

Maybe it's seeing that pregnancy test turn positive, waiting for that "Accepted Offer" notification on your dream house, anticipating the tearful "yes" after you pop the question, or the rush of seeing an extra digit on your paycheck. But again, why? Is it the need for love, yearning for safety and security, desperation to be accepted?

Are you all in, chips stacked high on one outcome because you feel this outcome will provide you with something that will make you feel whole? If life tosses you a curveball, are you centered to swing and hit a home run anyway? Wanting something higher and better is great, but if your entire emotional life savings are invested in a single event, dependent on a singular outcome, tread carefully.

Let's be real. These battles with ourselves and our lives? We've all got 'em. But it's high time we hit the reset button, find our center, and dance to our rhythm, not the rhythm of the Importance levels we've created, possibly blind to what was really going down. Time to groove, move, and prove that we're more than the sum of our anticipated results.

Are you game for a new game? How about mastering the art of staying unbothered, no matter which way the punches come? What if I told you there's a whole lot more to gain when you operate this way? Because trust me, there is.

Meet Karen

Karen's alarm buzzes at the crack of dawn, jolting her from a dream where she was, ironically, floating carefree in space. The first thought that hits her as her feet touch the cold floor? Her appearance. Today, she must look impeccable. The mirror becomes her first battlefield, scrutinizing every detail, every hair, every pore. Thousands of dollars of products, contouring like a pro, nearly 2 hours, as with each morning... poof. Gone.

Breakfast is a whirlwind of calories counted and Instagram stories scrutinized. Her oatmeal isn't just breakfast; it's a statement of health and discipline. The walk to work is no casual stroll; it's a parade of self-importance, her heels clicking on the pavement like a metronome of self-worth.

At work, Karen's world orbits around her email inbox. Each notification is a comet threatening to disrupt her Universe. The stakes? Astronomically high, of course. The presentation at 10 AM isn't just a meeting; it's the Apollo mission of her career. She navigates office politics with the grace of a diplomat during wartime, each interaction a delicate dance of alliances and rivalries.

Lunch with colleagues is a symphony of one-upmanship. The salad? An unspoken competition of who's eating healthier. The casual banter? A covert operation to gauge who's climbing the corporate ladder fastest. Karen's mind races faster than the speed of light, analyzing every word, every glance.

The afternoon brings the battle of personal finance. Checking her bank account feels like a deep dive into an abyss. Numbers on a screen aren't just figures; they're a measure of her life's success. The pressure to invest, save, spend, and flaunt jostles in her mind like a chaotic asteroid belt.

Post-work drinks with friends aren't about unwinding. It's a showcase of social standings, peppered with subtle brags about vacations booked and designer bags bought. Each story Karen tells is a calculated move in a chess game of social clout.

At home, Karen's apartment isn't just a living space; it's a museum of her tastes and accomplishments. Each piece of furniture, each artwork is a testament to her refined choices. Even relaxing involves curating the perfect Netflix playlist, portraying characters and storylines that display Importance levels out of control.

As Karen finally collapses into bed, her mind races with the events of the day. Did she win? Did she do enough? Her thoughts are a tornado of what-ifs and should-haves. Sleep doesn't come easy; it's another battle to fight.

In the world of Karen, every moment is a skirmish in the grand war of Importance. Every choice, every interaction, is laden with the weight of a Universe. But beneath the façade of control and perfection, there's a whispered cry for true self-love, a faint call for a truce. Maybe tomorrow, Karen will hear it. Maybe tomorrow, she'll realize that she's been fighting in a war that doesn't need winning, that doesn't even actually exist.

The Money Shot: Redefining Wealth – Beyond the Dollar Sign

> "Money never made a man happy yet, nor will it.
> The more a man has, the more he wants.
> Instead of filling a void, it makes one."
> —Benjamin Franklin

Why does Importance over financial matters drive so much of human life? It's deeply rooted in our survival instinct and our perceptions of self-worth. The Blackholes of society have been remarkably successful in convincing us of money's Importance, leading many astray in a deceitful game. The key point often missed in the pursuit of wealth is this: it's not about chasing money, but rather embodying the state of being you think wealth will bring. That's what truly leads you to prosperity, not the relentless pursuit of wealth itself.

Consider this: is endlessly wanting, grasping, and placing elevated Importance on money truly how you want to spend your precious moments? The irony is, the more you stress over finances, the less you tend to "bank"—both in terms of energy and actual cash. Next time you find yourself tripping over life's hurdles, pause for a moment. Remember, you're just stardust navigating this journey of life. It's time to let go of taking financial stresses so seriously. Does this mean you'll starve if you drop the Importance? Absolutely not. In fact, you're more likely to rise and thrive, which I'll show you in the upcoming lesson.

The Recap

Importance is often mistakenly ingested as a magic elixir, especially in the hustle and grind culture. Reflecting on my journey, I realized that once I started asking meaningful questions about my motivations and began to move away from a toxic mindset burdened with excessive expectations, life didn't just become easier—it became richer. More of everything started flowing my way with less effort. Believe it or not, it can indeed be that way for you too.

Poke the Brain

Reflect on where in your life you're battling due to elevated Importance levels. Be honest with yourself about where these levels originated. Do you believe there is another way to go about getting the things you want out of life?

Your Next Power Move

Juggernaut Journal Exercise: Peel the Onion.

Time to peel back the layers and figure out why you're stuck in this mess of Importance. It's time to get real and confront your attachments that are causing chaos. Let's do this!

Start with the little annoyances, like that neighbor blasting music all day. Ask yourself why it's bothering you so much. Keep digging! Each answer leads you closer to the root cause. This ain't rocket science!

This works even when it comes to the big stuff. You've gotta dig deep. Question those deeply embedded programs and societal beliefs. Unravel the knots in your reality, and you'll feel that sweet release!

Identify the Trigger

Jot down 3 things, whether significant or trivial, that have irritated, unsettled, or thrown you off recently. This could range from your neighbor's blaring music to a pivotal life event.

Dive Deep with "Why"

For each trigger, repeatedly ask yourself "Why does this bother me?" or "Why do I have so much elevated expectation over this?" Ask yourself this question at least five times. With each subsequent "Why?" you'll notice you're peeling back the layers and getting closer to the root of the issue.

Here are a few examples

Trigger List:

1. Colleague's Constant Criticism: every time you propose a new idea in team meetings, a particular colleague always finds something negative to say. This triggers you to feel discounted.
2. Friend's Canceled Plans: your best friend has canceled your planned outings multiple times in the past month. This triggers you to feel abandoned.

3. Pending Promotion: you've been waiting for news about a promotion, and the anticipation is eating away at you daily. This triggers you into feeling insecure.

Dive Deep with Why?

1. Colleague's Constant Criticism:
   - Why does this bother me? It makes me feel undervalued in team meetings.
   - Why? I've spent a lot of time and effort on these proposals.
   - Why? I want to contribute to the team's success and be recognized.
   - Why? Being recognized validates my hard work and makes me feel competent.
   - Why? As a child, I felt overshadowed and always sought validation.

2. Friend's Canceled Plans:
   - Why does this bother me? It makes me feel like I'm not a priority.
   - Why? I value our friendship and want to spend time together.
   - Why? Quality time with friends provides me with emotional support.
   - Why? I feel isolated and disconnected without regular social interactions.
   - Why? Growing up, I felt most secure and happy in social settings.

3. Pending Promotion:
   - Why am I so anxious about this? I've been working hard and believe I deserve it.
   - Why? This promotion symbolizes professional growth for me.
   - Why? I've always associated career growth with personal success and personal worth.
   - Why? Success in my career makes me feel more secure and confident in life and worthy.
   - Why? My family has always emphasized the Importance of professional success.

At the conclusion of this introspection, you'll likely find that much of your "Importance" is anchored in past experiences or entrenched beliefs. These culprits pump up those Importance levels. Tackling them head-on and at their root? That's your ticket to defusing the emotional fireworks. All it takes is a touch of heightened awareness. Dive deep, challenge the narrative, and watch the transformation unfold.

Lesson 15

Creating Chaos With Disproportionate Energy

In our previous lessons, we've pulled back the curtain on this concept of "Importance." We've pinpointed how you've been unknowingly hanging these "Importance" tags on parts of your life. Maybe it's the sneaky Matrix, or those scars from yesterday pulling the strings. But here's where the plot thickens: we're now diving into the deep end with "Importance in Action." This is where the energy gets all out of whack, where chaos waltzes in. Essentially, you're broadcasting on a frequency that's luring in everything you swore you didn't want.

Gear up, because we're about to embark on a quest into balance—nature's sole objective. In the realm of Quantum Capitalism balance is kind of a big deal, and you need it. Let's break it down.

The laws of nature don't come with explanations. They're just cold, hard facts. But let's get real here—the Law of Balance is the law of all laws, and it's the real deal. Earth without balance—it'd be like living in some funky, atmospheric jelly or a boiling furnace. So, are you ready to give props to balance and understand how the heck it keeps everything in check?

We've all experienced the ups and downs—the good and bad spells in life. Success and defeat, baby! That's just life playing the balance game, and it's got a master plan for everything. Day and night, incoming and outgoing tides, birth and death—it's all about perpetual balance.

When your sense of "Importance" skyrockets without a reality check, you don't just think differently—you act differently. And when you act from this heightened state of Importance, it's like throwing a rock into a pond—the ripples spread out, altering your reality. Think about it: you've been ghosted by your date, and instead of keeping your cool, you fire off a barrage of texts at an unholy hour. Ouch. That's you, generating Disproportionate Energy.

Here's another example: let's say I buy an overpriced t-shirt which boosts my self-worth, compensating for a perceived shortcoming. This act of assigning excessive value to the shirt represents "Importance in action," leading to the purchase—a manifestation of Disproportionate Energy.

But here's the twist: if everyone acted on these energy spikes without the Law of Balance showing up, the world would be one chaotic, unpredictable mess. Imagine that Universe for a second! Our world has its checks and balances for a reason. We'll dig deeper into that in the next lesson. But for now, just picture a world where every overreaction gets exactly what it's gunning for.

Just know that Disproportionate Energy is your energy running wild with Importance acting as its backup dancer. This is you operating in your Sector as moving matter while charged with Importance. Messing with the energetic field in this manner is akin to creating chaos like a nerd gone rogue on a science project. Think it's just in your head? Nope. Your thoughts pack a punch when it comes to action, and The Quantum Field and The Matrix can see that sh**.

When you're all gung-ho about something, and your Importance levels shoot through the roof, you're playing with fire. Disproportionate Energy is like a mischievous gremlin, inviting havoc in your life. It's a universal law—whatever can go wrong will go wrong if you're operating from a place of imbalanced energy.

So, when the world's already teetering on this tightrope of continuous balance, and you then toss Disproportionate Energy into the mix? KABOOM. When operating from a place of Disproportionate Energy you're a massive reality disruptor. When you go all-in on something, disrupting the peace and harmony, guess what? You're inviting a rollercoaster of polarity.

We've all been guilty of this groove more times than we'd like to admit. Want a few samples from the "Been There, Done That" playlist? Let's dive in:

Overbooked Overlord: ever cram your calendar so full, it's bursting at the seams? You think you're being the productivity master, but suddenly you're the star of "Burnout Boulevard". Juggling five coffee dates, three projects, two workouts, and a partridge in a pear tree? Hello imbalance, bye-bye zen!

Fitness Frenzy: so you decide, "I'm getting ripped!" and hit the gym like there's no tomorrow. But uh-oh, in this mad dash to chisel-town, you've skipped meals, canceled plans, and—would you look at that—pulled a muscle. Wasn't exactly the kind of ripped you were going for, was it?

Social Media Maniac: posting every second, every meal, every sneeze? Trying to curate that "perfect life" aesthetic? But then, you're bummed out because Janet from high school got more likes on her cat photo. That's The Quantum Field throwing shade, reminding you that there's more to life.

Relationship Rodeo: obsessed with that special someone? Texting 24/7, dreaming in Technicolor about your next date, and losing track of friends, family, and, well, reality? Cupid's got you in a chokehold, Romeo ain't texting back, and balance is gasping for breath.

Money Madness: whether you're hoarding every penny like there's a global coin shortage or blowing cash faster than a popped balloon loses air, extreme money moves shake your equilibrium. Trust me, neither Scrooge nor Spendy McGee has the right vibe.

Desperation Dive: ever lost a high-profit sale because you came off too eager? Maybe you kept dropping your price or followed up a tad too often? Desperation smells worse than week-old leftovers, and clients can sniff it out a mile away. Play it cool, or watch that big deal melt away.

Perfectionist's Pitfall: aimed to craft the "perfect" project? Maybe you nitpicked every detail, reworked every element, obsessed over every pixel? Instead of a masterpiece, you end up with an overcooked mess. Here's a tip: sometimes, less is truly more. When you micromanage perfection, you often invite imperfection.

And there you have it—a few head-nodding, "Whoops, that's totally me" moments. But remember, nobody's playing a perfect game here. We're all just trying to find that sweet spot in the middle where balance thrives. So next time you feel like going overboard in one direction, maybe—just maybe—pause and ask yourself, "Is this really the Quantum Capitalisty-brain move I think it is?"

Alright, you, let's finesse this:

Feeling confident, are we? Whispering to yourself, "I've got this under control... piece of cake." But don't get too comfy. Those sly Blackholes are always lurking, waiting for you to slip up. They feast on moments when you tilt into Disproportionate Energy territory because they know, oh they know, that's their time to go in for the kill. Picture this: You're burning the midnight oil, striving for pixel-perfect on that project. But if things don't align just right, you find yourself at that corner store grabbing a pack of smokes. Score: Tobacco Blackhole 1, You 0.

Take a step back from the relentless hustle and grind. Keep your wits about you, move with poised precision, and let clarity be your compass. Say goodbye to yanking yourself around by Disproportionate Energy! Keep an eye on your Importance levels, embrace your unshakeable calm, and watch any Disproportionate Energy vibes dissolve like a fleeting nightmare. Stay breezy, y'all.

The Money Shot: Balancing The Bank

Too often, we're stuck in the extremes. "Drowning in debt? Why not one more credit card binge!" "If I don't start saving today, I'm doomed!" We either go all in or completely pull back, either out of desperation or sheer exasperation. When Importance and money dance together, it's usually a mess. You find yourself losing or constantly sidelined because mastering the money game seems like a wild goose chase. But there's a smarter way: get intimate with balance. Spend, save, and give at the right times. Armed with the insights ahead, you'll master the art of stacking your wealth. But remember, don't let the pests of Importance and Disproportionate Energy nibble away at your fortune. Earning is one thing; maintaining it with balanced energy? That's how you build true wealth.

The Recap

Navigating the path to balance means understanding Disproportionate Energy and recognizing the chaos it births when we act from spiked Importance. Nature strives for balance, and when our heightened desires disturb that delicate equilibrium, we not only create chaos but also invite challenges that aim to restore the harmony we've disrupted.

Poke The Brain

Reflect on that recent moment when your heightened sense of Importance sent your energy spiraling out of balance, resulting in unintended chaos. With hindsight in hand, how might you have approached the situation differently, aligning your actions with a more favorable outcome?

Your Next Power Move

Meditation: Harmonizing Energy Waves.

Step 1: Tune In

Recognize a moment when you feel that surge of Disproportionate Energy—maybe it's stress, overwhelm, or intense excitement.

Envision this energy as a massive, unsteady wave, rising tall and ready to crash.

Step 2: Cosmic Balance

Take a deep, slow breath in for a count of four, hold for a count of four, then release for a count of four.

As you breathe, see yourself confidently hopping on a surfboard, ready to tackle that wave.

Now, let your intention settle on bringing balance to this energy.

Picture yourself skillfully surfing this cosmic wave, moving fluidly with its rhythm. Feel the exhilaration as you masterfully ride it, bringing harmony back into your being.

Repeat this quick meditation every time you sense the scales tipping, and soon you'll be adept at quantum surfing any challenge that comes your way!

Lesson 16

The Energetic Nosedive

Alright, let's connect the dots. We've chatted about Importance—that tricky habit of placing excessive value on just about anything. Then, there's its sidekick, Disproportionate Energy, which is basically Importance throwing a party. Now, every time you waltz through your Sector, juiced up on that Disproportionate Energy, you're rolling out the red carpet for the gangster of reality, Gravity. Remember the old saying, "What goes up must come down?" That's Disproportionate Energy and Gravity doing their thang. Go ahead, get all hyped up over some trivial stuff, but don't be shocked when Gravity swings by to bring you back down to Earth.

Today's lesson is all about Gravity, the counter-balance to Disproportionate Energy—the invisible force that shapes your reality when you veer too far off course and start acting or thinking in an imbalanced manner. Gravity is the metaphysical mutherf***** of our reality, ready to crack our quantum knee-caps when we go about operating from a place of Importance, disrupting the energetic balance.

Recall that T-shirt saga from the last round? Where I splurged on a ludicrously priced tee to patch up some insecurity, due to some funky Inner Importance? Enter Gravity, personified as a careless woman at a bar, slightly too inebriated to stand straight, spilling her red wine all over my treasured tee.

The Energetic Nosedive

Textbook cause and effect. Gravity is The Quantum Field's way of ensuring equilibrium, and believe me, it never takes a vacay. That shiny new car you've been worshiping since you bought it? Chances are, someone's going to leave a pretty little dent on it while you're shopping. Whatever you value disproportionately, The Quantum Field is watching. Gravity acts as the ultimate regulator, making sure that life's scales are always in a state of balance. Get used to it.

Or that other relatable scenario: that time you were ghosted after a Tinder date, and in your impatience to understand what's up, you bombarded them with texts, only to ensure they never reached out again. More often than not, Gravity serves us the exact scene we desperately wish to avoid.

Here's a fun one: a bunch of pals rent a chic beach pad for the weekend to raise a glass to their shared memories. Everyone's vibing, drinks are flowing, and there's just one pal fashionably late to the scene. Enter last-minute diva, making her grand entry onto the sunlit patio. Then, one of our over-eager friends, so pumped to see her, leaps up, ready to run her right into the biggest bear hug. But there's a twist—a freshly windexed sliding door, invisible as a ghost. BAM! The energetic field just served her a face-first slice of Gravity pie. Miss party girl and her friends spent the next 30 mins nursing a bloody nose. Disproportionate Energy meets INSTANT Gravity check.

Sometimes we're just one surprise event away from a wake-up call. Are you, my friend, strutting through life, thinking you're the kingpin, unknowingly setting yourself up to get a slap from reality? These stories? They are sly reminders that no matter how you think things are going to go, sometimes life whispers, "Watch this."

Remember the lyrics from Alanis Morissette's song "Ironic"? "Life has a funny way of sneaking up on you when you think everything's alright, and then everything goes wrong and blows up in your face. Isn't it ironic? Don't you think?" Well, Alanis, I've got news for you: it's not irony, it's Gravity.

So, when was the last time you felt that invisible smack? The kind where you were so sure of yourself, and then—plot twist! It's The Quantum Field's gentle (or not-so-gentle) nudge, telling you to cool those jets and maybe, just maybe, not take things too seriously.

Gravity, glass doors, that overpriced t-shirt, spooky Tinder dates... They're all waiting in the wings to remind you that balance isn't just a yoga pose. So, the next time you find yourself sprinting towards what looks like a clear path, maybe take a sec to pause, reflect, and check if you're about to run face-first into a lesson.

Here's the bottom line: the more you let go of specific outcomes, the more serendipitous life becomes. Have you ever been fortunate enough to ride the high of just letting everything unfold naturally? Admit it; when you ease off on a specific outcome, things often come to you much more easily and with less drama. This is how reality operates.

Now, if you're scratching your head wondering, "Why's life got these kooky rules, anyway?" Here's the tea: The Quantum Field is all about energy. Disproportionate Energy is like that awkward dancer at a party—chaotic, attention-grabbing (not in the good ways), and totally inviting in Gravity. But smooth, steady, and graceful moves on the dance floor? That's like you going into Stealth Mode.

Here's the secret: trust that when your desires align with The Quantum Field, your dreams begin to materialize without you needing to force anything. No need to desperately chase, beg, hope, and desire—just relax and let The Quantum Field do its thing. Without Gravity constantly wreaking havoc on your efforts, you obtain the ability to make moves without having to stop everything every five minutes to clean up a mess. Quantum Capitalism is all about operating in an energetically efficient manner and reaping the benefits of your well managed energetic resources.

Picture it like this: you have a glass of milk in your hand, and drinking this glass of milk represents your goal. But you set the glass of milk down on the counter, precariously positioning it halfway off the edge. Gravity steps in and causes it to spill everywhere and shatters the glass into pieces as well. Yes, you can go and get another glass of milk, but first, you have to clean up the mess you caused by inviting in gravity. This is why most people don't make it to their goals. Too much Disproportionate Energy leads to constant balance in the form of messes, letdowns, and eventually resignation because of exhaustion. There is an easier way.

The Money Shot: Cryptocurrency Chaos

Alright, time for a modern parable about our three amigos of mayhem: Importance, Disproportionate Energy, and Gravity. Enter the crypto craze. Picture someone with dollar signs in their eyes, dreaming of Bugattis, sprawling mansions, and that jet-set Andrew Tate lifestyle. Importance? We're talking stratospheric levels! Along comes the siren song of cryptocurrency investment. "Eureka! This is the golden ticket," cries our overeager, Importance-fueled hustler/grinder. "I'm going all in!" Classic case of Disproportionate Energy in the wealth game.

"Ima finally hit it BIG!" he exclaims, voice dripping with anticipation. "No more 9-5 for me!" he cries out. "Damn, this is it!" all juiced up on that Disproportionate Energy.

And the grand finale? Oh, just the dramatic crypto nosedive of the decade—Gravity showing up like a mutherfu****, delivering the reality check nobody wanted, but everybody needed. And a pathetic fizzle and rapid death of homeboy's capital, instead of a boom.

This ain't a one-time show, folks. Rewind to the 2008 housing meltdown, or the legendary tulip mania in Holland. Even you, perhaps once tempted to put all your eggs in one basket on a wild whim, have tasted this bitter pill. The moral? Take a moment, pause, reflect. Before you dive headlong into imbalance and chaos, remember: check it, before you absolutely wreck it.

The Recap

Gravity's out here playing referee for The Universe, while Disproportionate Energy? That's your caffeinated toddler messing up the game, especially when dollar signs are involved. Get a grip, folks!

Poke The Brain

How has your desperate chase for money pushed it further away in the past? What if you could harness the power of these ideas to create a more ideal environment for prosperity?

Your Next Power Move

Practical Exercise: Witnessing Energy in Action.

Step into your environment, any bustling spot will do, a dynamic canvas where life's drama and comedy play out in technicolor. This is no ordinary walk; it's a plunge into a living, breathing spectacle, a chance to witness the pulsating dance of Disproportionate Energy and Importance in its most unscripted form. You're not just passing through; you're an undercover anthropologist, decoding the language of the human dynamic dance with the energetic field.

Seek out your vantage point. Maybe it's a busy coffee shop, a park bench amidst the green oasis of a concrete forest, or a hidden nook in a happening marketplace. As you melt into the scenery, sharpen your senses to HD clarity. Tune in and witness the energetic dramas unfold.

Watch the high-heeled gladiator navigating the urban labyrinth. Each step is a statement, a testament to her crafted persona. But hold up, a rogue crack challenges her choreographed stride, sending ripples through her composure. Witness the interplay of emotions, the swift tumble or recalibration, a real-time lesson in the dance between self-image and life's unpredictability.

Or consider the driver speeding wildly, only to have to slam on the brakes for a red light. Then green, and he punches it, ultimately colliding with the tail end bumper of someone making a hasty turn across lanes unexpectedly. Both drivers jacked up on Disproportionate Energy, both fashionably late to those meetings that were, oh so important.

Then, zoom into the retail battlefield, where a customer and cashier are locked in a modern-day duel. The customer's mounting frustration crescendos against the cashier's fortress of rules. This standoff is more than a transaction gone awry; it's a live demo of Importance, Disproportionate Energy, and Gravity on both ends.

As these vignettes unfold, patterns emerge—the flux of energy, the aftermath of escalated Importance. It's akin to witnessing Gravity's invisible hand, orchestrating a symphony of balance and counterbalance. This street-side theater offers more than mere entertainment; it's a masterclass in the mechanics of human behavior and the force of nature.

Take this eclectic mix of urban tales, a smorgasbord of real-world insights, and weave them into your movements within your Sector. Identify where you're dialed up too high in Disproportionate Energy, where your scale of Importance is off-kilter. Remember, this dynamic interplay of energies is navigable, ever-present, and just reality doing its thing. Approach it with a mix of playfulness and a detective's eye, and let it reshape your interactions and perceptions. In the end, life's richest lessons aren't tucked away in textbooks; they're dancing in the streets, waiting for you to observe.

Lesson 17

Importance Pandemic

In our previous lessons, we broke down the concepts of Importance, Disproportionate Energy, and Gravity. It was engaging, wasn't it? I attempted to infuse some humor to lighten the mood, but the truth remains that Importance is not a trivial subject. This roller coaster—the intertwined dynamics of Importance, Disproportionate Energy, and Gravity—often leaves individuals feeling overwhelmed, intensely stressed, and thoroughly perplexed.

The Matrix is in a perpetual state of projecting what it believes we should value and deem Important. When we fall for this, we disconnect from our true and elevated selves. We become The Matrix version of ourselves and deviate from our Quantum Self.

Here's a metaphor to illustrate: celestial navigation, an old-fashioned term, describes sailors using the sun, moon, planets, and stars to navigate. When Importance enters the picture, it acts as fog, clouds, or sea mist, obscuring our view and preventing us from staying on course. We essentially become lost at sea, our vision obstructed and our direction therefore, skewed. This disconnection and inability to perceive the vital aspects of genuine navigation lead to a life marred by depression, emptiness, extended stress, and anxiety. I firmly believe that individuals who are unhappy or suffering have been led astray by external influences, pulling them away from their destined path. They feel out of sync, struggle to connect with the world in significant and constructive ways, and are, in essence, lost at sea within themselves. But there's hope; first, the fog must dissipate.

While understanding Importance takes intensive study, no truth offers more life enrichment or profound fulfillment. Consider this as shots fired.

"Importance" can be compared to a silent, undetected cancer. If left unchecked, it spreads rapidly, engulfing every aspect of one's life. An obsession with wealth may bring financial gains but simultaneously deteriorates personal relationships and emotional well-being. Similarly, being overly focused on getting married and starting a family might divert you from your true life's purpose and the creative fulfillment that would elevate you to your highest potential. Obsessed with the political twists and turns du jour or current events? Well, you might be burning it all down, feeding this ever-thirsty Blackhole.

In turn, placing excessive Importance on perceived shortcomings—whether it's learned helplessness, a lack of skills, or the ways in which The Matrix has labeled you as inadequate—leads to the same outcome. In this scenario, you also find yourself adrift and lost at sea.

The real tragedy? The damage isn't confined to the specific realm of Importance. Exaggerated Importance behaves much like a wildfire, sparing no field from its scorching wrath.

Allow me to paint a picture from my own life: a fervent ascent from poverty consumed my every thought. So engrossed in escaping my past, life's genuine joys were discarded for sheer monetary gain. By age 35, my existence wasn't fueled by a zest for life but by a relentless, never-ending race to a dead end. The closer I came to the image of the person I believed I wanted to be, the more I was tormented with feelings of desperation, loss, and self-loathing.

After a humbling wake-up call, I recognized that the unchecked Importance under which I operated was merely the beginning. I had become someone I no longer recognized. Understanding the fatal paths I had set by unchecked Importance and Disproportionate Energy was a pivotal first step. A brighter horizon beckoned, but first, I had to unshackle myself. This liberation wasn't instantaneous, but it was worth every bit of what I salvaged from the wreckage.

I relentlessly scrutinized my core beliefs, challenged societal programming, and questioned the narratives imposed on me that I had accepted like a poison apple. As I delved deeper, peeling back layers, I also micro-analyzed seemingly autonomous actions, such as excessive exercise and undereating. I re-evaluated my spending patterns, adopting a fresh perspective on wealth, and deeply appreciated the freedom from standards The Matrix had imposed. These shifts paved the way for the revelations I'll share in PHASE 2.

Assessing and managing your Importance levels will be forever worth your time and attention. The ability to modulate my Importance in real-time, averting relentless, overwhelming emotions and ceaseless havoc in my life, has been nothing short of a miracle. Finding and navigating my true course, free from many of the things I once deemed *so important*, well that's my Holy Grail.

The Money Shot: Digital Decadence

In an obsessive world where every click, swipe, and "like" fuels the Importance pandemic, the real price is often paid in emotional bankruptcy. The unchecked yearning for wealth and status might just rob you of not only life's truest treasures but the real opportunities for solvency. In the race to amass material treasures, we often sideline and overlook life's authentic riches: meaningful connections, genuine experiences, and avenues leading to tangible, lasting wealth.

The Recap

The "Importance" pandemic isn't merely about an inflated sense of self or misplaced aspirations; it's a ravenous beast, stripping away life's essence for many in the world. Yet, with realization springs hope, and with comprehension emerges the potential for metamorphosis.

Poke The Brain

When was the last moment you felt genuinely alive and connected? Was it amid the chase for worldly treasures, or during those rare, deep moments of insight and connection?

Your Next Power Move

Love yourself today. Love your world. Love others.

Lesson 18

A Band-Aid for Now

Alright, we've established the basics, haven't we? The chain of "Importance," which creates "Disproportionate Energy" and then "Gravity" as the consequence. When left unchecked and allowed to run through your life, elevated Importance behaves like the Hulk raging out in your Sector of Reality.

Quantum Capitalism promotes a profound shift in mindset. It's not just a handy guide sprinkled with candy-coated self-help "advice" that provides fleeting relief but sidesteps the real issues. However, in this lesson, I can only introduce you to a foundational solution. This step is pivotal though. Without a firm grasp on it, the potent remedies offered in Phases 2 and 3 might seem cryptic.

So, what's the trick to leveling out that sky-high Importance of yours? just the tiny task of reassessing and tweaking every last detail of your existence, no biggie.

Let's kick things off with some deep dive introspection: is what you're pining for really in sync with the true you? Or could it be a cocktail of societal ideals, standards, and the noise from your surroundings?

That itch for a baby—is it really yours, or is it a concoction brewed from all those baby showers you've been to? That dream job—is it something your heart truly desires, or just another shiny trophy to one-up your buddies? And when you daydream about having more money to lead your dream life, what would you actually spend it on?

In truth, many things we shroud in Importance in this world are material representations of intangible feelings we seek—love, security, good health, freedom. What we're genuinely pursuing is a state of being, and recognizing this offers the blueprint for success.

To simplify: it's not about the tangible "things" but the intangible state of being you're aiming for. If you can tap into that desired state-of-being, you'll naturally attract the physical manifestations aligned with that energy. Sounds pretty simple right?

This is about recognizing and harnessing the power to cultivate feelings, emotions, and ideals, where you perceive yourself as already possessing your desires. As an illustration, consider this: do you wish for $1 million? If you've placed an excessive emphasis on that figure, to the point of driving yourself to the brink, are you ready to consider a different approach? Instead of fixating on the financial sum, shift your focus towards cultivating feelings of wealth in your current situation. By doing so, you'll create a receptive environment, void of the sense of struggle, which is the antipode of your desire.

Instead of pursuing an endeavor from a stance of elevated Importance, can you shift to merely intending to access that state of being, knowing that there is a version of reality where you are absolutely content in this state?

There's a profound difference between "Importance" and the union of "Intention and Knowingness," one that can fundamentally alter your experience of reality. You see,

A Band-Aid for Now

when we label something as "Important," we inadvertently infuse it with a kind of anxious energy. It's a mix of desire, fear, and doubt—will we get it? What if we don't? This sort of apprehensive vibe can actually push away what we desire, keeping it tantalizingly out of reach.

On the flip side, blending "Intention" with "Knowingness" is a game-changer. "Intention" is about clarity of direction, while "Knowingness" exudes absolute confidence in the arrival to your destination. It's not just hoping; it's knowing with every fiber of your being that what you seek is already yours in an alternate version of reality. This combination acts like a magnet, pulling towards you the exact reality Sector that you wish to inhabit. Instead of standing in your own way with the shaky ground of "Importance," you pave a direct path to your desires with the solid foundation of "Intention and Knowingness." This mindset is a powerful tool, shaping and molding the reality you experience to align seamlessly with your deepest aspirations.

The Money Shot: A Rude Awakening

Before my Quantum Capitalist awakening, I was trapped in a relentless cycle of want, desire, and desperation. Money had ascended to the pinnacle of my priorities. Every dollar gained was ecstatically celebrated, and every dollar lost, deeply mourned. I reveled in the highs and lows of this financial roller coaster until one day, it sent my world spiraling into chaos. I found myself waking up in a lavish penthouse, surrounded by opulence, yet feeling utterly isolated and empty—a hollow version of who I truly was. The misery was palpable.

It's a universal pitfall: when you're unclear about the "why" behind your pursuits, you find yourself perpetually chasing, never attaining the ever-evasive feeling of having enough. I was that rabbit, forever running after an elusive carrot that seemed perpetually just out of reach.

Then, in a moment graced by the higher powers of The Quantum Field, a revelation struck. As The Matrix around me began to show its true essence, I caught a fleeting glimpse of my higher self. I recognized my folly: I had been chasing external validations instead of cultivating an internal state of being. This realization spurred a transformative journey, reshaping reality as I had known it for so many years.

Many things that once held immense Importance for me now barely register. Where I once sought validation from material possessions and societal metrics, I now find joy in the intangible—freedom from The Matrix's standards, the thrill of creativity, peaceful walks with my dogs, or the rush of embarking on a fresh, ambitious project. Have I renounced financial success? Far from it. Today, I am wealthier in spirit, well-being, and yes, even finances. The key was discerning genuine priorities from deceptive illusions that The Matrix had spoon-fed me. I'm convinced that this evolution is attainable for everyone. However, the crucial first step is surrender. By relinquishing our tight grip on preconceived notions and desires, we open ourselves up to a reality where we can truly manifest the state of being we seek.

The Recap

To "reset" is to reevaluate, re-understand, and redefine. By probing into the depths of our "wants and desires," we identify the state of being they correspond to. We can then actively fabricate that state of being, consistently nurture it and therefore reconstruct our reality.

Poke The Brain

Ok, have at it. Where do you need a reset?

Your Next Power Move

Challenge: 7-Day Introspection

Dive into a week-long adventure of self-discovery with this clarifying thought exercise. For the next seven days, you're going to embark on a mission of dual discovery: unveiling the areas in your life where Importance has taken an oversized role, and digging deeper to uncover what you're truly chasing after. This journey is more than just a mental exercise; it's an expedition to the core of your deepest desires.

Day 1 to Day 7: Unraveling the Layers

Each day, carve out a moment of tranquility for yourself. Begin by spotlighting the Sectors in your life where you've hoisted the flag of Importance—be it the relentless pursuit of career milestones, the complex web of relationships, the allure of financial security, or the quest for perfect self-presentation. Question why these realms have become so pivotal in your life. What's the real prize you're after here? Is it the warmth of acceptance, the armor of stability, the trophy of accomplishment?

Next, turn the spotlight inward. Imagine a reality where you're already basking in the glow of fulfillment, where every desire is not just a distant dream but a present reality. This part of the exercise is about syncing with contentment and openness, releasing the reins of your desires, and instead attracting opportunities that align with your genuine sense of fulfillment. Envision yourself welcoming these moments with newfound clarity and confidence.

What You'll Discover

At the end of this seven-day introspection challenge, expect to see a transformation in your world view and interactions. Realizing that stepping out of the maze of Importance isn't about dimming your drive but aligning it with your authentic self is a game-changer. This challenge is your portal to heightened self-awareness and a richer, more meaningful life experience. Get ready to step into the next phase of your personal evolution.

Lesson 19

The Downward Spiral

Alright, spark plug, it's game time. In recent lessons, we provided practical solutions for managing Importance and recognizing Disproportionate Energy. This way, you can save your valuable energy lost to the chaos that Gravity creates. But there's an additional reason you need to stabilize yourself within The Quantum Field.

We're diving into another treasure trove of knowledge, propelling you to greater heights—or, more fittingly, keeping you in an elevated Sector. The topic at hand: the Downward Spiral. Imagine this scenario: life pitches a curveball of negativity—be it an unforeseen event, a letdown, or unwelcome news. You take the bait and, in a flash, you're descending emotionally and experientially. But hang tight; in the upcoming lessons, you'll gain the tools to gain control.

The Downward Spiral isn't your typical amusement park ride; it's the real-life equivalent of stepping on a spiky thing in a Mario Bros video game. Then, emotions take the wheel and it's a non-stop trip to Downerville. And the main instigator? A Blackhole. Think of them as the most intrusive pop-up ads— irritating, destructive, and all-consuming. What's even more daunting? They masterfully leverage negative emotions like agitation, anger, and panic to draw you into their vortex. To triumph over this cunning game, you must remain cooler than a polar bear's toenail.

Remember the "Sectors" concept in Lesson 7? Well, it's the golden ticket to understanding your movement in The Quantum Field. Imagine you're riding high on an upper Sector, then one lousy phone call from a toxic family member throws you into the deep end. You get emotional, and suddenly your luxurious Sector feels like a distant dream. In short, that phone call was the sneaky Blackhole gunning for you, and you fell for it.

These Blackholes, along with the concept of "gravity," are the prime culprits in experiencing a Downward Spiral. You could be on Cloud Nine, waiting for that game-changing career upgrade call, and then Gravity plays its part, and suddenly you're in the basement. But as we journey together, you'll pinpoint the exact moments where you goofed up, compromised your reality and got stuck in the spiral.

So, what ignites this whirlwind of negativity? Spoiler: it's you. More precisely, it's your emotional response and reaction to a piece of negative information, news, or experience. A negative event drops by, you react adversely, and the dominoes start to fall. This event doesn't remain an isolated incident, oh no; it proliferates faster than rumors in a tight-knit community. You find yourself in a Downward Spiral, gathering speed and momentum, continuing until there's a shift in your energy and you manage to regain control. The concept of the Downward Spiral provides a deeper understanding of what we often label as "having a bad day." It's the underlying physics at play.

The Downward Spiral doesn't just cramp your style; it snatches you from your posh upper Sector where your dreams were taking shape. Being triggered into a Downward Spiral pulls you into a tour of a haunted house where you encounter everything you don't want, along with a few unexpected twists. First on the lineup: relationship tiffs, lost chances, doom and gloom from the headlines, the classic toe-meet-concrete scenario, or an out-of-the-blue bill—if it grinds your gears, it fuels the spiral. Then the emotional culprits come out to give you a spook—sadness, envy, anxiety, that gut-punch of depression, anger, confusion. Heck, even a sour look at yourself in a fitting room mirror can give it a nudge.

From here, things just continue to go off the rails. Lose your grip on this ride, and soon you'll have to expend precious energy trying to find your way back to where it all started. Are you passively riding through tumultuous Sectors with no hands on the wheel? Snap out of it!

Here's the deal; If a negative event hooks you, negative events will increase exponentially in your layer of reality. You can count on it. A tiny blip of negativity doesn't just birth its twin; it goes full-on rabbit mode, multiplying faster than you can track. Ever had one of those days where one misstep snowballs and suddenly The Universe seems out to get you? Classic Downward Spiral action.

Ready to switch lanes and play a whole new game?

Meet Lisa

Lisa, a vivacious lady in her sixties, usually finds her joy amidst the vibrant blooms of her garden and the infectious giggles of her grandchildren. Life for her is usually as sweet as the roses she tends to. But one morning, she hit a series of speed bumps that turned her day into an emotional roller coaster.

It all kicked off with a call from a relative, infamous for being a downer. The knot in her stomach twisted tighter with each grievance aired. As the call ended, she tried to shrug it off, thinking she could dodge the rain cloud of negativity. Oh, how wrong she was.

As the day trundled on, The Universe seemed hell-bent on testing her patience. Her favorite coffee? Sold out. Her beautifully manicured flower bed? Trampled by the neighbor's dog. Then, an unexpected bill arrived in the mail. And the cherry on top? News of the sudden death of a friend.

"What next?" Lisa thought. Each event felt like a jab to the ribs, leaving Lisa gasping for air under a cascade of frustration, disappointment, and anxiety. It was as if she was viewing the world through a pair of doom-and-gloom-tinted glasses. And the worst part? The more she stewed in negativity, the more it seemed to multiply.

By sunset, Lisa was spent. As she replayed the events of her day, a light bulb flicked on. It wasn't just the mishaps that had drained her, but her reaction to them. She'd unwittingly become the architect of her own demise, allowing each negative event to snowball into an avalanche of despair.

Determined to turn it around, Lisa chose to zero in on the positives. She nurtured her garden, had a heartwarming chat with her daughter, and even turned the last page of a book she'd been engrossed in.

As her mindset shifted, so did the weight on her shoulders. The ominous cloud that had cast a shadow over her day began to break apart, revealing hope and optimism again.

The takeaway? Life is a mixed bag of highs and lows. While we can't control the curveballs thrown our way, we do hold the reins when it comes to our reactions. By acknowledging our emotions and then consciously choosing to focus on the positive, we can snap out of the Downward Spiral and reclaim our joy.

The Money Shot: Panic? Ain't-nobody-got-time-for-that

Let's talk dollars and sense. Financial pitfalls—poverty, debt, that nail-biting panic over money—they're the norm in lower Sectors of Reality. Anytime you feel the Downward Spiral's nudge, take a step back. Reacting negatively? It's a one-way ticket down. But navigate wisely, and you'll be swimming in success sooner than you think.

The Recap

Reality isn't just something you live; it's something you shape. But the Downward Spiral, with its drama and negativity, can reshape your reality faster than you can say, "instant noodles." Stay alert, stay aware, and make sure you're always holding the joystick to your game of life.

Poke The Brain

When did you last feel like you were in free fall, spiraling down, with no parachute?

Your Next Power Move

Awareness Exercise: The Storm Chase.

Step 1: Stand Tall in the Storm

Prompt: throughout the week, when you feel negativity or drama approaching, pause for a moment. Instead of reacting, take three deep breaths, grounding yourself, while considering everything you've learned so far.

Step 2: Choose Something Different

Prompt: whenever you sense panic or unease, remind yourself: "I am in control. Disengaging is my choice."

Step 3: Blackhole Detection

Every evening, reflect on your day. Were there moments or situations that felt like potential "Blackholes" of negativity? Note them down. How did you handle them? Did you manage to steer clear?

This easy awareness exercise will help you build resilience against negativity, allowing you to navigate towards positivity effortlessly. Over time, you'll notice that the usual triggers lose their power, and being unbothered becomes your default state.

Lesson 20

Trauma Triggers

Ok, ok. I know this may all be feeling a bit doom and gloom, but don't trip. We've got to strip all this noise down to a fresh starting point, and then it will all be up from there. I promise.

Recall a moment when an unexpected memory or event struck you like lightning, leaving you reeling in a storm of emotions? That's the handiwork of a Trauma Trigger. We've previously explored the Downward Spiral and how external factors can abruptly drag you down. Now, let's shift our focus to a more subtle, yet profound challenge: the Trauma Triggers that reside within you. Yes, entangled in your own narratives, you often find yourself in the lower Sectors of your existence. In this lesson, we delve into the dynamics of the Downward Spiral and its shadowy accomplice, the Trauma Trigger. Prepare to embark on a journey of self-liberation because once you grasp this, you hold ultimate control over your position within The Quantum Field.

Have you ever experienced that sudden heart-pang or stomach-drop, as if your past just ambushed your present? That's a Trauma Trigger in action—a stealthy disruptor that can obscure your clarity like a fog. Picture it as the unexpected antagonist in your life's narrative.

We've all felt like emotional puppets at some point, our strings pulled by shadows of past hurts. A casual remark or an inadvertent action can unexpectedly transport us back to old battlefields. These are the moments when our traumas surreptitiously dictate our current scene. Yet, here lies the silver lining—while the external world may be beyond our control, the realm within us is ours to command.

Consider this mental toolkit your secret weapon. It's about cultivating FULL MENTAL AWARENESS, identifying the emotional upheaval, and gracefully sidestepping the Downward Spiral. Embrace this guiding principle: "I am the observer and the architect of my reality."

The truth is, you can dissolve the stranglehold these triggers have over you by not succumbing to the place they've taken you in the past. You need not completely dissect the trigger itself; it's more about not giving way to your natural propensity of spiraling downward once triggered. The key lies in recognizing the onset of a trigger and consciously choosing not to follow the familiar path that leads you into the depths of despair. By doing so, you're not only acknowledging the trigger but also actively preventing it from dictating your emotional response. This approach empowers you to maintain control and stay on a more positive trajectory.

The strategy is simple, yet powerful: identify the moment once triggered, acknowledge it, and transform it by not succumbing to the Downward Spiral. Pin down those triggers, be it rejection, criticism, or lingering insecurities. Embrace them, dissect their origins, and crucially, respond to them with this newfound control.

In essence, navigating Trauma Triggers is not just about healing; it's an opportunity to rewrite your script, redirect your narrative, and elevate your Quantum Capitalist journey.

Are you ready to turn your triggers into stepping stones towards a higher Sector?

The Money Shot: Unmasking the Ghosts of Your Money Past

In today's financial landscape, the bitter truth is that many people struggling with money are victims of trauma. Whether it's the weight of poverty mentality, the chains of a scarcity mindset, or the paralyzing grip of learned helplessness when eyeing the path to greater wealth, they are all manifestations of financial trauma. The underbelly of reality—the lower Sectors—is a breeding ground for poverty, debt, under-earning, and financial dysfunctions.

It's in these dimly lit Sectors that our money-related traumas, imprinted during our formative years by witnessing financial missteps by our role models, keep us anchored. When we internalize these experiences, we find ourselves perpetually resonating with these low-level financial frequencies. Both poverty psychology and ignorance of wealth-building are merely scars of financial wounds. Such wounds can be passed down generationally, like watching our parents make catastrophic financial decisions, or they can be self-inflicted.

Take this scenario: imagine diving headfirst into a booming housing market, only to helplessly watch as your investment plummets leading to foreclosure. Scarred by this experience, you vow never to purchase another house, and as a result, you miss out on potential profits for the rest of your life. This is a classic case of a financial trauma response.

It's paramount to step back and objectively pinpoint where your financial Trauma Triggers lie. Only by recognizing and navigating these triggers can we free ourselves from being perennially tethered to those bottom Sectors. It's not just about moving upwards; it's about healing yourself first.

Time is money, they say. But emotional energy? That's the real currency in the game of Quantum Capitalism. Every moment you spend stuck in a trigger is a moment lost, an opportunity squandered. But with mastery over your triggers, you're not just saving emotional energy—you're investing in yourself, reaping dividends in the form of clarity, focus, and unshakable determination. Higher Sectors beckon.

The Recap

So, we dove deep into the murky waters of Trauma Triggers. You've learned that a Downward Spiral isn't just triggered by the external but also internal. The path to higher Sectors is navigated by an awareness of the outer and inner events that trigger you either causing you to Downward Spiral or never leaving the lower Sectors to begin with.

Poke The Brain

Ever thought about how much wealth—emotional and financial—you've missed out on, because of unresolved trauma triggers? Chew on that.

Your Next Power Move

Juggernaut Journal Exercise: Trigger Throw-Down.

Trauma Triggers

In the spirit of leaving behind what pains you, because that's what Quantum Capitalists do best, let's create an exercise that you can use in your current place in space and time when confronted by a trigger.

For the foreseeable future, identify the moments when you are being triggered and use this exercise.

1. Remember the guiding principle, "I am the observer and the architect of my reality."
2. Identify the precise moment once triggered.
3. Acknowledge the trigger. This could be as simple as whispering under your breath "not this time, you little bitch."
4. Transform it by simply not succumbing to the Downward Spiral.

Do this as often as necessary, redirecting your focus in the moment to something that brings you joy, extracting some type of benefit from your reality instead. Maybe give yourself a treat or do something nice for yourself. Engage with somebody positively or spread some joy in your external environment instead. The key is to exit the routine you've succumbed to in the past, which involved getting triggered and giving in to the Downward Spiral.

Once you've grasped and cultivated the power of being able to stabilize yourself in your current Sector, only then can you truly begin to evolve to some of those upper Sectors. This exercise is pertinent in the process of stabilizing your place within The Quantum Field.

May the force be with you.

Lesson 21

The Upward Spiral

Alrighty, let's say goodbye to the gloom and zoom into the exhilarating essence of this system. Welcome to the Upward Spiral, the shining gem of Quantum Capitalism. Here, we're not just meandering along mundane paths; we're blasting off towards celestial heights, where we connect with higher variations of reality, upper Sectors, and serendipitous events that take us where we want to go. Strap in, because we're about to soar beyond the bounds of gravity!

Envision the Upward Spiral as The Quantum Field's ultimate thrill ride—a journey filled with exhilarating turns of events and intentions materializing before your very eyes. Here, you're perfectly attuned to The Quantum Field's rhythm, channeling your energy to launch into the upper realms of possibility, where opportunities don't just tap on your door— they roll out the red carpet and celebrate your arrival.

Our previous lessons? They were the runway to this grand takeoff. From honing your mindset to unloading past traumas (who needs extra baggage in zero gravity, right?), every tool, insight, and aha moment has been gearing you up for this ascent. Once you shed the shackles of internal and external obstacles, you're as light as a feather, bursting with energy, ready to explore higher Sectors and embark on new adventures. Prepare for liftoff!

The Upward Spiral

Recall the Sectors of reality, lined up from the penthouse at level 10 to the depths of despair at level 1? And those four dynamos from our 4 Qualifiers session—Guiding Theory, Thoughts, Action, and Frequency? They're not just theoretical concepts; they're the rocket fuel for your journey on the Upward Spiral, doubling as a force field against the drag of Blackholes and Gravity.

Let's refresh our memory of the essence of these pillars:

Guiding Theory: this is your master plan in The Quantum Field, your blueprint, your north star. Embrace the belief that YOU are the master builder of your reality. With a Guiding Theory aimed upward, you're already good to go.

Thoughts: consider these your sculpting tools. Like ripples across Sectors, they shape your surroundings. Opt for thoughts drenched in everything you intend, everything you like, everything that is working, and all that is good in your Sector of reality. This tunes you into the frequency of the Upward Spiral.

Action: this is the engine of progress—without it, potential remains untapped. Energize those vibrant thoughts with bold, intentional moves. Seize fresh opportunities. Watch as your path naturally aligns with the Upward Spiral's ascent. Unsure of your next step or can't spot new horizons? Keep your 4 Qualifiers aligned, and watch as pathways unfold before you. Action is your ticket to higher altitudes.

Frequency: your secret weapon, the silent force. Reflect on the aura you emit. Cultivating an energetic transmission that aligns with the positive attributes of your current Sector is key. Your frequency not only wards off Blackholes but also irresistibly draws in opportunities.

With the 4 Qualifiers fine-tuned, you're not just starting the Upward Spiral; you're donning an unbreakable armor, immune to any downward forces. Those Blackholes? They're mere specks on your interstellar dashboard.

So, are you ready to steer your Guiding Theory, Thoughts, Action, and Frequency? Are you set to wave goodbye to Blackholes and embrace the Upward Spiral, transforming into a powerhouse Quantum Capitalist?

Consider this: you've been navigating without a map, but now, with your destination on lock, you can expertly manage your internal landscape and external influences, keeping your eyes on the prize.

Just as negative experiences seem to snowball with the Downward Spiral, the same exponential growth happens with this upward counter-movement. Just like a stubbed toe can lead to a series of misfortunes, finding a coin can spark a chain of positivity if you maintain your focus there. Higher insights, innovative ideas, lucrative gains and positive encounters with all that will assist you on your journey are just a few of the treasures you'll unlock on this ride. The key is to deflect the negative and keep your Qualifiers and intentions aligned with the Upward Spiral.

Envision a spiral in motion: it begins modestly but gains momentum as it expands. Energy is constant, and matter is always in motion. Propel yourself in a positive direction, maintain this trajectory, and watch as your momentum builds, elevating you to greater heights.

The Money Shot: Rise & Thrive

The Upward Spiral is where real financial transformation happens. It's not just a concept; it's the highway to wealth, comfort, and security. Imagine trading in debts and scarcity for a life overflowing with opportunities and prosperity on your terms. Think of it as your personal accelerator, pushing you towards the horizon of financial freedom and stability. The Downward Spiral? That's the past, a distant memory. Ahead is a clear path, paved by your newfound Guiding Theory, Thoughts, Action, and Frequency. These aren't just buzzwords; they are the essential gears accelerating your success. The Upward Spiral isn't about hoping for better; it's about *creating* better. This is where you take control. Because with the Upward Spiral, you're not just dreaming of a richer life—you're designing it. Remember: the power to elevate your life, to secure a future of prosperity, is entirely in your 4 Qualifiers!

The Recap

With the Upward Spiral's potent quartet—Guiding Theory, Thoughts, Action, and Frequency—you're plotting a course for new paths to prosperity. These pillars serve as both your map and armor, shielding you from pitfalls and propelling you towards the pinnacles of success.

Poke The Brain

When was the last time you were on an Upward Spiral and didn't even realize it was happening? What Blackhole then sucked you into its vortex ending your ride prematurely?

Your Next Power Move

Juggernaut Journal Exercise: The 4-Qualifier Diagnostic.

Alright, Quantum Capitalist, it's time to put your spacecraft through a diagnostic. If you find yourself drifting rather than soaring, one of your 4 Qualifiers might just be off-kilter. This exercise will help you spotlight that misalignment and recalibrate, ensuring you're firing on all cylinders.

Let's say you dream of owning a bakery...

Step 1: Define & Visualize

Grab your Juggernaut Journal. Create a quadrant, labeling each quarter with one of the 4 Qualifiers: Guiding Theory, Thoughts, Action, and Frequency.

Guiding Theory

What's the overarching belief fueling your journey? Write it in this section. Example: "I am destined to be the most successful bread maker in town."

Thoughts

List down the top 5 thoughts associated with your guiding theory. Are they in alignment or are they contradictory? Example: "Every loaf I make will be loved by everyone."

Action

Here's where the rubber meets the road. Jot down the tangible steps you've taken or plan to take. Have you secured a lease? Created a business plan? Hired staff?

Frequency

This is the energy you project. How are you feeling about your journey? Excited? Doubtful? List emotions and factors that might be influencing your frequency (like that evening wine that has you down a few notches the next morning).

Step 2: Diagnose the Disconnect

Look at your quadrant. Is one section noticeably weaker or more uncertain than the others? Maybe your thoughts are on point, but your actions aren't matching up. Or perhaps your guiding theory is strong, but your frequency, affected by external factors, is lagging. Circle the weak link(s).

Step 3: Action Plan for Alignment

Now, for the circled Qualifier(s), jot down at least three concrete steps to strengthen them and get them back in alignment.

- If it's Action, maybe it's about finally signing the lease for the bakery or joining a baking masterclass.
- If it's Frequency, perhaps it's time to reconsider that nightly wine and replace it with a revitalizing evening ritual that keeps your energy high and resonant.

Complete this exercise, and you'll have not only identified the misaligned Qualifier but also set forth a roadmap to steer back on track and soar with the Upward Spiral. Remember, Quantum Capitalist, every tweak, every realignment catapults you closer to your desired destination.

Lesson 22

The Cosmic Comet of Fortune

Having explored the steady climb of the Upward Spiral, we now turn our attention to an even more exhilarating phenomenon: the Cosmic Comet of Fortune. This isn't just about maintaining a positive trajectory; it's about catching a wave of extraordinary, condensed success that amplifies the journey.

Picture this: you're on your Upward Spiral, aligning your 4 Qualifiers, when suddenly, you tap into something more intense, more immediate—the Cosmic Comet. It's a cascade of serendipitous wins and opportunities, materializing as if The Universe itself is conspiring in your favor. This isn't a fairy tale; it's a real, tangible burst of fortune that can manifest in myriad ways—be it the perfect networking connection, the right amount of capital at the right time, or even a surprise vacation win.

Think of the Cosmic Comet as a series of fortunate events, supercharged and condensed into a short timeframe. It's like catching a golden streak where everything you touch turns to success. But beware, this isn't an everlasting joyride. Much like a limited-edition sneaker drop, the Cosmic Comet is here in a flash and gone the next. Yet, what if you could extend this thrilling ride?

Here's the twist: the Cosmic Comet of Fortune is The Quantum Field's nod to those who excel in the game of Quantum Capitalism. But, as with any game, there are strategies to maximize your chances.

Your Comet Cheat Sheet

Align Your 4 Qualifiers: ensure your internal operating system is up-to-date. Negativity, inaction, and low energy won't summon the comet. It's time for an upgrade if needed.

Spot the Spark: it starts with acknowledging the small wins. Found a quarter on the street?

Celebrate it! These small moments are The Quantum Field's teasers, hints of the comet's trail.

Focus on these mini-triumphs, and watch them snowball into grand victories.

Fuel the Ride: once you're on the comet, keep the momentum. Maintain a positive outlook, engage in high-energy actions, and steer clear of negativity and mental clutter.

Graceful Exits: like all spectacular events, the comet's ride will eventually end. When it does, don't lament. Instead, recharge, stay alert, and be ready for the next cosmic opportunity.

Remember, the Cosmic Comet of Fortune is a magical, yet fleeting experience. Unlike the steady progression of the Upward Spiral, the comet offers a high-speed, high-intensity burst of wins and opportunities. It's a testament to the power of focused energy and alignment. Keep your eyes open, your spirit ready, and who knows? The next Cosmic Comet might just be waiting for you to hop on and ride it to your next quantum leap in success.

The Money Shot: Your Cosmic Jackpot

Beyond the playful metaphors and catchy phrases, there lies a profound truth: the Cosmic Comet isn't mere fantasy—it's an embodiment of how success compounds, how ideas crystallize into material reality, and how wealth begins to form. The patterns we're discussing here aren't just abstract concepts; they are time-tested principles upon which empires—both large and small—are built. By aligning with these principles and maintaining a focus on what you put out into the world, you're not just "playing" at success; you're constructing the foundations of lasting prosperity. This isn't just about immediate gratification; it's about building your legacy. As you grow in awareness and continuously align with your ambitions in concrete, actionable ways, you'll find that the Cosmic Comet isn't a rare visitor—it becomes a frequent spectacle, dancing brilliantly across the horizon of your Sector. Stay vigilant, stay aligned, and watch as The Quantum Field rewards your diligence with a wealth that transcends what you once believed was possible.

The Recap

The Cosmic Comet: Your Ticket to The Universe's Elite Circle. It's a simple formula, ride the Upward Spiral with unyielding positivity, and you could extend your journey on this comet of fortune. But beware, Blackholes are lurking, ready to disrupt your cosmic parade.

Poke the Brain

Ask yourself: what can I do right now to sync up with the Cosmic Comet's energy and dodge those pesky Blackholes?

Your Next Power Move

Meditation: Cosmic Comet Visualization.

Before we get started, let me just say, I know how this all sounds. I can hear you now... "Come on! For real?" Yes, for real. I know it sounds woo to the hilt, but hold up. What would it hurt to try it? What have you got to lose? Don't knock it until you've tried it.

1. Embrace the Cosmic Connection:
   - Find a peaceful spot to sit or recline. Gently close your eyes.
   - Imagine the boundless Universe above, a tapestry of twinkling stars. Amongst them, the Cosmic Comet blazes forth, its tail a shimmering spectacle of light.
   - Inhale deeply and envision the comet's radiant energy descending like a celestial waterfall, a fusion of gold and silver brilliance, embracing you in its cosmic glow.

2. Infuse and Intensify:
   - Sense this celestial light permeating every part of you, transforming you into a magnet for success and prosperity.
   - With each breath, this luminous energy intensifies, creating an aura of limitless opportunities and fortune around you.

3. Embrace The Universe's Offerings:
   - Whisper to yourself, "I am open and ready for The Quantum Field's opportunities and the abundance they bring. I welcome the success that is flowing my way."

- Feel a subtle vibration of energy as The Quantum Field responds to your openness.
- Take a profound breath and, as you exhale, imagine this cosmic energy grounding you in a new reality where success and prosperity are your constant companions.

Gently open your eyes, step into your day with the Cosmic Comet's radiant energy, and the assurance that The Quantum Field is bolstering your every stride towards triumph.

A QUICK NOTE

Before we delve deeper into this realm, let's pause for a moment. How are you adjusting to such a monumental shift in perspective? Is it overwhelming? If so, take a step back. Give yourself a day, maybe even a week, between lessons. Let each one marinate. Experience your reality through the lens of each lesson, familiarize yourself with it, then proceed. For many who embrace Quantum Capitalism, it becomes a lifelong commitment, a daily practice, an ever-evolving skillset applied in practical ways. If you're pacing well with us, that's commendable! However, we still recommend revisiting the material at least once more. We're traversing these concepts at warp speed, and to truly harness their full potential, deep absorption is crucial. Remember, our community is always here to provide additional support and clarification whenever you need.

Punch it!

Lesson 23

The Quantum Flow

Have you got all that?

- Picture the Sectors of Reality as unique layers within The Quantum Field.
- Remember, matter is always in motion. You're either spiraling up or spiraling down.
- Calibrate your 4 Qualifiers to guide your trajectory.
- Outmaneuver those pesky Blackholes.
- Keep your Importance and Disproportionate Energy balanced, or you might get snagged by Gravity, pulling you into the depths of lower Sectors.

Ready for yet another angle to this knowledge?

The Quantum Flow: it's The Quantum Field's heartbeat, the undiluted rhythm of reality itself. Here's where genuine breakthroughs, elevated solutions, and deep insights catapult you to realms you've only dreamed of. But watch out, The Matrix is clingy. It tries to shackle you to the mundane, obscuring the breathtaking vistas the Quantum Flow offers.

What exactly is the Quantum Flow?

Picture The Quantum Field as an intricate tapestry, rich with interwoven threads of data, events, and insights. It's the energetic autobahn, ushering reality forward, a fast track to those loftier destinations.

For instance, picture a night when you're awake in bed, contemplating a lofty desire, like backpacking through the Himalayas. Your heart ignites with enthusiasm, but your mind quickly chimes in, "Nah, too crazy." Yet, the next day, a friend calls, relaying that her divorce is almost final and she's ready to embark on an epic adventure. Then, an unexpected email about discounted flights, and a surprise bonus, converging at the perfect time, lead you to make the leap. These seemingly random occurrences are the Quantum Flow in action, inviting you to engage with a specific stream of reality.

These currents are omnipresent, and recognizing their patterns opens up a world of opportunities. The Quantum Flow facilitates the realization of your aspirations with less independent effort in solving problems or planning. It's akin to a luxurious, train car of knowledge, insights, and serendipity, waiting for you to hop on and enjoy the ride towards your higher destinations and goals. However, be mindful—The Matrix seeks to derail this journey, thriving on your stagnation and distraction.

Here's the lowdown: the Flow isn't just about a lucky break here and there; it's a transformative force. The golden threads of the Quantum Flow are your ticket to realities beyond your wildest imagination. But often, we're stuck outside, hypnotized by The Matrix's repetitive beats, blind to the possibilities.

Syncing with the Quantum Flow doesn't just tweak the game; it reinvents it. It's open to anyone bold enough to defy The Matrix and embrace the Quantum currents. Simple, right?

Quantum Capitalism is all about recognizing and acting on this flow.

Welcome to the next level

But let's face it: many are blind to this cache of insights and effortless paths. The Matrix, along with our own doubts, often clouds our judgment. Yet, your intuition, your gut feeling, is your hidden ace. Are you ready to trust it more?

Next time you stumble upon something that feels like a game-changer, ask yourself: "Is this lifting me up, or just more of the same?"

The Quantum Flow is your VIP pass to the hottest interstellar nightclub. It's where big ideas strike, opportunities glow red hot, and genius is unleashed. Your intellect is mighty, but it's your heart and soul that unlock the Quantum Flow.

So, what's it going to be? Stuck in The Matrix's echo chamber or surfing the Quantum Flow?

Meet Max

Max, a patron of reality's well-trodden paths in his quaint, predictable hometown. Life here ticks by like a metronome—steady, unchanging, and, to Max, increasingly monotonous. His dreams, once vivid and daring, now hang like faded movie posters on the walls of his mind. Max's existence is comfortable, yet it feels like a vortex of unfulfilled potential.

One evening, as Max sifts through the mundane, he stumbles upon a serendipitous invitation: an opportunity to housesit in a thriving metropolis, a stark contrast to his small-town cocoon. His heart skips a beat with excitement, yet his mind reels with cautionary tales. "It's a leap into the unknown," it warns. But beneath the chatter, a whisper from the depths of his being nudges him towards this unforeseen adventure. It's the Quantum Flow in action, calling him to a stream of reality rich with untapped possibilities.

Braving the unknown, Max steps into the city, a pulsating canvas of lights, sounds, and ceaseless energy. It's a symphony of chaos and harmony, and Max finds himself irresistibly drawn to its rhythm. The city, with its endless avenues and kaleidoscopic sights, breathes life into Max's dormant aspirations.

In this vibrant landscape, Max crosses paths with Ava, a beacon of creativity and zest. She's a soul sculpted by the city's relentless dynamism, her spirit a dance of light and shadow. Ava's world is a revelation to Max, a realm where passion and purpose intertwine. In her, Max discovers not just a partner but a kindred spirit who echoes the adventurous call of the Quantum Flow.

Ava introduces Max to a professional opportunity that lies in the heart of the city's creative vortex, a sector he'd never dared explore. It's a realm that challenges and exhilarates him, aligning with the newfound vibrancy within. Max finds himself not just embracing a new job title but stepping into a reality where his dormant talents and fresh passions converge.

In this bustling metropolis, amidst the whirl of new experiences and the warmth of newfound love, Max's life transforms. He sheds the skin of his former self, once confined to the predictable lanes of his hometown. Max now rides the Quantum Flow, a mover and shaker, in a reality where every day is a canvas of possibilities.

Max's story is a vibrant tale of change, a journey from the static shores of comfort to the dynamic waves of the unknown. It's a tale that weaves the magic of the Quantum Flow—a reminder that sometimes, the greatest discoveries lie just beyond the edge of our familiar world. In embracing the unknown and trusting the cosmic currents, Max finds not just fulfillment but a profound reconnection with the dreams he once thought lost.

The Money Shot: Who's Ready to Flow Like Mutherfu****?

Pumped and ready to reshape your reality? Take that plunge into the Quantum Flow! It's the Wall Street for your dreams, and guess what? The market's booming. Toss out that rulebook, and let's play Quantum Capitalism—it's the only game where everyone's winning.

The pièce de résistance de Quantum Capitalism? It's the flow, baby. With your Quantum Self firing on all cylinders and your connection to The Quantum Field on lock, life isn't just flowing—it's flooding. And the vision? HD clarity.

If you're not living your ideal reality, perhaps you've tapped out your current Sector. The Flow's got what you need. Our upcoming lessons will guide you out of the stale and into a current rich with everything you desire.

The Recap

Ready for an extraordinary journey? The Quantum Flow is your ticket, slicing through The Matrix's drama, guiding you into The Quantum Field's shimmering paths. Sync up with this expressway of higher insights, and you step out of The

Matrix's prefabricated realities and into the realm of infinite possibilities.

Poke the Brain

Think about the last time the Quantum Flow beckoned, but you hesitated. What opportunities did you overlook, and why?

Your Next Power Move

Practical Exercise: Spotting the Currents.

Matrix Illusions vs. Golden Threads

Remember that time The Quantum Field dangled an unconventional solution, a fresh path, or an alternate answer to your dilemma? Did you grab it, or did you dismiss it, trusting your own logic or buying into societal skepticism? Perhaps you wrote off the chance as unrealistic or not meant for you.

What held you back? Fear, skepticism, or maybe a bit of arrogance? Understanding this primes you to seize these golden moments in the future.

Embracing the Quantum Flow

Recall when you felt in sync with a higher wisdom. Maybe it was an intuitive hit, a creative burst, or a solution that just clicked.

How did this alignment benefit you? Notice the shifts in outcomes when you're in tune with this higher flow.

The Comfort Zone Dilemma

Pinpoint something in your life that you're clutching tightly. It could be your job, a relationship, a routine. Delve into why you're holding on.

Reflect: are you clinging out of genuine growth, or is fear keeping you anchored? Is your attachment fueled by love and progress, or fear and stagnation?

Now, picture this:

You're in a river, wide and deep, symbolizing The Quantum Field. You're clinging to a rock, representing your current reality. The Flow is trying to guide you to richer realities, but you're holding on, afraid of the unknown. Imagine downstream lie islands brimming with all you desire. Your reluctance to let go prevents you from reaching these havens. This journey is about shifting perspectives and tuning into these higher variations, seizing them for your gain.

Just by pondering these insights, you've got access to the Quantum Flow. The Quantum Field is always signaling; are you tuned in? Use these reflections to keep your Quantum Capitalist instincts sharp and your awareness keen to the Field's natural nudges towards higher Sectors.

Lesson 24

The Anti-Flow

In the last chapter, we dove headfirst into the game-changer called the Quantum Flow. Envision and harness those quantum currents ribboning through your reality, and suddenly, you're not just Quantum Capitalist-ing—you're in optimal human mode, baby. But, pump the brakes for a hot minute. We're delving into the treacherous territory of the anti-flow. *Cue dramatic music*

There are twin culprits holding us back from the tantalizing promises of the Quantum Flow. Number one: that pesky attachment to something you're just too darn stubborn to release. The second? That role—yes, that one—that's keeping you cemented in your current Sector. Remember reality as this vast, powerful river, with the Quantum Flow as the water currents, gushing, twisting, and turning. But—and it's a big "but"—there are these rocks. And you? You're clinging onto one, either because of some life event you've built up in your mind or some role that's become your comfort blanket.

If you're still struggling with the first type of rock, that *important* one, rewind and revisit the "Importance" chapter. Because here's the thing: Importance? That's the kryptonite to your Quantum Flow superpowers. The Quantum Flow? It's your ticket to that intergalactic evolution. But The Matrix? That's the meddling meddler, forever pitching outdated tales and wonky standards that either have you waiting to win the lottery or playing a role that's way beneath Quantum You.

This lesson? We're shining a spotlight on those roles. Let's crack the code of the role that's been your anchor.

Quick question: felt a tinge of guilt for reaching for the stars recently? Given capitalism in its traditional attire, the ol' stink eye? Or let envy and self-doubt fester? Newsflash: you're anchored to one of those rocks. Ready to cut the rope?

Let's explore these roles:

Needy Beggar: waiting for handouts? Darling, The Quantum Field isn't hosting a charity ball.

Radiating neediness while wanting more is like hoping for 5G in a dungeon.

This role stems from an unfulfilled desire for constant attention and affirmation. Are you someone who constantly seeks approval from others, whether for your fashion choices, life decisions, or even daily Instagram posts? Is your self-worth heavily reliant on external validation? If so, this could be your rock.

Indignant: feeling wronged? News alert: The Quantum Field isn't indebted to you.

This role stems from a deep-seated belief that the world owes you. Are you someone who always expects special treatment, be it cutting the line at a coffee shop or assuming you deserve the biggest slice of pie at a party. This sense of entitlement eclipses gratitude and understanding. If so, this could be your rock.

The Anti-Flow

Fighter: got that eternal war paint on? Heads up: The Universe isn't your opponent. Swap those fists for a strategy.

This role stems from a chronic need to prove oneself, constantly feeling under threat. Are you someone who treats every discussion as a debate to be won, always on edge, ready to dispute. Are you always geared up, even when there's no battle to fight? If so, this could be your rock.

Victim: feeling buried under life's weight? Shadows of the past dogging your steps? Time to soar, phoenix-style. Your destiny's calling, but it's on you to answer.

This role stems from a narrative where one's life is a series of unfortunate events, with you at the receiving end. Are you someone who, after facing a setback, always exclaims, "Why does this always happen to me?" Instead of developing into Quantum You, are you perpetually caught in the drama of your perceived misfortunes?

Listen up, buttercup: while these roles might seem like background noise, they're actually blasting on the main speakers of your life. Stuck in a rut but always hunting for reasons The Universe is ghosting you? Ranting about the latest social justice hashtag? Bemoaning your lot, thinking Lady Luck blocked your number? Or maybe waiting for The Universe to serve you success à la carte while you chill on the couch? Honey, with that mindset, the Quantum Flow will divert around that rock quicker than you can say: I hate Elon Musk.

TAKE THIS TO HEART: The Quantum Field is a treasure chest, not a battlefield. Ditch the drama. Move on from envy, resentment, and aggression. You can't run with the big dogs if you're stuck on the porch barking at shadows.

What to do instead?

After releasing yourself from the roles that are no longer serving you, dive into all you've learned. Maintain awareness of where your thoughts are lingering, the types of actions you're taking, and what your resident frequency is like. Being heavily involved in The Matrix dulls all this, steering you away from the flow and into standard narratives.

Give yourself a fighting chance here. Begin by cultivating luxurious thought loops, focusing on all that is good, all that is working, and all that is making your life beautiful. Listen to the quiet whispers of the Quantum Flow transmitting information to you in moments of pause and stillness. Listen. You've absolutely got this if you can shift your perspective. Upgrade your diet, your workout routine, and your relationships. Begin to view reality, just for the time being, as a polarizing dynamic energetic field with both Matrix information and frequencies, and Quantum Flow information and frequencies. Trust your instinct and check in with yourself: are you tuning into The Matrix or the Quantum Flow?

The Money Shot: The Ultimate Code Cracker

Your bank balance isn't just numbers—it's a reflection of where your mindset's at in The Quantum Field. Every moment you're stuck playing Victim, Needy, Indignant, or Fighter, you're tossing dollar bills into a cosmic shredder. Quantum Capitalism is your insider tip to The Quantum Field's stock market. Now, ditch the roles of old, and you're not just upgrading your mindset—you're unlocking the bank vault. Align with the Quantum Flow, and it's not just about feeling good—it's a calculated, smart strategy. Each mindset upgrade? That's you upping your net worth. So, level up, and let the Quantum Flow provide.

The Recap

Life ain't a sad story. The Quantum Field is not in the tissue business. Embrace Quantum Capitalism, navigate your destiny. Adjust, innovate; don't follow blindly. Let go of what holds you back.

Poke The Brain

What "anti-flow" role are you perpetuating? Is it adding to your life?

Your Next Power Move

Juggernaut Journal Exercise: Role Reversal.

Identify the Role

Put pen to paper and jot down moments from the past week where you've played the Needy Beggar, the Indignant, the Fighter, or the Victim. Think about what triggered these behaviors and the outcomes they resulted in.

Describe a situation where you exhibited one of these roles. What triggered it? Was there a specific incident or emotion?

Analyze the Impact

Now, focus on how that role impacted your decisions, your relationships, and most importantly, your alignment with the Quantum Flow. Assess if you've been blocking opportunities and prosperity by clinging to these outdated modes of operation.

How did embodying this role affect your day? Did it push away potential opportunities or strain relationships? Did you feel in tune with the Quantum Flow or distant from it?

Craft the Upgrade

Here's where you switch gears. For every role you identified in step 1, script a new response or behavior that's aligned with the Quantum Flow. Envision yourself operating in this upgraded mode, feeling confident, connected, and in sync with profitability.

Reimagine the situation from step 1 with your upgraded behavior. How would the Quantum Capitalist version of you have responded? How would this change in behavior realign you with the Quantum Flow and influence the outcome?

By taking the time to identify, analyze, and upgrade these behaviors, you're not only decluttering your mindset but also paving the way for Quantum Capitalism to flourish in your life. Each reflection and proactive change brings you closer to aligning with the boundless potential and prosperity of the Quantum Flow. Remember, Quantum Capitalism isn't just a concept—it's a lifestyle.

Lesson 25

Guiding Signs

Last round, we tackled the anti-flow, the cosmic chain around our ankles, pulling us away from our potential. Once you shed those weights, you're in the club. But I won't lie, being a newcomer can be dizzying. Which way do you go? Here's the thing: The Quantum Field is rich with signs, but don't turn this journey into a game of "Spot the Sign." Getting obsessed is a trap. Relax. *Let it happen.*

Let me break it down; The Quantum Field doesn't speak in riddles; it communicates with signs. While some of you might equate them to random omens or chalk it up to mere superstitions, wise up! This is the Quantum Flow nudging you, trying to show you the path drenched in opportunity for expansion. Stay awake, watch out for these signs, and lean into those sensations that seem to resonate with your very essence.

Recognizing Guiding Signs

Can you sense the atmospheric shift right before a thunderstorm? That's what these Guiding Signs are about—a hint of something changing. Watch, listen, feel. Intuition isn't just a fancy word; it's the compass you forgot you had. Start flexing that intuitive muscle, and it might lead you to the goldmine.

Embracing Guiding Signs

Don't just recognize these signs—embrace them like a lost love. They're your wake-up calls, saving you from pitfalls or pushing you towards that big break. That random advice from a stranger? That recurring symbol in your dreams? Don't dismiss them. Lend an ear to your gut, your intuition. It whispers tales of higher Sectors, if only you'd listen.

Interpreting Signs Wisely

You've got a message, but decoding it? Signs are about how your intuition responds. The sign itself is meaningless, it's what it evokes within that matters. Remember, when faced with life's convoluted crossroads, follow your gut. It's your silent partner in your shift to those higher Sectors.

Embracing Uncertainty and Potential

Guess what? There's a beauty in not knowing everything. Your understanding of the Guiding Signs might be evolving, but trust in those delicate feelings that tickle your core. Let these signs be your allies, guiding your voyage through Sectors, propelling you towards wealth and new prospects.

The Money Shot: Cha ching! Hear that?

You might wonder, "How do cosmic nudges and intuition sync with cold, hard cash?" Get ready for it: these Guiding Signs are like your personal stock market indicators for life. Just as traders make big bucks reading and predicting market signs, you can navigate life's opportunities with these universal cues. Each sign, each intuitive tug could be pointing you to a life-altering opportunity, a business deal, a career shift, or a venture that holds the potential for massive financial gain.

Ignoring them? It's like leaving money on the table or worse, missing out on a blockbuster investment. Master this ancient-yet-modern skill, and you've hit pay dirt. Your ability to read and act on these signs can directly correlate with seizing opportunities for wealth. So, every time The Quantum Field drops a hint, think of it as a potential gold coin gleaming in the distance. Your task? Spot it, check in with what your intuition has to say, and watch your prosperity multiply.

The Recap

Think of guiding signs as your Quantum road signs, guiding you through the unpredictable highway interchanges of life. They're your silent strategists, nudging you towards wise choices, steering you clear from dead-ends, and navigating you towards prosperous destinations.

Poke The Brain

Ready to challenge your status quo? How will you tune into The Quantum Field's whispers, amplify your intuition, and let these guiding signs elevate your game in the realm of prosperity?

Your Next Power Move

A Perception and Juggernaut Journal Exercise: Spotting Cosmic Nods.

Objective: become attuned to a single sign that whispers an opportunity from The Quantum Field. Simplicity is the essence!

Setting Your Intention

Close your eyes for a moment and take a deep breath. Ask The Quantum Field: "Reveal a sign to me that guides me towards an opportunity." Visualize yourself effortlessly recognizing this sign. Hold onto that feeling for a moment, and then release it. Remember, it's a relaxed request, not a demand.

Release & Trust

After setting your intention, let it go. Dive into your daily life without obsessing over signs. We can't force a sign to appear. It's about trust and patience.

Spotting the Sign

Throughout your day, if something catches your attention or resonates with you in a peculiar way, it might be your sign. It could be anything—a line in a book, a casual comment from a friend, a recurring theme in your day. Note this down in your journal or a note on your phone.

Acknowledging the Opportunity

Reflect on the sign you've noticed. Does it nudge you towards an opportunity? Maybe it sparks an idea or reminds you of a forgotten desire. Jot down any feelings, thoughts, or actions it inspires. If it doesn't immediately seem clear, that's okay too. Sometimes, clarity emerges with time.

Wrap Up: The Quantum Field operates in its own rhythm, often intertwining signs within our everyday life. By setting an intention and then releasing the need to control when or how the sign appears, we open ourselves up to serendipity. The key lies in balancing our intention with detachment. The Quantum Field has got your back—trust in its timing and enjoy the wondrous journey of discovery!

Lesson 26

Internal Guiding Signs

Let's rewind a tad. Last round, we dived into those subtle (sometimes flashy) external signs—subtle winks from The Quantum Field guiding our path to the upper Sectors of Reality. This chapter? We're diving deep into the pulse of those inner alerts. Ready to decode your Internal Signs? Let's go!

Life's a sassy teacher. It throws you hints, nudges, and if you're still acting dense—massive red flag signs screaming, "CHANGE COURSE!" When you decide to revisit that old romantic relationship that drained you more than it filled you, and you feel dread the moment you embrace, or that anxiety that builds up as you prepare to meet a childhood buddy, or the guilt creeping up as you binge-watch that show for the umpteenth time—these aren't just random feelings. Nope! They're The Quantum Field's way of sending SMS notifications straight to your soul.

Listen, The Quantum Field isn't always subtle. When things feel off-kilter, when your gut wrenches, when anxiety beats at your door like an unpaid landlord—it's life, shouting, "Hey you! Wake up!" It's about being in tune, in flow. And when you're not? Well, life has its ways of reminding you. But why do we often refuse to acknowledge the signs? Why, even when every bone in our body is screaming "LET GO," do we hold on with clenched fists?

Because letting go is scary. But the paradox is, the tighter you grip, the scarier it sometimes gets.

Cast your mind back to that moment when your Inner bell rang louder than a morning alarm after a sleepless night. You heard it, but chose to slap the snooze button, marching on until you face-planted, realizing that while life held out a neon "RIGHT" arrow, you went left. Why? Old trauma, rusty programming, or just that darn comfy rut you've danced in for too long. Look, you might not know me from Adam, and my "permission slip" might not hold much value, but let's shake things up. Next time that Inner alarm starts buzzing? Listen. Who knows? That might just be your golden ticket.

The Money Shot: Investing in Your Gut

Internal Guiding Signs can become your most trusted advisors on the journey to prosperity and higher Sectors of existence. This isn't just about listening to your gut; it's about transforming intuition into action, turning whispers of potential into roars of success.

Imagine your Internal Signs as the ultimate financial analysts. They don't just read markets; they read your life's patterns, emotions, and opportunities. When you experience a sinking feeling about a dead-end job or a flutter of excitement about a new venture, it's not random. It's your internal quantum system highlighting the stocks and shares of life's choices. Think of it as a sophisticated algorithm, uniquely calibrated to guide you toward the most prosperous paths.

These signs are the secret code to unlocking wealth in its most holistic form. They nudge you away from energy-draining endeavors and steer you toward activities and connections that amplify your personal and financial growth. It's a strategic shift from traditional wealth-building to a more dynamic, intuitive approach, aligning with The Quantum Field's rhythm of prosperity.

Every internal signal is an opportunity to recalibrate your route. It's about recognizing which doors to close and which windows to open, ensuring a constant flow of opportunities and growth. So, as you navigate the day-to-day, pay attention to these nuanced signals, both internal and external. Each one is a stepping stone to a richer, more vibrant reality, where success is not just measured in material gains but in the profound satisfaction of living in alignment with your intuition and potential.

The Recap

Life's a fun little game of reading between the lines. Both your personal life and your wallet benefit when you stop resisting and start listening.

Poke The Brain

Think about the biggest regret or missed opportunity of your life. What signs did you blatantly ignore?

Your Next Power Move

Juggernaut Journal Exercise: Considering Life's Red Flags.

Objective:

To cultivate awareness of The Quantum Field's nudges and apply intuitive insights to both personal and financial domains.

Reflection and Identification

- Sit comfortably and close your eyes. Take three deep breaths to center yourself.
- Reflect on the past month. Think about moments when you felt uneasy, anxious, or had that nagging gut feeling.
- Now, open your eyes and jot down three instances where you felt something within trying to send you a signal. This could be in personal relationships, career decisions, or financial moves.

Decoding The Signal

For each instance, answer the following questions.

1. What were the exact emotions or feelings you experienced?
2. Were there any external indicators or signs that accompanied this feeling? (For example, a random message, a conversation you overheard, etc.)
3. In hindsight, what do you think was trying to come through?

Applying The Insights

Reflect on how acknowledging and acting upon these signals could have (or did) change the outcome of the situation.

- Were there missed opportunities?
- Or perhaps you averted potential setbacks by heeding the signs?

Forward-Looking Intuition

- Close your eyes again, and visualize the month ahead.
- Set an intention to be more receptive to both Guiding and Inner Signs.
- Imagine yourself confidently navigating situations, with your intuition as your compass. Commitment and Closure

Write down a commitment statement in your journal. It could be something like:

"I trust and honor my intuition. I am open to The Quantum Field's guidance in all aspects of my life, and I pledge to be more attuned to its signals as well as my own."

Regular Check-ins:

At the end of each week, set aside a few minutes to revisit this exercise. Reflect on any new signals you've perceived and how you've responded. Adjust and refine your intuitive skills as needed.

By actively engaging in this exercise, you'll find yourself more in sync with life's ebbs and flows. Not only will you be able to navigate personal challenges with more grace, but you'll also develop a keen sense for financial opportunities and pitfalls. Remember, intuition isn't about predicting the future—it's about confidently riding the wave of the present.

Lesson 27

The Recalibration

Ah, brave soul, you've traversed the wilds of Phase 1, plunging into depths both mesmerizing and transformative. Let's pause, reflect, and ensure your roots are deeply entrenched in this newfound knowledge. If you sense a wobble, dare to dive back in for a second round, refine, and emerge triumphant!

Our odyssey into Quantum Capitalism began with the audacious act of breaking free from The Matrix's numbing lullaby. Recognize this: The Matrix seeks to ensnare, desiring you remain entrapped, ignorant of your boundless potential. This is a dance of liberation, recognizing and evading The Matrix's snares that stifle and limit.

Your initiation into the vast Quantum Field marked the dawn of true empowerment. Understand this duality: the constrained, Matrix-defined "you" and the boundless, Quantum Self. Comprehending their mechanisms, the realities each conjures, is your golden key. The Quantum Field extends a VIP invitation—but the question is, do you perceive your worthiness of the invite?

Have you fine-tuned your Guiding Theory? Are those 4 Qualifiers of navigation on lock? And the Blackholes, those reality-twisting vortexes; do they still pull you in, or have you mastered the art of zero f****? How about your Importance levels? Are you keeping them in check? And Disproportionate Energy and the chaos it unleashes? Don't worry if it seems overwhelming, it's a new language. Go easy on YOU. Soon, these Quantum laws will meld into your being, as effortless as a heartbeat.

This isn't a mere simulation though! You're on a trajectory—ascending to realms of prosperity or plummeting into scarcity. It's the principle behind wealth's exponential growth or rapid depletion. The rich get richer and the poor get poorer. So, where are you headed? Towards boundless prosperity or limiting paucity?

Have you truly surrendered to the Quantum Flow, or are remnants of The Matrix's illusion still ensnaring you, luring you into a mirage of lack and limitation? And those Guiding Signs, do you now move with awakened clarity, bypassing The Matrix's mirages and tuning into The Quantum Field's lush offerings?

The Recap

Your journey has reached an electrifying crossroads. Phase 2 beckons, promising an even grander, evolved version of Quantum You as you apply its lessons. But heed this: this alchemical system is mighty and transformative, yet it demands unwavering commitment. Let these teachings meld into your very essence or stay on the sidelines, believing it's just all for someone else.

Poke The Brain

Are you poised, ready to intensify your voyage, shed past constraints, and delve into the deeper enigmas of Phase 2?

Your Next Power Move

A Juggernaut Journal Exercise: The Recalibration.

Objective:

To reinforce and internalize the teachings from Phase 1 of Quantum Capitalism, ensuring a strong foundation as you progress into the deeper revelations of Phase 2.

Step 1: The Matrix Self-Reflection

- Reflect on a recent situation where you felt entrapped by The Matrix.
- Note down the exact emotions and constraints you felt. Was it fear, doubt, or another limiting feeling?
- What would Quantum You have done differently in that situation?

Step 2: The Quantum Declaration

- Write down a personal declaration, reminding yourself of your limitless potential within The Quantum Field.
- Example: "I am boundless, beyond The Matrix, and my potential is infinite."

Step 3: Your Guiding Theory Check

- Review the 4 Qualifiers of navigation. For each one, write a recent decision or action where you applied them.
- Reflect: are there areas where you need more practice or understanding?

Step 4: Blackhole Indifference Mastery

- Recall a situation where you almost got sucked into a Blackhole. How did you escape its pull? Or did you succumb?
- Strategize: if faced with a similar situation again, what will you do differently to maintain your composure and not give in?

Step 5: Importance Level Calibration

- Note down three things from the past week that you assigned high Importance to. Reflect: Were they truly deserving of that Importance?
- Think of ways you can recalibrate and reassign Importance levels more efficiently in the future.

Step 6: Acknowledge the Quantum Flow

- Close your eyes. Visualize The Matrix's illusion slowly fading away, revealing the vast Quantum Field. Feel yourself being drawn towards its abundance.
- Ask yourself: are there any Matrix remnants I still dysfunctionally cling to? Write them down and set an intention to release them.

Step 7: The Guiding Signs Journaling

- Dedicate a page in your journal to document any Guiding Signs you've recently encountered.
- Reflect: How did these signs steer you toward any higher opportunities?

Closing Reflection

Revisit your initial state of mind from the beginning of Phase 1. Compare it to your current mindset. Write a short reflection on your growth, breakthroughs, and areas needing further exploration.

With this exercise, you solidify the foundation built during Phase 1. The path to Phase 2 will be clearer and more enriching when you're deeply rooted in the lessons of Phase 1. Celebrate your progress, and remember, every step forward in this Quantum journey is a leap towards boundless prosperity.

PHASE II

QUANTUM YOU

Lesson 28

Mirror | rorriM

Think you've got a handle on reality? Time to rethink, friend, because we're dialing up the intensity on the "awareness creates reality" concept. Welcome to the game-changer, the eye-opener, the hidden track of life's album: The Mirror World. Are you ready for the ultimate cosmic twerk-off?

Think your days are just a random jumble of events? Think again. Those terse exchanges in the coffee line, unexpected acts of kindness, the sudden outpouring of affection—they're all part of a synchronized routine with The Quantum Field. You're not just moving to its beat; you're leading the dance.

Let's delve into this: life isn't a series of random events. It's a dynamic duet with The Quantum Field, where your every action invites a mirrored response. But here's the catch: the Field's response isn't always immediate. It's like a boomerang you've forgotten you threw, coming back to you unexpectedly.

Imagine skipping a pebble across a pond. The initial splash is instant, but the ripples spread, reaching far shores long after the stone has sunk. Similarly, your actions, whether noble or not, resonate like that pebble. The Quantum Field might take its time responding, echoing back your actions at the most unexpected moments.

Here's where many stumble. They dabble in positive thinking for a short while and then dismiss it as ineffective when they don't see instant results. Or they observe a slight shift in their world, only to be blindsided by an event that leaves them puzzled, thinking, "Where did *that* come from?" Welcome to the mysterious ebb and flow of the Mirror World.

Life is the grandest of mirrors, consistently reflecting your thoughts, actions, and vibrations. Cast a shadow, and The Universe mirrors it back. Radiate joy, and life brightens, akin to adding a perfect filter. Ever snapped at someone, then unexpectedly faced someone else's ire? That's life's quirky way of saying, "Gotcha!" Contrastingly, spread genuine kindness—assist someone or tip generously—and watch as life opens doors to the finest experiences. It's not just cosmic reciprocity; it's the Mirror World in real-time action.

So, as you go about your day, remember: each act, each thought, is a step in the grand choreography of your reality. The Mirror World is ever-present, responsive, mirroring your moves in this cosmic ballet of existence.

Meet Jake

One particular morning, Jake awakens enveloped in a cloud of irritability. He bypasses his usual pleasantries with his neighbor, opting instead for a scowl. "Why is he always in such a good bloody mood?" Jake wonders. As he hurries to work, the Universe seems to conspire against him. His coffee betrays him, spilling over his crisp shirt and then a minor fender bender pulling into the parking lot. Then at work, his computer scowls at him too with a sudden crash and loss of work. And, as if in cahoots with his crappy mood, an important call slips through his fingers and he loses a deal as a result.

The day feels like a relentless echo of his morning mindset, an unyielding reflection of his internal storm.

But here's the script flip. The following day, Jake, aware of the Downward Spiral he's set in motion, decides to turn it all around. He greets the dawn with a stretch and a smile, despite the residue of yesterday's chaos. He shares a genuine moment with his neighbor, replacing the scowl with a friendly nod and a few kind words, attempting to relish in his neighbor's perpetual positivity instead. On his commute, he takes the scenic route, letting the beautiful scenery soothe his soul.

As if by magic, Jake's day transforms. His boss, often indifferent, takes a moment to acknowledge Jake's hard work with unexpected praise. In his pocket, he discovers a long-forgotten $100 bill, as if the mind shift is winking at him. And the cherry on top? An unexpected call from an old client offering him a solid opportunity, brightening his day further.

This shift in Jake's reality isn't just serendipity; it's a testament to the power of a positive focus and emotional consistency. It illustrates a crucial principle: The Quantum Field mirrors our thoughts, actions, vibrations and our emotional states. Sometimes instant, sometimes with a delay.

The lesson here is profound yet simple. The chaotic ups and downs of life are often a mirror of our inner turmoil. When Jake's world seemed unreliable, it wasn't The Quantum Field being a little bitch; it was a reflection of his own erratic emotional state.

Jake's story teaches us that we're not just passive observers in life; we're active participants. Our emotional and mental states are like signals sent out into the Mirror World, only to be reflected back in the form of experiences and encounters.

So, remember, influencing The Quantum Field isn't about control; it's about understanding and curating the energy you emit. Project negativity, and you'll find yourself alone in a gloomy theater of life, where the popcorn is stale, and the audience is noisy. But approach life with positivity, grace, and a desire for goodness, and watch as The Quantum Field offers you a front-row seat to a story that unfolds just as you wish.

The Money Shot: The Quantum Exchange

Consider wealth and prosperity not merely as dollars in your bank, but as an energetic exchange with The Quantum Field. When you're stuck in a mindset of scarcity, constantly lamenting what you lack or resenting others for what they possess, The Quantum Field picks up on this frequency. It hears, "I don't have enough." And guess what? It responds in kind, echoing back, "Here's just a little bit." Why? Because The Quantum Field delights in mirroring your tune right back at you.

However, flip the narrative. Begin operating from a space of feeling as though you have plenty, even if your current circumstances suggest otherwise. When you invest in yourself, learn a new skill, appreciate small victories, or even give—be it time, money, or effort—without immediate expectation of return, you're sending out a powerful signal. This says, "I am prosperous. I am worthy. I am open to receive." And The Quantum Field? It listens and responds.

Money is merely a tangible representation of an intangible concept: value. And The Quantum Field is the greatest arbitrator of value. When you genuinely believe in the value you bring to the table, in the worthiness of your skills, ideas, and ventures, you begin to align with opportunities that reflect this value back to you. Deals fall into place, investments flourish, unexpected avenues of income appear. But it's not magic—it's Mirror. The Quantum Field simply reflects the value you see in yourself. To truly magnetize wealth, you don't need to chase money; you need to resonate with its frequency.

The Recap

Your world is a high-definition, responsive mirror. It doesn't just display; it delves deep, picking up your actions, intentions, emotions, and even the subtleties you forget. It might seem unpredictable, but in truth, it's just playing your tune.

Poke The Brain

If today was a reflection of your past actions, what kind of echoes are you setting up for your future? Where are you leading the dance, and where are you merely reacting to the world's lead?

Your Next Power Move

Thought Exercise: The Quantum Mirror Reflection.

This exercise aims to provide a vivid and educational experience to help you understand and visualize the power of the Mirror World concept. It guides you in observing the relationship between your internal state and the external world's responses.

Step 1: Recall and Reflect

- Think back to a recent interaction or event where you noticed a clear response from your environment to your emotional state.

- Was it positive, like a smile from a stranger that mirrored your own cheerful mood? Or was it negative, like an argument that escalated because of your agitation?
- Write down this event in your notebook.

Step 2: Connect the Dots

- Draw connections between your internal state during that event and the external response it elicited. This is your personal demonstration of the Mirror World in action.
- Reflect on how your thoughts, feelings, and vibrations might have influenced this interaction. Were you projecting positivity, negativity, or something else?

Step 3: The Change Experiment

- For the next week, consciously alter your internal state before engaging with others or starting your day. Choose a state of being like calmness, kindness, or positivity.
- Observe how people and situations around you respond to this change. Note any differences in interactions, opportunities, and even your own feelings during the day.
- Write down your observations and any shifts in the quality of your experiences in your notebook.

Conclusion

This exercise is designed to make you deeply aware of the reciprocal relationship between your internal state and the world around you. By actively participating in this experiment, you'll gain a visceral understanding of how The Quantum Field mirrors your internal world, empowering you to navigate life with greater awareness and intention. Remember, the world is a reflection of your Inner state; change the latter, and watch the former transform.

Lesson 29
Your Algorithm

In our lesson of the Mirror World, we've seen how life mirrors our projections. We've introduced this concept, but it runs deep, observing the tangible impact of our thoughts and actions just scratches the surface. Now, we delve deeper, tuning your personal algorithm to align with your desired Sector. Our mission? To attract what you truly crave and discard what's been holding you back.

Think you've nailed the art of curating your Instagram feed? Cute. Let's now focus on curating the perfect reality feed. Like choosing the perfect filter, you're subconsciously selecting life's tone. But are you consciously crafting your selection?

Remember that day where a grumpy start spiraled into a series of misfortunes, like Jake in the last lesson? That's your "negative" algorithm at work. Your mood set the tone, and your reality echoed it back. Conversely, when you're riding high, your day reflects that too, with unexpected joys and wins. This is no coincidence; it's the art of reality curation.

If you're aiming for financial growth but constantly dwell on scarcity, on what you lack, and how others surpass you, you're misaligning yourself from the prosperous reality you seek. Similarly, if you desire personal evolution yet constantly ruminate over your flaws, fixate on your shortcomings, and project a fragmented, discordant self-image, you'll find progress elusive.

Conversely, if you can pivot this mindset and start recognizing the overflow in your life, acknowledging your strengths, and affirming that you're on the right path, you initiate a transformative shift. By embracing these positive feelings and expanding them within, you effectively rewrite the code of your personal algorithm. This change broadcasts potent new signals to your environment, aligning you with those exact versions of reality you aspire to. This is the key to unlocking the life you envision.

Your experience of reality is shaped by your internal algorithm—a mix of thoughts, beliefs, feelings, emotions, and actions. This personal algorithm influences The Quantum Field's responses to you, functioning as life's feedback mechanism. Our mental and emotional patterns, much like our dietary habits, shape our experiences. Understanding which patterns serve us and which require modification is key to mastering this process.

Counterproductive Patterns - What not to do and when it's time for a change

Listen, doom and glooming, catastrophizing and woe is me-ing has got to fuckin' go. If you find yourself often expecting the worst, it's time for a clean-up. But that's not all. Comparing your life to others' highlights reel can distort your sense of achievement. Waking up without direction can lead to aimless days. Holding onto past hurts or constantly voicing grievances without seeking solutions keeps you stuck in a negative feedback loop. Feeling isolated, resisting change, surrounding yourself with negativity, anticipating the worst, or allowing past mistakes to overshadow your present—all these patterns can derail your journey to a better reality.

Constructive Patterns - Blueprint for a Better Life

Luxurious thinking, being delusionally positive and hyper focusing on all that is good in your Sector is your new jam. Got it? Setting a clear, positive intention each morning can transform your day. Practicing gratitude and being present in every moment enhances your life quality. Continuous learning and connecting with nature contribute to your growth. Establishing healthy boundaries, mindful eating, engaging in joyful activities, using positive affirmations, and visualizing your goals are practices that can shape a fulfilling life.

By identifying your prevailing patterns, you can make conscious choices that resonate with your desired experiences. Life reflects our internal algorithms; adjusting them leads to enriched living. It's about recognizing and embracing the power we have to shape our reality. Just as we curate our online presence, we can curate our life experiences. So, are you ready to recode your algorithm and transform your experience of reality?

The Money Shot: Cashing In On Your Algorithm

Let's talk cold, hard cash. You want more of it, right? Now, consider your financial reality as an Instagram feed exclusively dedicated solely to wealth. The content? Opportunities, investments, raises, savings, and all that jazz. How you curate this "wealth feed" plays directly into how fat your wallet gets. When you curate your general life with positivity, confidence, and determination, you're not just improving your mood or relationships, you're directly impacting your financial future.

Want to see more dollar signs in your life's feed? Then adjust your inner wealth algorithm. Curate a mindset of prosperity, see the value in every experience, and trust that with the right mental tools, the ROI (Return On Intention) will be lucrative. Financial prosperity doesn't just stem from wise investments of money, but also from wise investments of thought and actions. Remember, in this grand market of life, you're both the broker and the asset. Make every thought count, and watch your wealth grow.

The Recap

Your life isn't a series of random events. It's a carefully curated feed, influenced by your mindset and reactions. The events in your life, both good and bad, are often a reflection of your internal state. To change your Outer World, start by tweaking your Inner settings.

Poke The Brain

If your life was a social media platform, what kind of content would dominate your feed? Is it time for a digital detox or a new curation strategy?

Your Next Power Move

Practical Exercise: Curate Your Reality Challenge.

Objective: to consciously influence the "feed" of your daily life by curating positive experiences, thoughts, and reactions.

Duration: one week.

Instructions:

Morning Tone Setting

Start each day by choosing a "tone" for your life's feed. It could be "opportunity," "prosperity," or "determination." Post a note with the day's mood on your bathroom mirror.

Daily Content Creation

- When faced with a challenge, think: "How can I frame this for my life's feed?"

Example: you keep running up against a problem at work. Could it actually align with the tone of "opportunity" you set? Maybe it's not a problem at all but an opportunity to create a useful solution that all in your office would benefit from.

- Actively seek three positive experiences or moments in your day that align to the tone you've set. These could be as simple as a pat on the back at work, finding the solution to the problem that has perplexed you, or spotting a fresh offer for something that excites you.
- Snap a photo or jot down a note of these moments representing a "post" to your life's feed.

Evening Reflection

- Review your "posts" for the day.
- Think about how they made you feel, and how they contributed to the overall "theme" or "tone" you set for the day.

Adjusting the Algorithm

- What can you adjust in your "algorithm" (mindset, reactions) to improve your feed next week?
- Celebrate the positive themes and patterns. These are the "trending tones" in your life that you'll want to keep amplifying.

Lesson 30

Boomerang

In our previous lesson, we dived deep into shaping the algorithm of your life. We talked about setting a tone, spotting aligned events, and dialing into your desired vibe. Now, it's time to reverse it. We're going to examine what we're projecting to the Mirror World. See, the Mirror World is like a two-way street, functioning in dual directions. Feels complex? Hang tight; I've got your back.

On one side, there's the world, flinging a multitude of experiences your way. From this vast array, you cherry-pick what to zoom in on, crafting your internal ambiance, which in turn shapes your reality even more. This is the magic of multiplication—the more you focus on something, the more of it you seem to attract.

Then, there's the other side—the proactive stance. Here, you're the initiator, releasing into the world the images, events, and vibes you wish to see more of. We term this the "Boomerang Effect." Intrigued? There are two core facets to understanding the Mirror World's dual dynamics:

Observation: noting what you're seeing and deliberately tuning into what resonates with your desires.

Initiation: mindfully dispatching into the world the energy, actions, or vibes you wish to amplify.

Picture it as a boomerang toss. You fling it out, The Quantum Field sends it back amped up, and then you consciously choose to engage with it. This cycle is not just perpetual, it's potent, serving as the engine that propels your desired energies within your reality. To manifest a desire, you need to recognize its presence in your world, no matter how tiny, while simultaneously emitting that exact energy.

Example: let's say you're feeling a lack of opportunities. Your task? Spot even the tiniest openings around you while simultaneously creating opportunities for others. This simple act stirs the energy of opportunity, making it ripple, expand, and then... snowball.

Glitch: that incessant chatter in your mind. It's like a hyperactive child on a sugar binge, always leaning towards mischief. For many of us, this inner monologue tends to drone on about our fears, dislikes, and all the undesirable facets of our lives. Evolution has hardwired our brains to zone in on potential threats, making us hyper-alert to potential pitfalls in our everyday activities. Let's face it: if our ancestors were perpetually distracted by every beautiful butterfly or rainbow, they might have missed the lurking dangers and, well, we might not be here. However, those tangible threats of yesteryears, like imminent predators or the looming cold of winter, aren't prevalent concerns today. Yet, here's the twist: many of us are still broadcasting these fear-based, scarcity-driven vibes into our realities. And the result? We're caught in this mental whirlpool, oscillating on a frequency of negativity.

Let's paint a picture here. Imagine your mindset is your home. If you're stuck in a loop of complaining about your current digs, well, you're just packing those nasty feelings in your suitcase and sending them over to your future reality. So, that dream house you're moving into? Expect it to come with leaky pipes and annoying neighbors. And that fat paycheck you just started earning? Watch it disappear under a pile of unexpected expenses.

Whatever energy you put out there—good vibes or bad vibes—it's going to come back at you just like a boomerang. Your mindset, your vibe, is the power behind your throw. So, if you want to shift your life, if you're looking to fill up that bank account, or just have a better life, you gotta change the frequency of your thoughts.

First off, give your present circumstances a big, warm hug. Let go of that whiny dissatisfaction and go on a scavenger hunt for joy. Express some gratitude for the things you have now, and let it radiate like a dang lighthouse. This positive energy? It's gonna act as your beacon for better opportunities.

Second, imagine your best life like you're watching it in IMAX. Visualize the home you want, the money you want. Go window shopping for beautiful homes, take a financial planning course, and immerse yourself in thoughts of the things you intend to have. Keep in mind, you usually get what you think about the most. Your thoughts, boo, they're Boomerangs waiting to be thrown.

Lastly, keep a check on the energy you're pushing out. Firing off a rant at someone? You can bet your boots that you'll soon stumble into some trouble. Every time you let off negative steam, you're basically stepping onto a path littered with some bullsh**. So, do yourself a favor, and keep that energy positive.

The Money Shot: Fake or Financially Sound?

Maintaining positivity and choosing to focus on the positive in any scenario doesn't have to be contrived or seem fake. What you focus on exponentially increases in your realm of reality.

So, view this as a valuable investment in the bank of life, rather than as forced happiness. Quantum Capitalism isn't asking you to pretend or act like someone other than yourself. This is about choosing to concentrate on the good in your world and avoiding anything that might lower your mood, frequency, and mindset. Engaging with reality in this negative way offers no benefits. If you aspire for more and better for yourself, you'll need to evolve your thoughts. PERIOD.

The Recap

Your thoughts, feelings, and reactions, they're like Boomerangs. They'll swing right back at you, shaping the kind of life you lead. If you're dreaming of the sweet life, flush with opportunity and wealth, tune your thoughts to the frequency of positivity. Embrace the present moment, express gratitude, dream about your success, and keep a leash on your negative reactions to ensure your Boomerang brings back stuff you can actually use to create your ideal reality.

Poke The Brain

What frequency are your thoughts buzzing on? Is it time to tweak your mental radio for a station playing the tunes of success and prosperity?

Your Next Power Move

Thought & Juggernaut Journal Exercise: Boomerang Bootcamp.

Objective: to become hyper-aware of your thoughts, ensuring you're releasing positive Boomerangs, and prepping yourself for prosperous returns.

Duration: one week (with potential to make it a lifelong habit)

Instructions:

Morning Declaration

- Start each day by choosing a positive statement that resonates with you.
- This statement or declaration could be: "Today, I attract success and prosperity."
- Repeat it aloud 10 times, really feeling its truth within you. This primes your mind to release similar frequency Boomerangs.

Thought Trackers

- Carry your Juggernaut Journal or use your mobile to track your thoughts.
- Divide a page into two columns: Positive Boomerangs & Negative Boomerangs.
- Every time you have a significant thought, jot it down in the appropriate column.

Positive Pivot Practice

- Whenever you catch a negative thought, challenge yourself to pivot. Find a way to rephrase it or shift your focus to something positive.
- For instance, if you think: "I always mess up," pivot to: "Every mistake is a learning opportunity."

Evening Reflection

- Review your Thought Tracker. Notice any patterns? Are there triggers for negativity that you can avoid or address?
- Celebrate the positive Boomerangs you released and recognize your efforts in pivoting from the negative ones.

Visualize Victory

- Close your eyes and imagine yourself throwing out a Boomerang loaded up with all the best parts of you. Visualize it coming back to you, loaded with success, prosperity, and exciting opportunities.
- Feel the joy of receiving this Boomerang back.

Wrap-Up

At the end of the week, check the balance of your Positive vs. Negative Boomerangs. Hopefully, you'll notice an increase in positive ones. Celebrate this shift! Remember, you're training your brain to be an expert Boomerang thrower, ensuring your returns are always beneficial. This might happen quickly and it might take time. Try not to focus on the results yet stay consistent in what you are throwing out.

Master the throw, and you'll master the game of life.

Lesson 31

Blackhole Slingshot

Alright, in our previous lesson, we delved deep into the art of refining what we project into the world to amplify the quality of our reality. Do you spot a pattern with the last few lessons? Let's recap. On one side of the Dual Mirror World concept, we selectively choose and interpret what comes our way, using that feedback to craft our internal vibe. On the flip side, we launch our finest intents into The Quantum Field with a metaphysical Boomerang, ensuring this vibrant energy exchange keeps churning and forming our ideal reality. The crux? Positive engagement with both sides of our reality, the input received from the world and the output we project to our world. Engage with what reality offers you, and in return, send out your consciously crafted message.

But wait, there's more depth to dive into! Time to learn the art of positively interacting with those seemingly destructive Blackholes. Yes, you read that right. While a tranquil reality requires disassociating from the downers that Blackholes can be, a thriving reality necessitates leveraging them to your advantage. Enter the Blackhole Transmission Triumph. Ready to tune in and level up?

Each day, you're flipping through the frequencies of life, sometimes stumbling upon a rockin' track and sometimes a cacophonous noise. These frequencies are driven by the information you choose to dial into. Think of destructive

Blackholes as those static-filled stations, giving you nothing but static noise. But what if I told you, Blackholes play different tunes for different folks? Some might just have the beat to get you grooving to higher Sectors.

You see, it's not all about what Blackholes take from you but also what they can potentially give back. There are Blackholes that uplift, that inspire, that challenge you in the most invigorating ways, while others may have a different relationship. Instead of focusing on the negative Blackholes that drain you, why not shift your perspective and find those that boost your signal?

Meet Jamie

Jamie had a habit. Every weekend, she'd plunge into the Blackhole that was YouTube. From cat videos to travel vlogs, she'd dive headfirst into this digital vortex, emerging only when Monday came knocking. Before she knew it, her weekends vanished into pixelated memories, leaving her wondering, "Where'd all the time go?"

But one fateful Sunday, as Jamie was watching her 67th consecutive DIY video, she stumbled upon a video titled "How to Become a YouTube Superstar." "Hey, I can do this!" Jamie thought. Instead of being a passive consumer in this Blackhole, she decided to become its star.

Jamie bought a light-ring and started her own channel. Her weekends were now dedicated to creating content she loved. From her misadventures in baking to her thoughts on trending topics, she shared it all. Not only was she now productive during her weekends, but the Blackhole that once consumed her time was now working in her favor.

As her subscriber count grew, so did her confidence and sense of purpose. The Blackhole, which once sucked her weekends into a void, was now propelling her into YouTube stardom.

The moral? Blackholes can be as destructive or as beneficial as you make them. Jamie could've continued her endless watching spree, but she chose to tune into the Blackhole at a different frequency. She eventually transformed her passive consumption into passive income.

Like Jamie, it's essential to recognize that sometimes, the very Blackhole that appears to be draining us can be the one that also catapults us to new heights. It's all about how you interact with it.

Meet Alex

Once upon a tipsy time, Alex was hopelessly lost in the Alcohol Blackhole. Nights blended into mornings, and hangovers became a permanent fixture. Friends worried, family intervened, but the seductive pull of the bottle was just too strong for him to resist.

However, one particularly rough morning, the weight of his addiction bore down on him. It was an existential dread he couldn't shake off. Recognizing the damage he was doing to himself and the relationships he cherished, Alex decided to dive into sobriety. With rehab, counseling, and the unyielding support of his loved ones, he managed to break free from the shackles of his addiction.

But here's the twist: Alex's love for the vibrant and intricate world of cocktails didn't vanish. He remembered the delight he took in mixing flavors, creating new drinks, and the showmanship that went with it. But could he still be part of that world without falling back into its darker corners?

Determined, Alex enrolled in a bartending course, focusing on flair bartending. Juggling bottles, spinning shakers, and wowing audiences with his cocktail-making dexterity, Alex became a maestro of the bar. He innovated non-alcoholic cocktails, elevating them to a level of taste and sophistication that rivaled their alcoholic counterparts.

Years passed, and Alex became a legend in the industry. Winning award after award, he was hailed not just for his unmatched skills, but for his inspiring story of transformation. Alex had managed to reverse out of the Blackhole's pull. From self-destruction to self-actualization.

He often said, "It's the same stage, just a different show."

The Alcohol Blackhole that once threatened to consume him was now the same platform from which he shone the brightest. Same Blackhole, different relationship.

The Money Shot: Blackhole Benefactor

Here's the key insight you've been overlooking: some Blackholes can actually be your financial allies. They're not solely about the void they pull you into; sometimes, they're about the value they can bring to your life.

When you start looking at the world from a perspective of it all being about energy, everything changes. Blackholes thrive on the human energy that they can captivate and suck into their vortex. Here's the cool thing though: there is an accumulation of energy there for anyone to tap into. With this knowledge, you can easily pinpoint opportunities nearly anywhere you look. Start to see where human energy collects and then begin to recognize where you can tap into that arena and collect some of it for yourself. This is an incredibly enlightening concept and way to look at the world. Blackholes can propel you to a prosperous new Sector, leveraging the energy the Blackhole accumulates for your own good. The fact of the matter is nearly all Blackholes can be flipped to your favor. It's about recognizing how something is affecting you and flipping it to how you can benefit from it instead. Have at it! As long as you are not hurting anyone, you can do anything you want to do in this world. Don't let the Matrix or Blackholes tell you otherwise. The main thing to keep in mind and ask yourself is, is the Blackhole getting the best of me or am I getting the best of it?

The Recap

Life's Blackholes aren't just energy drainers. Some can transmit the signals that lead to growth, prosperity, and wisdom. It's all about dialing into the Blackhole in a way that benefits you. Reject the static and embrace the symphony.

Poke The Brain

So ask yourself, which Blackhole is feasting on you, and how can you have a slice of its pie instead?

Your Next Power Move

A Practical & Juggernaut Journal Exercise: Blackhole Flipping.

Objective: to transform the way you interact with a specific Blackhole in your life, turning a negative energy source into a positive one, thereby redefining your relationship with it.

Duration: one month (You'll start to see changes within the first week, but for a lasting impact, give it a full month.)

Instructions:

Identify Your Blackhole

- Take a moment to think about what drains your energy or mood on a daily basis. It could be mainstream media, social media platforms, politics, or any habitual activity.
- Write down this identified Blackhole in your journal.

Research Your Alternative

- Now, seek out a positive alternative to your identified Blackhole. If it's mainstream media that's bringing you down, consider platforms like Positive News (http://www.positive.news) or similar uplifting news sources.
- Note down this alternative in your journal next to your identified Blackhole.

Commit to the Switch

- For one month, commit to switching from your draining Blackhole to your chosen positive alternative. If your Blackhole was spending hours aimlessly scrolling on social media, replace that time with engaging with uplifting content or creating meaningful content instead.

Daily Check-In

- At the end of each day, reflect on your interaction with the alternative. Write down how you felt, any challenges you faced in making the switch, and the positive impacts you noticed.

Weekly Reflection

- At the end of each week, go through your daily notes. Identify patterns, observe how your mood and energy levels have changed, and note any other positive ripple effects in your life.

Celebrate Small Wins

- Each time you successfully flip a Blackhole, even if it's just for an hour or a day, acknowledge and celebrate that victory. This is you becoming a practical magician!

Wrap-Up:

At the end of the month, reflect on your journey of Blackhole flipping. How has your relationship with the original energy drainer changed? Do you feel a tangible difference in your overall well-being? Has your perspective on other potential Blackholes in your life evolved?

Remember, this exercise isn't about demonizing or completely cutting out the original Blackhole. It's about becoming aware of its impact on you and consciously choosing how to interact with it in a way that serves you. The power is always in your hands.

Lesson 32

Inner Force

Imagine this: you're the protagonist of your own action-packed movie. Every morning, the camera zooms into your intense gaze, ready to conquer the world. The soundtrack? The deafening chants of "hustle," "grind," and "push." This fiery spirit, this unyielding determination? That's your Inner Force. It's the modern hero's anthem, with moguls like Gary Vaynerchuck and Grant Cardone as the poster boys. Instagram reels are flooded with it—"No days off!" or "Push until it hurts," It's seductive, the idea of being this lone wolf, cutting through challenges with sheer will.

You, wielding your Inner Force, can feel invincible. Like a surfer riding the biggest wave, there's a thrill, an adrenaline rush. But there's also the looming danger of wiping out if that wave isn't ridden with precision. And just like a surfer, there's a need to respect the force, understand it, and not get consumed by it.

Now, don't get me wrong, Inner Force is powerful. It's the engine that can drive your dreams to reality, propelling you into Sectors of success you've only daydreamed about. But like all powerful engines, without the right checks and measures, it can overheat, it can malfunction, and it can crash, sending you on that Downward Spiral to lower Sectors.

Remember, even superheroes have their Kryptonite.

Meet Mia

She was a live wire from the start. Always up at dawn, her days were packed to the brim with tasks, each accomplished with a fierce intensity that left others in awe. The word "quit" wasn't in Mia's vocabulary. Gym sessions at 5 AM, managing her start-up till late at night, and in those rare moments of stillness, her fingers would be busy scrolling through motivational clips, fueling her Inner Force even more.

But there was a cost. While Mia's startup was a booming success, her health and relationships began to crack under the pressure. Friends began to call her "The Ghost," as she seemed to fade from their lives. Dark circles took permanent residence under her eyes, and her once radiant energy now seemed more like a flickering bulb, threatening to go out.

One day, while Mia was on a treadmill, pushing beyond her limits yet again, she collapsed. The diagnosis? Extreme exhaustion. The prescription? Complete rest and a reevaluation of her priorities.

Mia's recuperation was an eye-opener. In the silence of her room, away from the blaring anthems of "push harder," she had an epiphany. Her Inner Force wasn't meant to be a wrecking ball, smashing through every barrier in a frenzied haste. It was a power within, but best used in measured doses.

Emerging from her hiatus, Mia transformed her hustle into a dance. Yes, she still chased her dreams, but now with grace. She took breaks, reconnected with loved ones, and even started a YouTube channel sharing her story, teaching others the balance of force and flow.

Her channel "Forceful Grace" became an emblem of the new age hustle—one of passion and purpose, without the burnout. Mia's message was clear: Your Inner Force is a tool, not the only tool. Handle with care.

Every video ended with her new mantra, "Harness your force. But dance, don't destroy."

The Money Shot: The Inner Force Paradox

The challenge with using Inner Force to amass wealth? Often, the returns aren't built to last. You end up shackled to the empire you've built, anxiously aware that a single misstep—which, let's face it, is inevitable—will send you plummeting Sectors downward. It lends depth to the term "crash and burn," doesn't it?

Today's culture might celebrate the non-stop hustle. But the true champions? They know the value of pause, reflect, recalibrate and let their world do some of the heavy lifting (more on this to come). It's in those moments of stillness that clarity emerges, and the path forward becomes evident. By merging the vigor of Inner Force with the wisdom of The Quantum Field, you create a formula not just for success, but for sustained, meaningful, and joyful achievement.

In this era dominated by "hustle hard" anthems, you can be that luminary, crafting a legacy without the constant dread of maintaining it. Think back to Disproportionate Energy and Gravity: what goes up must come down. The golden rule? Stay grounded while aiming for the stars. Balance is the name of the game.

The Recap

Inner Force is the intense personal drive championed by many. It's about using every ounce of your personal energy, mentally and physically, to achieve your dreams. It's appealing, prevalent, and for some, quite successful. But unchecked, it's a path to burnout, isolation, and often, profound disappointment.

Poke The Brain

Are you riding a wave of Inner Force, or are you just being swept away by it?

Your Next Power Move

Awareness Exercise: The Inner Force Balance

Reflect on those intense moments in your journey, where your relentless drive pushed you to the extreme, leading not to triumph but to exhaustion and eventual surrender. This scenario, marked by a relentless hustle and an overpowering Inner Force, is all too common in today's entrepreneurial culture. But take a moment to ponder: how often has this overwhelming Inner Force led to outcomes that starkly contrasted with your intentions?

As we gear up for our next lesson, which promises to offer a transformative alternative and a complete shift in perspective, it's vital to first recognize instances where your forceful inner drive may have backfired. Consider times when your unwavering determination resulted in unintended consequences, or when your intensity transformed into Disproportionate Energy, ultimately leading to more work or significant challenges to overcome. Remember, it's all about the balance and utilization of your energy.

This exercise aims to heighten your awareness of such instances where your energy might have been misdirected. By acknowledging these patterns, you're preparing yourself for our next session, where we'll delve into a practical and almost miraculous solution. Stay tuned for an enlightening shift in your entrepreneurial approach.

Lesson 33

Outer Power

Alright, got the memo? It's not just about racing to burnout, hustling hard, and carrying the world solely on your shoulders with brute Inner Force. Strap in, because I'm about to drop a metaphysical bomb on you. Ready?

Quick refresher: remember those nights burning the midnight oil, sweating out every deadline, riding high on the hustle wave, and wearing it as a badge of honor? But what if there's a smoother path? Say hello to: Outer Power.

You know those moments? The random luck, the unexpected success, or that perfect timing? That isn't coincidence; it's The Quantum Field doing you a solid, or if you're more spiritually inclined, it's God giving you a nod and a wink.

Think of it like this: you're at a theme park. You could spend hours in line for the roller coaster, using every ounce of patience and Inner Force. Or, someone from the park staff could spot you, walk over, and hand you a fast pass, letting you breeze right to the front. That's Outer Power in action. It's The Quantum Field's way of saying, "Hey, I've got your back!"

You've been operating like a manual car, shifting gears, grinding clutches, using that Inner Force to push the pedal. But what if I told you there's an automatic mode? A mode where the gears shift seamlessly without you having to do much. It's like upgrading from manual to a self-driving car.

Meet Leo

A dynamic young clinical therapist, Leo is convinced his voice has the power to shift perspectives. He's fueled by ideas advocating for mental health awareness and the need to break down the stigmas surrounding mental illnesses. Every night, post office hours, Leo is found hammering away on his blog, sharing stories, insights, and research. But he senses a greater pull—an urge to reach more people, to foster a larger conversation. Podcasts? That sounds right for Leo.

With unmatched determination, Leo looks to plunge into the realm of podcasting. Each night, after clocking out from his regular job, he's crafting perfect pitch emails. And weekends? They're booked solid with advanced workshops, diving deep into the podcast booking scene, and occasionally letting himself fantasize about being heard in a big way. There's no doubting it; Leo's zeal is at its peak. But it seems he's just spinning his wheels.

Days become weeks, then months, and the inbox? Disheart255eningly barren. But just when the relentlessness seems to wear him down, making Leo question if his advocacy is getting lost in the vast digital wilderness, The Quantum Field winks. While skimming through his social media feed one evening, a new notification appears. A direct message from "MentalMatters," a leading podcast that dives into mental health topics. The message is simple but promising, "Hey Leo, chanced upon your blog. The depth of your content? Exceptional! How about a discussion on our upcoming episode?"

After the airing of Leo's episode, the reception is overwhelming. Invites from numerous other podcasters start pouring in, placing Leo in the delightful dilemma of choice. The twist? None of these are from the podcasts he initially set his sights on. It seems The Universe had better, more fitting platforms in store for him. All Leo had to do was stay aligned with his vision and allow this perfect opportunity to come his way.

That, right there, is the magic of Outer Power. It's when the world recognizes you, sees the light of your passion, and decides to amplify it in all the ways you had dreamed. Outer Power is the world bringing you something in line with your intention or goal... or maybe just a little bit of exactly what you need.

The Money Shot: Becoming The Quantum Field's Favorite Child

Outer Power isn't about flexing your muscles; it's about letting The Quantum Field (and The Matrix) flex its muscles for you. The Quantum Field is bursting with opportunities and solutions tailor-made for you. It's that secret sauce that elevates the ordinary to the extraordinary. And guess what? It's limitless. No burnouts. No hitting brick walls. Just pure, effortless magic that you hold the power to initiate.

The Recap

Remember that time you hustled so hard you felt like you hit a dead end? That's because you were so focused on wielding your Inner Force that you overlooked the helping hand of Outer Power. It's not about working harder; it's about working smarter with Quantum energies.

Poke The Brain

When was the last time something unexpectedly awesome happened to you? Could it be that Outer Power was trying to give you a taste of its magic?

Your Next Power Move:

Practical Exercise: Neutralizing Inner Force and Engaging Outer Power.

Feeling a bit baffled? Don't worry. Grasping the concepts of Inner Force and Outer Power in these teachings can indeed be a head-scratcher. I've been there, but fear not, I'm here to guide you through. Let's break it down with a simple exercise to put everything into perspective.

Here's a quick example to illustrate:

First, consider Inner Force in action: picture yourself in a hotel in an exotic city, yearning for a coffee, but room service is unavailable. Annoyed, you get dressed and set out to find a café. You walk around, ask for directions, and constantly check your phone's Maps app. Despite the effort, you finally find a café, but you're still irked when you get your coffee. In this scenario, your intense focus on needing coffee led to frustration and a lack of appreciation for your surroundings.

Now, let's see how Outer Power changes the game. This time, upon realizing room service can't help, you decide to relax in bed a bit longer before casually strolling through the city. You admire the architecture and enjoy your walk, keeping the thought of coffee in mind but not obsessing over it. Lo and behold, you stumble upon a renowned café with a welcoming table in the sun just for you. Here, without the urgent need to find coffee, the world pleasantly surprises you, presenting a delightful, stress-free coffee experience.

In both scenarios, you achieve your goal of getting coffee, but the experiences are worlds apart. The first is stressful and narrowly focused, while the second is enjoyable, filled with unexpected delights.

Now, here's your task for the next week. Identify a moment in your life driven by Inner Force. Then, consciously shift gears, send out your intention to The Universe, and carry on with your day, allowing the possibility of it materializing on its own through Outer Power.

By recognizing when you're overly reliant on Inner Force, you can open yourself to the magic of Outer Power. The art of transitioning from energetically draining efforts to letting life effortlessly bring opportunities to your doorstep is a game-changer. Master this, and you've just leveled up like a boss.

Lesson 34

Harnessing and Leveraging

Let's go deeper. Reflect for a moment on how you've been running on Inner Force. Picture all those epic goals you've chased, the mountains of ambition you've tried to climb, and the relentless grind you've endured. Sure, you've snagged some wins, but at what price? Endless nights of zero z's, missing out on precious family time, and that never-ending burnout—sound familiar? And then there's the allure of Outer Power, seemingly too good to be true. But wait, what if I told you there's a third way? A path that doesn't leave you wrung out or chasing shadows. Intrigued? Let's peel back the layers.

In the standard hustle, most of us are blind to the mystical beast that is Outer Power. We're all about that Inner Force life—the relentless push that gets us through the Monday blues and beyond. But here's the game-changer: have you ever stopped to feel the energy buzz of others around you? Their Inner Force could be the missing beat in your life's soundtrack.

You see, while capitalism is built on the labor and man-hours of the working person, Quantum Capitalism has a refined and superior approach to this energetic exchange, one that benefits both the one working from a place of Inner Force and you, dear reader, seeing the value in capitalizing off of it. Quantum Capitalism spins a different yarn. It's about a win-

win energy exchange where both the Inner Force hustler and you, the savvy Quantum Capitalist, score big.

Inner Force is all about that burning desire, the single-minded pursuit of a dream. But here's the twist—when you help someone else catch their dream, their Inner Force becomes your power-up. Imagine tapping into their drive and using it as fuel for your own Quantum journey.

Let's break it down. The Inner Force of those around you— their ambitions, drives, and desires—becomes your secret sauce, your Outer Power. It's about flipping the Script, transforming their energy into a catalyst that propels both of you towards greater heights.

In this lesson, we're not just talking theory—we're talking street-smart Quantum Capitalism. It's about sensing the energy around you and harnessing it to elevate your path and theirs. This is modern-day alchemy, where Inner Force meets Outer Power, and together, they create something extraordinary. Ready to tap into this power and turn your world upside down? Let's do this.

Meet Jane

A zealous entrepreneur with an unwavering dream: a sustainable fashion line that doesn't just follow trends, but sets them. Jane's brimming with ideas, armed with deep insights into sustainable materials. However, she's hitting walls left, right, and center. From the elusive funding to nitty-gritty supply chain mechanics. But then, stars align, and into her orbit come Raj and Alex.

Raj: a marketing maven. His social media accounts aren't just "followed"; they're celebrated. Drowned in likes, shares, and

Harnessing and Leveraging

the "heart eyes" emoji. Raj, deep down, is an eco-warrior at heart. His Inner Force? To reshape consumer behavior and be known not just as a marketer, but as the harbinger of green marketing.

Alex: picture a supply chain maestro with an impressive resume flaunting collaborations with fashion bigwigs. But here's the twist: Alex is on the brink of a professional existential crisis. The waste, the carelessness of the industry has been eating away at him. His Inner Force screams for change, a shake-up, and most importantly, responsibility.

Jane, being the visionary she is, doesn't merely see two potential team members. She sees a reservoir of raw, untapped energy. So, she goes beyond the usual elevator pitch. She speaks directly to their Inner Forces.

To Raj, she paints a picture of a world where marketing is not just about selling but about educating, about creating waves of change, starting with sustainable fashion.

To Alex, she lays out a vision of a supply chain that's not just efficient, but conscious. An approach where every link in the chain is a testament to responsibility and forward-thinking.

The Outcome?

With the trio's combined might, they don't just carve a niche; they sculpt a legacy. Raj's campaigns are no longer just posts; they're movements. Movements that ripple across the globe, reshaping perceptions, and realigning consumer preferences toward sustainability.

Meanwhile, Alex crafts a supply chain blueprint so avant-garde, it has industry stalwarts scrambling for notes.

Jane's fashion line? It's not just a brand. It's a revolution. All because she recognized the Inner Forces at play and harnessed them not just for her dream, but for a shared vision. A masterclass in creating symphonies out of solo acts!

The Money Shot: Harnessing Inner Force

The secret lies in not just understanding your Inner Force, but learning to harness the collective Inner Force around you. Each person you interact with has their motivations that propel them forward. Now imagine, what if you could align these individual energies to create a shared momentum towards your vision?

The idea is not to drain or manipulate others, but rather to cultivate their Inner Force for your benefit. When individual Inner Forces align towards a common goal, everyone wins. This concept moves away from the over-glorified hustle culture to a space of shared success. Instead of "I win, you lose," it becomes "We win together."

The Recap

Tapping into the collective Inner Force involves shifting from a self-centric approach to a collective one. It means finding shared goals, empowering others, actively listening, and balancing importance in you being solely in the spotlight.

If this resonates, great. If not, welcome to a whole new perspective.

Poke The Brain

Reflect on a moment when you felt truly heard and valued. How did it influence your motivation and alignment with the person or group who made you feel that way? How can you recreate that for others, creating a collective Inner Force for you to harness for your benefit?

Your Next Power Move

Practical Exercise: Energy Spotting.

Imagine seeing the world not just as a collection of objects and events but as a vibrant dance of energy. That's the essence of Quantum Capitalism—recognizing and tapping into the dynamic flow of energy that underpins everything from wealth and love to happiness and well-being. Every human experience, at its core, is an energetic phenomenon.

This exercise isn't just a task; it's an awakening. Your mission: to become an astute observer of energy in its myriad forms. It's about developing an eye for the energetic currents that swirl around you. Notice how people and systems harness the Inner Force of others to achieve dual goals. Observe those who exert energy without a meaningful direction or purpose. Where do you see wasted potential, untapped resources, or misdirected efforts?

Then, shift your focus inward. How can you, in your unique position, start leveraging the energy around you to your advantage? This isn't about exploitation; it's about recognizing opportunities for mutual benefit and growth. How can you channel the energy you observe into productive, fulfilling avenues that elevate not just you but those around you?

Embrace this new lens of perception. See the world as an energetic playground where your understanding of Inner Force, Outer Power, and the interplay between the two can lead you to higher sectors of existence. Acknowledge your Inner Force, appreciate the force in others, and open yourself up to the enchanting possibilities of outer power.

As you begin to view life through this energetic prism, you'll notice a shift in your reality. It will take on a new hue, a more vibrant and dynamic quality, as you align more closely with the rhythms of The Quantum Field. The path to higher sectors is not just about physical movement but about an energetic evolution. Are you ready to transform your perception and embrace the full potential of Quantum Capitalism?

Lesson 35

Quantum Dance

Got the gist of Outer Power from our previous lesson? Great! It's a doozy. But this powerhouse concept is like an onion. Let's peel back another layer and uncover even more of its essence, shall we?

In essence, Outer Power is The Quantum Field's intention working in conjunction with your desires. The allure of Outer Power is undeniable, and timelessly, it's been echoed across a myriad religions and philosophies. Here's a snapshot:

- **Taoism's "Wu Wei":** often translated as "non-action" or "non-doing," it underscores the art of living in harmony with the Tao—the primal order of existence. Align with the Tao, and actions seamlessly flow.
- **Law of Attraction:** rooted in New Thought philosophy, it asserts that our thoughts—whether positive or negative—magnetize corresponding experiences. Cultivate a positive mindset, and you'll naturally draw in uplifting opportunities.
- **Christianity's Promise:** "Ask, and it shall be given unto you." At its core, this belief encourages faith, prayer, and living according to divine principles. In return, believers find their needs met and wishes granted.
- **Sufism's Call to Surrender:** in this strand of Islamic Mysticism, surrendering to Allah's will harmonizes one

with the divine blueprint, allowing life to unravel with purpose and grace.
- **Rastafarianism's "I and I":** a belief in the God within and the interconnectedness of all. By acknowledging this innate divinity, we can better synchronize with The Universe's rhythm.
- **Shamanism:** across its diverse traditions is a shared conviction: by fostering a bond with the spiritual realm and nature, one attracts healing, insights, and providential moments.
- **Zen Buddhism's Zazen:** this meditative practice beckons one to be present, letting thoughts and feelings ebb and flow, which nurtures non-attachment and lets The Universe manifest uninhibitedly.

Consider this analogy: Inner Force is like swimming tirelessly against a current, while Outer Power feels akin to effortlessly riding a supportive wave. It's the distinction between tirelessly pushing against your world and being gracefully carried by it.

Consider dreams. Ever dreamt you were soaring above the clouds? You weren't consciously thinking, "I insist on flying!" Instead, it was a realization, "Oh! I'm flying!" There's a subtle yet Quantum Field-sized difference between the two. Inner Force charges at goals like a bull, while

Outer Power strolls with the elegance and assurance of a cat, knowing its desires are already met.

Need more contrast? Picture this:

Inner Force is the muscle-bound guy trying to force open a jammed door.

Outer Power is the suave dude who simply knocks, and the door magically swings open.

Or think of it as the battle of space. With Inner Force, you're tirelessly pushing your existence into the vast space, trying to make a mark. Outer Power, however, makes it all come to you like you're the center of The Quantum Field.

The Money Shot: The True Catalyst to Wealth

The road to amplified wealth is built on the bedrock of Outer Power. While the lesson on Inner Force makes it clear that our personal drive can propel us to a point, it has its limits. Relying solely on Inner Force can sustain you, but it's through harnessing the world's collective intention—tapping into Outer Power—that you truly skyrocket to success. When you're perfectly attuned to The Quantum Field, there's no need to strain or strive. Simply set your sights, radiate your passion, and before you know it, opportunities will come knocking. With this synergy, there's no need to force things; The Quantum Field starts conspiring in your favor.

The Recap

It's not just about achieving goals, but how you get there. Remember, you can choose to wrestle with reality or let it serenade you with opportunities. Don't believe it? Go Back to the lesson on GUIDING THEORY.

Poke The Brain

Reflect on a recent goal you achieved. Was it through sheer Inner Force or did you allow The Quantum Field to pave a path for you?

Your Next Power Move

Meditation: Outer Power Assistance.

Get Comfortable

Find a quiet and comfortable place to sit or lie down. Close your eyes and take a few deep breaths to center yourself and get into a meditative state.

Set Your Intention

Quietly ask The Quantum Field for assistance with your intention. Be clear and specific about what you are asking for.

Visualize the Door Opening

Imagine a door opening before you. Visualize the energy of Outer Power assistance coming to your aid, streaming through the open door.

Embrace the Gifts

Visualize yourself embracing all the gifts, opportunities, signs, and offered assistance without questioning, judging, or refusing because it doesn't seem like exactly what you had thought it would look like. Open yourself to new possibilities and outcomes in unexpected ways.

Commit to Keeping the Door Open

Set a commitment to yourself to keeping the door for Outer Power open. Feel the energy of this commitment deeply.

Close the Meditation

Leave the meditation knowing that Outer Power is behind you, moving you along without you even knowing it. Take a moment to express gratitude for this support.

Carry the Energy

As you slowly open your eyes and return to your day, take the energy of this meditation with you. Carry the knowledge that Outer Power is assisting you, and stay open to the signs and opportunities that present themselves.

Remember to revisit this meditation whenever you need a reminder of the support available to you from The Quantum Field and Outer Power.

Lesson 36

Face-Off

You think you know yourself? Time for a recalibration. Your existence operates ad infinitum: there's the Quantum You, able to successfully navigate the realm of endless possibilities, juxtaposed against the static Matrix You, tethered by conventions, standards, and limiting beliefs, and every version in between.

Quantum mechanics doesn't merely exist in academic journals and labs; it's the undercurrent of your life's narrative. Imagine a vast array of selves: one end is the embodiment of aspiration, and the other? Well, let's call it "garbage you." You get to toggle between the highest version of yourself (think penthouse Sector level #10 you and the lowest, that dusty old basement Sector level #1 you). Your Qualifiers decide your floor and self. But don't just take my word as gospel. Jump into this perspective and confirm it for yourself. The challenge isn't just acknowledging this spectrum, but mastering the art of the toggle.

Amidst the sprawling expanse of Quantum realities, countless versions of you exist. Not all versions are animated at once in the infinite Sectors, but a single version gets invited to take center stage courtesy of the quartet: Guiding Theory, Thoughts, Action, and Frequency. Remember those? In essence, your avatars are all waiting behind the Mirror

Face-Off

of reality, available to become animated, and you decide which version is brought to life. Comfortable playing a lower version, or are you ready to choose another?

Enter Quantum You

Close your eyes, if you dare, and envision Quantum You. Not the know-it-all, superficial, ego version, but the distilled and unapologetic version. Quantum You is the optimal, risk-taking, theoretical skull-crushing version of you. This isn't a mere alternate ego; it's a paradigm shift. While the current you may get lulled into societal algorithms, Quantum You is the disruptor, the system hacker, the winner. Every choice you face? Quantum You is the audacious voice challenging convention, questioning, "Why this path? Why not another?"

Quantum You then guides the way to higher Sectors via higher information and opportunities accessed via The Quantum Field. But the narrative isn't devoid of antagonists. Matrix You thrives on predictable, mundane cycles. It's the echo of the status quo, a vortex that Quantum You consistently attempts to prevent you from getting sucked into. If life seems to offer monotones, chances are Matrix You has been dictating the script. Ready for a narrative shift?

Quantum You and Matrix You, engaged in a perpetual dance-off, each strategizing moves and countermoves. If life's been a predictable loop, it's likely Matrix You holds the dominant moves. But with Quantum You on the dance floor? Expect some trophy-winning voguing.

Why this dynamic, though? Why isn't identity straightforward? For insights, we can't bypass the spiritual prowess of G.I. Gurdjieff. He didn't just illuminate this idea; he tore the fabric to expose an intricate tapestry. Prepare for a metaphysical death-drop.

Diving into the Many "I's": Gurdjieff's Key to Unlocking Your Real Self

George Gurdjieff: a name that stands out in those pioneering the intricacies of the human psyche. Born around 1872 in the mystic landscapes of Alexandropol, Asia Minor, Gurdjieff was a wanderer, an explorer of esoteric knowledge. His travels through the East brought him a treasure trove of insights, which he generously gifted to the West.

His revelation? Humanity is in a cosmic slumber. Every gesture, every decision, every giggle, and every tear—borne out of a state of unconsciousness. It's like we're all in a dream, believing it's real. "Can truly aware individuals," Gurdjieff muses, "plunge themselves into the abysses of war and hate?" The chaos around us? It's because most of us are asleep at the wheel.

But here's where Gurdjieff turns the tables. This somnambulist state isn't a life sentence. You can, he assures, awaken. You can evolve from an automaton to a conscious dynamo of your existence.

The Quest to Know Thyself

How do you break the trance? Begin with brutal honesty. Confront the chasm between the person you believe you are and the reality of your behavior. Although this mirror may reflect some unsettling truths, it's the starting point of profound transformation.

Delve deeper, and Gurdjieff's philosophy reveals the multiplicity of selves within. We aren't unified entities.

Instead, we're a cacophony of voices, each proclaiming to be the true "I." This insight resonates with observations from many thinkers, but it was Gurdjieff who spotlighted it with piercing clarity.

These many "I's" manifest in our paradoxical behaviors. Ever sworn off sugar but found yourself gobbling down a chocolate bar moments later? That's a different "I" having its say. It's like having a committee in your head, each member with its own agenda.

Gurdjieff's antidote? Become an observer. Detect the shift from one "I" to another. Recognize that these transient selves are often mere echoes of societal conditioning, compliments of The Matrix. By shedding light on them, you weaken their stranglehold, paving the way for your real I—the luminescent Quantum You.

The Illusion of External Thrills

A pitfall many fall into is equating excitement with happiness. The surge of adrenaline, the highs of external stimuli—they're fleeting. In your introspective journey, realize that real excitement isn't in external theatrics. It's in the thrilling unveiling of Quantum You.

Don't mistake the serenity that will follow as boredom. In fact, without the chaotic interference of artificial thrills, what emerges is authenticity. Get off the rollercoaster of perpetually entertaining Matrix You.

The exhilaration of this quantum self-discovery surpasses any ephemeral rush. When you truly awaken to yourself, even the quiet moments hum with an underlying current of joy. The tranquility that follows isn't loneliness—it's profound peace.

The Money Shot: Banking on Your Best Self

You're probably wondering, "What's this got to do with my bank account?" Here's the scoop: Quantum You is swimming in success. They're making smart, savvy decisions, spotting golden opportunities, and living a life of prosperity. The more you listen to Quantum You, the more you align with this prosperous reality. Matrix You? They're stuck in a scarcity mindset, missing opportunities, and clinging to financial instability. The one you give the wheel to drives your financial journey.

When you let Quantum You take the wheel, you're positioning yourself right at the intersection of Materialization Avenue and Opportunity Street. The real currency in The Quantum Field isn't just cold hard cash, but the quality of the version you have chosen to animate.

The Recap

1. Infinite versions of you are out there in The Quantum Field.
2. Quantum You = the best version of you, ready to help you level up your game.
3. Matrix You has had its time, but it's time for an upgrade.

Poke The Brain

If Quantum You showed up at your doorstep right now, what's the first piece of advice they'd give you?

Your Next Power Move

Juggernaut Journal Exercise: Upgrading from Matrix You to Quantum You.

Objective: this exercise is designed to help you actively shift from the limiting patterns of Matrix You to the empowered state of Quantum You. Through reflection, awareness, and action steps, you'll transition from a passive observer of life to an active creator of your destiny.

Awareness & Acceptance

1. **List Matrix You Characteristics:** in one column, jot down habits, beliefs, and patterns that define Matrix You. Examples might include procrastination, self-doubt, or resistance to change.
2. **Acknowledge Without Judgment:** recognize that these patterns served a purpose at some point but may no longer align with who you want to be now. No self-blaming; just pure acknowledgment.

Visioning Quantum You

1. **Describe Quantum You:** in another column, describe the characteristics, habits, and patterns of Quantum You. What qualities do they possess? How do they respond to challenges? What actions do they take daily?
2. **Feel It:** visualization is key. Imagine a day in the life of Quantum You. What does it look, feel, sound, and taste like? Dive deep into this exercise to anchor the sensations and emotions.

Bridging the Gap

1. **Pinpoint Key Differences:** identify the main disparities between Matrix You and Quantum You. For example, if Matrix You tends to overthink decisions, Quantum You might be more intuitive and decisive.
2. **List Down Practical Shifts:** for each of the disparities identified, list a practical step or action that can help bridge the gap. Using the example above, you might decide to practice meditation to enhance intuition or set a time limit for making decisions.

Implementing Change

1. **Daily Commitments:** every morning, choose one practical shift to focus on for the day. Commit to practicing it wholeheartedly.
2. **Evening Reflection:** before bed, spend a few moments reflecting on your day. How did you embody Quantum You? Where did you fall back into Matrix You patterns? Celebrate the wins and learn from the slips.

Celebrate & Connect

1. **Acknowledge Your Growth:** every time you notice a positive shift, no matter how small, take a moment to acknowledge and celebrate it.
2. **Connect with Quantum You:** set aside a specific time each week to deeply connect with Quantum You through meditation, visualization, or any other technique that resonates with you.

Remember, the journey from Matrix You to Quantum You isn't about perfection but progress. It's about gradually aligning with a version of yourself that is empowered, proactive, and in sync with the infinite possibilities of The Quantum Field.

Embrace the journey, trust the process, and watch as the world transforms around you.

Inviting in Quantum You Meditation

Objective:

This meditation aims to create a profound connection between you and your Quantum You. Through visualization and inner dialogue, you'll meet, communicate with, and integrate aspects of this higher version of yourself.

Preparation:

1. Find a quiet space where you won't be disturbed for about 20-30 minutes.
2. Wear comfortable clothing and either sit on a cushion with a straight spine or lie down.
3. Take a few moments to relax, deepening your breath and grounding yourself.

Meditation Steps

Begin with Breathing: focus on your breath, inhaling deeply through your nose and exhaling through your mouth. With each exhale, release any tension or stress. With each inhale, draw in peace and calm.

Enter The Quantum Field: visualize yourself standing in a vast, open space filled with shimmering, silvery energy. This is The Quantum Field, a realm of limitless possibilities. Feel its boundless energy wrapping around you.

The Golden Door: in the distance, see a magnificent golden door, emanating a warm, inviting glow. Know that behind this door is Quantum You, the best version of yourself.

Begin walking towards Quantum You with confidence and anticipation.

The Meeting: as you approach the door, it slowly opens to reveal Quantum You. Take a moment to absorb their presence. How do they look? What energy do they radiate? How are they dressed? Notice their posture, the confidence in their gaze, the wisdom they exude.

Embracing Quantum You: allow Quantum You to step closer. Feel the resonating energies between the two of you. As they approach, note the similarities and differences. Acknowledge this higher version of yourself with gratitude and admiration.

Open Dialogue: now is the time to communicate. Ask Quantum You any questions you have. It can be about life choices, challenges you're facing, or simply seeking guidance on a matter. Listen intently to their responses. Trust the wisdom they offer.

Merging Energies: once the dialogue concludes, Quantum You steps even closer, and the two of you start to merge into one being. As this happens, you feel an infusion of their wisdom, confidence, clarity, and love. This merging symbolizes the integration of Quantum You's characteristics into your daily life.

Gratitude and Farewell: thank Quantum You for their guidance, wisdom, and energy. As you part, the golden door gently closes, but you know you can return anytime.

Returning to the Present: slowly become aware of your breathing again. Feel the ground beneath you. Wiggle your fingers and toes. Whenever you're ready, gently open your eyes.

Post-Meditation Reflection:

Take a few moments to write down any insights, messages, or feelings you experienced during the meditation.

Reflect on how you can integrate Quantum You's guidance into your daily life. What actionable steps can you take?

Remember, this Quantum You Meditation isn't just a one-time exercise. Regularly revisiting this meditation will strengthen your connection to Quantum You, facilitating a seamless integration of their wisdom and energy into your daily life.

Lesson 37

The Purge

Now that you're cozying up to your Quantum You and peeling away that Matrix You, like last year's fashion disaster, it's prime time for some cosmic housekeeping.

I'm about to serve you a piping hot plate of truth with a side of reality check. As you vibe higher with Quantum You and your Matrix persona becomes a shadow of the past, you might notice your reality—everything from your pantry to your playlist—yearning for a makeover. Is it that pile of guilty pleasures you munch on? The incessant hum of news that's creating a background score to your life? Or that energy-vampire in your life who's suddenly all up in your business as you are trying to evolve? Time to trim the fat.

You see, every choice you make, every habit you indulge in, slots you into one of these versions. Ever done a tequila shot and immediately regretted it? That's Mr. Matrix having a go. Or have you ever chosen a calming tea instead of that fifth coffee? That's Ms. Quantum giving you a gentle nudge.

Do you always want to be stuck in a loop, making the same ol' mistakes? Or are you itching for some real transformation, some next-level existence?

Here's a cosmic cheat code for you: The Quantum Field has this quirky way of gifting those who vibe with its principles an uncanny flexibility. Yeah, the kind that lets you effortlessly dance around life's curveballs. Stubborn old habit? Poof, it's history! Family drama spiraling out of control? You're the Zen master in the eye of that storm.

Now, think of the guy who's always blowing his lid, swearing, "This is the last time!" only to rinse and repeat. Why does he falter? Simple. His Matrix, false self is running the show, and let's be real, it thrives on chaos. It's like expecting a cactus to sprout roses. As Marcus Aurelius wisely put it, "Why be shocked when a fig tree sprouts figs?"

Real growth happens when deep self-reflection joins the chat. Otherwise, it's just a loop of mess up, confession, rinse, repeat. Another myth to bust? Your past missteps looming over you like some dark cloud. Newsflash: once you set on the path to your Quantum Self, every hiccup, stumble, or faceplant becomes a stepping stone. Wake up from the drowsy trance of Matrix reality, and you'll find the key to nixing the screw-ups.

Wrap your head around this: the mistakes of your yesterdays weren't the deeds of your Quantum Self. It was The Matrix self, now on its way out.

So, have you felt a tugging duality within recently? A little bit of yin-yang, the classic light and shadow? We humans, you see, we're a fascinating blend of The Matrix and Quantum versions of ourselves. Sometimes, we're swiping left and right in The Matrix, and other moments, we're floating on a Quantum level. Either way, let's lay it out, shall we?

Matrix You Habits, Tendencies, and Patterns:

1. Flipping the bird more than you change gears. Anger at every red light.

2. Emptying your bank account while filling your shopping cart. Retail therapy, they call it.
3. Overeating, especially when the emotions come out to play.
4. Lighting up a cigarette as a buffer between you and your stressors.
5. Netflix until 4 am, then knocking out with sleeping pills.
6. Downing alcohol to drown out that inner voice or to "loosen up."
7. Excessive masturbation as an escape from boredom or emotional emptiness.
8. Gorging on the latest drama like it's the main course.
9. Arguing just to "win," not to understand.
10. Anything that brings the quickest pleasure, no matter the cost.

Those habits dragging you down, the instant-gratification shopping sprees, and anything that's feeding your Matrix desires? Hit pause and take a deep, judgment-free look.

Quantum You Habits, Tendencies, and Patterns:
1. Deep breathing exercises when traffic tightens.
2. Thoughtful spending based on needs, not fleeting wants.
3. Mindful eating, savoring each bite, acknowledging hunger cues.
4. Opting for walks or meditation during breaks, not the familiar pull of nicotine.
5. Choosing content that uplifts, educates, or inspires.
6. Drinking socially, and in moderation, or opting for mocktails.
7. Recognizing the difference between self-love and using physical relief as an escape mechanism.

8. Seeking conversations and experiences that spark genuine introspection.
9. Engaging in dialogues to gain perspective, not just to rebut.
10. Embracing the journey and the growth it brings, even if the rewards are slow to show.

Now, let's get personal. I've been on this journey, too, and let me tell you—tidying up your personal Universe? Worth it. My space now radiates joy. My tribe vibrates at the same frequency as my Quantum Self. And those pesky habits? Most of them are history. But here's the twist: every now and then, I indulge in a little Matrix mischief. Example: My old smoking habit? Yup, started at 13. Today, it's mostly kicked, but every blue moon, when a friend sparks one up at a café, I'll join in. Not out of craving, but as a nod to my Matrix days. That, or maybe indulging in a mindless Netflix binge. Why? It's a little reminder that while Quantum Me is at the wheel, Matrix Me is still chilling in the backseat.

Here's my golden nugget for you: when you occasionally vibe with your Matrix Self, do so without the guilt-trip. Dabble in a "guilty pleasure" if it doesn't trigger a craving or a bout of

self-reproach. If there's even a whiff of either, it's time for a heart-to-heart with Quantum You.

After all, this journey is all about balance, not banishment.

The Money Shot: Show Me the Money

Now, let's get real and talk about the Benjamins. Every Matrix You choice isn't just chipping away at your mental and physical wellbeing, but it's also siphoning off your wealth, your opportunities, and your financial security. Those impulsive buys? They aren't adding value. They're short-lived pleasures with long-lasting consequences. Embracing the Quantum You is like investing in stocks that promise steady, long-term returns. It's about creating wealth in all aspects of your life.

The Recap

You have two distinct versions of yourself: The Matrix, who's about the now, the quick fixes, and the instant (often regretful) choices. And then there's the Quantum, who's all about the bigger picture, the growth, and the long haul. Your life's quality, wealth, and opportunities? They're directly tied to which version of you is calling the shots.

Poke The Brain

Ask yourself: when was the last time you made a choice that screamed Matrix and when did you embrace your Quantum side?

Your Next Power Move

Juggernaut Journal Exercise: Introspective Power Move.

Divide a page right down the middle.

Matrix Eyeballing

On the left, jot down all The Matrix patterns, habits, and indulgences you reckon need some serious eyeballing. Let's be brutally honest here; no one's peeking but you.

Quantum Gold Mines

On the right, make a note of those Quantum You patterns and habits you believe can be dialed up a notch. These are your gold mines, your strengths.

Awareness Key

Remember, awareness isn't just the key, it's the whole darn treasure chest. So, gear up and let's dive deep.

Flex Your Muscles

Knowing yourself, both The Matrix and the Quantum versions, is the ultimate power move. Now, go on and flex those introspective muscles!

By taking time to identify both your Matrix patterns that need addressing and your Quantum strengths that can be amplified, you are taking control of your narrative. This exercise empowers you to break free from The Matrix and harness your Quantum potential to create a more intentional and prosperous reality.

Lesson 38

Your Real Dream

In our last pow-wow, we dived deep into the rabbit hole of human quirks. Remember? We laid bare the tango between our Matrix shenanigans and our Quantum masterstrokes. But hold onto your latte, because this lesson? It's all about one of Matrix You's most toxic flings: the relentless pursuit of Matrix standards.

Imagine this: a cosmic DMZ. On one side stands Quantum You—empowered, tapping into unparalleled abilities, and embracing the unique nuances that make you genuinely extraordinary. But lurking on the other side is Matrix You—caught in the web of vanity metrics, always chasing the latest trend, and constantly wondering if you're checking the right boxes. Eye roll, right? Time to snip that toxic tie. This madness? Yeah, it's got to bounce.

So, you feel like a rat in a maze, blindly following cheese, huh? That cheese, often crafted by the omnipresent Matrix, seems so appetizing, but is it genuinely what you hunger for? Think about it. Every billboard, every ad, every influencer paints a glamorous picture: big houses, luxury cars, and a life of opulence. The Matrix dangles these tantalizing carrots in front of you, making you believe they're the epitome of success. But dig deeper. Maybe your heart doesn't beat for a Bugatti but yearns for a simple bike ride through winding countryside roads. Perhaps the high-rise penthouse doesn't excite you as much as a cozy cabin nestled amidst the mountains, where you can pen down poetry as the sun dips beyond the horizon.

The Matrix's standards? It's akin to fast food: tempting in commercials but often leaving you with an emptiness, a hunger for something more nourishing, more real. Now, ask yourself: have you been dining on The Matrix's menu or creating a fulfilling recipe for yourself?

Here's a hard truth: if you don't set your own standards of wealth, The Matrix will gladly do it for you. Remember, every time you chase someone else's dream, you stray further from your own.

Personal Note

Once upon a time, my life mirrored the pages of a luxury lifestyle magazine. My sleek BMW wasn't just a mode of transportation—it symbolized who I had become. From the lofty heights of my penthouse, I looked out upon a sprawling cityscape, feeling like royalty in their castle. Every accolade, every material gain, was a nod from The Matrix: I had made it.

But as my collection of "successes" grew, so did an inner emptiness. Each new achievement was like pouring water into a sieve—momentarily satisfying but quickly drained away. Surrounded by the finer things, there were moments when I'd pause, a quiet voice within asking, "Is this all there is? What comes next?" The Matrix's version of success felt hollow, a shimmering illusion that, no matter how much I chased, always remained just out of reach.

What shocked me further was realizing I wasn't on this treadmill alone. Discussions with contemporaries, some even more "successful" by conventional metrics, revealed similar sentiments. From property tycoons to finance gurus, a recurring theme emerged: beneath the facade of vast wealth and acclaim, many grappled with an undercurrent of discontent. Some admitted feeling ensnared by their own success, yearning for freedom despite being surrounded by luxury. It became painfully clear that The Matrix's glossy promise of "arrival" seldom equates to happiness or inner peace.

This realization serves as a stark reminder: perhaps our true quest isn't about collecting the world's trophies, but about understanding what genuinely enriches our souls.

The Money Shot: Awakening from The Nightmare

Adopting society's yardstick for success feels like being trapped in an endless loop—forever chasing, never truly attaining. Genuine wealth, prosperity, and satisfaction stem from aligning with your core desires. It's not about the flashiness of what you possess, but the authenticity of what you pursue. When you chase genuine passion and align with Quantum You, prosperity isn't a far-off dream—it becomes an attainable reality. Opportunities arise, not because you're conforming to someone else's standards, but because you're forging your own path, remaining true to your Quantum Self. The money you earn carries meaning because it springs from a genuine place within—your creativity—contributing to something greater than yourself. It's rooted in ideas birthed from The Quantum Field, not some blueprint handed down by The Matrix. And as you transition to Quantum You, realizing wealth beyond your wildest dreams, you find you crave it less and less. Your benchmarks evolve. Quantum You revels in simple pleasures, often requiring little to no money, or in the joy of creativity. Everything starts to shift and transform before your eyes. Those standards you once strained to meet? They now seem like a distant nightmare, barely remembered.

The Recap

The Matrix, with its flashy lights and loud promises, can be enticing. But remember, it often sells a one-size-fits-all dream. Your journey to prosperity must resonate with your Quantum Self's desires, not what's plastered on a billboard. Find your authentic aspirations, go for them, and watch as real prosperity envelops you.

Poke The Brain

Are you running someone else's race, or have you carved out your own path, lined with your dreams and desires?

Your Next Power Move

Juggernaut Journal Exercise: Authentic Aspiration Audit.

Navigating the maze of Matrix-inspired goals can be dizzying. Often, the line between what you truly desire and what The Matrix prescribes blurs. This exercise aims to help you gain clarity on your authentic aspirations, ensuring that every step you take aligns with your Quantum You.

Objective: distinguish between Matrix-imposed desires and your Quantum You intentions, and recalibrate your life to resonate with genuine ambitions.

1. The Desire List

Start with a blank page. Draw a vertical line down the middle, creating two columns.

1. On the left, list down everything you currently aspire to or are working towards (e.g., owning a fancy car, a big house, a high-paying job, etc.).
2. On the right, jot down reasons why you want each of those things. Be brutally honest. If it's for societal validation or to fit in, note that down.

2. The Quantum Filter

Review each aspiration and its associated reason.

1. Does the reason resonate with your heart's true desire, or does it feel superficial and imposed by external pressures?
2. Circle the aspirations that genuinely align with Quantum You. Strike through those that seem Matrix-imposed.

3. Visioning Quantum Success

For each aspiration that you've circled.

1. Visualize what achieving it would look and feel like. Bask in the state of being. If the state of being feels uplifting, genuine, and fulfilling, it's a keeper. If it feels hollow or unfulfilling, reconsider its place in your life.
2. For the aspirations you've struck through, think of what a more aligned, Quantum version might look like. For instance, instead of the high-rise penthouse, maybe it's that cozy mountain cabin.

4. Blueprint of Authenticity

Having sifted through your aspirations.

1. Create a plan for the coming months, prioritizing those goals that resonate with your Quantum You.
2. Ensure your actions, decisions, and investments (time, money, and energy) align with these authentic aspirations.

5. Daily Check-in

Each day, as you work towards these aspirations.

1. Pause and ask yourself, "Is this choice bringing me closer to my Quantum aspirations or pushing me into The Matrix maze?"
2. Over time, this will become a habit, guiding your decisions and actions towards genuine fulfillment.

Reflection Time

At the end of a month, sit with your list. Reflect on the progress you've made.

- Celebrate the steps you've taken towards your Quantum aspirations.
- Note any moments you felt pulled into The Matrix's illusion and contemplate what triggered it.

This awareness will arm you against future such diversions.

Committing to this exercise will help you continually recalibrate your path, ensuring you're not aimlessly chasing The Matrix's cheese but dining on a fulfilling feast of your making. Remember, prosperity doesn't lie in acquiring what's on the billboard but in achieving what's in your heart.

Lesson 39

Soul Code

Do you sense it? That gentle pulse of your Quantum Self, emerging from beneath the layers you're steadily shedding? It's intoxicating in all the right ways, isn't it? The newfound lightness, the whispers of promise, and that profound connection to something greater—a connection that remains unfazed by The Matrix's need for affirmation.

Now, we're hitting our stride. We're in full swing. In our upcoming lesson, we'll elevate our journey even further. By distancing yourself from Matrix-imposed standards and tuning into the true essence of your soul, you're preparing for a profound transformation. Ready to dive deeper? Let's go.

Think of The Quantum Field as a colossal radio, teeming with infinite channels, each broadcasting its own unique frequency. You probably go about your life, randomly flipping through these stations, occasionally resonating with a tune, but never quite understanding why. Herein lies the secret: to harness the power of The Quantum Field, you must tune into your own soul's unique frequency, your Soul Code.

Picture the vast Quantum Field. It's not some distant realm; it's right here, intertwined with your reality. Each Sector of this field vibrates with its own distinct melody. Your job? To find your song and sing it unabashedly. When you sing in harmony with your Soul Code, the song matches a Quantum

Field's Sector, and presto! That becomes your reality. This isn't just spiritual mumbo jumbo; it's Quantum Capitalism in its purest form.

What exactly is the "Soul Code"? It's a composite of all your unique traits: your strengths, talents, and the very elements that make you, authentically YOU. The Matrix may want you to blend in, but it's your Soul Code that ensures you stand out. However, over time, The Matrix has tinkered with and altered this intrinsic code. In essence, The Matrix has attempted to overwrite your original programming. But here's the good news: you can revert to your genuine self. How? By attuning to your Soul Code. This isn't about transforming into a different person; it's about rediscovering and embracing who you truly are.

However, there's a catch. Your Code isn't written in the lines of your palm or the constellations above. It's buried deep within, veiled by societal standards, personal insecurities, and matrix-imposed beliefs. Yet, when glimpsed, it holds a magnetism that's beyond captivating.

You've met them, haven't you? Individuals who defy societal standards of beauty, success, or charisma, yet leave an unforgettable mark wherever they go. They are the soulful sages amidst a sea of superficiality. Their charm? They've tapped into their Code. It's an allure that doesn't comply with worldly standards; it transcends them. Keep a lookout, you might spot one.

Meet Dr. Alex Carter

The city was always abuzz, a cacophony of sirens, honks, and the distant murmurs of a million conversations. In the heart of it all was Dr. Alex Carter, a renowned physician with accolades aplenty. Patients waited months for an appointment, and his peers revered him as one of the best in the field. His parents proudly showcased articles about their son in their living room, basking in the reflected glow of his success.

Yet for Alex, something was always amiss. His sprawling apartment overlooking the park, his friends who were quoted in medical journals, the expensive wine he sipped—none of it felt truly his. It was as if he were living someone else's life. Every night he would return home, and the hollow echo of his footsteps in the marble hallway would serve as a stark reminder of his disjointed reality.

Unbeknownst to many, Alex harbored a secret passion. As a child, he was enchanted by tales of mystery and suspense. The twists, the turns, the unraveling of enigmatic plots—these tales captured his imagination like nothing else. Under the blankets with a flashlight, young Alex would devour pages, losing himself in worlds far removed from the pragmatic path his life had taken.

As years turned to decades, the weight of this other life, this "should-have-been" began to press upon him. The city, with its towering skyscrapers, felt suffocating. The parties, brimming with medical anecdotes, grew tedious. One evening, after a particularly grueling surgery, Alex found an old notebook from his childhood. Flipping through, he stumbled upon a half-written mystery tale, a relic from a time when dreams were unbridled.

A fire ignited within him. That night, Alex wrote. He penned down thoughts, feelings, and mysteries, unraveling stories from the depths of his soul. With each word, the grip of The Matrix began to loosen. It was as if The Quantum Field enveloped him, guiding his hand, drawing him closer to a Sector of Reality that felt unmistakably...right.

Six months later, Alex took the most courageous step of his life. He resigned. Word spread like wildfire, peers were flabbergasted, and his parents struggled to comprehend. But Alex had caught a glimpse of his Soul Code, and there was no turning back.

He sold his city apartment, packed his essentials, and journeyed to a quaint mountain town in a foreign land. Surrounded by nature, he found a little house overlooking valleys and peaks. There, with pen and paper, Dr. Alex Carter began his second life, this time as Alex Carter, the mystery novelist.

The transition wasn't without challenges. Doubts and fears occasionally knocked on his door. But every time he wrote, every time a new mystery unraveled on his pages, The Universe seemed to affirm his choice. Soon, his novels gained traction. Readers from around the globe were captivated by his tales. In the town, he found kinship with a close-knit group of artists and writers, each on their own journey of self-discovery. Their evenings were filled with discussions on their projects, and the mysteries of life.

Years later, as the sun painted the morning sky with hues of gold, Alex sat on his porch, a manuscript on his lap that he knew would be a bestseller. Looking out over the vast expanse, a serene smile played on his lips. Life felt dreamlike, unreal in its perfection. His every day was a testament to the magic that happens when one truly tunes into their Soul Code, merging with a Sector of The Quantum Field designed especially for them.

CAVEAT

Alright, a little side note to Dr. Alex's narrative. Let's not get it twisted. Happiness isn't about a change of scenery, new friends, or a shiny new job title. Trying to snatch a fresh slice of reality, while still marinating in the same old personal muck, will always, always, circle back to a dead end. But here's the kicker—change the inner landscape, and voila, you slide into a different slice of reality where the scenery is, dare we say, refreshingly better.

Dialing to your Soul Code is where you find inner freedom. Freedom from what, you ask? A little Soul-Coding and you purge your private collection of angers and anxieties. It's freedom from the haunting fear of ending up alone, unloved, unimportant. Freedom from the confusing mess in your head that pushes you into doing things you later wish you hadn't. Freedom from the desperate longing that tricks you into believing that having this person or that thing will magically make everything alright. Simply put, happiness is breaking free from everything that makes you unhappy.

Now, here's the tricky bit. Happiness doesn't have a shape, size, or color. It can't be squeezed into the boxes of our demands. We stamp our feet and demand this partner, that career, this house, that sense of security, thrill, or distraction. And even when we get everything on our wish list, surprise, surprise, we're not dancing with joy. We've just papered over our unhappiness. It's still lurking in the shadows, ready to jump out in those moments when you see through the illusions. The way out? Smash the Sector altogether, and just let life unfold. Suddenly, we find ourselves in a world we never knew existed.

Try this. Quietly question every belief you hold about yourself. Ask, "Could it be that the person I believe I am is entirely different from my actual self?" Consider the possibility.

When you do that, you set off a chain reaction. It's like waking up to a whole new world. You start feeling differently about yourself. You can't quite put your finger on it, and guess what, you don't need to. It's a faint stirring of something new, something different. Dip your toe into this mighty Quantum Flow, and you feel its force right away. That's how it hits you.

Sure, money can't buy happiness, but when you're raking in the dough doing something that sings to your soul, thriving in the slice of reality that's tailor-made for you, well, let's just say it's a whole lot of... fuck, yes.

The Money Shot: The Anti-Matrix Move

Here's the kicker. This harmony, this alignment, is your ticket to unparalleled prosperity. When you resonate with your Soul Code, you're not just attuned to your soul, but to the very fabric of The Quantum Field. Discord with the Code, on the other hand, closes doors and misses beats. Syncing with your Soul's Code isn't merely about finding inner tranquility; it's the blueprint to a prosperity that's uniquely tailored for you.

The Recap

To unlock the boundless affluence of The Quantum Field, you must first discover and align with your Soul's Code. It's your map, guiding you through the Sectors of The Quantum Field. The true treasures aren't out there in the cosmos; they are buried deep within. The Holy Grail is internal.

Poke The Brain

Is your current Sector of Reality genuinely tailored for you? If the answer isn't a resounding "YES," are you prepared to discover why?

Your Next Power Move

Meditation: Soul-Coding.

Dive deep into The Quantum Field to uncover and attune to your unique Soul Code. This meditation will guide you to connect with that intrinsic rhythm, harmonizing your frequency with The Quantum Field.

Objective: discover and align with your unique Soul Code, unveiling a map to the treasures of The Quantum Field.

1. Preparation

Location: choose a quiet and comfortable spot where you won't be interrupted.

- **Posture:** sit comfortably, with your back straight, either on a chair or cross-legged on the floor. If you prefer, you can also lie down.
- **Intent:** before starting, mentally affirm, "I am on a quest to discover and align with my Soul Code."

2. Breathing Technique

- **Inhalation:** take a deep breath in through the nose for a count of 4.
- **Hold:** hold the breath for a count of 4.
- **Exhalation:** release the breath through the mouth for a count of 8.

Repeat this breathing cycle for a few minutes until you feel calm and centered.

3. Visualization

- **Quantum Field:** picture yourself standing at the edge of an infinite, luminous field, stretching as far as the eye can see. This is The Quantum Field, alive with countless melodies and frequencies.
- **Radio Tower:** in the distance, you see a towering radio mast. Approach it. This tower represents your current connection to The Quantum Field, broadcasting your current frequency.

4. Soul Code Discovery

- **Old Station:** notice that the radio tower is currently tuned to a certain station. This station, emitting a discordant tune, symbolizes The Matrix's influence on your life.
- **Tuning:** now, gently turn the dial on the tower. As you do, different melodies emerge. These represent various parts of you—some might be influenced by societal expectations, some by personal fears, and some, your genuine Soul Code.
- **Resonance:** continue tuning until you come across a melody that feels intrinsically "you." It's a melody that feels familiar yet extraordinary. It resonates deep within, awakening a sense of profound recognition. This is your Soul Code.

5. Embracing the Code

- **Harmony:** allow this melody to envelop you. Feel every note, every rhythm. As you immerse yourself, notice how The Quantum Field responds, lighting up in vibrant colors and patterns.
- **Affirmation:** as you resonate with your unique tune, affirm, "I embrace and honor my unique Soul Code. I align my frequency with the infinite Quantum Field."

6. Integration

- Slowly bring your awareness back to your physical surroundings, carrying with you the melody of your Soul Code.
- Gently open your eyes, taking a moment to internalize this newfound awareness.

Post-Meditation Awareness Exercise

Throughout the day, whenever you're faced with decisions, choices, or actions.

- Pause and ask, "Is this in harmony with my Soul Code?"
- This consistent check-in will serve as a compass, guiding your actions and choices towards authentic prosperity and Quantum Field alignment.

Remember, every time you align with your Soul Code, you're not just finding personal harmony, but tapping into the abundant reservoir of The Quantum Field.

Lesson 40

Unleashing

Remember "The Wizard of Oz"? The Tin Man, Scarecrow, Lion, and Dorothy—each searching for something they believed they lacked. Only to find, after a whirlwind of adventures, that they always had what they sought. The wizard didn't give them magic; he gave them belief in their own magic. The power to see and connect with what was there all along. Just like Oz's gang, you've got a power within, and it's not stashed in some distant "Emerald City." It's nestled right inside: your Soul Code.

The dark forces—The Matrix and Blackholes—love to have you believe that you're just another cog in their vast machinery. They thrive when you're blind to your own potential, just spinning in place. But why? Well, a person aware of their unique essence challenges the status quo. And that, my friend, is a direct threat to The Matrix.

Yet, the irony is palpable. Societies need rules, yes. Without them, chaos reigns. But when the price of societal order is your individuality, you're robbed. Stripped of your dreams and aspirations, replaced with molds that hardly fit. Your divine essence? Forgotten.

So, ask yourself: is the Sector you inhabit genuinely crafted for your essence? If not, warning: Transitioning from the Matrix You to the attuned Quantum You, aligned with your Soul Code, isn't achieved with the mere flip of a switch.

Your starting point? Prioritizing some genuine self-reflection. Instead of the endless scroll on your social media, take a moment. Feel the dirt beneath your feet on a hike, breathe in nature, and let the fresh air clear your mind. Ask yourself: "What is it that I truly want? Why do I feel stuck in a loop? And who put these perceived barriers in front of me? And why did I allow this?"

Reflect upon Dr. Alex Carter's narrative. It wasn't reluctance that kept him from acknowledging his dream; it was sheer obliviousness. The only thing he really knew was that something just didn't feel right. His concern for societal reputation, professional stature, and familial expectations veiled his heart's true yearnings. This is often our plight. We stray from our destined paths, seduced by external voices, until we become numb, ceasing to question. Such disconnection sows the seeds of existential crises. When one seeks fleeting solace in stuff, it's a desperate attempt to soothe the cries of the soul seeking acknowledgment.

This is the exact making of a midlife crisis. When the middle-aged, overworked dad goes out and buys a red Corvette to drive around town, the soul is screaming out for help. Yet the man doesn't know how to help it, so he reaches for a material possession he's always wanted, to create some relief. And this probably does provide some relief, although fleeting.

True fulfillment is found when you intimately understand your Soul Code—those facets that render you distinct and gifted. Challenges will persist, but the haunting question, "Is there something more?" diminishes. That "something more" is your Soul Code.

However, venturing this deep can be unsettling for those firmly anchored to The Matrix's rigid benchmarks, or those who prioritize familial and societal validation.

Undeniably, transitioning to a higher vibrational realm may stir discomfort, akin to shifting gears to ascend a steep incline. If you find contentment in your current reality and deem this exploration excessive or even overwhelming, it's understandable. Delving into the profound recesses of one's Soul Code is a pilgrimage reserved for those yearning for radical transformation. Remember, genuine paradigm shifts happen first within, which inevitably ripple into your external world. These ripples can create discord initially, and many might not be ready for this level of work.

The true magic unfolds when you genuinely listen to your soul's whispers. Once you act in harmony with your soul's deepest desires and recalibrate your life accordingly, you attain a steadfast, inner grit that remains unshakable by outside forces.

That Soul Code harmony, it was in Dr. Alex Carter's eyes as the dawn bathed him in gold, manuscript in hand. No longer seeking validation, he had transformed into the composer of his life's symphony. He had evolved into the masterful architect of his destiny, profoundly aware of his newfound sovereignty.

The Money Shot: There's No Place Like Home

You'll find that your Soul Code isn't just a philosophical concept—it's the yellow brick road to unparalleled prosperity. Envision the moment a key perfectly fits a lock, turning smoothly, opening a door with ease. When you're attuned to your Soul Code, opportunities aren't just available—they feel custom-tailored, designed just for you. The wealth you'll create isn't about mere numbers on a screen; it's the kind of affluence that feels right, resonating with your very essence.

This isn't about chasing after fleeting financial gains; it's about unlocking a Sector where your wealth mirrors your soul's purpose. When you align, you don't just succeed—you thrive on your own terms, basking in a prosperity that feels divinely intended, just for you.

The Recap

When you harness the magic generated via your Soul Code, you align with The Quantum Field in unstoppable ways. Authenticity isn't just a personal triumph; it's the business strategy for those brave enough to deploy it.

Poke The Brain

So, ask yourself, are you still searching for the Emerald City, or are you ready to recognize the wizardry of your own Soul Code?

Your Next Power Move

Observation Exercise: Self-discovery through Observing Others.

Are you ready to unmask the wizard within? I can imagine that much of this may seem ambiguous and confusing. Yet, once you gain a sense of what the Soul Code is, you can begin the fine-tuning process. Often, we are challenged to connect with qualities within ourselves because they are obscured by standards, programming, and beliefs that no longer serve us. We have tailored ourselves to fit within the confines of The Matrix, and realigning ourselves can seem daunting. I encourage you to shift your focus outward to gain insights.

Start by observing every person you come into contact with on a daily basis and acknowledge those who possess a certain "je ne sais quoi." Look for individuals who seem aligned, charismatic, and energetic. Seek out those who appear to be in a state of flow, living in the moment, and positively impacting the people they encounter.

Then, shift your focus to the antithesis of these people. Observe those who are bogged down by The Matrix, like the person yelling at traffic in their car, the grocer who seems to hold contempt for every customer, or the family member who is eternally miserable. Try to pinpoint the moments when you recognize that a person is tapped into their innate talents and special abilities. Absorb their energy. In turn, recognize individuals who seem disconnected from their true selves and commit to disengaging from your own self in the ways that you observe.

If you spend just a single day observing reality through this lens and aligning with these ideals, by the end of the day, you will see the magic in front of you. Reality might take on an entirely different hue and transform before your eyes. Things will begin to look up, and The Matrix will seem much more recognizable and manageable. It is by tuning into the code of our souls that we truly exit The Matrix. Try it for yourself and see.

Lesson 41

Heart and Mind Synchronization

I can almost hear the gears in your head turning..."Alright, alright, I get it. Tuning into my Soul Code is crucial, but where the heck do I start?" Don't worry, upcoming lessons will relay everything you need to know. Here's a little insider secret: you don't need to "try" to do anything. Just start tuning in deeply to yourself while staying mindful of external factors. Everything will start clicking into place.

At the core of your Soul Code is the art of discerning and choosing things that are expressly meant for you. Things that make your heart sing and get a nod of approval from your brain.

Let's face it, we exist in a world teetering off-balance. Even though nature is forever hustling to restore equilibrium, The Matrix seems hell-bent on throwing us through a loop. Here's a simple way to visualize it: nature equals balance, Matrix equals imbalance. But guess what? You hold the scales of balance within you, and the key to unlocking it is heart and mind synchronization.

I see you hustling, crunching numbers, and analyzing every little detail. That's your brain, the analytical powerhouse, taking charge. But let me ask you: where's the heart in all this? Your gut feelings, your raw passion, your core desires? Too often, we're so lost in logic we forget the fire. Imagine Elon Musk's tech genius without his passion for Mars, or Oprah's business acumen without her empathy. Yeah, it falls flat, doesn't it?

Your heart is a wild horse, galloping towards fantasies and desires, while your mind is the stern rider, pulling back the reins, trying to stick to the safe, paved roads. But what if I told you that the secret to achieving the level of wealth that's perfect for you, exciting success, and a life sizzling with satisfaction, is not about choosing one over the other?

That's right. It's not heart vs mind, but heart AND mind. It's a symphony, not a solo. It's the Heart-Mind Harmony—your ticket to a prosperous life. And no, I'm not hawking some cheap, shamanistic potion here. This is science, psychology, and good old common sense, all packaged into a neat life hack.

Think of it like cooking a gourmet dish. Your Heart is the raw ingredient, full of natural flavors and freshness. Your Mind is the chef, knowing when to chop, when to stir, and when to let it simmer. The outcome? A Michelin-star worthy life.

Meet Jasmin

Story 1: Mind Overdrive: Heart on Standby

Jasmine, the modern marvel of meticulous planning, breezes through a day that is charted down to the second. Waking up at the precise chime of her alarm, she knows the number of steps to her caffeine drip. Breakfast? A strategic blend of nutrients perfectly designed for her energy burn-rate.

As the day unfolds, Jasmine zips from one task to the next, navigating her urban jungle with military precision. Lunch invites? Declined for optimized solo meal multitasking. But even in this streamlined Universe, life throws its curveballs. On her way back from work, the faint strumming of a street musician's guitar brushes past her. A melody, unfamiliar yet haunting, tries to tug at a corner of her armored heart. However, encased in her bubble of efficiency, the evening shadows find Jasmine untouched by the tune's gentle pull, replaced instead by a quiet, encroaching emptiness.

Story 2: Heart Unleashed: The Emotional Rollercoaster

In another corner of reality, Jasmine awakens to the caress of sun rays, not an alarm. She's captivated by the world's spontaneous wonders. Breakfast? Whatever her whims dictate—a decadent slice of cheesecake, perhaps?

She ditches work because, well, the sky looks like a Van Gogh painting. The city becomes her playground. Sidewalks transform into dance floors. Chance encounters with street artists lead to deep philosophical exchanges, her wallet draining on whimsical keepsakes. As dusk descends, so does the weight of her unrestrained day. The starlit night witnesses Jasmine wrestling with her unchecked passions, the consequences of her heart-first approach becoming all too palpable.

Story 3: The Perfect Cocktail: Heart & Mind Synchronized

In the most captivating of realities, Jasmine has awakened her entrepreneurial spirit. The morning starts with a blend of mindful meditation and enjoying the success of her new business venture. Work is no longer a 9-5 chore; it is a dance of productivity interwoven with moments of whimsy and wonder.

During an afternoon break, she steps out for a walk, and the familiar sound of the street musician fills the air. This time, she doesn't just pass by. She stops, listens, and allows herself to dance on the sidewalk, fully absorbing the music and the moment. The notes weave through her, each strand a blend of emotion and intellect.

Later, she sits down to refine her business plan, fueled by the energy of her Heart's desires and the clarity of her Mind's strategies. This version of Jasmine has found the alchemy of Heart and Mind, living a life filled with color, purpose, and joy. No longer confined to the 9-5 grind, she has unleashed her potential as an entrepreneur, thriving in a reality specifically intended for her, where her Heart chooses, and her Mind crafts a plan to make it all possible.

Insider scoop: the Mind is often like a toddler in a toy store—utterly befuddled, not knowing what it wants. Classic indecisiveness is the telltale sign of someone who's dancing to the beat of their brain, not their Heart. They look to the Mind for answers, and the Mind, bless its Heart, is a whimsical, willy-nilly entity. But here's the kicker—your Heart, that's your true north. It knows with absolute certainty what it doesn't want. Sure, it might take a hot minute to decode your Heart's desires, but it's got the "no-go" zone down pat, right from the get-go. Facing a head-scratcher of a decision? Consult both your brain and your Heart. Let your Mind chime in, but listen to your Heart with the ears of a hawk. If your Heart says, "Nah, this ain't it, chief," there's your answer, clear as day. No need to dig any deeper.

The Money Shot: When Passion Meets Pragmatism

Heart-Mind fusion isn't just a jazzy idea; it's about gaining an edge in a competitive world. When your Mind's strategies resonate with your Heart's desires, your potential becomes limitless. Your motivation soars, decision-making sharpens, and avenues to wealth and prosperity open up. It's like having the perfect algorithm for success: your Heart sets the goal (the "what"), and your Mind crafts the roadmap (the "how"). Together, they can build an empire, whether it's monetizing your passion, innovating your current bread and butter, or spearheading a movement.

The Recap

Syncing your Heart's dreams with your Mind's logic is like merging the fire of a rocket with its precision-guided system. It's not just about chasing passions; it's about channeling them effectively, ensuring they lead to tangible rewards. The age-old debate of "follow your heart" versus "mind knows best" is outdated. The new mantra? Unite and THRIVE.

Poke The Brain

What's the boldest dream your Heart's whispered, and how can your Mind craft a plan to grab it?

Your Next Power Move

Practical Exercise: How to Choose Your Things -The Art of Harmonious Selection.

In a world saturated with trends, ads, and the incessant push to keep pace with society's ever-shifting desires, how do you make choices? Let's start with clothes shopping. Are you swayed by the latest cover of a fashion magazine? Or do you prioritize comfort, putting function above form? What if there's a different way—a path that doesn't just cater to the world's whims or your comfort, but resonates with your very essence? Although clothing is our focal point here, this practice is all-encompassing. It's relevant whether you're deciding on a menu item, a holiday destination, a home, or a vehicle, and even down to the most significant choice of all, your life path and Sector of Reality. Perfecting the real-time synchronization of your Heart and Mind is a powerful navigational tool for ascending to higher Sectors.

Let's dive into an enlightening exercise called "How to Choose Your Things."

The Quantum Shopping Experience

Much like navigating The Quantum Field where every decision resonates with your unique frequency, shopping can become an exploration into your personal essence. This isn't just about choosing clothes, but about aligning choices with your Soul Code.

The Heart-Mind Dress Rehearsal

Next time you're out shopping, instead of being swayed by sales tags or brand names, try this.

1. Seek The Spark: try on an outfit and stand in front of the mirror. Now, don't just look—*feel*. Does your Heart flutter? Does a surge of confidence wash over you? That's your Heart saying, "YES!"
2. Rational Reflection: now, let your Mind chime in. Is the outfit versatile enough for different occasions? Is it durable? Does it offer value for its price? If your Mind nods in agreement, then it's a harmonious choice.

Serendipitous Discoveries

Sometimes, this alignment might strike when least expected. You could be walking past a store, and something in the display window catches your eye. Without even trying it on, your Heart and Mind might chorus, "THIS IS FOR YOU!" This spontaneous certainty is The Quantum Field's way of guiding you towards choices that resonate with your essence.

Harnessing This Power Beyond Shopping

This sensation, where your Heart's desires and your Mind's logic unite in perfect harmony, is invaluable. Recognize it. Cherish it. And most importantly, use it as a compass, not just in shopping but in navigating the vast expanse of The Quantum Field. When both Heart and Mind affirm a choice, be it in fashion, relationships, or career moves, that's The Quantum Field's way of whispering, "You're on the right track."

Synchronicity is Sacred: when Heart and Mind agree, it's a sign that your choice resonates with The Quantum Field.

Shopping as Soul Exploration: every choice, even the seemingly mundane ones, can be a step closer to understanding and aligning with your true self.

Expand Beyond the Mall: harness this harmonious decision-making in all facets of life.

So, next time you're out shopping, remember—it's not just about the clothes. It's an opportunity to synchronize with The Quantum Field, to choose things that are a genuine reflection of you. Happy shopping and harmonious choosing!

Lesson 42

Quantum GPS

You've got a top-of-the-line, sophisticated navigation system built right within you, yet most of us are blissfully unaware of it. Imagine strapping yourself into the pilot's seat of life, ready to navigate its ups and downs, twists and turns. But, instead of tuning into that inbuilt GPS, you're trying to read a torn, outdated map while simultaneously being bombarded by random directions shouted from the backseat. That chaotic backseat driver? Your over-stressed Mind, which too often gets confused and distracted by its own "Importance" and the Blackholes in daily life. That advanced GPS? The gentle dictates of your Heart, oftentimes barely heard.

Your Heart doesn't argue, fuss, or overthink. Your Heart doesn't get tangled in the cobwebs of logic or the chains of societal expectations. Instead, your Heart taps directly into the Quantum Flow—a limitless reservoir of ideas, optimal paths, and energy-efficient ways to solve problems. Your Heart feels and knows, while your Mind seeks to control and often complicates. Too often, your Mind acts like a toddler with a crayon, scribbling over the elegant designs the Heart perceives from The Quantum Field.

Imagine the Quantum Flow like an expansive river. In its natural state, the river finds the path of least resistance, flowing smoothly and effortlessly. But with the burden of

Inner Force, the overthinking Mind and Importance, the river is dammed, rerouted, and often spills over, causing chaos and confusion. Your Mind, driven by Importance, creates these blockages, straying from the optimal stream of new insights and solutions, steering you right to the edge of a waterfall.

Meet Carlos

Carlos had always been a man of logic. A software engineer in a bustling city, he tackled problems with algorithms and clean lines of code. But his life felt like an endless loop of the same variables—code, sleep, and occasional social gatherings, which he approached like debugging sessions. Analyzing, dissecting, but never really feeling good.

One day, Carlos stumbled upon the idea of Quantum Capitalism. He considered it esoteric nonsense at first, but a persistent emptiness led him to lean in. With a skeptical Mind, he sat still for a while and tried to listen to the dictates of his Heart and perceive The Quantum Field and Flow. He allowed himself to feel his Heart for the first time in a long time, muting the blaring noise his Mind usually generated. Carlos then received an idea that seemed to have been birthed out of nowhere.

At that moment, he felt something strange in his chest, call it a ping from The Quantum Field. The idea was simple yet profound: "Create art through code." It went against his pragmatism, against the linear career graph he had plotted for himself. But the sensation was undeniable, like the perfect fit of a puzzle piece.

The next day, Carlos started working on a side project—coding intricate digital landscapes that were visually stunning and emotionally resonant. Through social media feedback, he discovered that his art could actually improve people's mental health and well-being just by looking at them. Mental health professionals became interested, and he found himself at the intersection of technology and human psychology, exactly where his Heart's Quantum GPS had directed him. For the first time, Carlos felt vibrantly alive yet tranquil, stimulated yet calm, purposeful and effective. It felt nothing short of a miracle to him.

And as for that incessant, Importance-driven chatter from the backseat of his Mind? It was still there, but its voice grew fainter each time he tapped into his Heart's guidance. The sophisticated internal GPS was steering him clear of life's treacherous waterfalls as he navigated his new endeavor, and reality, with ease.

Now, Carlos wasn't just solving technical problems; he was resolving emotional equations, all while significantly enriching his own emotional quotient. The best part? He had tapped into the limitless stream of the Quantum Flow, where optimal solutions weren't just probable—they were inevitable.

Carlos realized his inner Quantum GPS was like having an ace up his sleeve in the poker game of life. No more needless detours or exhausting internal work conflicts. Every decision was a royal flush, optimizing his life for maximum impact and personal fulfillment.

The Money Shot: Cashing In On The Quantum Flow

When you harness the power of the Quantum Flow through the dictates of your Heart, it's like having insider trading information in the stock market of life. You're cashing in on the best solutions and optimizing every move for wealth, prosperity, and well-being. Remember, it's not about complicating the process but rather understanding that every answer, solution, and idea you need already exists within The Quantum Field, delivered by its streams, the Quantum Flow. All you need to do is tune in with both Heart and Mind. New information is not generated within the Mind but is infinitely abundant within the Quantum Flow. It is the Heart that accesses this information and the Mind that makes sense of what your next move is. Master this and you have hacked the wealth equation.

The Recap

Your Heart serves as the direct line of communication to The Quantum Field and Flow, offering optimal solutions to all problems and challenges. While your Mind is invaluable, it often becomes entangled in the noise of The Matrix and your Importance levels. Learn to balance the two: let your Heart guide, with the Mind serving as the executor. Embrace simplicity, shift from control to observation, and release into the Quantum Flow to access everything you need to optimize your sector of reality.

Poke The Brain

Remember, Carlos' quantum pivot didn't involve advanced algorithms or groundbreaking tech. It was a simple call to blend emotion with logic, an answer that existed in the Quantum Flow all along. What about you? What solutions are within reach, waiting for your Heart to tune in?

Your Next Power Move

Heart and Quantum Flow Data Exchange

Life is a delicate balance, and at times, we may find ourselves leaning too heavily on one side. It's easy to let our Minds dominate, especially in our fast-paced world. Here's a straightforward exercise to help your Heart tap into the infinite data within the Quantum Flow and identify what might be off-balance in your life.

1. Find Your Center:

    - Sit or lie down in a quiet space. Close your eyes and take deep, slow breaths. Envision your Heart at the center of your being, glowing with a warm light. With each breath, see this light grow brighter and more expansive, radiating calm and clarity.

2. Ask and Listen:

    - Once you feel centered, ask yourself, "What in my life feels out of balance?"
    - Wait patiently. Do not force an answer. Instead, be open to sensations, images, emotions, or thoughts that arise. These are messages from the Quantum Flow.

3. Reflect and Journal:

    - Open your eyes and grab your journal. Write down what you felt, saw, or thought during the exercise. Did any specific areas of your life stand out as being off-balance? Was it a relationship, career, health, or perhaps a personal goal?

- Once you've identified this area, let your Heart access insights and guidance. Ask, "What can I do to navigate this situation?" Listen, and then jot down any messages that emerge.

This exercise, though simple, can be profoundly revealing when done with genuine intent. You can practice it weekly or even daily to consistently check in with your Heart and ensure proper navigation. Remember, the Quantum Flow holds wisdom and true guidance—it's up to you to give your Heart the opportunity to listen.

Lesson 43

There's a Better Way

Ready to shake things up a bit? This lesson is all about "materialization," a whole new ball game from the tired old manifestation rituals. Remember our Heart-to-Heart in the last lesson? Your Heart knows the way and it's when your Mind gets involved in the logic of the Heart's decisions that a powerful energy emerges, Heart and Mind Synchronization. That's where the real magic happens—when your Heart and Mind team up and start navigating Sectors of reality. Dreaming of something grander? Time to level up from the tired old techniques, my friend.

Mainstream "manifestation" is like a desperate attempt to yank gains into your current reality using just your brain power. No shocker that the results are usually lackluster. No judgment, though—we've all been down that road. But take a deep breath, there's a way better route!

The Mirage of Classic Manifestation

Old-school manifestation vibes, like the Law of Attraction and The Secret, have swept the globe with their tantalizing promise of endless possibilities. But they often hinge on the idea of "willing" your desires into your current reality. You're told to believe and visualize, fingers crossed that The Quantum Field will miraculously change its trajectory to hand-deliver your wishes. The snag? This method is all about Inner Force, Importance and strong-arming the world to bend to your will.

Now, let's flip the script. Instead of trying to drag The Quantum Field towards you, what if you maneuvered yourself within the vast Quantum Field to where your desires are already chillin'? That, my friend, is Materialization. It's the heartbeat of Quantum Capitalism.

Recall the Sectors of Reality depicted as layers stacked upon each other in a linear fashion—from the dreary ones at the bottom to the dreamy ones at the top. Quantum Capitalism is your express elevator. But you've got to press the "up" button.

Switching from a manifestation mindset to a materialization mindset is like swapping out your old, clunky gears. We're programmed to desire, to hope, and to ask. But how often do we actually get in sync with those desires, putting ourselves smack dab in the middle of environments and mindsets where our dreams are just par for the course?

Here's the skinny: manifestation is all about Inner Force, Importance, and Matrix You.

Materialization is all about Outer Power, Quantum Flow, and Quantum You.

Meet Sam

Sam was just your run-of-the-mill mid-western guy with dreams as boundless as the oceans he ached to sail. Despite being a country mile away from any coast, Sam harbored a deep-seated desire —to own a yacht. For years, he visualized himself as the proud owner of a yacht, sailing across the shimmering open seas, the wind tousling his hair. He took sailing and deckhand lessons on the Great Lakes, and even slapped up a picture of a yacht on the whiteboard behind his desk, fingers crossed that The Universe would, by some miracle, hand-deliver his wish.

Eventually, Sam waved the white flag on wishing for a yacht and took the picture down. However, out of the blue, a LinkedIn job offering landed in his inbox: "Junior Deckhands Needed for Long Haul Delivery Voyages." He knew the drill—long hours on the blue water seas, sailing brand-new yachts to their eager owners waiting with bated breath for their purchase. Sam took a gutsy leap of faith, relocated to the coast to establish a new base, and embarked on his journey as a Junior Deckhand.

In this new playground, where yachts were a dime a dozen, Sam stumbled upon a bounty of opportunities to materialize his dream in a concrete way. Over time, he was presented with the opportunity to join financial forces on a modest sailing yacht with four other deckhands. His Heart nodded, "Yeah, dude. This is it," and his brain agreed that having four savvy partners for his maiden voyage into yacht ownership was a stroke of genius. They called her "Goodbye 9-5." They reveled in their collective purchase for a few years, taking turns embarking on blue water voyages, renting it out for charter, and showering it with care. Eventually, they opted to sell, once the second-hand market started sizzling. With their astute investment and a surging market, they all sailed away from the deal with their pockets brimming with enough cash to buy small yachts of their own.

Sam secured his very own yacht, which he also made his home. Life took on a dreamlike hue, and he felt a wave of satisfaction wash over him, grateful for where his leap of faith had steered him. He named her "Flow, Baby."

For Sam, the moment he let his Heart join the fray and pivoted from "craving" to "action," the magic started happening. With a little help from Outer Power and the Quantum Flow, Sam materialized his precise desire in a Sector of Reality where everything fell into place with ease.

So, what's the takeaway from Sam's odyssey? It's not merely about picturing your desires; it's about aligning yourself with the Sector of Reality where those desires are par for the course. When Sam took the bull by the horns, relocated to the coast, and plunged headlong into the yachting world, he merged with the Quantum Flow, and his dream materialized organically. Sam's tale is a masterclass in how, by taking the reins and aligning ourselves with the right environments, we can materialize our desires effortlessly. It's all about harnessing the Outer Power, letting your Heart throw in its two cents, and hauling yourself off the couch.

The Money Shot: Reality Hopping 101

Here's a game-changer for you: your current financial struggles? They aren't your forever. And while The Matrix might whisper that wealth and success are reserved for a few "lucky" ones, Quantum Capitalism begs to differ. Lean in, because you deserve to hear this: there's a quantum reality where a financially secure, thriving version of YOU exists. It's not about praying for a sudden windfall or waiting for a miracle. These teachings are your tools to navigate through Sectors, moving closer to the reality where opportunities are abundant. Yes, even for you, especially for you. Let's be real—money matters can appear daunting if you are overly tuned into The Matrix. But with every conscious decision, you're not just hoping for better days, you're taking quantum strides towards them. You've got this, and The Quantum Field, with its infinite wealth possibilities, is cheering you on. Get ready to embrace a version of you, where you're not just surviving, but flourishing.

The Recap

Manifestation—the classic method? It's like yelling at the TV because your favorite team isn't winning. Materialization, on the other hand, is like flipping channels until you find a game where your team *is* winning. Quantum Capitalism isn't about bending The Quantum Field to your will. It's about navigating to where in The Quantum Field your will is already the rule.

Poke The Brain

When was the last time you asked someone how they snagged that amazing opportunity or got their hands on something super valuable, and they hit you back with, "Oh, I manifested it"? Exactly.

Your Next Power Move

Juggernaut Journal & Meditation Exercise: Reality Channel Flipper.

Objective: shift from a Manifestation Mindset to a Materialization Mindset by actively placing yourself in the desired Sector of Reality.

Reality Visualization

Step 1: close your eyes and take five deep breaths. With every exhale, release any tension or stress.

Step 2: visualize your current reality. How does it look, feel, and sound? Recognize it as one layer among countless others.

Step 3: now, imagine a vast expanse of layers above you. These layers represent better and improved realities, holding all the good stuff you would love to come in contact with.

Destination Selection

Step 1: think of one desire you've been trying to manifest or create (e.g., financial security, a loving relationship, a career achievement).

Step 2: instead of focusing on the desire itself, visualize the version of you that already exists in a reality where that desire is fulfilled. How does this version of you look, feel, act, or think differently from the current you?

Quantum Channel Flipping

Step 1: imagine a remote control in your hand. This remote has the power to change your channel, or "reality."

Step 2: begin "flipping channels" by visualizing different versions of you. With each "channel," you are getting closer to the version of you that has what you desire.

Step 3: when you've found that desired version, delve deeper. What are the daily habits, thoughts, and beliefs of this version of you? How do they react to challenges? What do they prioritize?

Anchor in the New Reality

Step 1: focus on one specific habit, belief, or action from the desired version of you. Write it down.

Step 2: over the next week, adopt this trait. Embody it as if it were already second nature. Allow it to lead your decisions, actions, and thoughts.

Reflect and Repeat

At the end of the week, reflect on how embodying this trait has influenced your actions, thoughts, and experiences. Did you notice a shift in your reality, even if it was subtle?

Closure

Remember, Quantum Capitalism is an active pursuit. It's about consciously placing yourself in the desired reality. While one week might not catapult you entirely into a new layer, repeated and consistent shifts in mindset and behavior will. Embrace your power to "channel flip" and watch as your reality begins to align with your desires. Onward to your chosen reality!

Lesson 44

Spotlight

Alright, let's rewind. In our last tete-a-tete, we unpacked the difference between classic manifestation and materialization. Now, we're diving deep into another facet of materialization that usually gets brushed under the carpet.

Ever noticed that after deciding on a dream car, that model suddenly seems to be EVERYWHERE? It's like some cosmic joke where The Quantum Field starts spamming your life with pop-up ads. But here's the thing—it's not The Quantum Field playing the games, it's you.

The mechanism is simple. Picture reality as an infinite dark room, and your focus is like a spotlight. This vast realm? Yep, it's The Quantum Field. Jam-packed with potential events and material things just biding their time until they get their fifteen minutes of fame. When you shine your light on something specific, even if it's as trivial as a jerk driver who cuts you off, reality's mirror flashes back with a "ta-da!"

Let's take this neat little phenomenon positive and practical, shall we? Enter the "Magic Quantum Card Trick." It's a crowd-pleaser in our quantum community, and for a good reason. Ever found a playing card randomly on the street? Weird, huh? Never happened to you? No worries. Just imagine finding one. But don't overthink it; just let that thought slide into your mind like a song request to a DJ and watch it happen when you least expect it.

Believe it or not, this is a real thing. People all over the world piece together entire decks of playing cards just by gently focusing their intentions on finding them. And guess what? The cards seem to be everywhere. This trick doesn't just work for cards though. It works for opportunities, relationships, and even that ten bucks you find in your jeans. Just remember, there are infinite variables out there; gently focus on what you want and let things unfold.

So, what's on your agenda to spotlight today? Opportunities? Networking buddies? Or maybe just the stain on your shirt? The choice is yours.

What's crucial here is understanding the value of your intention. The Quantum Field doesn't discriminate; it will magnify whatever you put your focus on, no matter how minute. Are you stressed about work? Expect more stress. Focusing on the beauty of something you're creating? Expect more beauty to be presented to you by your world. Your mental spotlight has a butterfly effect on your reality.

Therefore, be deliberate with your attention. If you constantly worry about the worst-case scenario, The Quantum Field will echo your fears. However, if you channel your focus into positive and proactive actions, you'll see a ripple effect in your life.

But remember, don't stress over the details. The Quantum Field takes care of the minutiae. Your job? Direct your focus with intent. The specifics of how things materialize? That's The Quantum Field's department. Trust the process, keep your eyes on the prize, and let The Quantum Field do its thang.

Let's nerd out, shall we?

Ever heard of Schrödinger's cat? No, it's not a new internet meme, but a famous thought experiment that gives us a peek into the wild world of quantum mechanics and the observer effect!

Picture this: a cat, a sealed box, a radioactive atom, and a vial of poison. Sounds like the setup for a bizarre thriller, but stay with me! In this thought experiment, the cat is placed in a sealed box with a radioactive atom that might decay and kill the cat. According to quantum mechanics, until someone opens the box and checks, the cat is both alive AND dead at the same time. Yep, you heard that right. Alive and dead. Simultaneously.

This strange state is called "superposition," and it's one of the reasons quantum mechanics gives even the smartest cookies a headache. The act of observing the cat forces it into one state or another—alive or dead. This is what's known as the "observer effect."

So, how does this relate to your life?

Well, while it's a stretch to say that just thinking about a yacht will manifest it into your life (sorry!), the observer effect does highlight the fascinating ways in which our observations can affect reality at the quantum level. And while many scientists and philosophers reject the idea that these principles can be applied to the macroscopic world, it does make you wonder...

Could focusing your thoughts and observations on positive outcomes affect your reality in some way? Could softly focusing on an intention, like finding playing cards on the street, increase the likelihood of it happening?

Remember, The Quantum Field's library is vast; softly cue up your track and let it play out. So, what are you going to spotlight today?

The Money Shot: The Quantum Field's Request Line

By choosing to connect with specific events in The Quantum Field, you essentially request their presence in your reality. It's your world; you control the track list. But here's the real kicker: it's not about craving or desperation. Oh no, it's about softly setting your intention to experience that variable and then trusting the rhythm of the Quantum Flow. When you master the Quantum Capitalist shuffle, you're not just wishing upon a star for some extra cash; you're moonwalking to a Sector where money, opportunities, and luxury abound. So, groove to the beat, fine-tune your Qualifiers to resonate with a higher frequency, and watch as your reality transforms into a VIP club of infinite possibilities. Doubt it? Back to the "Guiding Theory" lesson or bust.

The Recap

Your attention in the expansive DJ booth of The Quantum Field sets the rhythm of your life. From playing cards to profound opportunities, your intentional focus is your universal request line. So, what track are you queuing up next?

Poke The Brain

If you had the power to request an event from The Quantum Field right now, knowing it'll play, what would it be?

Your Next Power Move

Practical Game Exercise: Card Counting.

Objective: explore the power of your focus in the vast Quantum Field by setting a light intention and observing its materialization.

Setting Up

Choose Your Item: decide on a quirky item or symbol you'd like to spot. It could be a playing card, a specific animal like a butterfly, a particular kind of car, or anything else that resonates with you, something you don't already notice daily.

Intention Setting: spend a moment visualizing your chosen item. See it clearly in your mind, feel the excitement of spotting it, and then release the thought. Remember, this isn't about force; it's about setting a gentle intention and letting The Quantum Field do its thing.

Rules of the Game

Daily Logging: over the course of the week, whenever you spot the item or symbol you chose, jot down a quick note in your journal or tally it on your phone notes. Write the date, time, and context in which you found it.

No Obsessing: the key is to not obsess over your chosen item. Trust in The Quantum Field and go about your daily activities. Your chosen symbol will show up when you least expect it.

No Limits: there's no cap to how many times your item might appear. It could pop up once, or it could become a recurring theme throughout your week.

End of the Week Reflection

At the end of the week, take some time to review your notes. Reflect on the moments your chosen symbol appeared and how it made you feel.

Bonus Round

For those who want to dive deeper into The Quantum Field's playful side, try setting a new intention every week. This way, you can keep the game going and continuously test the boundaries of your focus and The Quantum Field's responsiveness.

Remember: this game is not just about spotting an item; it's about understanding the power of subtle intentions, your awareness, and The Quantum Field's playful way of responding with Outer Power. Enjoy the Quantum Spotlight Game and happy spotting!

Lesson 45

Raiding the Vault

Alright, my doom-scrolling friends stuck in mom's basement, let's have a little chit-chat, shall we? We've been yakking about materialization, and I'm here to drop a truth bomb on you: materialization of your desires takes energy. Remember that little chat we had about The Quantum Field, at the very beginning? Everything—and I mean EVERYTHING—material in this world passed through that bad boy, before arriving here. That Chapstick you just slathered on your lips? Bingo! Someone's bright idea turned into reality through energy in manufacturing. That salad you just ate? You betcha! Someone played Mother Nature, planting seeds, watering them, and setting up the sunny environment, all energy in action. And that book you're clutching or the YouTube video you're glued to? Do you think they just popped out of thin air? Nada! It was energy in action that pulled them into the material realm. So, let's slice and dice this, shall we?

You've heard it countless times: "Time is money." Let's twist that just a tad—"Energy is wealth." In the realm of Quantum Capitalism, where infinite realities and potentialities dance before you, *how* you choose to spend your energy is the single most crucial factor determining whether you'll be lounging in the penthouse suite of Sector #10 or remaining stuck in the grimy basement of missed opportunities, Sector #1.

The digital age's glittery Matrix is designed to suck you in. Social media platforms and streaming services are built to devour your attention, your time, —your energy. But here's the catch. Every minute spent doom-scrolling or drowning in Netflix is a minute *not* spent moving towards that higher Sector of Reality you so deeply crave. It's not just about the Netflix subscription dollars or ad revenues from social platforms. It's about the cost of opportunities foregone, your dreams delayed, and your potential unfulfilled. The Matrix thrives while you stagnate. Sounds sinister? That's because it is.

Here's the hard-hitting truth: energy is finite. Time is limited. Every moment squandered is a moment you won't get back. Your physical vitality, mental prowess, and the life force pulsating within you are your most precious commodities and they do have expiration dates. They're the currency of Quantum Capitalism. You've got two options:

1. Invest it: channel this energy into endeavors that amplify your wealth, knowledge, and growth.
2. Waste it: drown it in mindless escapism, handing it over to The Matrix's ever-hungry maw.

The stark reality is this: if you're not where you want to be right now, it's not The Quantum Field's fault, or your boss's, or the market's. It's that you've been *spending* instead of *investing* your energy.

THE SHOCKER

Consider this: 78,000 hours. That's how much TV the average human gobbles up in their lifetime. That's NINE years of potential squandered. Imagine, in that same time, you could earn multiple degrees, master skills, or even establish an empire! The wasted potential is beyond staggering.

The Money Shot: The Quantum Currency Shift

Your energy? It's more valuable than the most luxurious gem, the rarest metal, or the most dominant cryptocurrency. But how often do we donate it into the Blackholes of The Matrix, expecting no return? The heart of wealth-building isn't just about smart investments in stocks or real estate. It's about investing in your energetic potential. Every time you shift an ounce of your energy from passive consumption to active creation, you're minting your own Quantum currency. This is how you break free from the constraints of traditional capitalism and step into the boundless realms of Quantum prosperity.

The Recap

Quantum Capitalism is not about abstract theories or metaphysical nonsense. It's anchored in something incredibly tangible and real: your energy. Realize its value. Begin to see yourself as a dynamo of energy, and the world as a vast canvas awaiting your unique mark.

Poke The Brain

If you were to reclaim just one hour of your energy from The Matrix daily, what could you accomplish in a year? In a decade? Where have you been squandering your energy?

Your Next Power Move

Juggernaut Journal Exercise: Energy Audit.

Objective: reclaim your energy from The Matrix and redirect it towards wealth-building activities of the Quantum Capitalism kind.

Setting Up

Identify Your Energy Sinks: before starting the audit, list down typical activities you believe suck up most of your time and energy. These could be binge-watching TV, aimless social media scrolling, or even daydreaming.

Define Your Wealth-Building Activities: determine activities that would contribute to your personal growth, professional advancement, or general well-being. This could range from taking an online course, reading a book, practicing a hobby, or working on a side business.

Rules of the Exercise

Hourly Check-in: set an alarm to ring every hour (hardcore, right?). When it goes off, pause and jot down what you've been doing for the past hour. Be honest—this exercise is for your benefit.

Energy Classification: at the end of each day, categorize each hour spent into two columns: "Matrix Time" (passive consumption) and "Quantum Time" (active creation or personal development).

Weekly Assessment: at the end of the week, tally the total waking hours spent in both categories. Reflect on the balance. How much of your energy went into The Matrix versus quantum growth?

25% Challenge: for the next week, aim to shift 25% of your Matrix Time into Quantum Time. For instance, if you spent 20 hours on passive consumption, aim to redirect 5 hours towards your defined wealth-building activities.

End of the Second Week Reflection
Reflect on the shifts you've made

- How do you feel mentally and emotionally after redirecting your energy?
- What have you accomplished or learned in your Quantum Time?
- Do you notice any changes in your motivation, productivity, or general outlook on life?

Continuation & Expansion

Keep refining and expanding on this exercise as you progress.

- Can you shift even more time from The Matrix to Quantum endeavors?
- Introduce new wealth-building activities as you master or complete the old ones.
- Seek out like-minded individuals and share your journey. Perhaps join our support group or find an accountability buddy.

Remember: the true essence of wealth is not just financial; it's the accumulation of knowledge, skills, experiences, and personal growth. The Quantum Energy Audit is designed to help you realize where you're investing your most valuable resource and guide you towards maximizing its return. Commit to the exercise, and witness the transformative power of Quantum Capitalism.

Lesson 46

Hard Money Truths

In our last lesson, we confronted some uncomfortable truths about your energy, its immense value, and the loss incurred when it's frittered away. This round, we're diving headfirst into another chilly ocean—the hard truths about money. Many shudder at the mere thought of facing their financial narratives, but we're about to flip those narratives on their heads and give them a good, hard shake. Punch it!

Ever felt like money is this mystical, elusive entity, forever playing a game of hide and seek with you? Well, it's time for a reality check: money is nothing but energy materialized. That's it. No mysticism involved. Our world runs on energy, which is why its material form—money—holds such sway. It's time to start seeing money as a physical extension of your own energy and power. More money equates to more freedom. And more freedom? That means you get to brazenly toy with The Matrix, rather than being its plaything.

Do you feel that itch at the back of your mind? That's realization.

Money is the confluence of thought energy, physical effort, and the pure brilliance of ideas pulled from The Quantum Field. Capture this trifecta, and congratulations—you've unlocked the vault.

Hard Money Truths

Look at Bill Gates. He didn't just stumble upon a fortune. He extracted a revolutionary idea from The Quantum Field—an operating system that would change the world. He invested attention, time, and sweat equity into realizing that idea. And what was his reward? Billionaire status.

But let's get real for a second. Think about the person sweating under the sun, earning a minimum wage to dig a hole. Their physical energy earns them their day's wage. Here's the thing: the quality of the idea, combined with shrewd thinking and execution, determines the quantity of money one gets in exchange for his output.

Consider jobs with a low barrier to entry, like trench digging. Essentially, they'll hand that position to nearly anyone with a pulse. Just show up, and you're in. Contrast that with high-barrier jobs. These are reserved for the elite, the individuals attuned to their higher selves, who've dedicated time to mastering valuable skills. These are the people with an open line to The Quantum Field, effortlessly drawing out revolutionary ideas. See the difference?

Our prior lesson on not wasting your energy wasn't just whimsical chatter. Notice how many individuals are trapped in a perpetual grind, inefficiently using their energy? Their pockets feel the weight—or lack thereof.

The Money Shot: Fun and Shadowy Money Tidbits

The Dark Side of the Money Moon: sure, we talk about energy and money a lot, but let's dive into the darker, more mysterious waters of wealth. Money gained by shady means is just the human attempting to circumvent the balanced energetic exchange, or die tryin'.

Criminal Enterprises: ah, the classic shortcut to riches! These aren't just people bending the rules; they're bending their entire moral compass in hopes of a fat payout. They account for the risk of being caught and the price of possible jail time. More risk, more reward, right?

High-Profile Divorces: poured all that time and energy into a relationship only to see it crumble? Time to cash in! They want all that time and energy back, and then some. A broken heart often demands the most significant compensation.

The Passive Income Myth: it sounds like a dream, doesn't it? Hit a button, watch the cash roll in. But surprise, surprise! It requires a hefty investment of attention, time, and energy upfront. But, once you've set the stage, The Quantum Field does indeed shower you with dividends.

Strip Dancing and Morally Questionable Endeavors: the extra cash earned for shaking that booty? It's because the cost of your reputation (and your sanity) is baked into the price.

Celebrities: why do these people make so much money? Well, they are dialed into their Soul Code in ways that The Matrix approves of. This valuable combination is rare and highly lucrative.

Rarities: diamonds? Jewelry? Watches? Pure, unadulterated energy channeled into a material object. Take diamonds, for instance. Imagine how many impoverished Africans dig for how many hours to find a diamond, let alone one worthy of a royal title. It involves strategizing, immense physical energy, pain, and suffering. That's precisely why those prices are sky-high.

Insider Trading: this is when someone uses confidential information to trade a company's stocks or bonds. It's illegal, but some people risk it for financial gain. Talk about defying The Matrix!

Ponzi Schemes: this is the ultimate energy drainer, inspired by none other than Charles Ponzi from the 20th century. It's a deceitful vortex that attracts investments by promising to fuel the energy (original investment) of earlier investors with the fresh energy (profits) injected by the newcomers. The illusion created is one of a thriving energy field, bustling with legitimate business exchanges, while in reality, it's merely a recycling of new energy to placate the old. Eventually, the energy well runs dry—there simply isn't enough new energy to sustain the old, or the masterminds behind the scheme can no longer lure more energy donors. The entire facade crumbles, leaving a trail of drained and depleted investors.

Gambling: a masterstroke on the poverty mindset. Lotteries and casinos ingeniously capitalize on the belief that for some, the only conceivable way to amass a fortune is through a windfall.

The gambling matrix seductively whispers that wealth could be just a roll of the dice away for anyone and everyone. This wafer-thin glimmer of hope nestles deep within the psyches of the impoverished, because, without it, the prospect of wealth would be utterly non-existent.

Patent Trolling: this involves buying a patent, often from a bankrupt firm, and then suing another company by claiming that one of its products infringes on the copyrighted idea. It's less about innovation and more about making money from lawsuits.

Art World Shenanigans: art is a feast for the senses, but the art market? A whole different kettle of fish. Counterfeit masterpieces, dodgy transactions, and orchestrated price surges barely scratch the surface. Some artists, in a twisted dance with their own energy, even annihilate their creations to inflate the worth of their remaining body of work. Captivatingly ruinous to distill one's energy into inciting scarcity, wouldn't you agree?

Now, we're not saying you should turn to a life of crime or go shaking your booty for some extra cash (unless that's your thing; no judgment here). But understanding the energy (and sometimes the lack of morals) behind these avenues of wealth can offer some fascinating insights into the world of money, energy, and The Matrix.

The Recap

Money is fundamentally about optimizing your energy. While there are numerous shortcuts in this game, never forget that each comes with its hidden costs. Everything in this world bears a price tag—absolutely everything. At the very least, you pay with your time.

So, ditch your naïveté. Stop viewing money as some esoteric force. It's merely the sum total of focused energy. If you're continuously drained, bleeding energy into The Matrix and getting zilch in return, whose fault is that? Yours. The moment you take control, prioritize, and harness your energy towards achieving financial wealth, the game changes. Stop pointing fingers at The Matrix or blaming your programming. The real culprit? Your mismanagement of your energy. You're now in the know. So, are you just going to sit there, or are you going to start Quantum Capitalist-ing?

Your life, your choice. What's it going to be?

Poke The Brain

Reflect for a moment on all the time, energy, and attention you've squandered over the years. Just for fun, can you imagine how much wealth that would have equated to long term, had you known all this earlier? How might your life look different now? Are you ready to channel it into creating something better?

Your Next Power Move

Juggernaut Journal Exercise: Pathways to Higher Wealth Creation.

Objective: to challenge and stretch your mind in identifying and brainstorming avenues for higher wealth generation, shifting away from traditional and low-barrier methods.

Steps

Baseline Evaluation

- Write down your current income sources.
- Next to each, mark whether it's a low, medium, or high-barrier source of income.
- Reflect on the amount of energy and time you invest in each of these sources.

Brainstorming Burst

- Set a timer for 15 minutes.
- Rapidly jot down as many ideas as possible for creating wealth. Don't filter or judge; the goal is quantity.

Evaluation

- Review your list and circle the top 5 ideas that excite you the most or seem the most viable.
- For each of these ideas, consider:
- What skills or resources would you need?
- What barriers might you face, and how could they be overcome?
- How scalable is this idea?
- What's the potential return on investment (time, energy, money)?

Deep Dive

- Select one idea from your top 5.
- Spend 30 minutes researching this idea online. Look for success stories, strategies, potential pitfalls, and market demand.
- Jot down key findings and insights.

Planning

- For your selected idea, draft a basic plan:
- What are the first three steps to get started?
- How can you acquire any necessary skills or resources?
- Set a tentative timeline for when you'd like to kick-start this venture.

Visualization

- Close your eyes and imagine yourself successfully implementing this idea. Feel the emotions tied to the increased wealth and freedom this venture brings.

Commitment

- Make a commitment to take one small action towards this idea within the next 48 hours. It could be as simple as reading a book, enrolling in a course, or having a conversation with someone in that field.

Reflection

At the end of this exercise, reflect on the following question.

- How did it feel to shift your mindset towards higher paths of wealth creation?
- What beliefs or fears surfaced during this exercise, and how can you address them?
- Are there individuals or communities who can support you in this new venture?

Notes

- Revisit this exercise periodically, especially as your skills, interests, and the economic landscape evolve.
- Remember, the path to higher wealth often requires continuous learning, adaptability, and resilience. Stay informed and remain proactive in seeking opportunities.

Lesson 47

Dreams Are Your Unlived Realities

Alright, let's pivot, shall we? We're transitioning from the daytime hustle and bustle to the tranquil nighttime. From active, awakened energy to those serene, restful hours. There are plenty of them, after all. Roughly one-third of your life is spent in a state of sleep, dreams being your consistent companions. But what if I were to tell you that the dreamworld isn't just your brain playing games while you're "offline"? Rather, it's your unhindered soul soaring through The Quantum Field, a realm teeming with boundless possibilities and paths yet to manifest in your physical reality. Let's dissect this a bit.

Modern psychology posits that dreams are merely nonsensical and arbitrary reverberations bouncing around in your mind as you sleep—fragments of the day's events or past memories kaleidoscoping into fragmented experiences. However, from the Quantum Capitalist perspective, it's actually your essence navigating diverse Sectors of Reality. While conscious, our awareness anchors us to the physical realm. Conversely, during sleep, this tether is liberated.

Lucid dreams: mastering the art of controlling this flight, your actions, or the sequence of events in your dreamscape. Now, imagine applying this control to your waking life, where you could navigate the realm of possibilities and realize the ones that serve you best.

Your dreams are not illusions; they are projections from unmaterialized Sectors of The Quantum Field. Bizarre architecture you've never seen, people you know behaving out-of-character, even seeing a different reflection of yourself in a dream mirror—these are all glimpses into unmaterialized realities. And just as you can tune into different TV channels, your Heart—serving as a conduit—can tune into various Sectors of The Quantum Field while you sleep.

Cue the baffling part. Your mind is the overthinking bestie who tries to rationalize everything. "Oh, that dream where pigs were flying? Must've been that leftover pizza." Nope! What if, instead, that was a glimpse of an alternative reality where physics works differently?

Meet Anna

Anna had become fascinated by the concept of Quantum Capitalism. The idea of merging quantum physics with the economic principles to redefine value, not just in terms of money, but in terms of energy and possibilities, resonated with her deeply. She was a successful venture capitalist, but the traditional ways of doing business felt soulless and, frankly, outdated. Anna had been educating herself on The Quantum Field and practicing lucid dreaming, recognizing its potential to revolutionize not just her life, but the world's economy.

One night, after a particularly exhausting day of meetings, Anna had a lucid dream. She found herself in a bustling marketplace, unlike any she had seen. People were trading not just goods and services, but ideas, energy, and even emotions. It was a marketplace of possibilities, and she felt an electrifying sense of potential all around her. Anna encountered a vendor who offered her a seed. "This is not just any seed," the vendor explained. "It's the seed of an idea, a business that can change the world. But it needs the right soil, the right energy to grow." Intrigued, Anna took the seed and woke up feeling euphoric and invigorated.

Inspired by her dream, Anna started developing a new business model, one that leveraged the principles of Quantum Capitalism. She envisioned a platform that connected people not just based on their professional skills or financial capital, but on their energy, their intentions, and the possibilities they could create together. It was a radical idea, but Anna believed in it with every fiber of her being.

Anna gave it her all to bring her vision to life. She faced skepticism and resistance from traditionalists, but she also found allies who shared her vision for a more equitable, sustainable, and innovative future. Together, they built the platform, and it quickly gained traction. It became a hub for creative collaboration, groundbreaking ideas, and positive energy.

In a few short years, Anna's platform transformed the way business was done. It enabled people to tap into the limitless potential of The Quantum Field and materialize their dream lives, quite literally. Anna knew that her lucid dream had been more than just a flight of fancy; it was a glimpse into an unmaterialized reality that she had brought to life.

The Money Shot: Financial Freedom via Lucid Living

Are you getting the connections yet? Understanding your dreams as travels through The Quantum Field isn't just some mind-bending philosophical concept; it can be the key to your financial freedom and personal success. As you become conscious of your "lucid living," akin to lucid dreaming, you can tap into the limitless potential of The Quantum Field and materialize your dream life—quite literally.

The Recap

In essence, your dreams aren't illusions, but snapshots of unrealized Sectors within The Quantum Field. And by treating your waking life like a lucid dream, you can navigate through this Quantum Field to materialize the life you desire. This requires you to challenge your mind's inclination to separate dreams from reality, and to understand that The Quantum Field is real, even if not physically tangible.

Poke The Brain

Are you truly awake or just dreaming? Ever wonder why certain dreams stick with you more than others? Could those be signals or opportunities you're overlooking in your waking life?

Your Next Power Move

Awareness Exercise: Lucid Wakefulness.

Objective

To cultivate a heightened sense of awareness and marvel in your daily life, enabling you to view the waking world as a lucid dream and make empowered choices.

Steps

Morning Intention Setting

As you wake up, sit quietly for a moment and set an intention for the day: "Today, I will view my world with wonder, as if I am in a lucid dream."

Reality Checks

Several times a day, pause and ask yourself:

Is this a dream?

What makes this moment magical or out of the ordinary?

This practice will blur the lines between the dream world and waking reality, allowing you to appreciate the magical nuances of daily life.

Mindful Exploration

Dedicate at least 15 minutes each day to explore your surroundings as if you've never seen them before. This could be your home, a local park, or even your workplace. Approach everything with a sense of curiosity and wonder, as if you are exploring a dreamscape.

Empowered Choices

Recall a decision you made in a lucid dream, where you had complete control. Now, as you face decisions in your waking life, channel that same sense of empowerment and confidence. Remind yourself, "I have the power to shape my reality, just as I do in my dreams."

Nightly Reflection

Before sleeping, reflect on the magical moments you noted.

Ask yourself: how did perceiving the world through a dreamer's lens influence my choices, actions, and emotions today?

Reflection

After practicing this exercise for a week, consider the following:

How has viewing waking life as a lucid dream affected your overall perspective and appreciation of daily events?

Were there moments where you felt a deep sense of control and empowerment, akin to a lucid dream?

What magical moments stood out to you the most?

Notes

As you delve deeper into this exercise, you may begin to notice synchronicities or seemingly coincidental events. These are your markers that you're actively engaging with the magic of waking life.

Remember, the intention isn't to dissociate from reality but to embrace it with the same wonder, empowerment, and control that you would in a lucid dream.

Lesson 48

Sleep Spell

"Ugh, I wish I could lucid dream! Instead, I just lie here, overwhelmed with anxiety and frustration!" Sound familiar? Don't worry, we've got you, boo. Tonight, let The Quantum Field be your personal therapist. Turn those sleepless nights of staring at the ceiling into exploratory journeys through The Quantum Field. Too good to be true? Think again. This approach offers a novel way of dealing with insomnia, restlessness, and anxiety. Embrace the opportunity to transform your nightly struggles into enlightening experiences.

When anxiety and restlessness cloud your mind, they create feelings of disconnection and chaos. Picture using the breadth of the Quantum Capitalist knowledge as a propulsion into The Quantum Field in these moments. Seek insights to overcome, self-heal, and connect to higher Sectors where a serene version of yourself awaits. This version does exist.

Is your anxiety potentially a quantum wake-up call? Reflect on this—have you excessively focused on your anxiety, insomnia, and restlessness? Perhaps it's time to redirect that focus. Consider the possibility that these nighttime disturbances are signals from your environment, gentle nudges from The Quantum Field. Hush the jibber-jabber of your Matrix Self and let your Quantum Self establish a connection.

As you prepare for sleep each evening, remind yourself of the power you hold to traverse The Quantum Field. Instead of fearing the night, eagerly anticipate these explorative journeys, even if restful sleep seems elusive. The Quantum Field stands by you, as does your Quantum Self. You do not have to be frightened, agitated, or restless anymore. Indulge in this newfound peace. Allow yourself this luxury.

Embracing Quantum Capitalism entails recognizing your sleep and waking life as two sides of the same coin, both influenced by your mind. This realization can empower you to bring desired change into your life, making way for tranquility and control, replacing insomnia, restlessness, and anxiety.

Reflect on These Perspectives:

- Could your insomnia be an opportunity? Is it possible that nighttime is your sole quiet moment, the only time The Quantum Field can subtly convey your next significant move?
- Is it possible that your anxiety represents a Quantum version of you attempting to capture the attention of your Matrix self?
- Perhaps your restlessness is a materialization of potent energy within, yearning for a purposeful release.
- Is it possible that your insomnia could be a sign of a disconnect between your conscious and unconscious mind? What buried truths or unresolved conflicts might you be ignoring during your waking hours?
- Could your anxiety be a sum total of unmet needs or unfulfilled desires? Could it be that your mind is urging you to address something that you've been avoiding or postponing?
- Have you considered that your restlessness could be a physical manifestation of mental or emotional stagna-

tion? Is there a situation, relationship, or decision that you're hesitating to address?

By acknowledging these perspectives and considering these insights, you can begin to understand the underlying causes of your insomnia, anxiety, and restlessness. Rather than viewing them as purely negative experiences, see them as opportunities for self-reflection, self-improvement, and personal growth. Embrace the teachings of Quantum Capitalism and use your newfound awareness to make positive changes in your life, ultimately leading to a more fulfilled, purposeful, and tranquil existence.

Poke The Brain

Could your waking reality be mirroring your nighttime experiences? If restful sleep eludes you, is your waking life filled with similar challenges? Maybe the solution is to truly awaken to find deeper sleep.

Your Next Power Move

Sleepytime Meditation

Objective

To redirect moments of restlessness, anxiety, and insomnia into opportunities for insight by accessing The Quantum Field.

Sleep Spell

Steps

Center Yourself

Find a comfortable position, either sitting or lying down.

Take three deep breaths, inhaling calmness and exhaling any immediate tensions or worries.

Close your eyes

Visualize the Quantum Window

Picture a radiant window in front of you, your gateway to The Quantum Field. If you have a window in your room, open it. Visualize that beyond the window frame lies the vast expanse of The Quantum Field, and you are on its threshold.

Your channels of communication are wide open, baby. Lie still and either initiate a dialogue with The Quantum Field or simply allow it to whisper secrets to you. This is also a fantastic opportunity to engage with the Quantum You. Let any feelings of unrest seep into this realm, making room for insights and messages to reciprocate. Engage in this practice for moments, minutes, or even hours.

Capture and Reflect

When you feel a sense of relief or receive any insights, slowly open your eyes. Jot down these insights or feelings on a notepad, ensuring you capture the essence of what The Quantum Field communicated.

Note: remember, each time you feel restless or anxious, especially at night, consider it an invitation to tap into The Quantum Field. Over time, this simple exercise can transform these challenging moments into opportunities for profound understanding and peace.

Lesson 49

Waking Up

Cock-a-doodle-doo! Rise and shine, sunshine! The rooster's belting out its morning anthem, and a pot full of endless possibilities is brewing away. A brand-new day is upon you, and it's your cue to sparkle, Quantum Capitalist style. So, grab that coffee mug of reality, gulp down a mouthful, and let the caffeine of awareness zap you awake. Ready or not, we're embarking on a journey of transformation. Bid adieu to dreamland and embrace the world of wakefulness.

The Awakening: Life's Screenplays

As you savor your cuppa, soaking in the warmth, let's spill some tea on this thing we call "waking reality." Ever thought that, just like you're the protagonist in your dreams, you play roles in your waking hours, too? Your daily grind? Scripted. You've been reciting your moves like lines in a play.

And the most common Script? Oh, it's the classic life timeline—birth, school, work, love, marriage, house, kids. Hold up, though, I'm not bashing the storyline. But what if your soul is yearning for a plot twist?

If your Script is more "Titanic" than "La La Land," more "Psycho" than "Ferris Bueller's Day Off," maybe it's time to holler "cut!" To switch Scripts, you gotta be ready to ditch your current narrative. A mere plot twist won't cut it; you need a whole new screenplay.

Here's the deal, the Scripts are all laid out, ready, and waiting. It's like a cosmic library, every storyline you can imagine, from the mundane to the magnificent, it's all there. And guess what? You're able to choose. You get to pick your plot.

Most folks, they go for the bestsellers. You know the ones, "The 9-5 Grind," "The Suburban Dream," "The Marriage-Kids-Retirement" trilogy. Why? Because they see everyone else reading them, and they think, "Hey, that must be a good read."

But then there are the trailblazers, the mavericks, the ones who dig deep into the dusty shelves and pick out a story that speaks to their soul. It's the road less traveled, and it's a bumpy ride, but oh boy, is it worth it.

So, what's it going to be? Are you going to follow the herd, or are you going to carve out your own path? The choice is yours, and it's one of the most important decisions you'll ever make. Choose wisely.

Now, let's talk "rebellion." Being labeled a rebel is just a fancy way of saying you don't stick to the norms of the Script you've picked (consciously or subconsciously). Remember, The Matrix spotlights the chosen ones and the standard-breakers; bypassing the mediocrity and those stuck in the middle. So, are you ready to break out of your humdrum Script?

Breaking free from the norms can be unsettling; you're wired to adhere to the rules to avoid embarrassment or ostracism. But here's a magic trick: there are very few repercussions from defying the standards, other than some side-eyes from those around you. Dare to try it.

Also, striving for Script perfection and then stumbling shines a spotlight on your flaws and failures. However, if you embrace the maverick Script and celebrate your blunders as tiny triumphs and essential steps towards progress, you unshackle yourself.

This is a game-changer for creativity. Fear of failure or ridicule stops many from even starting. Give yourself permission to fail, to look silly, to be mocked. Is your ego really that delicate?

So, what's holding you back? Awaiting approval from an unknown entity? Trying to fit into a specific mold before switching Scripts? Convinced there's a workaround?

Sometimes, we initiate Script jumps ourselves. We can opt for the maverick or the rebel blueprint and find alternate routes intentionally. Other times, unexpected opportunities arise in the most surprising ways. Spotting these golden threads woven into your Sector is a skill; seizing them and riding them to success is an art, but anyone can master it.

Quantum Capitalism underscores the value of being open to unexpected ways of achieving your goals. It also highlights the need to explore different Sectors of The Quantum Field where our desires are more accessible. Imagine a highway interchange, and you're just choosing a new road. Your only limit is your imagination. Also, consider your own flexibility and ability to switch Scripts when you spot a new one. If you see a new Script today, will you give yourself the green light to jump on it?

Flex, Film, and Governance: The Arnold Schwarzenegger Script Choices

Waking Up

A shining example of an expert Script jumper would be Arnold Schwarzenegger. Yes, that's right, the Terminator himself. Arnold's life is a masterclass in Script-jumping.

Born into poverty in Austria, Arnold started his career as a professional bodybuilder, a Script that was already off the beaten path for most. He went on to win the Mr. Olympia contest a whopping seven times. Talk about flexing, right?

Our man Arnold wanted more than just muscles, though; he eventually chose the Script of a shrewd businessman and real estate mogul. In between bench presses and protein shakes, he was wheeling and dealing in the property market, a completely different Script that he managed to ace as well. Talk about multitasking, eh?

But here's where the plot thickens: instead of just pumping iron and closing deals for the rest of his life, Arnold decided to switch Scripts entirely and entered the world of Hollywood. A muscle-bound Austrian with a thick accent, becoming a leading man in Hollywood? Preposterous, right? WRONG. Arnold landed iconic roles in films such as "The Terminator," "Predator," and "Total Recall."

It wasn't smooth Script jumping, however. Arnold faced a storm of ridicule in his early acting days. Imagine a muscled-up Austrian with a tongue-twister name trying to make it in Hollywood. The auditions? A laugh fest, but not for Arnold. Critics had a field day roasting his acting chops and that accent, oh boy, that was fodder for comedians. His initial films? Box office disasters. Arnold was the punchline in a Matrix joke.

But, did he let the laughter of The Matrix drown his spirit? Nope. He wore that ridicule like a badge of honor and soldiered on. He knew that every jeer, every mocking review, every flop was just a stepping stone on his path to greatness. Arnold was on a mission to redefine the Script, and he wasn't about to let a few chuckles stand in his way.

Now, if that wasn't a plot twist enough for you, Arnold decided to throw another curveball and jumped into politics, eventually serving two terms as the Governor of California. Remember that? He faced backlash, mockery, and doubt at every turn, but did he let that stop him? Absolutely not.

Each Script change came with its own set of challenges, from language barriers to a lack of political experience, and let's not forget the "Governator" jokes. Yet, he defied the naysayers and continued to redefine himself, achieving success in multiple arenas. And let's be honest, who doesn't love a good underdog story?

So, what's stopping you from being the "Terminator" of your own life Script? If Arnold can transition from being poor and uneducated to a bodybuilder, business mogul, actor, and politician, you can certainly take the leap to a new Script too. Be your own action hero. Hasta la vista, baby!

The Money Shot: Lights, Camera, Action!

Forget the overplayed narratives and tired tropes; it's time to Script your own tale of triumph, complete with plot twists, daring leaps, and a grand finale that leaves the audience (including your bank account) on their feet, applauding. Picture Arnold Schwarzenegger, flexing his muscles against the naysayers, shifting from Scripts of poverty to bodybuilder, actor, and politician. Now, picture you, rewriting the rules of your financial game, dodging the bullets of convention, and leaping into a reality where your net worth matches your self-worth. Forget the critics; this is your show, baby!

Embrace the stumbles, chuckle at the laughs, and bask in the knowledge that every choice, every shift, is shaping a narrative of wealth, opportunity, and financial evolution that's all your own. Buckle up, the ride might be bumpy, but the destination? Oh, it's sweeter than a Hollywood ending. Ready to roll?

The Recap

Just as a new day dawns, you can start a fresh chapter in your life. When you're ready to ditch your current Script, a new one will unfurl. The question is, are you prepared to choose a new Script?

Insider Tip: the Script lets go of you, once you let go of the Script.

You must let go of your current Script with solid resolve and your commitment to jump Scripts must be unwavering. Doubts and fears can drag you back into the old Script. Think of Script-switching as a road under construction. It requires effort and occasional detours before you can cruise smoothly. Trust the process and don't micromanage the journey. Have faith in the Script-switching process and let it unfold naturally.

Poke The Brain

How often do you feel like you're on autopilot, being led by a Script that may no longer be serving you? If you could pick a new Script today, what would it be?

Your Next Power Move

Practical Exercise: Coffee Cup Clarity.

Objective: to awaken your awareness, reflect on your current life Script, and visualize the narrative you genuinely desire. This exercise harnesses the power of morning routines to help you break free from auto-pilot and curate your own story.

Materials: your morning coffee or tea, a quiet spot, and your Juggernaut Journal (optional).

Preparation

Begin by preparing your coffee or tea as you usually do. However, with each action, be fully present. From boiling the water to pouring it over your brew, immerse yourself in the process.

The Seat of Reflection

Find a quiet spot, preferably where you can get a view of the morning sky. Sit comfortably.

Sip and Identify

Hold your coffee cup with both hands, feeling its warmth. Before taking a sip, close your eyes and ask yourself, "What Script am I currently living?"

Take a sip and let the flavors, warmth, and sensation of the drink seep in as you consider the question.

Note any feelings or thoughts that arise.

The Desire Declaration

Now, ask yourself, "What Script do I wish to live in?" Visualize a day in your ideal life.

As you do this, take slow sips of your coffee, imagining each sip infusing you with the energy and intention of your desired Script.

The Daily Scene

Finally, think of one small action you can take today that aligns with your desired Script.

This could be as simple as reading a book related to a new hobby you want to pick up, making a call about a job you're interested in, or even just deciding to break a routine.

Jot or Commit

If you have your journal, write down the insights from your reflection and your chosen action for the day. If not, mentally commit to it.

Conclude and Carry On

Finish your drink with gratitude for this moment of clarity. As you proceed with your day, let the sense of intention guide you.

Tips

This exercise is not just about the major shifts but also about the subtle nuances that make your day uniquely yours.

Engage with this exercise as often as needed, especially during moments of transition or when feeling stuck.

By starting your day with this Coffee Cup Clarity exercise, you're consciously stepping out of auto-pilot and allowing yourself to choose your narrative for the day ahead.

Lesson 50

Reality Flip

Down the rabbit hole we go! In our last session, we dove headfirst into the game-changer of all game-changers: Script-jumping. That powerhouse technique is all about taking the reins of your life's overarching narrative. But today, we're zeroing in on the nitty-gritty: seizing control of those smaller, everyday scenarios instead of just standing by, passively watching life unfold. Mastering this knowledge will not only turn your reality upside down but will also arm you with a skillset that'll prove invaluable on your Script-jumping journey.

To truly navigate the scenes of life, you need to toggle between being the actor and the audience. The Quantum You, that's the audience—always vigilant, but shouldn't be taking popcorn breaks. This observer just tracks everything, like a live reviewer rating the performance on stage.

Ever had a dream where you're just dragged along with zero control? That's your actor self with no backup from the observer. When dreams "just happen," it's because the Quantum You took a nap. Wake that dude up, and you're suddenly lucid dreaming, designing the narrative. It's the exact same deal in lucid reality.

The more conscious we are, the more control we have over our life situations, the less susceptible we are to external influences, or Blackholes that can suck us into problematic Scripts. Sleepwalking through life, we become victims of our own conditioned perceptions, bound by Scripts written by external forces.

Picture yourself at work. A colleague dumps a problematic task on your desk. You feel the anxiety creeping in, the dread of the daunting task. In this moment, you've slipped into the "nap mode," falling prey to the Blackhole's Script. You've dozed off, and you're about to be led into a room of taxing work, ending up in a Sector filled with strife.

But now, let's consider another scenario. You see the same colleague approaching with the same task. This time, you shake yourself awake and decide whether this issue will become your problem or not. You program yourself to perceive whatever comes your way as a minor hiccup. You participate, but not as a pawn. You're now the witness, attentive, yet detached, understanding that you hold the power to turn a potential tragedy into something much lighter.

Here's the cheat sheet

The Quantum You is your key to awareness and control—in dreams and reality.

Be both an actor and an observer. Participate, but always have that vigilant Quantum You at your back.

Don't let external issues hypnotize you. Be aware, stay detached, and assess problems as if you're watching a play—sometimes dramatic, sometimes comedic. Choose the genre you like.

Trust the Quantum Flow. It's The Quantum Field's way of giving you mind-blowing solutions.

The Money Shot: Your Quantum Superpower

Why does this matter? The more aware you are, the less you're at the mercy of external factors, especially those pesky Blackholes that suck you away from opportunities and financial gains. Zombies are fun in scary movies, but in real life, walking around like one makes you susceptible to external influences. You're stuck in a nightmare where you're more of a prop than a protagonist. Control and choosing your narrative? Kiss that goodbye!

The Recap

In life, we often find ourselves as actors, lost in our roles, unable to see the bigger picture. But you can switch your perspective, step back, and become the audience, the observer. Quantum You is constantly vigilant, assessing soberly, but never entangled.

Poke The Brain

Recall a situation recently where you felt you were merely reacting rather than consciously acting. How would Quantum You have observed and acted in that same scenario?

Your Next Power Move

Practical Exercise: The 10 Second Pause.

Objective

To cultivate a habit of conscious decision-making by tapping into the Quantum You. This exercise helps in enhancing clarity, reducing impulsive reactions, and aligning actions with a broader understanding.

Recognize the Trigger

Whenever you're faced with a decision, problem, or a situation that demands a response, recognize this as your cue. It might be an emotional response like frustration, confusion, or excitement. Or it could be a logical challenge, like making a choice.

Initiate the Pause

As soon as you recognize your cue, mentally say "Pause."

Start your 10-second count. Close your eyes if it's feasible (especially if it helps reduce distractions).

Summon Quantum You

In these 10 seconds, envision the Quantum You, the observer part of you, stepping back from the immediate situation.

Imagine this observer looking at the bigger picture, untouched by immediate emotions and pressures.

Assess

Let the Quantum You assess the situation. Is the initial reaction or decision you are about to make in line with the larger goals and perspectives?

Would the Quantum You agree or suggest a different response?

Proceed with Intention

With the insights from Quantum You, consciously decide on your next step.

This might be the same action you were initially going to take, or it might be something different.

The key is that it's now a conscious choice.

Tips for Success

Start Small: begin with everyday decisions to get into the habit. "Should I have that third cup of coffee?" "Is now the right time to send this email?"

Set Reminders: it's easy to forget to pause, especially when starting out. Set periodic reminders on your phone or leave sticky notes in strategic locations.

Reflect: at the end of the week, review your notes. Identify patterns, shifts in perspective, and any improvements in decision outcomes or emotional responses.

Extend the Duration If Needed: while 10 seconds is a good starting point, some situations might demand a longer reflection. Adjust accordingly.

By making "The 10 Second Pause" a regular practice, you'll find that you're not only reacting less impulsively but also aligning your actions and decisions with a more holistic and grounded perspective. Over time, this can lead to improved decision-making, better emotional regulation, and a deeper understanding of yourself and your goals.

Lesson 51

Turbo Allowing

Do you see a theme playing out here? Script-jumping, flipping reality on its head by activating Quantum You mode in the heat of the moment, and not allowing yourself to be swept away by a Script that does not serve you. All of these lessons prepare us for the granddaddy of all lessons having to do with choice:

ALLOWING

Let's break it down: Script-jumping is about you choosing a new path altogether, and our last lesson was about you choosing your reactions within day-to-day scenarios. The idea of "allowing" is the absolute rocket fuel of choice, however. It signifies you declaring to your world that you are deserving of your choice—which you are—and that you are opting for a higher and better option.

The hard truth is: you will only go as far as you allow yourself to go. You can never go any further than that. And allowing is the ultimate choice; it's the ultimate navigation tool within your Quantum Capitalist journey.

So, have you been dilly-dallying long enough? If you're ready for this grand adventure, ready to flip reality on its head, activate observer mode, and stop getting swept away by a

Turbo Allowing

Script that doesn't serve you, then you must unabashedly allow yourself this option. Your life will only soar as high as you allow it to. Your potential is a beast, but it's on a leash, and you're holding the reins.

On the flip side, do you think allowing yourself to have means that your desires will magically appear? I hope not. It means you're open to the Scripts showing you the way to onboard to that Sector of Reality. Allowing also means choosing that same Script, day after day, until your desired Sector materializes. Allowing also means trashing The Matrix programming, the wants and shoulds of others, and all the corrupt data overwriting your Soul Code.

Brace yourself, because this is where Quantum Capitalism truly takes off. Allowing yourself to have is staking your claim. It's declaring to yourself and your world that you're choosing something higher, something better. The Quantum Field doesn't care who you are; it's not prejudiced. Sure, there are different paths that lead to different Sectors, some more bumpy than others, but everyone has access to all Sectors. Sure, it's a controversial fact because The Matrix wants you shackled to the idea of people trapped in their lives, wealth hoarded by a select few, and those people labeled as the big bad wolves. The truth? Once you resonate with the idea that we all have access to the same stuff, despite our challenges or distances, playing the victim isn't an option any longer.

Enough with paddling in the shallow end of your potential. Listen up, there's no cosmic rulebook saying you can't have what you want. You've been playing the role of the naysayer, telling The universe, "Wrong number, buddy. This much abundance must be for someone else." Cut the crap.

Again, allowing doesn't mean you're waiting for The Quantum Field to hand you everything on a silver platter. It means you're tuning into the Outer Power that's going to guide you to your ideal destination. You're not just window shopping; you're committing to buy. So, toss out those secondhand beliefs and societal presets. Is it time to push the "ALLOW" button on your spacecraft and fire that motherfucker up?

Is it time to jump on the Script that will take you there, and allow yourself to take that ride?

Newsflash: the people living their dreams chose themselves. They stopped asking for permission and began taking what was theirs to take. Dreaming without permitting yourself to actually catch up with those dreams is like window shopping without money—you can't buy what you're drooling over. But you have the quantum capital to allow yourself anything. So, what is your choice?

Imagine a homeless person staring longingly through a window at a festive feast unfolding inside a house. The spread is there, but for the homeless person, it seems to exist in someone else's reality. The question isn't whether they deserve the feast, but whether they can envision it in their own world. If they were invited to join the luxurious meal with wealthy players in the game of life, do you think they would come in and sit down? Common sense might suggest they aren't ready, but what if they allowed themselves to be?

Remember, The Quantum Field is a colossal treasure chest overflowing with all of life's possibilities. The moment you make a choice, the Mirror starts reflecting back all you need to see that choice to fruition. It's like ordering a meal—you pick from the menu, and the kitchen whips it up. Do you question that your meal will come out? It's no different with your other, meatier desires in life.

Where things go haywire, it's usually because we've let our fears, doubts, and insecurities eclipse our desires, and we never actually press that "allow" button. Here's a revolutionary idea: stop wrestling with The Quantum Field. Let go of the incessant need to control. Smash that "allow" button and don't look back. We will cover exactly how you will get to your destination in PHASE 3 THE EXPLORER. But for now, all you need to know is that the "allow" button needs to be activated. Otherwise, your spacecraft will remain stalled.

The Money Shot: A Quantum Slice of Wealth Pie

This is the realm of Quantum Capitalism, my friend. You don't just exist in this marketplace; you own stock. When you "allow," you're essentially telling The Universe, "I'm open for business." It's not a zero-sum game. The wealth pie isn't just for the 1%; you can grab a slice or even cook up your own. Forget the scarcity mindset; The Quantum Field is the most unbiased venture capitalist you'll ever meet.

The Recap

"Allowing" is the ultimate Quantum Capitalist tool, an unshackling of your potential that signifies to The Quantum Field your readiness for a higher and better option; it's not about waiting for desires to magically appear but an act of active co-creation, tuning into the Outer Power, staking your claim, and committing to the journey.

Poke The Brain

Think about this: what if you had no limitations, and you were free to "allow" yourself to have anything? What Sectors of your life would you revolutionize?

Your Next Power Move

The Permission Ceremony: A Quantum Key to Unlocking Choice

Objective

To harness the vastness of The Quantum Field, granting yourself the freedom to actively choose and shape your reality. The Permission Ceremony is your ritual to tap into this potential, ensuring you're not on autopilot, but deliberately carving your destiny.

Recognize the Crossroad

Every time you're faced with a decision, big or small, understand that you're at a quantum crossroad. Multiple realities beckon.

Close your eyes and take a deep breath.

Whisper to yourself, "I am at the crossroad."

Grant Quantum Permission

With the crossroad recognized:

Hold your hand over your heart.

Say aloud or in your mind, "I allow myself to choose my reality."

Visualize The Quantum Field, vast and endless, waiting for your command, ready to reflect your decision.

Embrace the Outcome

After making your choice:

Take another deep breath, releasing any doubt or fear.

Whisper, "I trust the Quantum Flow."

Believe that The Quantum Field is now adjusting, preparing to materialize your choice, and reflect it back to you.

Tips for Success

Cosmic Confidence: trust in your innate power to shape reality. The more you believe in your ability to choose, and allow yourself this luxury, the clearer the reflected reality will be.

Celebrate the Small Choices: every decision, no matter how small, is a step in shaping your reality. Celebrate them. They're the building blocks of your chosen Sector.

Regular Reflection: take time weekly to review your Juggernaut Journal. Recognize patterns, celebrate successes, and identify areas where you can grant yourself even more permission.

The Permission Ceremony isn't just an exercise; it's an act of empowerment. By recognizing your crossroads and granting yourself permission to choose, and allowing yourself to have that choice, you're taking charge of your destiny. Remember, The Quantum Field is ever-responsive. You have the power. You hold the key. Now, boldly choose YOUR reality.

Lesson 52

Cognitive Dissonance

(The Sugar in Your Spacecraft Fuel Tank)

So, you're on your spacecraft (that's your ambitious self, just in case you were wondering), all primed and ready for an interstellar voyage to your dream galaxy. But there's a snag: instead of high-octane rocket fuel, someone's poured sugar in the tank (you)! That sticky, gummy mess slowing down your ignition? Oh no! It's cognitive dissonance! It's not the sweet treat it sounds like, but a hindrance to your meteoric rise.

Ever tried to take off in a rocket with sugared-up fuel? Neither have I, but the point is, it won't go very far. Cognitive dissonance acts in a similar way. Your mind is battling between the ambition to soar to the stars and the past doubts and fears anchoring you to the ground.

Classic definition:

Cognitive dissonance is a psychological theory developed by Leon Festinger in 1957. It refers to the discomfort one feels when holding two conflicting beliefs, values, or attitudes. For example, if someone values health but smokes, they might experience discomfort because smoking is not consistent with valuing health. People are motivated to reduce this discomfort by changing one of their beliefs, values, or attitudes. In this example, the person might quit smoking or might change their belief about its health effects (e.g., convincing themselves that smoking isn't that harmful or that it has some health benefits).

So, imagine you're piloting your spacecraft, ready to cruise through the vastness of The Quantum Field. Your onboard computer relies on two main sources of information: one from your reliable, time-tested star charts and another from a state-of-the-art space probe that is mapping uncharted territories. Cognitive dissonance occurs when you receive conflicting signals from both sources. One is guiding you to stay on a well-trodden path based on past journeys, while the other is urging you to venture into the unknown. It's the unsettling feeling of spatial turbulence when the gravitational pull of the past clashes with the magnetic draw of the undiscovered. Until you reconcile these conflicting forces, your celestial voyage may be a tad wobbly or you will simply remain grounded.

Nitty-Gritty of the Gooey Mess: What to do

Identify the Sugar Crystals: before you can clean out your tank, you need to know what you're dealing with. Recognize when your brain is playing those old, grainy recordings of self-doubt.

Refine Your Fuel: take the sugar-laden thoughts, filter them, and reframe them. Find success stories, gather new evidence, and challenge those outdated beliefs.

Ditch the Sugar Suppliers: there's always that one alien—er, I mean, person—who sneaks negativity into your tank. Identify them, and create some space from their sugar supply.

Ignite with Pure Rocket Fuel: remember the "why" behind your mission. Tap into your Soul Code and don't forget to burn that good old dependable fuel that's generated by the Heart and Mind.

The Money Shot: Balancing the Brain's Portfolio

Think of your Mind as the most advanced financial portfolio. Diverse investments, some old-school blue chips and some exciting new startups. Cognitive dissonance? It's like having stocks that pull in opposite directions. Your old limiting beliefs are those sinking stocks, weighing you down. But the new choices, the belief in boundless possibilities—those are your rising stars. And every savvy investor knows: to maximize returns, you need to recognize the underperformers and bolster the ones with potential. Your wealth, your success, hinges on harmonizing this portfolio of beliefs. Time to re-evaluate, trader. Don't let that internal conflict bankrupt your future.

The Recap

Your spaceship deserves the finest fuel. Cognitive dissonance, with its sugar-laden stickiness, keeps you grounded. Cleanse the tank, refine the fuel, and set your sights on the stars.

Poke The Brain

Ever felt like your spaceship's stuck in the mud, unable to take off? What sugary thoughts are clogging up your fuel?

Your Next Power Move

Juggernaut Journal Exercise: The Cognitive Cleanse.

Objective:

To close the gap of cognitive dissonance.

Step 1: Awareness Check

Every morning, after waking up:

Close your eyes, take a deep breath, and ask yourself: "What's in my fuel today?"

Quickly jot down the first three thoughts or feelings that come up, without overthinking it.

Step 2: Reframe and Replace

For each of those thoughts or feelings:

Ask, "Is this thought sugar or pure rocket fuel?"

If it's sugar (a negative belief, doubt, or past limiting narrative):

1. Challenge it: ask yourself, "Is this thought based on fact or fiction?"
2. Reframe it: replace the negative with a positive. For example, replace "I might fail" with "Every step I take brings me closer to success."

Step 3: Nightly Reflection

Before going to bed:
Reflect on the day, think about moments you felt doubt or conflict.

Acknowledge them, then mentally toss them out of your spaceship.

Envision yourself filling up with pure, unadulterated rocket fuel, ready for tomorrow's journey.

Tips for a Smooth Ride:

1. Stay Consistent: your spaceship needs daily maintenance. Stick to this simple routine. Over time, you'll naturally begin to filter out the sugary thoughts.
2. Celebrate Small Wins: each time you successfully reframe a negative thought, give yourself a pat on the back. Remember, space voyages are made up of small, consistent moves.

The Cognitive Cleanse Exercise is a continuous process, much like maintaining your spacecraft. It's not about reaching the destination but ensuring you're always in optimal flying condition. Remember, Quantum Capitalist, your journey is as infinite as space itself. Keep your fuel pure, and the stars will always be within your reach.

Lesson 53

Hyperspace Odyssey

It's time to take a breather and reflect on the path we've traveled so far. Let's do a pre-launch check to make sure we are ready to blast off. In the next phase, you will transform into the explorer, learning all the ways to traverse The Quantum Field with everything you've already learned. It's all waiting for you. Are you ready?

Pre-Launch Checklist

- **Embrace The Mirror:** have you embraced the "Mirror World" principle, taking accountability for your thoughts, actions, and focus?
- **Boomerang:** have you recognized that the energy, thoughts, and actions you send out into The Quantum Field are what will come back to you?
- **Inner Force:** have you checked your Inner Force to prevent early burnout?
- **Quantum You in the Cockpit:** have you made sure that Quantum You is in control, making the decisions and at the control panel?
- **Matrix You in the Backseat:** have you put Matrix You in the backseat, acknowledging its presence but limiting its time at the controls?

- **Outer Power:** remember you're not entirely on your own. The Quantum Field is at your back with its infinite Outer Power.
- **Soul Code:** your ultimate map! Don't forget that!
- **Heart and Mind Synchronization:** have you synchronized your Heart and Mind, ensuring they work together in harmony to guide you through The Quantum Field?
- **Harness Your Energy:** don't forget you'll need plenty of free energy traversing The Quantum Field.
- **Materialization vs Manifestation:** have you acknowledged that what you want is out there, and instead of trying to will it to you, you must journey to it?
- **Tackle Cognitive Dissonance:** have you addressed cognitive dissonance by letting go of old, limiting beliefs that conflict with new, empowering ones, and stopped the sugar from clogging your engine?
- **Script Spotting:** remember, all the cosmic roads are there; now it's just about choosing.

Poke The Brain

With the vast expanse of knowledge now filling your database, ask yourself: With all this knowledge, what will I do and where will I go now?

Your Next Power Move

Juggernaut Journal Exercise: Astro-Reflection.

Objective:

Before diving into Phase 3, take a moment to reflect on the knowledge and lessons from this phase.

Step 1: Quick Recall

In your Juggernaut Journal, quickly jot down.

1. One belief you've changed or strengthened during this journey.
2. A moment when you felt empowered.
3. An instance where Quantum You and Matrix You had a tiff. Who won?
4. A time cognitive dissonance had you second-guessing.

Step 2: Chart Your Course

Think of one goal you want to achieve using what you've learned.

1. Write it down.
2. Underneath, note three simple actions you can start with to move toward that goal.
3. Step 3: Reflection

Take a quiet moment to think about your answers. Feel the weight and value of each.

Remember, every lesson is a building block. They're setting the foundation for your next phase in Quantum Capitalism. Onwards!

PHASE III

THE EXPLORER

Lesson 54

YOUR Project

Strap in! We are going warp drive into Phase 3. This is where you choose your next destination. We are going to go over exactly how to choose something new and then uncover exactly how to get there. Are you ready?

You've been spoon-fed ideas of what success and purpose look like for far too long. But you know what? Those generic, one-size-fits-all goals? They're outdated as last year's memes. You deserve better.

Ever felt like a fish trying to climb a tree because that's where everyone else is heading? Well, no more! It's time to splash back into your waters and find where you truly shine. You've got a compass within you—it's just buried beneath layers of expectations, fears, and societal noise.

Now, I won't sugarcoat it. You're at the precipice of a challenging journey, but every thrilling quest demands you showing up as Quantum You. Your mission? To fuse the new wisdom of Quantum Capitalism with the unbridled passion of your Heart.

You know those goosebumps you get when a piece of music resonates deep within? That's how a real goal feels—it's a symphony that moves every cell in your body, not just a random jingle playing in the background. It's that electrifying surge that courses through your veins, making every obstacle seem like child's play.

Listen, society has a crafty way of making us dance to its chaotic tunes. But you? You need to find your rhythm, your beat, the baseline that gives your life the bounce it truly deserves. A genuine goal isn't just a destination on a map; it's the magnetic North on your personal compass, an irresistible siren's song that makes every challenge, detour, and pitstop a thrilling part of the voyage.

Determining The Goal That's Right for YOU

Here's the raw deal: not every shiny object is your gold. Just because Joe next door is chasing a million Youtube subs or Jane on Instagram is flaunting her third pop-up location this year doesn't mean you should be doing the same. Your goals shouldn't be a messy scrapbook of other people's highlights.

Dig deep. what stirs the storm inside you? Is it creating art that will be remembered for eons, or is it helping one person each day connect with knowledge that will enrich their life? Maybe it's both, or neither. But remember, a goal that's authentically yours will never feel like borrowed robes. It'll fit you perfectly, tailor-made for the royalty that you are.

Picture two diverging paths, each with its own character. One stretches out smooth, paved, and bustling, hosting the masses—the Toms, Dicks, and Harrys of the world. The other, however, meanders through rugged terrain, wild and untamed, but undeniably majestic. The journey toward your true goal may not always be the easier route, yet it promises to be worth every bruise and every breathtaking vista that awaits you.

YOUR Project

Now, let's dive into the art of distinguishing whether a goal is genuinely yours or if you're simply riding the wave of societal expectations.

Consider the "Oh Hell Yes" factor

It's all about that deep-dive resonance—that exhilarating moment when your goal strikes a chord deep within, like the bass drop in your favorite song. This isn't just alignment; it's a seamless fit, like slipping into your most comfortable pair of jeans. You're not merely interested; you're on fire with a passion that rivals spontaneous human combustion. Your strengths and talents take center stage on this path. Embrace growth, like a Pokémon evolving, but with fewer battles and more self-discovery. Your goal extends beyond yourself; it's a force for positive change in the world. This isn't about external validation or impressing others; it's an intrinsic desire that comes from within.

Now, let's address the "Nah Bro" indicators

If your primary motivation for a goal is the pursuit of likes, shares, comments, or nods of approval from others, it's time to reconsider. Are you striving to keep up with the Joneses? Remember, they might be drowning in debt and misery. If the goal lacks the spark of excitement and is as thrilling as watching paint dry, it's probably not your jam. A goal that feels like a perplexing maze, leaving you lost and bewildered without any cheese at the end, is likely not your true calling. Feeling like a pressure cooker about to blow its top? It's a sign to release the steam and seek a different recipe. If the path to your goal leads you through a graveyard of your values and integrity, it's time to make a U-turn. Beware of goals that function like Blackholes, consuming positivity and leaving only darkness in their wake.

Always remember, your goal should be the wind in your sails, propelling you forward, not an anchor holding you back. Ensure it's a goal that sets your soul on fire!

Laying it down

Alright, let's cut through the fluff. Remember that band-aid I handed you in phase 1? Time to toss it, because we're diving into the cure. We're talking goals, but not just any goals—the kind that make your heart race and your brain light up like a pinball machine. This is the Quantum Capitalism playground, and it's time to dominate.

Got a goal? Good start, but crank up the volume. Put some muscle into it. And if you're still searching, lost in space, make finding that goal your number one mission. It's not just about surviving in this game; it's about owning it.

Here's the deal: when your day-to-day feels like a biblical feast, everything else just clicks into place. It's like unlocking a secret level in the game of life. You don't just deserve this level up; you've earned it. So go out there and grab life by the horns.

The Money Shot: The Soul's Spotlight

Here's the raw truth: The Quantum Field doesn't really give a fuck about generic goals. It resonates with audacity. It leans in when YOU dare to carve out a path that's authentically yours. Forget the world's checklist. Your goal? It should make your heart race, palms sweat, and be so damn magnetic that it pulls you from bed each morning with a fire in your belly.

The Recap

Navigating towards your true goal isn't about fitting in—it's about standing out, and lighting up the world with the unique flare only YOU possess.

Poke The Brain

If you could achieve one thing without the fear of judgment, failure, or societal expectations, what wild dream would you chase?

Your Next Power Move

Juggernaut Journal Exercise: Is It For Me?

Objective

Align your desires and intentions with your Quantum Capitalist mindset by discerning which goals truly resonate with both your Heart and Mind.

Step 1: Consider Your Options

Task: start by listing down every potential goal or aspiration that floats in your mind. These can be anything from professional achievements to personal milestones. Give yourself the freedom to think wide and broad. This is your chance to list down every option without judgment or inhibition. You're merely gathering the stars from the galaxy.

Step 2: Dual Resonance—Which Options Do Both Your Heart and Mind Love?

Task: review each goal you've listed. As you read each one aloud, place one hand on your heart and one on your forehead. Ask yourself, "Does this resonate with both my Heart and Mind?" Feel the answer. If it's a "yes" from both, circle that goal. If it's a mixed response, put a question mark beside it. And if it's a "no," simply cross it out.

Step 3: Quantum Quest—Setting the Intention for a New Path

Task: if you find that none of the options truly sing your tune, it's okay. Sometimes, the path isn't clear yet, and that's a part of the journey. Sit comfortably, close your eyes, and take three deep breaths. Whisper to yourself, "I set the intention to realize a new goal or discover a path that resonates with my Quantum Self."

Concluding Thoughts

Whether you've found a goal that aligns with your Heart and Mind or you've set an intention to find one, you've made significant progress. By doing this exercise, you're actively participating in shaping your reality. Revisit this exercise anytime you feel misaligned or unsure about your path.

Gone are the days of settling for the ill-fitting, second-rate crap that wasn't hand-stitched by The Quantum Field just for you.

Lesson 55

Leveling Up

Okay, we've covered the huge value of choosing a goal tailored just for you. Now, a question—ever had a goal that you let slip through your fingers because you couldn't map out every step from start to finish? Classic human move. When our brains can't connect the dots from dream to reality, we often bail, assuming it's unreachable. But not you, not anymore. With your new knowledge, you'll be bursting with a kind of quiet confidence that shifts tides because you'll know The Quantum Field is about to shower you with opportunities. And guess what? These opportunities will appear as "Doors."

Now, don't overthink it. You've set a goal, so what's next? The Quantum Field isn't playing games with you. Your opportunities will show up, no doubt about it, if you know where to look. Not convinced? Just watch. When your Heart and Mind synchronize, the world not only listens but joins the chorus.

Quick tip: leave behind that exhausting Inner Force—it's outdated. With the magic of Outer Power, you're on the fast track.

Let's say you're itching to start that trendy business downtown. What's next? Stop overthinking and stay alert. That prime spot on the corner is available—THAT'S YOUR DOOR.

An email with a fantastic business loan offer appears—ANOTHER DOOR. The Quantum Field is in a perpetual state of generating opportunities; you just need to pay attention and act when you see one that aligns with your goal. It may not happen instantly, but trust the process. With your Heart and Mind synchronized, the path will reveal itself, trust. All you need is the awareness to spot these Doors and the courage to walk through.

Meet Max

Reality One: The Overwhelmed Overthinker

A dynamo of innovative ideas and ambitions. One sunny morning, Max awoke with a sparkling vision of opening a boutique virtual reality gaming studio in his city. The surge of excitement in his chest was undeniable, and his Mind swirled with the potential impact this studio could have on local gamers and tech enthusiasts. Max could feel it in his bones; this was *the* goal. His Heart and Mind were singing in perfect harmony.

However, as the days unfurled, Max's Mind spun into overdrive. He started to obsess over every microscopic detail, from the software, the gaming equipment, marketing strategy, and finances. The how and the when consumed every moment of his waking life. Anxiety swelled like a thundercloud in his chest, and the initial burst of inspiration seemed like a distant mirage. Overwhelmed by the magnitude of it all, Max decided to abandon the idea entirely. He

convinced himself it was just too intricate, too mammoth a task. In this reality, Max's overthinking led him to lose sight of his goal, leaving him feeling defeated and deflated.

Reality Two: The Trusting Trailblazer

In this alternate reality, Max adopted a different tack. When he awoke with the idea of the virtual reality gaming studio, he felt that same initial exhilaration, the same alignment of Heart and Mind. But this time, he resolved to focus solely on the "what" and the "why," entrusting that The Quantum Field would unveil the "how" and the "when" in due course.

Max clung to his vision and the reasons behind it. He envisioned the joy his studio would bring to local gamers and the opportunity it would create for tech enthusiasts to connect and collaborate. He remained devoted to the bigger picture rather than getting mired in the minutiae. Max took the first logical step, which was to research potential locations. To his astonishment, he stumbled upon a vacant space in a bustling tech hub—his first Door. Next, he discovered a local grant for tech entrepreneurs—another Door. Each step he took, another Door materialized. Max stayed vigilant and acted when opportunities presented themselves, trusting the process every step of the way.

In this reality, Max managed to transform his dream into reality, and his virtual reality gaming studio became a resounding success, setting a precedent for others in the tech community.

In both versions of Max's reality, he initially set a goal with his Heart and Mind perfectly synchronized. However, the trajectory of his journey was determined by how he navigated the subsequent steps. In the first reality, Max succumbed to the overwhelming pressure of needing to figure everything out, leading him to abandon his goal. In the second reality, Max focused on what he was doing and why he was doing it, trusting that The Quantum Field would provide the how and the when. This trust and focus allowed him to spot the Doors that appeared along his journey, leading him to perfect success.

In conclusion, it's essential to maintain the synchronization of the Heart and Mind throughout the journey, not just in the goal-setting stage. Trusting the process and staying alert for the Doors that The Quantum Field presents will lead to a path of success, prosperity, and fulfillment. Keep your eyes peeled, your Heart open, and your Mind clear, and watch as The Quantum Field rolls out the red carpet of opportunities for you.

But wait, hotshot! Not every Door deserves your knock. It's a skill to discern the Doors that lead to green pastures from those that lead to dead ends. Aligning your Heart and Mind isn't just for setting goals, it's for navigating the path, too. If your Mind isn't feeling a Door? Walk on by. If your Heart is raising red flags? Double bolt it. But when both give the green light? Burst through like there's a million bucks waiting on the other side. Because, who knows, maybe there is.

The Money Shot: Tickets Here! Get Your Golden Tickets Here!

Hold up! This isn't just philosophical jargon. Recognizing Doors is your real, tangible shortcut to the big bucks. Every Door is a golden ticket, a step closer to the prosperity you're after. While others are lost in the maze, you've got the cheat codes. With Heart and Mind aligned, each Door you dare to step through could mean something big.

Remember, what you focus on exponentially increases in your Sector of Reality. Choosing to focus on Doors will never disappoint. So, when that intuitive light bulb flickers, and a

Door beckons, stride through with confidence. This is more than just wealth—it's your ticket to opportunities, networks, and untapped gold mines of success.

The Recap

Recognizing the right opportunities is a skill that involves aligning your Heart and Mind, not just for setting goals, but throughout the journey. Listen to your instincts and logic; if a Door doesn't feel right, shut it tight, but if both your Heart and Mind agree, walk through it, into your next Sector, like you own the joint.

Poke The Brain

Are you ready to trust the synergy of your Heart and Mind to guide you, even when the path isn't clear, and seize the Doors that could lead to your most fulfilled and successful self?

Your Next Power Move

Mental Exercise: The Door Detective.

Objective

Develop your intuitive and analytical skills to recognize genuine opportunities that align with your goal, ensuring you step through the right Doors towards success.

Visualize Your Goal

Close your eyes and vividly picture your primary objective. Embrace the feelings that arise when you achieve it. This emotional resonance will be your guiding light.

Spotting The Doors

Throughout your week, maintain a heightened awareness of potential opportunities or Doors that crop up. These can be unexpected offers, chance meetings, or even intriguing ads you come across. Jot them down in your notebook or on your phone.

Heart-Mind Analysis

Review the Doors you've noted. Ask yourself: does this resonate with the feeling of my goal? Is it logical and aligns with my strategy? Mark the Doors that get a "yes" from both your Heart and Mind.

Take Action

For each marked Door, determine one actionable step you can take within the next 48 hours.

This could be making a call, sending an email, or conducting research.

Concluding Note

As a Door Detective, your primary job is to filter out the noise and focus on genuine opportunities. With practice, you'll become adept at spotting and capitalizing on the right Doors, guiding you faster towards your objectives. Embrace your role and step confidently towards your goals.

Lesson 56

Mindfilm Mastery

The biggest tragedy? Finding your goal, having the power to sculpt reality, and just... letting it sit there. Dust collecting. Potential wasted. I'm dragging you out of that pit and into the dazzling arena of the "Mindfilm"—the exhilarating fusion of your senses, metaphysics, and yes, *magic*, where you craft your desired reality straight from your Mind's vivid palette.

The Mindfilm is not your grandma's "visualizing." That's child's play. It's diving deep, mixing quantum mechanics, your goals and the high-octane energy Outer Power of the Quantum Flow. Here's where you take the director's seat in your life movie. This is *Inception* level, where you craft layers of reality and your role in it.

Ever found yourself stuck in the "outtake scenes" of your own life? The tragedy isn't in not knowing your goal or lacking the power to shape your reality. The tragedy is in letting your masterpiece rot in the dark recesses of your mind, unseen, uncelebrated. No more! It's time to grab the director's chair, slap on that beret, and start rolling.

Welcome to Mindfilm, your ticket out of mediocrity and into the Oscar-worthy life you deserve.

Crafting your Mindfilm is not just some fancy daydreaming. It's the living, breathing storyboard of your desired location in

The Quantum Field. It's the lens through which you view the world you currently experience, bridging realities, and setting the stage where you play out your role in your current Sector. When you release into the Quantum Flow, your Mindfilm serves as the blueprint, steering the energy to serve your desires.

Now, crafting a Mindfilm isn't about just picturing a beach and a pina colada (unless that's your Oscar-winning moment, in which case, go nuts!). It's about immersing yourself in the experience as if it's already real. Engage all your senses, sensations, and even the complexities and nuances of the scenario you wish to manifest. The more detailed and dynamic your Mindfilm, the stronger its magnetic pull on the Quantum Flow, guiding it with precision and power.

Meet Daphne

For as long as Daphne could remember, movies served as an escape, a window into worlds where anything was possible. Inspired by the silver screen, Daphne dreamed of starting a production company and making films that would inspire others the same way.

Fast forward to a drab Wednesday afternoon, Daphne found herself stuck in a 9-to-5 grind, miles away from the dream. The film posters adorning the walls of Daphne's cubicle served as a constant reminder of the dream that felt more like fiction than a potential future. Each day blended into the next, a reel of monotonous scenes that nobody would want to watch.

One fateful evening, after a particularly soul-draining day at work, Daphne stumbled upon a video about the Mindfilm—a method of materializing one's desires by creating a dynamic mental imagery, infused with sensory details, sensations, and beliefs. Intrigued and desperate for a change, Daphne decided to give it a shot.

Daphne began by articulating the goal—starting a production company that made heartwarming and inspiring films. The desire was clear, but now it was time to infuse it with life. Daphne spent the entire evening meticulously crafting the Mindfilm.

In Daphne's Mindfilm, the office was alive with creativity, scripts scattered across desks, storyboards pinned on walls, and a team of passionate individuals discussing ideas animatedly. Daphne could hear the hum of conversations, the clinking of coffee mugs, and the rustling of papers. The aroma of freshly brewed coffee filled the air, mingling with the faint scent of ink and paper. Daphne could feel the smooth surface of the director's chair, the weight of a script in hand, and the warmth of a congratulatory handshake from a satisfied client.

Daphne then infused the Mindfilm with emotions. The feeling of accomplishment after wrapping up a successful shoot, the joy of a team member's breakthrough idea, the gratitude for a supportive and creative team. Finally, Daphne infused the Mindfilm with a firm belief that this scenario was not just a fantasy, but a reality waiting to materialize in The Quantum Field.

For Daphne, creating the Mindfilm was a transformative experience. It was more than just a vivid daydream; it was a dynamic design of the future. The Mindfilm served as a reminder that the dream of starting a production company was not just a fanciful desire but a potential reality.

As Daphne closed her eyes that night, the images of the Mindfilm danced across the mind's eye—a reel of scenes that held the promise of a brighter, more fulfilling future.

The Money Shot: Crafting Your Quantum Blueprint

Think of your Mindfilm as your blueprint. It's not just a fun mental exercise; it's the master plan for your blockbuster life. The more vibrant your Mindfilm, the stronger it attracts the Quantum Flow, opening up Doors to untapped opportunities and financial growth. Your Mindfilm is not just your mental playground; it's the architect of your fortune. So, what's it gonna be? Another rerun of yesterday's drama or a red-carpet premiere of your dreams?

The Recap

Your Mindfilm is more than a visualization; it's a dynamic design that dictates your reality, influences your experiences, and shapes your future. By consciously crafting and focusing on your Mindfilm, you command the Quantum Flow to align with your desires, sculpting your ultimate reality.

Poke The Brain

Reflect on your current Mindfilm. Is it a chart-topping blockbuster or a straight-to-DVD flop?

Does it cease to exist at all?

Your Next Power Move

Practical Exercise: Crafting Your Mindfilm.

The journey towards your dream starts with a single thought, and the Mindfilm is a powerful tool to help you materialize it. So, let's roll up our sleeves and get started on creating your dynamic mental imagery.

Define Your Goal

Be as specific as possible. Don't just say, "I want to be successful." Carefully consider what success looks like for you. Is it starting your own business, getting a promotion, finding a new home, or perhaps something completely different?

Detail The Scene

Imagine a scene that represents your goal being fulfilled. Picture it as vividly as possible. Who is there? What are you doing? What can you smell? What can you hear? How do you feel? The more details, the better.

Infuse Emotions and Beliefs

Lastly, infuse the scene with sensations. How would accomplishing this goal make you feel? Proud, happy, relieved, excited? Really feel those sensations. Then, infuse the scene with belief. Know that this is not just possible, but it is happening.

Remember, this is a Juggernaut Journal exercise, then a mental exercise. Put pen to paper first and let your imagination run wild. Capture the essence of your goal, the sensory details of the scene, and the sensations and beliefs that will bring it to life.

And here's a little teaser: in the next lesson, we're going to delve into what to do with this Mindfilm. Trust us, it's going to be game-changing.

Lesson 57

SectorSyncing

You've built the blockbuster of your life, scene by scene, in your Mindfilm. Now, it's showtime. Roll out the red carpet and welcome yourself to the world of SectorSyncing. No more sitting in the audience of your life, it's time to take center stage, direct the scene, and call the shots. This is not just a leap of faith; this is a quantum leap into a new reality, crafted by you, for you.

Ok, you've got your Mindfilm, but now what? It's not just a mental movie to play on a loop in your head. It's your key to SectorSyncing. Your Mindfilm is the lens through which you align and sync with your desired Sector.

When, how, and the frequency you SectorSync is a question only you can answer. You may have to experiment with various timings and methods of running your Mindfilm until you find what materializes tangible results. Whether with eyes wide open or shut, multitasking, strolling, meditating, exercising, before bedtime—my personal favorite—or any other way that suits you. You can observe your Mindfilm from a third-person perspective or first-person, from a bird's-eye view or a worm's-eye view, for an hour or a minute—as long as you're seeing results.

SectorSync in parallel to your goals. For instance, immerse yourself in activities that align with your desired role. Dream

SectorSyncing

of owning a bakery? Start baking and doing everything a baker does as frequently as possible.

The true power of SectorSyncing lies in aligning with your Quantum Self while running your Mindfilm. As you start living and feeling as if this reality is an absolute certainty, merely being previewed in your current Sector, the Quantum Flow kicks in, revealing pathways to materialization.

SectorSyncing doesn't just stretch your comfort zone; it obliterates it, making room in your current reality for your growth into the desired role. It creates a "waiting room" atmosphere in your present reality—but you're not idly waiting. You're letting The Quantum Field guide your journey to achievement.

Hold your horses, though! It's not just about visualizing your goals and hoping for the best. This is a full-throttle, pedal-to-the-metal kind of operation. The 4 Qualifiers (remember those?)? They're your nitro boost. Your supercharger. Your rocket fuel. SectorSyncing isn't just about dreaming with your eyes open (or closed); it's a full-bodied experience that demands action, thoughts aligned with your destination, and a frequency that matches your desired outcome, all underpinned by a robust Guiding Theory.

This is not a sit-back-and-let-the-Universe-do-its-thing kind of deal. This is an active, participatory process that requires your engagement. It's about being in the driver's seat, not just along for the ride. So, buckle up, buttercup, because we're about to dive deep into how you can supercharge your SectorSyncing practice with the 4 Qualifiers.

When you unify these Qualifiers in your SectorSyncing practice, you create a coherent and powerful force that can bring your desired reality into materialization quickly. It is about assembling a solid belief system, clear and focused thoughts, aligned actions, and a harmonious frequency to create a fruitful and effective practice.

Meet Shannon

Shannon is a dynamic and ambitious individual who stumbled upon the concept of Quantum Capitalism. Intrigued by its transformative potential, she decided to dive headfirst into this revolutionary approach to life. Shannon had always aspired to venture into a foreign real estate market. A dream that seemed overwhelming, given the language barriers and unfamiliarity with international market dynamics. However, she was determined to make it a reality.

Once she learned about the Mindfilm concept, Shannon devoted herself to crafting a detailed mental movie of her life as a successful international real estate investor, living in a foreign city. This wasn't just a daydream; it was a vivid visualization of her desired reality, down to the minutest detail. From conversing fluently in a foreign language to confidently closing deals and celebrating her successes, her Mindfilm was a masterpiece, a mental blockbuster that she was ready to bring to life.

Understanding that creating a Mindfilm was only part of the process, Shannon embarked on integrating SectorSyncing into her nightly routine. Every night before sleep, she would dedicate 20 minutes to running her Mindfilm, immersing herself entirely in the world she had created. It was more than just a visualization exercise; it was a visceral experience. As she closed her eyes and let her Mindfilm play, she could feel the energy of her desired Sector pulsating through her veins, could hear the buzz of conversations in a foreign tongue, could smell the scent of foreign cuisine that permeated the air.

This nightly ritual became a sacred practice for Shannon, a time when she could align with her Quantum Self and let her senses play. As she engaged in this practice, she noticed her comfort zone expanding each day, creating a "waiting room" of sorts in her current reality where she could apply the 4 Qualifiers—Guiding Theory, Thoughts, Actions, and Frequency—to her intended reality.

With a solid belief system as her foundation, thoughts aligned with her desired outcome, actions that reflected her intentions, and a frequency that resonated with her goals, Shannon found herself growing into the role she had envisioned. The act of SectorSyncing had not only widened her comfort zone but had also created a space for her Quantum Self to take action.

Today, Shannon is a thriving international real estate investor, navigating the foreign market with ease and confidence. Her journey from crafting a Mindfilm to engaging in nightly SectorSyncing

practices and applying the 4 Qualifiers to her daily life is a testament to the power of Quantum Capitalism. It's not just about dreaming with your eyes open; it's about actively participating in the creation of your own reality.

So, what's holding you back?

The Money Shot: Crafting Your Quantum Cocktail

SectorSyncing is the star ingredient of your Quantum Cocktail, a mix that's one part Qualifiers, one part Mindfilm, and a splash of SectorSyncing magic. Mastering this blend is your ticket to untapped opportunities and financial growth. Remember the 4 Qualifiers (Guiding Theory, Thoughts, Actions, Frequency)? Combine these with the power of SectorSyncing, and you've just become the cosmic bartender of the millennium. This is your concoction for a wealthier existence. Cheers!

The Recap

SectorSyncing is not about daydreaming; it's about taking an active role in creating your reality. You're the director, the actor, and the audience, all rolled into one. You've crafted your Mindfilm, now use it as a tool to align with your desired Sector, embrace the unknown, and engage with your reality on a whole new level.

Poke The Brain

How have you been SectorSyncing in your life already? Remember, we are utilizing these techniques in various ways at all times, sometimes without even knowing it. Sometimes we even do it in fatal directions. Are you prepared to evolve your current game?

Your Next Power Move

SectorSyncing Exercise

Objective

To practice engaging with your desired Sector by immersing yourself fully in your Mindfilm and taking action aligned with that reality.

Preparation

Have your Mindfilm juiced up with detail and ready and find a quiet space where you won't be disturbed.

The Exercise

Revisit Your Mindfilm. start by immersing yourself in your Mindfilm. Play it in your mind with as much detail and emotion as possible. Stay there for as long as you feel comfortable.

Take Aligned Action: identify one action that you can take today that aligns with the reality portrayed in your Mindfilm. It doesn't have to be big, but it has to be meaningful.

Reflect and Adjust: at the end of the day, reflect on your action. Did it bring you closer to your desired Sector? What can you do differently tomorrow?

Make a commitment to practice this exercise daily. The more you engage with your desired Sector, the closer you'll get to making it your reality.

Lesson 58

The Negative Mindfilm

While the sunny shores of the Positive Mindfilm have been powerful, there's a hidden cove not many dare to explore: the realm of the Negative Mindfilm. This tool, although it may initially seem counterintuitive, carries with it potent power. Now, before you start questioning my sanity, it's best to approach with an open mind. And if this concept isn't for you, feel free to ditch it, but it has proven to be an absolute game changer for me and countless others. Let's dive into a technique so powerful, it's like sneaking into the back door of The Quantum Field.

The technique...

Imagine, for a moment, your meticulously crafted Sector of Reality failing to materialize. Your Mindfilm has gone bust! That's right. Envision the unraveling of all your dedication; the deal dissipates, the much-anticipated call never comes through. Bask in this alternate reality for a brief moment, in the same immersive manner as when you positive SectorSync.

Perceive the scene, resonate with its emotions, and let it flow through your very being. By doing so, you foster resilience. Embrace the perspective: "If it works out, fantastic! If not, even better!" With unwavering trust, believe that The Quantum Field has an optimized plan in store. If one door closes, it's only because there's a grander gateway awaiting your entry in the vast Quantum Field.

Succumbing to despair when plans veer off course is detrimental to your evolution. Remember, such setbacks don't just drain your emotions, they also zap your energetic resources. And in our voyage of Quantum Capitalism, energy is our prime currency. Why frivolously expend it if there is another way?

A Negative Mindfilm acts as your secret weapon to diffuse Importance and Disproportionate Energy. By periodically engaging in this process, you ensure that you remain energetically balanced, allowing you to navigate your path with unwavering focus. But heed this advice: employ the Negative Mindfilm sparingly. Once you've run your Negative Mindfilm, promptly revert to your routine Positive Mindfilm. Master this subtle dance between the two, and watch as the reality you craft becomes more robust and resilient.

The Negative Mindfilm is not about pessimism, nor is it about self-sabotage. Instead, it's an exercise in grounding, a recalibration technique that works in direct contrast to its positive counterpart. By actively envisioning and fully feeling a scenario where your goals go astray, you do a couple of pivotal things.

Eradicate Importance: by visualizing the worst, you're stripping the event or goal of its inflated Importance. No longer is there this looming pressure of it being a make-or-break scenario. It's just one of the many outcomes, and by experiencing it mentally first, you're neutralizing its shock value.

Neutralize Disproportionate Energy: disproportionate Energy, that sneaky force that can easily spiral out of control, is reined in. By confronting your fears head-on, you dissipate the energy they carry.

Defy Gravity's Pull: ahhh, Disproportionate Energy's BFF; it's the force that pulls you back down when things get a little too hot and heavy. By preemptively experiencing the "down," you build resilience. There's no unexpected plummet; you've already felt the fall and risen back.

The Negative Mindfilm is the audacious play of prematurely accepting defeat of your goal. It's not about dwelling in misery. It's about short, controlled bursts of embracing the worst-case scenario. In the game of quantum mechanics, it's your slick counter-move.

The Comedy of Human Disappointment

Life is full of disappointments, big and small. You save up all year for a sunny tropical vacation, and what do you get? A hurricane, that's what. Or that Tinder date, the one where you were absolutely nailing the conversation, and they seemed so into you. You were already planning date number three in your head, and then...ghosted. Poof! Vanished into the digital ether. And don't even get me started on Netflix canceling your favorite show. You've been religiously following it for seven seasons, you've bought the merchandise, you've converted all your friends into fans, and then BAM! Canceled. Devastation doesn't even begin to cover it.

The Buffer of the Negative Mindfilm: it's like the superhero that swoops in to save the day, except it helps you navigate through life's disappointments with grace, humor, and resilience. Imagine having already experienced that hurricane-ridden vacation in your mind. You've felt the disappointment, the frustration, and then let it go. You've visualized that

Tinder date never texting back and felt the sting of rejection, then shrugged it off. You've even mourned the loss of your favorite show before it was canceled. If these events actually happen, you'll be prepared. If they don't, you'll be elated.

The Negative Mindfilm helps you preemptively experience and process any possible disappointments, so you can navigate your life with resilience, humor, and an unshakeable sense of self.

The Money Shot: The Power of Preemptive Defeat

In the financial world, panicking and making impulsive decisions can often lead to a downward spiral. Instead, learn from the savvy and wealthy—maintain emotional composure and have contingency plans in place. Running your Negative Mindfilm allows you to preemptively experience defeat, keeping you alert and proactive instead of reactive in crucial moments. This preemptive visualization equips you with the mental fortitude to make informed decisions, not impulsive ones. It's not about wallowing in negativity, but strategically preparing your mind for all possible outcomes. By doing so, you cultivate a mental resilience that empowers you to stay steadfast, even when the tides of fortune seem to be turning against you. Remember, it's not about the setbacks you face, but how you respond to them that ultimately defines your journey in Quantum Capitalism.

The Recap

The Negative Mindfilm is like taking a power drill to your bloated expectations, letting out the air, and then moving forward smoothly. By embracing potential failure, you're removing pressure, and in doing so, you're gaining a tactical edge in the world of Quantum Capitalism. You're playing 4D chess while everyone else is fumbling with checkers.

Poke The Brain

How different would your life be if you walked into every situation without the heavy weight of expectation? What if every outcome was just a bonus on top of your well-managed expectations?

Your Next Power Move

Mental Exercise: The Negative Mindfilm Game.

Objective

Harness the untapped power of the Negative Mindfilm to supercharge your Quantum Capitalist journey. By daring to visit potential "failures" or setbacks, you'll craft a resilient and grounded mindset that turns every situation into an opportunity for growth.

Preparation

Choose a quiet space free of distractions. This is a mental game, so you don't need any props. However, you might want your journal nearby to document insights or feelings after the exercise.

The Game

Setting the Stage:

Close your eyes. Take three deep breaths, centering yourself. Acknowledge that you're about to play a game, a mental exploration, nothing more.

Choose Your Scene

Think of a goal or an upcoming event that holds significance. It could be a business pitch, a personal project, or any endeavor where there's a desired outcome.

Diving into the Negative

Let your mind wander into the "worst-case scenario." Visualize every detail. What does this setback look like? How does it feel? What are the immediate consequences?

- Sight: identify the people, the setting, and the visual cues of this scenario.
- Sound: what are the sounds associated with this setback? Disappointed sighs, silence, or maybe even comforting words?
- Emotion: allow yourself to truly feel the disappointment, the initial shock, and perhaps even the subsequent relief.

Resilience Reboot:

Having experienced this setback, now focus on your rebound. How do you pick yourself up? What lessons do you derive? How does this setback pave the way for a new opportunity or an unforeseen path?

Anchoring Positivity:

Conclude by re-centering yourself in the present moment. Recognize that you've just played a game, a "what if" scenario. Remember, this is not a prediction but rather a resilience-building exercise. Anchor yourself in the belief that, regardless of outcome, you're equipped to handle and grow from it.

Re-emerging:

Slowly open your eyes, coming back to your current reality. Acknowledge the strength and grounding you've just cultivated.

Post Game Reflection:

Take a moment to document any new insights, feelings, or revelations you've had during the exercise. Do you feel more prepared moving forward towards a goal or intention?

As long as you keep your 4 Qualifiers aligned with the Positive Mindfilm, your Negative Mindfilm cannot harm your progress when used in moderation. So, go ahead! Embrace defeat, failure, and disappointment for a few moments and feel the relief. It's all good.

Lesson 59

Transport Links

Alright, so you've got your goal in sight (or one is hurtling its way towards you), your Mindfilm is masterfully designed, your SectorSyncing practice is on point, and you've even mastered the art of maximizing benefits from the Negative Mindfilm. But does your goal still seem overwhelming? Do pangs of anxiety hit you when you think of navigating through all the steps from point A to Z? Well, fret not. We've got the solution right here! Step right up and get your solutions, hot and ready!

Transport Links, in Quantum Capitalism, represent the successive steps or stages you take towards realizing your ultimate goal. Picture them as individual links of a chain, your goal being at one end and you at the other. But instead of worrying about every link all at once, you simply focus your mind on one link at a time, pulling yourself along. Every achievement, every lesson, and every step are links that align you closer with your goal.

Imagine trying to get from your couch to a marathon finish line without any prep. Ouch! Skipping stages of progression (attempting to jump several Transport Links at once) may leave you bewildered at why things have fallen apart on the way to your goal, missing out on essential experiences and learnings that prepare you for the bigger game. Transport

Links ensure you have the resilience, the knowledge, and the stamina to embrace your goals when you get there. They also make the path to the goal less of a question of "will this work?" Transport Links almost ensure arrival if you follow the simple formula here.

Transport Link Formula for Success

1. Draw a Chain

Sketch a chain with a number of links, and place your goal at the end.

2. Fill in Known Links

Fill in as many links as you can with the significant milestones you know are needed to reach your goal. Don't worry about the links you don't know yet; they will present themselves as you move along.

3. Be Open to Change

Be prepared to shift links around, add more links, or remove links as the situation evolves.

Sometimes the path may reveal a shortcut or a necessary detour.

4. Focus on the First Link

With your chain built out as much as possible, turn your attention to the first link and focus only on that. Put all your energy into completing this first step.

5. Cherish Each Link

As you progress, cherish each link as a significant accomplishment and an essential part of your journey.

Transport Links

Pro-tip:

Focus on one link at a time. Don't worry about the entire journey, just focus on the link right in front of you. Trust that the next link will reveal itself when the time is right. One link at a time.

Remember, each step, each link, is a crucial part of your journey towards realizing your ultimate goal. Treat them as such, and success is just a matter of time.

Meet Sofia

You might've seen Sofia on the covers of those glossy business magazines last month, hailed as the "Quantum Queen of Condos." But rewind five years, and Sofia was sleeping on friends' couches, her pockets filled with dreams but not a dime to her name.

Did she just stumble on a real estate goldmine overnight? Nah. But Sofia also knew it was going to take some Quantum Capitalist-ing to get there. Juiced up with her goal in mind, Sophia kicked into gear, wrote her goal down, and began to utilize Transport Links like a pro.

Link 1: Sofia started small. She picked up books, podcasts, anything that could teach her about the real estate world. Her initial goal? Grasp the basics without her eyes glazing over.

Link 2: with newfound knowledge, she interned at a real estate firm. Days filled with fetching coffee? Sure. But also, picking up golden nuggets of insider wisdom.

Link 3: Sofia saved every penny and made her first move: a rundown studio apartment. Not exactly a penthouse, but it was hers. She rolled up her sleeves, renovated it, and flipped it for a neat profit.

Link 4: rinse and repeat. With every property, Sofia grew bolder, eyeing bigger spaces, better neighborhoods. Her reputation grew, too.

Fast-forward to today, and Sofia owns a skyline's worth of apartments in the city. How? She embraced The Quantum Field, realizing dreams aren't about huge leaps but mastering each and every Transport Link.

Think you can't turn couch crumbs into a condo empire? Sofia begs to differ. Go link by link. It's the Quantum way.

The Money Shot: Your Quantum Passport Anywhere

Transport Links aren't your everyday self-help nonsense; they're your chain pulling you along. Think of them as assets. Each Link you conquer? That's equity in the bank of life. Play your cards right, and by the end, you're not just rich in experience but rolling in the real deal.

The Recap

In this lesson, we explored the idea of Transport Links, a strategic approach to breaking down a goal into manageable, sequential steps or stages. This approach not only simplifies the path to achieving your goal but also maximizes your chances of success by focusing your energy and attention on one link at a time.

Poke The Brain

Think back. That achievement you're so proud of—can you spot the links? Did they catch you off guard or did you dance through them?

Your Next Power Move

Creative Exercise: Chart Your Course.

Materials Needed:

- Whiteboard
- Colored Markers

Step 1: Set Your Goal

Clearly define your goal and write it at one end of the whiteboard.

Step 2: Break it Down

Break your goal down into smaller, more manageable milestones, or "Links." Each one is a step towards your ultimate goal.

Step 3: Color Code

Assign a different color to each Link, the goal, and a separate area for uncertain Links.

Step 4: Draw Your Chain

With your colored markers, draw a chain across the whiteboard, making each Link a different milestone towards your goal. Remember, it's okay if you don't know all the steps yet. Just fill in the ones that are known and leave spaces for those yet to be discovered.

Step 5: Uncertain Links

In the separate area you've assigned, jot down any Links that you're uncertain about where to place or any that might be subject to change. This space is dynamic and meant to evolve as you progress towards your goal.

Step 6: Stay Flexible

Be open to the chain evolving. You might need to add Links, remove some, or even shift them around as you progress and as situations change.

Step 7: Focus

Start working on the first Link of your chain. Focus all your energy and attention on this single step until it's complete. Then, move onto the next Link.

Remember to hang your whiteboard somewhere visible so you can see your chain every day.

This will serve as a constant reminder of your path and the progress you are making.

As you work through each Link, remember to cherish each one. They are all vital steps in your journey towards your ultimate goal.

Lesson 60

Triple-Threat You

Oh, snap! Feel that tingling? That's you leveling up! You're diving into some seriously transformative stuff here. If you're all geared up to bag that massive goal, give your life a 180, or just jazz up your current Sector, you are on the right track. You've unlocked a secret level: The Triple Threat. What's that? It's someone who embraces top tier self-development, leverages The Quantum Field in all aspects of life, and catapults themselves towards their goal, all at the same time. If you're hitting all three, life's about to get a whole lot sweeter.

Still challenged to unlock this level? There's no magic wand. This is all about you and your intention to work this knowledge. Lean in. It won't happen while you're Netflix-and-chilling. Goals are achieved quickest when you start operating as Triple-Threat you. So, keep yourself tuned to the frequency of pure magic, shaking off stagnation and degradation while staying focused on finding your life purpose, your true goal, marching towards it. Even if you're unsure of your purpose, your Quantum Self knows. Be patient, while holding the intention.

Need a little reminder?

Stop the Shortcoming Syndrome: those "imperfections" you mull over? They're what make you. Stop focusing on what's lacking. Instead, channel your energy into growth. Turn away from degradation, and face magnificence head-on.

Remember: you're either evolving or eroding. Never both.

Be a Seeker, Not a Sleeper: still feeling blah about life? It's 'cause you're missing a destination. The world is filled with bystanders, folks yawning their way through life. Don't be that. Have a goal, an ambition that makes you jump out of bed. If the sight outside your window doesn't excite you, you're looking in the wrong direction. Change the view or change the window!

Quantum Leap Like a Motherf*****: embrace the Quantum You. How? Invest in yourself. When you fine-tune yourself, three things happen. You break free from stagnation, you begin evolving, and you realize or start achieving your grander vision. It's real.

Think of yourself as a software. Constantly update, upgrade, and reboot. By actively Syncing with Quantum You, you not only evolve but also light up the path to that thing that is going to light your Heart up. Look, there's no magic button. There's time in, commitment, and the merging to your Quantum Self. And yes, it's not all rosy. But stagnation? It's a swamp. Are you a swamp creature?

Meet Rachel

Rachel, our go-getter, always considered herself the ambitious type. Top of her class, nailed a fantastic job, and was living what society deemed "the dream." Yet, she found herself stuck in a Groundhog Day scenario, minus the humor. A loop of checkboxes yet no sense of direction. The quintessential high-achiever, who, despite ticking all those boxes, felt she was just part of a never-ending cycle, eroding away her dynamite potential.

Enter Quantum Capitalism. A friend recommended it, and curious cat Rachel decided to dive into its pages. Eureka! It hit her like a ton of bricks; she was miles away from operating as a Triple Threat. She'd been riding the self-development train but totally out of sync with The Quantum Field and neglecting her true goal.

Fired up by her revelation, Rachel went full throttle. She first identified her passion and set a goal that made her heart do somersaults. Time to start her own business, a dream she'd parked in the "someday" garage.

Clear goal in sight, Rachel became a Quantum Field supernova and actively worked toward her ambition. She invested in herself like a queen—self-development workshops, an improved diet and workout routine, and a new level of luxurious self-care. Plus, she began to really see her world through this new Quantum Capitalist worldview.

As Rachel took action like a pro and embraced her Quantum Self, The Quantum Field reciprocated. Opportunities knocked, she connected with like-minded souls, and her fulfillment meter was off the charts. No more yawning bystander, she was the captain of her ship, steering towards her destiny.

Fast forward, and Rachel's business was booming. Making a difference, building wealth, and living her grand vision. Triple-Threat mode activated, and life was sweeter than a bowl of cherries.

Looking back, Rachel realized the golden ticket was connecting with her Quantum Self and the relentless pursuit of her goal. She shook off societal weights, zeroed in on what set her heart on fire, and supercharged her personal development. A trifecta of awesomeness that was unbeatable.

Rachel's journey is a wake-up call for all of us. We've got the potential to be a Triple Threat. It starts with finding your purpose, embracing The Quantum Field, and going all in towards your goal. So, ditch the swamp creature vibe; get moving, and Sector jump.

The Money Shot: Develop or Deteriorate

Here's the golden nugget: in the world of finance, economics, and opportunity, the same principles apply. You either move with the market, adapting, learning, and growing, or you stagnate and miss out. When you're in tune with Quantum You, making money decisions, spotting opportunities, and building wealth becomes second nature. It's the same energy; channel it.

The Recap

You're Quantum, baby. Shed societal weights, zero in on your life, what gets your heart LIT, and turbocharge your personal development. It's a trifecta that's unbeatable.

Poke The Brain

Think of the last time you felt truly alive, charged, and unstoppable. What were you doing? How can you harness that energy and make it your everyday vibe?

Your Next Power Move

Juggernaut Journal Exercise: Triple-Threat Transformation.

Unlock your potential and keep your progress in check with this straightforward daily journaling exercise. Designed to align with your aspirations, it sharpens focus, boosts self-awareness, and propels action.

1. Knowledge Nugget

Purpose: cultivate a habit of lifelong learning and recognize daily growth.

How to do it:

- Reflect on your day.
- Identify and jot down one significant thing you've learned. It could be a fact, a self-realization, an insight into your work, or even understanding someone else's perspective.
- Over time, these nuggets of knowledge compound into wisdom.

2. Spotlight Self-Reflection

Purpose: maintain an ever-evolving mindset by spotting areas for improvement.

How to do it:

- Engage in a few moments of introspection.
- Acknowledge one area or aspect of yourself or your skill set that you believe needs refining or enhancement.
- By shining a spotlight on this area daily, you foster an environment of self-improvement, ensuring you're always in growth mode.

3. Goal Getter

Purpose: ensure consistent forward momentum towards your aspirations.

How to do it:

- Think about your bigger picture, your ultimate goal.
- Note down one tangible step you've taken towards this goal during the day. Whether it's a task you've accomplished, a connection you've made, or even just a relevant thought or idea that has sprung up.
- Witnessing daily progress is a powerful motivator, pushing you closer to your aspirations.

Recap

This Juggernaut Journal Exercise is your daily passport to personal evolution. By breaking down growth into these three actionable checkpoints, you stay aligned with your Quantum You, ensuring you're not just moving but evolving. Challenge yourself to maintain this journal for a month and observe the quantum leaps in your progress.

Lesson 61

The Labyrinth

Caught in an intricate maze of insecurities and self-doubt? Don't fret! Quantum Capitalism is here to light your path, sprinkling some magic to help you dance through the maze of self-doubt. Let's twist and turn our way to the exit.

Every goal you've set is like setting out to retrieve something precious. But guess what's standing between you and your dreams? It's not some external force or its minions; it's your own inner demons of self-doubt and insecurity.

Just as an intricate maze seemingly shifts and changes, so does the weight of your insecurity. The tighter you grip, the more complex your journey becomes. It's like you're racing against time, and the clock keeps ticking.

Those swirling thoughts? They disorient you even more, drowning you with negativity, while energy vampires hover, feasting on your sinking spirit. Do you want to be trapped here forever?

In the grand scheme of Matrix mazes, it's not the meticulous mapping or perfecting of every trait that leads you to the exit. Quite the contrary. There are two magic keys that unlock these winding paths:

Dissolving the Illusion of Importance: think back to a time in your life where everything seemed utterly disorienting.

That's what plays out every time you inflate the Importance of your every flaw and solely focus on your idiosyncrasies. It's time to see those barriers for what they are: mere illusions. Because, newsflash, the mazes in life are built by your over-inflated sense of Importance. Drop that weight and watch the walls dissolve. Magic? Nope. Just a change in perspective.

Dancing Through The Maze: waiting for perfection to act? Ha! You'll likely wait forever—prepare to be endlessly frustrated. Every moment you stand still, gazing at your own reflection, focusing on ways you perceive yourself inferior, the maze grows a little more complicated. Dance your dance, jump into the fray, face those inner demons, and turn things upside down. Move forward regardless of what you feel is keeping you back. Remember, these illusions have no actual power over you.

While the maze of life is fraught with riddles and misdirections, the key to navigating it isn't in waiting for the stars to align perfectly. It's in realizing that every twist, every turn, every setback, is just a part of your story. So, embrace your power, tell those self-doubts "You have no power over me!" and walk out with your head held high. Because at the end of this maze, you're the hero, not the lost child.

Meet Renee

Once upon a time, Renee harbored a passion that burned brighter than a supernova, yet her voice was muted by daunting shyness. She longed to step onto the world stage, but the spotlight of public speaking, especially on a platform as intimidating as YouTube, seemed like an insurmountable challenge. Alone in her room, she faced the mirror, her reflection starkly illuminating her fears. The words she yearned to speak were tangled in a dance of stuttering and self-doubt.

Facing the camera lens felt like staring into an abyss. Her heart raced uncontrollably, her mind clouded by the imagined judgments of unseen viewers. The red record button loomed as a formidable barrier to her dreams.

Then came a pivotal moment: Renee thought, "Who the hell cares if people laugh?" and "What does it really matter if I make a fool of myself?" She decided right then and there that the Importance she had attributed to her image, how people would perceive her, and all the ways she felt inadequate was meaningless. Renee made the decision to cut the crap, venture into the unknown, and film her first video. This journey was fraught with inner turmoil—her stomach churned, her heart echoed her fears with each thudding beat, but deep down, she knew it was all just her Matrix Self throwing shade at her. She stepped into this uncharted territory, each recorded second a step into a realm shadowed by her anxieties, but her Quantum Self had her back. "Keep going," she could hear the whisper.

She persevered. The video, raw and genuine, was uploaded to YouTube. Something magical then unfolded. The viewers, whom she had feared would be harsh and unforgiving, greeted her with warmth and encouragement. Her audience, far from being critical, became her support system, spurring her on.

Empowered by this surprising reception, Renee embarked on a 30-day odyssey, challenging herself to confront her fears daily, camera in hand. She committed to filming a video every day, come hell or high water, despite the storm of internal feedback. Each day was a battle fought, each video a small triumph. There were moments of extreme frustration to the point of tears, a steep learning curve, a refinement of skills never used, and an epic overhaul of a scared part of herself she never thought she could overcome. Gradually, the labyrinth of self-doubt that had imprisoned her began to crumble.

Fast forward to today, and Renee stands as a YouTube sensation, her voice resonating with nearly 30,000 followers. Her channel boasts an astonishing 1.5 million watched hours. Fathom that. Her journey has transformed her, turning her crippling fear of the camera into a beacon of inspiration and a personal miracle to counter any creeping self-doubt. The revenue from her channel represents more than financial gain; it symbolizes her triumph over the internal mazes that had once held her captive.

Renee's story is a powerful testament to the might of stepping forward despite fears and self-doubt. It's a tale of transformation, showing how consistently facing our fears can dissolve

the barriers we erect around our potential. Her journey from paralysis to empowerment lights the way for all who are lost in their own mazes of doubt.

So here's to you, embarking on that courageous journey. May you find the strength to face your fears, turn on your camera, and dance through the labyrinth of self-doubt. May you, like Renee, discover that in vulnerability lies the power to transform both self and reality.

The Money Shot: Dissolving Walls

In the enchanting realm of wealth and opportunity, the maze symbolizes the intricate web of beliefs and fears we hold about money. Just as the goal seems distant and unattainable, so too might prosperity feel out of reach. It's not the gold or the glittering treasures that elude us, but the doubt-infested beliefs we harbor about our worthiness and capability. When we let our self-doubt shape our monetary decisions, we inadvertently hand our inner demons the keys to our treasury. However, by recognizing that the walls of financial constraints are often self-imposed, we can dance our way to opportunities and success. Money isn't just currency; it's a story we tell ourselves. Rewrite your tale.

The Recap

From the whimsical corridors of indecision to the deceptive allure of negativity, we've laid it out: the maze of self-doubt is self-constructed. By living with Importance over your shortcomings, you're trapping yourself. But by taking action regardless, by dancing through the maze instead of fearing it, you wield the power to dissolve its very structure.

Poke The Brain

Are you letting your inner demons dictate your path or are you ready to defy their games and move forward regardless?

Your Next Power Move

Challenge: Step into the Unknown.

Inspired by Renee's journey? It's time for your own. Identify something that scares you, something you feel unprepared for. It doesn't have to be a giant leap; small, consistent steps can lead to significant changes.

In your Juggernaut Journal, list the top three fears holding you back. Lower the volume on these fears, and take that first step towards your goal. It's not about having all the answers or being perfect from the get-go. It's about embracing the imperfect journey and learning as you go.

This isn't just a challenge; it's an invitation to explore uncharted territories of your potential. Who knows, you might just find a new passion, skill, or even a hidden talent waiting to be unleashed.

Embrace the uncertainty, trust the process, and remember—every great journey begins with a single, brave step.

May the force be with you.

Lesson 62

Navigating NPCs (Non-Playing Characters) & Narcissists

Alright, you've smacked down that inner Debbie Downer and given a solid "no thanks" to the sun-slapper in your psyche. High five! But don't start the victory dance just yet. As we're about to rip off this next Band-Aid, there are peeps in your life who, plot twist, don't exactly want to see you rise. Say what now? Yep, when we marinate in self-doubt and focus on our not-so-awesome traits, we often end up in a conga line with others who amplify our not-so-great beliefs about ourselves. As you start to ditch this self-inflicted baggage, it's time for a relationship spring clean. Today, we're diving deep, challenging those relationships, and reclaiming our damn thrones. Let's do the thing!

Engaged? Check. Confronted? Check. Time to dive into the nitty-gritty and rise like the phoenix you are.

Ever considered the characters in your own life story? You know, the sidekicks, the villains, the cheerleaders? It's a wild thought, but your circle might just be filled with NPCs (non-playing characters) and not genuine stakeholders. And trust me, in the game of life, these characters determine your power-ups or setbacks.

Life ain't a solo game. It's an open-world adventure, filled with allies and foes. But here's where things get spicy. Some people around you are NPCs—background characters that might be keeping your avatar from reaching the next level. Who are the classic culprits? Let's break it down.

The Narcissist: someone who thinks they're the sun and you're just a planet revolving around them? Yup, that's them. They'll craft your reality, expecting you to play by their rules. Don't. You're no satellite; you're a star in your own right. Time to use the energy they are siphoning for your own good.

The Artificial Satellite: no ambition, no direction, just dead weight. Sounds familiar? They're like gum stuck to your shoe; everywhere you go, they're right there, not contributing, just... being. Maybe they tell you what you want to hear, but are they just an artificial satellite?

The Crash and Burner: evolution or degradation, baby. There's no in-between. Got someone spiraling downwards to Sector #1 and trying to make you their parachute or use you to soften the impact? Gross. Time to cut the cords.

Bottom line: you're the sum of your top three contacts. So, do some quick math. Liking what you're adding up to?

The Money Shot: Balancing the Ledger

Listen up: in the grand bazaar of life, your network is your net worth. The people around you either grease the wheels to the bank or slam the vault shut. When you're shackled by the insecurities and whims of NPCs, you're trading pure gold opportunities for mere copper pennies. Remember, time and life force are limited reserves. Are you squandering your resources? Prosperity isn't about hustling; it's about smart alliances, empowering partnerships, and surrounding yourself with visionaries. You could either let dead weight drag you into financial quicksand or cut ties, soar, and watch as the riches—both tangible and intangible—flow effortlessly into your treasury. Time to make your circle a golden one. After all, you're here to mint coins, not lose them.

The Recap

Navigating life requires discerning the characters in your story. From narcissists to clingers to crash and burners, knowing who to team up with and who to steer clear of makes all the difference. Remember, it's your game. Play it right.

Poke The Brain

Think of the three closest people in your life right now. Are they co-op players boosting your game or NPCs dragging your storyline?

Your Next Power Move

Juggernaut Journal & Practical Exercise: Level Up Your Circle.

Objective: the goal of this exercise is to introspectively analyze the characters that are active in your life. By understanding their roles, you can strategize your interactions and build a network that propels you forward, both personally and professionally.

1. Character Inventory:

- **List Down:** make a list of the top ten people you interact with most frequently.

- **Tag Them:** now, label each person with a category: Narcissist, Artificial Satellite, Crash and Burner, or Co-op Player (someone who genuinely supports and uplifts you).

2. Power Interactions:

- **Frequency Analysis:** next to each name, write down how often you interact with them (daily, weekly, monthly).
- **Quality Time:** mark whether these interactions are positive, negative, or neutral in terms of their impact on your emotional and mental well-being.

3. Reflect on Reciprocity:

- **Energy Check:** beside each person, write down how you feel after interacting with them. Drained? Energized? Indifferent?
- **Value Offered:** what does this individual bring to your life? Is it advice, resources, perspective, or maybe just stress?

4. Re-evaluate & Rebuild:

Priority Check: based on your findings, prioritize these individuals. Who adds value to your life?

Who sucks the energy out of you?

Action Plan: now, create a game plan. Maybe you need to have a heart-to-heart with a friend, or perhaps it's time to distance yourself from a negative influence. Maybe it's time to strengthen a bond that positively impacts your life.

Execute: take action. Adjust your interactions and invest your time and energy where it will yield the most positive return.

5. Reflect & Reset:

Mirror, Mirror: take a look at yourself. What role do you play in other people's lives? Are you an MVP, or are you a Puppet Master? Be honest and make the necessary changes.

Affirm: acknowledge the progress you've made and affirm your commitment to fostering positive relationships moving forward.

6. Rinse & Repeat:

Remember, people evolve, and so will your relationships. This exercise isn't a one-time deal.

Make it a habit to regularly check in on your relationships and adjust accordingly.

Closing Thoughts

You've just taken a significant step towards optimizing your life. Remember, your network is a reflection of you. Surround yourself with those who inspire you, challenge you, and make you a better version of yourself. It's not about the quantity of friends, but the quality. You're not just building a network; you're building a power circle.

Lesson 63

Stealth Mode

Alright, you've identified some relationships that need a tune-up. But, what about the human wrecking balls that smash into your Sector, yanking you from your orbit while you're in full on upper Sector power drive? We're about to confront the chaos creators—the Meteors! You know, those folks in your Sector that collide with you like dark matter? Unpredictable, disruptive, yanking you off course. Hang tight; we're going space-age on this one, teaching you to zig-zag through the Meteor people and engage full-on Stealth Mode!

First off, what's a Meteor person? Picture this: you're cruising through space and time, enjoying the beauty of the stars (or handling your life like a pro Quantum Capitalist), when suddenly dark matter (or in this case, a demanding, drama-loving person) throws you off your trajectory. These Meteors can pop up anywhere—at work, at home, or even in the digital realm as you're building your empire and nailing those Transport Links like a metaphysical maestro.

Now, here's the catch. These Meteors have this wicked talent to trap your thoughts in a cycle that revolves entirely around something other than where you want to maintain focus. They distract you, steal your attention, and hold your brain captive in their gravity. Are you ready to master the art of dodging these Meteors, tuning into different frequencies, and soaring high in The Quantum Field?

Next time you spot a Meteor headed your way, don't panic. Activate your Stealth Mode. Keep things in perspective. Stay cool, calm, collected. Engage, but don't get emotionally tethered. Remember, Meteors thrive on pulling you into their gravitational pull of chaos. Counteract with detachment, observe from the outside. Problems thrown by Meteors are never as complex as they seem. There's always a simple solution lurking around.

Face a challenge with a Meteor? Shift your attitude. Stay empty. Dive deep into that massive quantum database—your subconscious. Let go, mute Matrix You, and harness the power of intuitive thinking, powerful, unbothered you. You might surprise yourself with a solution so simple; you'd wonder why you never saw it before. Keep practicing this, and soon, dodging Meteors will become your second nature.

Meet Riley

A modern-day maven, teeming with ambition, fueled by a desire for success, and, not to forget, a sucker for space analogies. One morning, while sipping a galaxy-themed smoothie, an epiphany struck like a shooting star—she had to dodge the Meteors in her life, and fast, as her energy levels were at critical levels and a red light was flashing internally!

Fresh off a lesson about navigating the chaos creators, Riley felt a jolt of determination. Today, she would dodge those Meteors like an astronaut navigating dark matter with skillful precision.

First on the agenda was the daily team huddle. As the Zoom call lit up, Darren, the office chaos-creator-in-chief, started his usual spiel. This guy could turn a cup of coffee into a crisis. But today, Riley was ready. She engaged with Darren's dramatics but didn't let it get under her skin. She nodded, offered constructive feedback, but remained an observer, not a participant, in the chaos. What once seemed like a vast wormhole of doom suddenly felt like a navigable Meteor.

Feeling empowered, Riley geared up for her next task—a call with a notoriously demanding client. This client had a talent for making it seem as though the Earth was about to be incinerated by the Sun. But Riley, armed with her new perspective, saw the challenge as an opportunity, not an obstacle. She tapped into her subconscious, silenced her inner critic, and harnessed her intuitive thinking. As a result, she presented solutions so straightforward and effective that even the client was left impressed.

As the day unfolded, Riley encountered various forms of Meteors—a passive-aggressive email from a supplier, a vague text from a friend, and unsolicited advice from an internet stranger. But by maintaining her cool and keeping things in perspective, she dodged them all with grace. She realized that the problems Meteors throw your way are never as complicated as they seem. There's always a straightforward solution waiting to be discovered.

For the grand finale, the ultimate challenge arose. As Riley drove home from the gym that evening, she received a phone call from the mother of all Meteors—Meteor Mom—a call that, in the past, would surely have spiraled into her spacecraft engine catching fire again. But not this time. Riley took a deep breath and activated Stealth Mode. She put the call on speakerphone and engaged only partially in the conversation, instead focusing her attention on the beauty of her surroundings as she navigated home, her mind filled with thoughts of the healthy meal she was excited to prepare, and the soothing hot bath that awaited her later. By the time the call ended, Riley's energy levels had only taken a minor hit, nothing that a nice meal and a hot bath couldn't revitalize.

By the end of the day, as she soaked in her tub, Riley felt invincible. She realized that every moment spent dodging a Meteor was energy reserved for her own ventures. By not letting the chaos get to her, she tapped into a deeply nourishing sense of empowerment that helped her to feel in control of her Sector. Avoiding Meteors wasn't just about inner peace—it was about connecting yet another powerful tool to navigate life. Riley's ability to sidestep the drama and keep her eyes on the prize was not only liberating but long term, incredibly rewarding.

The Money Shot: Cash Over Chaos

Remember, every time you successfully dodge a Meteor is energy reserved to fuel dreams. In the grand scheme of life and success, being unbothered by these Meteors means more energetic resources for opportunities, growth, and, yes, financial prosperity. Evading Meteors isn't just about peace—it's about prosperity. Your ability to sidestep their drama and keep your eyes on the prize, will literally pay off!

The Recap

Meteor people? They're the drama magnets trying to pull you into their chaos. But you've got the tools: go into Stealth Mode, detach, keep problems in perspective, and tap into your intuitive problem-solving. By mastering these, you're not just surviving, you're thriving in The Quantum Field.

Poke The Brain

When was the last time a Meteor person tried to throw you off course? How could going into Stealth Mode have changed the outcome?

Your Next Power Move

Practical Exercise: Spot the Meteor.

The objective of this practical exercise is to equip you with a simple, three-step approach to quickly identify and navigate encounters with Meteor individuals. By following these steps, you'll be better prepared to maintain your focus and composure in the midst of chaos.

Observation and Recognition

- **Awareness Check:** regularly assess your surroundings and interactions. Notice if someone's behavior seems disruptive, dramatic, or attention-seeking.
- **Energy Meter:** pay attention to your own energy levels. If you suddenly feel drained, overwhelmed, or off-center after an interaction, there might be a Meteor in your vicinity.
- **Patterns:** look for consistent patterns of behavior. If someone tends to bring chaos or negativity to your interactions, it's likely they're a Meteor.

Detachment and Perspective Shift

- **Breathe and Pause:** when you sense a Meteor, take a moment to breathe deeply. This brief pause gives you time to gather your thoughts and emotions.

- **Zoom Out:** mentally step back from the situation. Imagine viewing it from a distance, as if you're an observer. This helps you detach from immediate emotional reactions.
- **Perspective Check:** ask yourself if the situation is as significant as it initially seems. Will it matter in the bigger picture of your goals and aspirations?

Redirect and Refocus

- **Stealth Mode Activation:** imagine yourself activating your Stealth Mode shield. This visual metaphor helps you mentally shield yourself from the chaos and drama.
- **Positive Pivot:** redirect the conversation or interaction towards a more positive topic. Gently steer away from the disruptive topic or behavior.
- **Maintain Your Path:** keep your focus on your own goals and objectives. Politely disengage from drama or negativity, and remind yourself that you're on a mission to achieve greater things.

End Note

By following these three steps, you'll become skilled at spotting Meteor individuals and smoothly navigating through their disruptions. Remember, you have the power to choose how much influence these individuals have over your thoughts and emotions. By detaching, refocusing, and staying true to your course, you'll maintain your momentum toward success and prosperity. Practice this approach regularly to strengthen your ability to identify and manage chaotic encounters.

Lesson 64

Cracks in The Matrix

The real game-changer in engaging with reality with a heightened state of awareness is the broader perspective you gain on your current circumstances. When you're not sidetracked by Meteors, embroiled in negative interactions with people in your life, or tangled up in your own internal dialogue due to the discord present in your layer of reality, you acquire a superpower: the ability to spot glitches and cracks within The Matrix. Ever noticed that momentary blip in the mundane, a split-second glitch where The Matrix momentarily lifts the veil? It's more than just a glitch. It just might be your cue, your golden ticket.

Chances are your everyday is a tapestry of repeated routines and echoed conversations. But occasionally, there's a tear, a discrepancy, a "crack." I'm not narrating a sci-fi thriller; I'm talking about "Cracks in The Matrix." These aren't system errors; they're your green light to an elevated Sector. But you've got to slide in.

It's like that heart-stopping moment when you dash for the subway and slip in just as the doors are sealing shut. It's the same with spotting and moving on Cracks in The Matrix. That's The Quantum Field nudging you. It's whispering, "This way."

These cracks? They're divergences, deviations from the Script. Moments when you resonate with a higher frequency,

Cracks in The Matrix

an upgraded version of reality. Perhaps it's an impromptu trip to an unexplored country, where every alley feels like déjà vu. Or a call from a long-lost friend, dangling a tantalizing business idea, as if destiny dialed your number.

Or maybe, just maybe, it's spotting an overlooked item in a thrift shop that you just *know* has a history and a hefty resale price. These aren't coincidences. They're cracks. Opportunities. And they're everywhere. The act of sliding into one of these cracks is Quantum Capitalism in its purest form.

Navigating the vast expanse of reality, Cracks in The Matrix present themselves as golden opportunities, beckoning us towards untapped potential. Yet, discerning which crack to leap into is an art cultivated not just by logic, but by a profound alignment of Heart and Mind. When these two powerful forces—the emotional compass of our Heart and the analytical prowess of our Mind—synchronize, a distinct clarity emerges. It's as if The Quantum Field itself whispers the right direction in our ear. This synchronicity is our internal barometer, a fine-tuned instrument that discerns the difference between a fleeting distraction and a genuine, life-altering opportunity. When Heart and Mind resonate in unison, hesitation diminishes and confidence flourishes. It's in this harmonious state that we truly recognize which Crack in The Matrix is our destined route, our quantum leap into the boundless possibilities of existence.

Meet Steve Glew

Steve was a guy stuck in the wrench-turning, oil-splattering loop of a job he loathed. Imagine a hamster wheel but with more grime and flickering fluorescent lights. Steve was hungry for more, but he had no idea what more looked like.

Steve began entering sweepstakes and cereal box contests in need of some therapeutic escape. This led Steve into the exhilarating, dynamic Universe of toy collecting, and his Heart and Mind started playing a duet that would make Mozart envious. When Heart meets Mind, The Quantum Field tends to pay attention.

Cue the scene change to a U.S. toy fair that was basically a candy store for grown-ups with jobs and nostalgia to burn. The air was thick with childlike wonder, and not just because of the nacho cheese fountain in the corner. It was here that The Universe dialed Steve's number. Not literally, of course, but through a mysterious stranger, the carrier of a tantalizing tip: a cache of Pez dispensers, the Holy Grail of toy collectors, hidden in the wilds of a Slovenian warehouse.

To most, war-torn Eastern Europe sounded like a bad idea. To Steve, it was the neon sign pointing to destiny. Remember, this was a time when Eastern Europe was about as inviting as a piranha pool, and not many were diving in for a swim. But when your Heart and Mind are throwing a rave, you don't just listen; you dance. Steve booked his ticket.

Navigating a labyrinth of red tape, black markets, and gray morals, Steve struck gold: a bonanza of Pez dispensers. He started importing them stateside and soon became the Pez dispenser don. Collectors tossed their cash at him like he was the star of the show, and before he knew it, he was waving goodbye to grease-stained overalls and hello to a life less ordinary.

Steve's journey from wrench jockey to Pez outlaw shone as a beacon of Quantum Capitalism in action. Attunement, receptivity, audacity—these are the tickets to the cosmic roller coaster, where the ups, downs, twists, and turns reveal opportunities that can catapult us into realms previously unimagined.

Steve's saga reflects a potent truth: every day, we pass by Cracks in The Matrix deemed too perilous, too far-fetched, too outside the box. Yet, somewhere in the "too hard" basket lies the key to unlocking a life less ordinary. As Steve's journey from the daily grind to Pez Outlaw shows, with the right blend of Heart, Mind, and guts, one person's "too hard" can be another's ticket to the ride of a lifetime.

The story ends here, but the lesson lingers. Slide into the Cracks, no matter how far-fetched they appear. Sometimes, these Cracks in our Matrix are where the light we catch a glimpse of leads to gold.

The Money Shot: The Riches Between Reality's Stitches

Most people hustle in life, desperately chasing opportunities. But in the realm of Quantum Capitalism, opportunities find you, especially when you are navigating Sectors with Heart and Mind Synchronization. These cracks? They're Doors to prosperity you didn't account for. They're the whispered secrets of The Quantum Field, begging you to seize the moment, to capitalize, to profit not just in currency but in experiences, wisdom, and growth. Slide in.

The Recap

Cracks in The Matrix are not mere accidents or illusions to be brushed off. They're The Quantum Field's nudge towards greater Sectors, often dripping with golden opportunities. They are Quantum Field's secret passageways to prosperity. Recognize them. Trust them. Dive into them.

Poke The Brain

Have you ever disregarded an opportunity due to fear or uncertainty? What might have transpired if you had taken that leap?

Your Next Power Move

Connecting with Cracks in The Matrix Meditation

Objective: this guided meditation will lead you through a step-by-step process to connect with Cracks in The Matrix and carry this awareness into your practical daily life.

Instructions:

Settle into Meditation

Find Your Quiet Space: choose a comfortable and quiet place where you can sit or lie down.

Relaxation Breathing: close your eyes and take a few slow, deep breaths. Inhale deeply through your nose for a count of four, then exhale slowly through your mouth for a count of six. Feel yourself becoming more relaxed with each breath.

Body Scan: shift your focus to your body. Start at your feet and mentally scan upwards, paying attention to any areas of tension. With each exhale, release any tightness you feel.

Connect with Cracks in The Matrix

Visualize Awareness: imagine a warm, glowing light radiating from your Heart center. This light expands with each breath, filling your body and surrounding space. As you bask in this gentle radiance, bring your attention to the concept of Cracks in The Matrix. These are moments when the usual patterns of reality shift slightly, revealing hidden opportunities or insights.

Opening the Cracks: now if you sense or see any Cracks, deep within this meditation, acknowledge the same glowing light radiating from them that is radiating from your Heart. Allow as much light to shine through these Cracks as you can imagine, connecting it with the light from your Heart. Take this sensation with you as you bring your awareness out of meditation.

Carry This Light into Practical Life

Daily Reminders: as you go about your day, whenever you encounter something that feels even slightly out of the ordinary, gently bring this light to mind. Let it serve as a reminder to stay open to the potential within these subtle shifts.

Embrace Curiosity: when you recognize these moments, resist the urge to dismiss them as mere coincidences. Instead, approach them with curiosity. Ask yourself: "Could this be a Crack in my Matrix, leading to an opportunity?"

End Note: by engaging in this guided meditation, you're cultivating an increased sensitivity to the possibilities within the ordinary. As you integrate this practice into your daily life, you'll find yourself naturally drawn to these Cracks in The Matrix, unlocking hidden potentials and embracing unique opportunities that can lead you to greater levels of insight and success.

Lesson 65

Candy Bridges

Transitioning now from the luminescent Cracks in The Matrix, those extraordinary moments when you're fully in your zone, and suddenly, something extraordinary appears that could catapult you onto a higher path. Here's another delightful facet of Quantum Capitalism: the phenomenon of unexpectedly discovering shortcuts on your journey towards a goal, long before you even deemed it possible. Enter, The Candy Bridge.

Remember the dazzlingly colorful trail of Candyland? As you maneuvered your piece, you always hoped for that sweet spot—the Candy Bridge. That delightful shortcut, skipping past the Peppermint Forest and the Licorice Lagoon, was every player's wish. It wasn't just about advancing in the game; it symbolized a magical leap, surpassing numerous steps, hurdles, and competitors.

The Candy Bridge in Quantum Capitalism works in a strikingly similar fashion. Think of it as your shortcut to a final result. The Quantum Field is generous, sometimes weaving enchanting Candy Bridges into your path. These are accelerated routes, bypassing the routine drudgery, catapulting you to realms you hadn't imagined you'd reach so soon.

Whether it's a podcast platform offering to showcase your new idea, or an unexpected investor expressing interest in your venture, these are your Candy Bridges. Retirement, seemingly decades away? Spot a Candy Bridge, and you could be lounging in the sun much earlier!

Now, let's unwrap the Candy Bridge cheat sheet:

Don't Stick to the Recipe: while you might have a specific recipe to reach your goal, be prepared for surprise ingredients. Candy Bridges can shorten time-frames dramatically. Be open to the unexpected sweetness.

Sample Others' Sweets: sometimes, the best treats aren't the ones you've concocted, but ones shared by friends. When someone offers you a piece of advice, consider it. They might be showing you a Candy Bridge you haven't seen yet. Listen, taste, and decipher.

Avoid the Sour Patch Kids: you'll meet skeptics, warning you of treats that seem "too good to be true." In the vibrant world of Quantum Capitalism, your journey is dotted with magical sweets and shortcuts. Be discerning, but don't let naysayers prevent you from savoring genuine opportunities. Quantum Capitalists believe in everyday miracles.

Remember, in the grand game of Quantum Capitalism, Candy Bridges are the delightful shortcuts, the sweet surprises that make your journey not only shorter but also much more enjoyable. So, keep your 4 Qualifiers on point, and be ready to leap over the Gumdrop Mountains!

Meet Renee (again)

A goal-getter, dream-chaser, and a living, breathing embodiment of Quantum Capitalism. From juggling passion projects to nurturing grand visions for her future, Renee was no stranger to the magic of The Quantum Field. Her big, far-off goal? A mortgage-free life abroad, filled with book-writing, dog-cuddling, and adventure.

Enter Andrew, the friend with a penchant for spontaneous vacations. A text from him about a trip to Tbilisi, Georgia, and Renee was all in. Georgia, with its mystic aura and rich history, had always intrigued her. The duo hit the streets of Tbilisi, soaking in every bit of the city's charm. Strolling past a real estate office, Renee did a double-take at the property prices showcased in the window. A seed was planted. Was this The Quantum Field fast-tracking her dream of living abroad?

Fueled by her love of Tbilisi, Renee dived into research mode. She found that with a property purchase, obtaining a residency permit was a breeze. Plus, the tax, legal, and banking systems were a dream for Quantum Capitalists. Game on. She held a yard sale, sold all her US possessions, packed her bags, and, with her two dogs in tow, embarked on an exhilarating new chapter.

Fast forward to today, Renee is living her dream in a stunning home in a land that captivates her imagination daily. Her days are filled with writing, doggy playdates, and exploring her magical new surroundings. While she had earmarked this dream for the distant future, The Quantum Field had other plans. She acknowledged the Candy Bridge and danced across it straight up a few Sectors.

Renee's story is a masterclass in Quantum Flow. When you align with the principles of Quantum Capitalism, your dreams don't just take flight; they soar. It's a wild ride of unexpected "Candy Bridges," those delightful shortcuts to dreams you thought were years away. Renee's journey is a vibrant reminder: when you're in sync with The Quantum Field, incredible things happen at warp speed.

The Money Shot: Candy-Coated Capital Gains

In the game of Quantum Capitalism, Candy Bridges aren't just whimsical shortcuts—they're the golden pathways to rapid financial elevation. Imagine fast-tracking your wealth goals, leaping over market lulls and bypassing pitfalls. Every Candy Bridge you courageously cross could be translating to exponential monetary returns, turning your financial graphs into delightful roller coasters of rising success.

The Recap

Candy Bridges, inspired by our beloved Candyland, are the unexpected shortcuts in the game of Quantum Capitalism. They're The Quantum Field's way of sprinkling a little magic on your path, offering opportunities that can accelerate both your journey and your prosperity.

Poke The Brain

What if your next big breakthrough, your financial jackpot, is just one Candy Bridge away? How will you spot it, and more importantly, do you have the audacity to cross it?

Your Next Power Move

Practical Exercise: Spot The Candy Bridge.

The Candy Bridge represents those serendipitous shortcuts that effortlessly connect you to your goals. It's a vibrant, quantum leap in your journey, a materialization of your focused intentions, transforming into tangible opportunities.

Candy Bridges

Now, here's your challenge: in the coming week, become an explorer in your own life, seeking out your next Candy Bridge. This could manifest in numerous ways: a shortcut that accelerates a long-term goal, a direct path to a near-term objective, or even an unexpected journey towards a desired state of being.

Keep in mind, Candy Bridges are not just about luck; they're about heightened awareness and recognition. Tune into the nuances of your daily experiences. Be on the lookout for anything that resembles a Candy Bridge—it could be a piece of timely advice, an out-of-the-blue invitation, or crucial information that appears just when you need it. These are not mere coincidences; they are your Sector's way of offering you a quantum shortcut.

When you spot this Candy Bridge, don't just acknowledge it—seize it! Embrace the opportunity, no matter how small or insignificant it may seem. Each Candy Bridge you cross brings you one step closer to the higher Sectors of reality, navigating you towards success and fulfillment with ease and grace.

Remember, The Universe is abundant with these hidden pathways, waiting to be discovered by those who are ready to see them. Are you prepared to find your Candy Bridge and take that daring leap towards your aspirations? The journey to the higher Sectors awaits you.

Lesson 66

Magic and Miracles

Your life is a theatrical display of magic and miracles, a grand spectacle just waiting to be appreciated. Your day-to-day reality is bustling with whimsical whispers, all you need is to train your senses to catch their fleeting tune. Don't think I've gone cuckoo; I'm just here to uncloak the extraordinary hidden in the ordinary.

Envision this: you're strolling to work, the same old route, but you're not just a participant, you're a seeker of magic. You notice the way sunlight filters through the leaves, creating a kaleidoscope of shadows on the ground. A vibrant bird flutters past, its flying dance moves matching the rhythm of your music. A rainbow from a mysterious prism dances across parking lot asphalt. It's all around you every day, if you choose to see it.

This isn't an exercise in delusion; rather, it's a recalibration of perception. It's about learning to resonate with The Quantum Field—the vast cosmic canvas—and spotting serendipities as plentiful as the stars. This practice will whisk you away from oppressive negativity, buffer you against the onslaught of bullshit and inferior information, and set you on a path of dazzling opportunities and experiences. Need to be pulled out of your over-thinking head? Well, here's your ticket. This

Magic and Miracles

practice can have the exact same effect and work just as well as meditation. Don't knock it before you try it.

Tuning into magic and miracles isn't a flight of fancy, it's the red pill that breaks you free from The Matrix of mundanity. By training your senses to spot the extraordinary in the ordinary, you're not only amplifying your daily dose of childlike wonder and awe, but also unlocking streams of synchronicities and opportunities. This isn't just about making your walk to work more exciting, it's about transforming your reality into a playground. You're not just spotting magic; you're becoming a magician of miracles.

The Money Shot: The Lens of Magic

Imagine this: you're not just cruising through your day-to-day life, you're on a constant scavenger hunt for the magical and miraculous! You're the Indiana Jones of the mundane, transforming your world from black and white into technicolor. This shift of perspective lights up hidden pathways to wealth and prosperity. How? As you dissolve those mental chains and welcome the everyday magic, you don't just get freedom —you get the all-access-pass, keys-to-the-city kind of freedom. Seeking daily miracles isn't just a fun game, it's your golden ticket out of The Matrix.

The Recap

Tuning into magic and small daily miracles is all about cultivating a keen sense of awareness and expectation for high frequency opportunities. It's about seeing the magic in the mundane, spotting synchronicities, and understanding that every moment carries a potential miracle. The act of looking for these instances doesn't just make your world more wondrous, it makes it more abundant with opportunity.

Poke The Brain

Do you think this all sounds like a crock? Go back and reread the Guiding Theory lesson.

Your Next Power Move

Awareness Exercise: Tune into Everyday Magic Game.

Objective: engage in this simple and delightful game to tune into the magic and small daily miracles that surround you. By shifting your perspective and seeking out these moments, you'll cultivate a greater sense of wonder and abundance in your life.

Instructions

Game Start: begin this game with an open Heart and a curious mind. Decide that for the next week, you'll be on the lookout for small daily miracles and moments of magic.

Magic Moments Hunt: throughout your day, actively seek out instances of magic or miracles. These could be simple things that catch your attention, surprise you, or make you smile. Look for signs, coincidences, or moments of unexpected beauty.

Spot the Magic: when you encounter a moment that feels like magic or a small miracle, pause for a moment. Take a mental snapshot or even a quick photo if you can. Acknowledge this moment as something special.

Acknowledge the Magic: whenever you spot a magic moment, whisper to yourself, "There it is!" This simple phrase serves as a reminder to embrace and appreciate the magic in your life.

Reflect: at the end of each day, take a few minutes to reflect on the magic moments you've encountered. Write down a short description of each moment in your Juggernaut Journal. Recall how they made you feel and the impact they had on your day.

Stay Open: throughout the week, stay open to the possibility of magic and miracles. Keep your senses heightened, and be ready to spot these moments in unexpected places.

End Note

Cheesy as fuck, I know. Ten years ago, if someone had asked me to do this, I would've blocked them from ever contacting me again. But it works. Listen, there's The Matrix's grid of negative information, tragedy, and limiting beliefs, and then there's all the other, better stuff that these things shroud from our perception. This isn't a woo-woo overdose; it's your intention to focus on something other than what The Matrix would prefer you to be spinning in.

Lesson 67

Turning Lead Into Gold

Alright, we've delved into the practical magic of various kinds in recent lessons, from luminescent Cracks in The Matrix to Candy Bridges, and even random displays of the world delighting our senses. These have tuned us into auspicious and serendipitous events, helping us to transcend The Matrix that ensnares us with overthinking, worrying, and fretting. Now, are you ready for some magic that has the potential to utterly transform every aspect of your life, should you choose to embrace it?

Imagine, for a moment, that life is this intricate web, beautifully complex yet sometimes confining. The more you resist its design, the tighter it binds you. The twist? You don't need to break free. These Scripts that make up this intricate web are moldable, bending and adapting according to your wishes.

Your life, with all its unexpected turns, isn't trying to trip you up. But your resistance? That's the real tripwire. Rejecting, resisting, or resenting circumstances distorts the potential to mold the events that you experience in life.

Now, here's the pivot: instead of wrestling with life's challenges, what if each held something crucial for your current mission? Every single event is dual; they are woven with both setbacks and opportunities. The amazing part is, you can switch your focus to the opportunities and stick steadfastly to your course.

Turning Lead Into Gold

The setbacks? They are just illusions. Your mission isn't to brawl with the setbacks but to leverage them. You can actually use them to go warp speed towards your destination. You heard me right. Every challenge, every setback holds power you can use to gain momentum.

Every pitfall, every pothole you encounter isn't out there to puncture your tires. Think about it. What if every setback is just a slingshot stretch, priming to launch you into your best Sector? Perceive negative events as positive, and voila, they will be.

We call this the Law of Advantage.

Sounds too good to be true, right? But hold up. Let's play a little imagination game. Something annoying happens. Before you label it as a disaster, calamity, misfortune, or any other doom-and-gloom term, hit the pause button. Swap that negativity with an assumption of this law. Say to yourself, "Wait! It's just a game with a Blackhole. Alright, Blackhole, bring it on!" Stay upbeat, pretend you're thrilled, and hunt for the silver lining. Believe that everything is unfolding perfectly for your benefit. Sometimes the benefits are glaringly obvious; other times, you'll need to trust that they're there, guiding you to a higher Sector. Sounds absurd? How can something unfortunate be positive? But here's the kicker—it works. Every. Single. Time.

Seeing the silver lining in every cloud will catapult you into a favorable Sector. Accepting and pretending that every event is exactly what you needed empowers you to dynamically control unexpected changes. Paradoxically, relinquishing control over a scenario grants you control over it and aligns you with the Quantum Flow, rather than battling against the current and veering off course. The beauty of The Law of Advantage lies in this paradox: surrendering control while simultaneously taking the reins. From now on, be mindful of your attitude towards life's happenings. Treat every event as an Advantage, foster positivity with your world, and your thoughts will be mirrored back to you flawlessly. Embrace your foolish trust in the world, believe it has your back, and ditch the ingratitude. Doing so will keep you on a successful trajectory, beautifying your reality. This simple technique holds immense power. Give it a whirl before passing judgment!

Meet Sarah

Sarah, a talented artist hustling to make a name for herself in the cutthroat world of modern art. One day, she received a phone call that would, she believed, make or break her career. It was from The Modern Edge Gallery, the most avant-garde art gallery in town. They wanted to feature her work in their next exhibition. Elated, she spent weeks creating a masterpiece that was a culmination of her years of hard work and creativity.

On the day of the exhibition, Sarah's painting was placed at the entrance of the gallery, the first thing people would see when they walked in. As the evening progressed, she noticed the crowds gathering around other artworks, but hardly anyone was stopping by hers. Anxiety crept in as she overheard a group of art enthusiasts commenting that her piece seemed "out of place" and "trying too hard." Devastated, Sarah perceived the event as a massive failure and a public humiliation. As a result, she fell into a spiral of self-doubt and negativity, questioning her talent and even considering quitting art altogether. This mindset affected her creativity, and she found herself unable to paint anything for months.

Now, let's rewind and explore an alternate reality.

In this version of events, Sarah still overheard the negative comments about her painting. However, instead of letting it crush her spirit, she decided to find the Advantage in the situation. She approached the group and introduced herself as the artist behind the piece they were discussing. She asked them for constructive feedback and engaged in a lively discussion about modern art, trends, and their expectations as art enthusiasts. The group appreciated her openness and courage to seek feedback, and one of them, an art critic with a popular blog, decided to feature her in an article about up-and-coming artists. This exposure led to more people discovering her work, and eventually, she was commissioned for a mural by a trendy local cafe.

In this reality, Sarah used the negative comments as an opportunity to engage with her audience, learn from them, and gain exposure that eventually led to more opportunities. Instead of a cascade of negativity, she experienced a series of positive events that boosted her career.

In both scenarios, the event was the same, but Sarah's perception and reaction to it made all the difference. By seeking the Advantage in a seemingly negative situation, she was able to turn it into a blessing in disguise. This story highlights the power of perception and the value of maintaining a positive attitude, even in the face of adversity.

The Money Shot: Absolute Alchemy

Money's got ears. Whisper constantly about your empty pockets, and The Quantum Field will keep 'em that way. But what if, in every financial hiccup, you sought the silver lining? Maybe that bad investment sharpened your strategy skills. Got fired? Maybe it's The Quantum Field's way of yelling, "It's time to be your own boss!" Dig for the Advantage, and watch your financial garden bloom.

The Recap

Your power lies in finding the Advantage in every situation, big or small. By aligning yourself with this Law of Advantage, not only do you sway The Quantum Field to favor you, but you also unlock unparalleled growth and potential in every Sector of your life.

Poke The Brain

Ever had a bad day where something unexpected turned out to be the best thing ever? That's The Quantum Field showing you the Advantage. Think back to such a moment. How did it make you feel? And how can you recreate that feeling daily by always seeking the Advantage?

Your Next Power Move

Juggernaut Journal Exercise: Embracing Setbacks.

Objective: this reflective Juggernaut Journal writing exercise encourages you to revisit moments in your life when you faced setbacks or challenges. By shifting your perspective, you'll explore how these perceived negative events held hidden opportunities and became catalysts for growth and positive change.

Example: one of the setbacks that stands out in my life was the painful breakup of a romantic relationship. At the time, the emotions were overwhelming, and I couldn't see beyond the heartache. However, as time passed and I began to heal, I realized that this breakup was a pivotal moment of growth. It pushed me to reevaluate my priorities and rediscover my sense of self. The void left by that relationship allowed me to invest more time in my personal interests and reconnect with friends and family. What initially felt like a devastating loss eventually became an opportunity for self-discovery and self-love. I learned to value my own happiness and recognize that I deserved a relationship that aligned with my Quantum Self. Looking back, I see that the breakup was not an end but a beginning—a stepping stone toward a healthier and more fulfilling chapter of my life.

Instructions

Recall Three Setbacks: choose three specific moments from your life when you encountered setbacks or faced challenges. These could be situations that initially felt discouraging or difficult to navigate.

Describe Initial Reactions: for each setback, write about your initial reactions and emotions.

How did you feel when faced with these challenges? What thoughts crossed your mind?

Describe any frustration, disappointment, or anxiety you experienced.

Identify Hidden Opportunities: reflect on how each setback eventually led to unexpected opportunities or positive outcomes. Explore the ways in which these challenges pushed you to think differently, take new paths, or seek alternative solutions.

Recognize Personal Growth: describe the ways in which each setback contributed to your personal growth and development. Did these experiences teach you new skills, enhance your resilience, or broaden your perspective? Write about how these challenges transformed you.

Highlight Quantum Alchemy: consider how each setback turned into an opportunity for alchemical transformation. How did you leverage these situations to your Advantage? Write about how you turned setbacks into stepping stones, priming yourself for greater success.

Express Gratitude: conclude each reflection by expressing gratitude for the setbacks that turned into stepping stones. Write about how these experiences, in hindsight, helped you become a more empowered and evolved individual.

End Note

This writing exercise invites you to recognize setbacks as powerful catalysts for growth and positive change. By exploring how these challenges held hidden opportunities and transformed into stepping stones, you're acknowledging your ability to leverage adversity for your Advantage. Embrace the concept of quantum alchemy and the Law of Advantage in your journey towards prosperity and personal evolution.

Lesson 68

Chaos Theory & Quantum Disturbances

Alright, let's dive into the good stuff—pure quantum alchemy. It's a blast, right? Until something explodes. And yes, when you're messing with the laws of reality, The Matrix, and The Quantum Field, expect a few experiments to go awry. But don't worry! It happens to the best of us, and we've got your hazmat cleanup tools ready. So, fasten your lab coats and tighten those safety goggles. We're about to explore the intricate dance of chaos in The Quantum Field, and trust me, it's more riveting than any equation you've tried to solve.

Ever heard of the butterfly effect? A tiny wing flap in Brazil setting off a tornado in Texas? That's Chaos Theory for you. It's eerily similar to what happens when you decide to make a change in your life. This is life's inherent unpredictability at play. Every action, every shift in your mindset or life direction, resonates in the fabric of your reality, sometimes creating waves of chaos. Think of it as a quantum disturbance.

Choosing a new trajectory? Expect a ripple effect. Changing your life's Script or shifting to a new Sector in your quantum reality isn't a silent transition. The elements of your life—people, situations, your daily routine—they're like particles in a state of flux. Disturb one, and the whole system responds.

Let's use an analogy here. Imagine your life changes are like observing a quantum particle. The act of observation—or in our case, change—disrupts the natural state. Your friends, family, and even your favorite barista might react unpredictably, thrown out of their orbits. Suddenly, everyone has an opinion or emotion, making you question if chaos is the price of evolution.

Scientifically, everything vibrates, from the smallest atom to the most complex system. As you raise or shift your frequency, expect some fascinating vibrational feedback. It's like tuning into a new radio station; you might get static before the music comes through crystal clear.

So, if you're met with confusion, resistance, or drama, know it's just The Quantum Field recalibrating. You've thrown a pebble into the pond of predictability, and those ripples are The Quantum Field saying, "Change detected! Recalibrating..."

Ready to Give Chaos a Bear Hug?

Setting sail on a transformation adventure is a total rush, but let's not beat around the bush—it can get a smidge...chaotic. When you start messing with the quantum threads of your very being, don't act all shocked if things start to wobble. It's just par for the course, folks!

Most people think of chaos as the big bad wolf, something to dodge like that awkward hug from your weird uncle. But here in the quantum hood, we know chaos is just The Quantum Field doing a little spring cleaning. It's a heads-up that things are getting jiggy with it and realigning with your new vibe. So, instead of running screaming from the chaos, lean in, manage the mayhem, and spoon that chaos like you're on a romantic weekend retreat. Because if you're making moves, if you've galvanized, chances are you've got chaos stepping in. Don't trip, dawg. We got you. Let's do the thang.

Identifying Chaos in Your Life:

Does your brain feel like it's endlessly twerking while juggling flaming torches? That's overwhelm for you—the first sign of chaos making itself at home in your life, transforming your day-to-day into a circus act.

Now, consider the people in your life. When your inner circle starts acting like critics, it's a clear sign that chaos is getting cozy. And when life, despite your meticulous planning, throws you a curveball, that's chaos playing its game.

Emotional turbulence is like a roller coaster from euphoria to doubt, making you the star of your emotional drama. And if conflicts are suddenly on the rise, whether related to your changes or not, it's chaos directing the show.

But how does chaos manifest? Small changes, like tweaking your coffee order or adding someone new to your circle, can cause ripples, unsettling your routine or altering social dynamics. Big changes, like a career move or relocating, are tidal waves of uncertainty, self-doubt, and disorientation.

Remember, chaos is not just a nuisance; it's an opportunity for growth and transformation. Embrace the chaos, ride its waves, and trust the journey. You have the tools, skills, and mindset to dance with this turbulent energy and emerge not just intact but empowered.

Taming Chaos:

Mindfulness is your anchor in the storm of anxiety. Journaling is your heart-to-heart with your soul, providing clarity and catharsis. Positive affirmations are your mental pep talks. Physical exercise is your stress relief valve, and seeking support, whether from a Quantum Capitalist buddy, a friend, or a professional, helps air out your doubts, refreshing your mental space.

Look at it like this: chaos equates to Sectors of reality opening before you. Existing within your well-worn Reality Rut keeps you and your Sector protected from chaos but also means no new pathways for growth and evolution. To truly level up in your Quantum Capitalist game, you need to open yourself to the new while cleaning out the old. Often, chaos is this exact stimulative energy, ushering in all that is to come and clearing the debris of all that needs to go.

The Money Shot: Frequency Fortunes

Think about stocks for a second. Market volatility is just like the chaos of changing frequencies. Traders, the wise ones, don't panic during the wild swings. Instead, they see an opportunity. Every dip, every high, an avenue to make bank. Your life's frequencies are no different. As things shake up, as some investments (relationships, habits, jobs) go bearish, there's always a bullish opportunity lurking. So, next time the chaos seems overwhelming, remember this: you're not in a crash; you're in a prime market to capitalize on your new frequency. Time to trade up and reap the quantum profits.

The Recap

Life's chaos is like quantum fluctuations—unpredictable, but essential for growth. As you step out of your Sector comfort zones, remember: every great scientific discovery emerged from the heart of a chaotic experiment. So, embrace the disorder. It's all part of the grand equation.

Poke The Brain

Einstein once said, "Order is needed by the ignorant, but it takes a genius to master chaos."

Your Next Power Move

Juggernaut Journal Exercise: Embracing Chaos.

Engage in this exercise to shift your perspective on chaos and disruptions, and to harness their potential for personal growth and evolution.

Instructions

Take a few moments to think back on your life journey. Recall moments when you faced unexpected chaos, disruptions, or major changes. These could be personal, professional, or any aspect of your life.

In your Juggernaut Journal, write down at least three instances where chaos or disruption seemed challenging at first. Describe the situation, your initial feelings, and how you perceived the chaos.

Now, revisit each of these instances and reflect on the outcomes. Were there any positive changes, growth, or opportunities that emerged as a result of the chaos? Write down how the situation eventually turned out and how it contributed to your personal development.

Consider how your perspective on chaos has evolved through these experiences. Did chaos actually lead to new beginnings or positive shifts? Write a short paragraph about how you now view chaos as an essential part of growth and change.

Review your reflections and look for patterns or common themes. Do you notice any recurring lessons or benefits that chaos has brought into your life? Write down these insights.

Based on your reflections and insights, think about how you can apply this new perspective to future chaos or disruptions. How can you harness the energy of chaos to create positive outcomes and quantum leaps in your personal and professional life? Write down a few strategies or mindset shifts you can adopt.

Throughout the upcoming week, whenever you encounter chaos, disruption, or unexpected changes, remind yourself of the lessons you've learned from this exercise. Embrace the chaos with an open mind, knowing that it holds the potential for positive transformation.

End Note

By completing this exercise, you're expanding your understanding of chaos as a catalyst for growth and transformation. As you embrace chaos and decode its patterns, you'll be better equipped to navigate life's disruptions and turn them into opportunities for quantum advancement.

Lesson 69

Magical Middle World

When chaos comes a-knocking, there exists a secret sanctuary that provides not just a respite from the tempest of turbulent energies but also a golden opportunity for exponential growth. This magical realm is more than just a safe haven; it's a transformative zone that, when frequented, aids you in evolving your reality in novel and transformative ways. This is no exclusive club for Quantum Capitalists, oh no; this notion has reverberated throughout history by a number of great mystic thinkers, yet in today's world, it seems to have been utterly erased from the collective memory of humankind. Indeed, The Matrix is hell-bent on making you erase this place from your memory, lock it up, and chuck the key into oblivion. It pulls out all the stops to keep the doors to this magical realm hidden away... But guess what? You've got the power now. So, punch it!

G.I Gurdjieff, the mystical thinker, once spoke of three worlds:

> "There are two struggles: an Inner-world struggle and an Outer-world struggle...you must make an intentional contact between these two worlds; then you can crystallize data for the Third World, the World of the Soul."
>
> —G.I Gurdjieff

Sounds trippy, right? Stick with me, and let's unpack this.

Here's the Quantum Quickie: we've got the Inner World, where daydreams and midnight existential thoughts thrive; the Outer World, bustling with every imaginable external stimuli, from the allure of flashy tech to the chaos of a city's hustle and bustle. And now, the pièce de résistance—the Magical Middle World.

When you daydream about the million dollars you want to make or sulk about yesterday's missteps, you're basking in the Inner World. Meanwhile, if you're gawking at the latest iPhone or stuck in traffic hating it, you're trapped in the Outer World. The magic is in the Middle World.

So where's this Magical Middle World? It's the Goldilocks zone, not too hot, not too cold—just right. It's where you're in control, both of the spiraling thoughts in your mind and of the external world trying to sway you. The Middle World is where you can tap into the Quantum You and take the reins of your reality.

Too deep? Let's simplify. Tap your fingers around your nose. Now, think. Where was your mind? Floating in space or fixated on your screen? Observing both? Congratulations, you've just tiptoed into the Middle World!

Forget balancing on life's seesaw, teetering between internal chaos and external clamor. In the Magical Middle World, you become the fulcrum, the cosmic conduit. By mastering this nexus, you don't just straddle realities; you mold them. It's not just about existing or reacting—it's about creating. The Quantum Field doesn't just speak to you here; it listens. Tap into this realm, and you're not just playing the game; you're designing the board.

Alright, time for some real talk. Life's a roller coaster, and we're all just strapped in, holding on for dear life, right? Wrong! Let's break it down. There are two worlds we get trapped in—the Outer World, filled with shiny gadgets, social media spirals, and the never-ending "keeping up with the Joneses" saga. Then there's the Inner World—a labyrinth of overthinking, self-criticism, and FOMO. Sound familiar? We've all been there. Let's dive into the nitty-gritty of these two worlds that keep us stuck in a never-ending loop of distraction.

Getting Stuck in the Outer World:

Hypnotized by Technology: spending hours scrolling through social media, binge-watching Netflix, or gaming.

Materialistic Obsessions: constantly craving the latest gadgets, fashion, or other material possessions.

External Conflicts: getting entangled in arguments, gossip, or drama with others.

Environmentally Captivated: being overly affected by your surroundings, whether it's noise, crowds, or the chaos of urban living.

Sensory Overload: becoming overwhelmed by the barrage of information and stimuli from the external world.

Social Pressure: conforming to societal expectations or norms, despite personal beliefs or desires.

Getting Stuck in the Inner World:

Overthinking: obsessing over past mistakes, future anxieties, or hypothetical scenarios.

Self-Criticism: focusing excessively on your flaws, shortcomings, or perceived inadequacies.

Envy and Comparison: constantly comparing yourself to others and feeling envious of their achievements or possessions.

Obsession Over Relationships: overanalyzing every interaction or becoming overly dependent on others for validation or happiness.

Ruminating on the Past: dwelling on past experiences, missed opportunities, or past grievances.

Worrying About the Future: being consumed by anxieties, uncertainties, or fears about the future.

The Magical Middle World is where you are in a state of "flow," fully engaged, creative, productive, and present. It's when you are harnessing the best of both your Inner and Outer Worlds to create something new, solve problems, and engage with life in a meaningful way. Here's a list of what being in the Middle World might look like:

Being Creative: engaging in any creative activity, whether it's painting, writing, playing music, or dancing.

Working on a Project: being fully immersed in a project, whether it's for work or a personal hobby.

Building or Designing Something: engaging your mind and hands to create something tangible, whether it's a piece of furniture, a website, or a piece of art.

Creating To-Do Lists and Workflows: organizing your thoughts and tasks to create a plan of action.

Setting Up an Environment for Maximum Efficiency: organizing your physical space to minimize distractions and optimize focus and productivity.

Staying Focused on a Task: engaging in deep work, where you are fully concentrated on a task that requires cognitive effort.

Engaging a Group of People: leading or participating in a group discussion, brainstorming session, or collaborative project.

Brainstorming and Coming Up with Higher Ideas and Insights: engaging your mind to think creatively and strategically to solve problems or generate new ideas.

Practicing Mindfulness: being fully present in the moment, whether you are meditating, practicing yoga, or simply taking a walk in nature.

Engaging in Physical Activity: being fully engaged in a physical activity, whether it's playing a sport, exercising, or doing manual labor.

Learning Something New: engaging your mind to learn a new skill, language, or piece of information.

Helping Others: engaging in acts of service or kindness towards others.

Remember, the Middle World is not just about what you are doing, but also how you are doing it. It's about being fully present, engaged, and intentional in whatever activity you are participating in.

The Money Shot: Quantum Wealth Junction

Imagine a realm where your internal convictions synchronize flawlessly with external opportunities. The wealth you've been chasing in the Outer World? It's already encoded in Quantum You. All you need to do is bridge them in this Middle zone. Opportunities won't merely knock; they barge in. You then harness everything you need, to turn them into reality. Welcome to the financial fast lane of the cosmos. You're not just spending or saving money here; you're sculpting it.

The Recap

There are three worlds: Inner, Outer, and the Magical Middle World. The true magic, the real quantum energy, flows in that Middle. It's the space where you can exit both your internal narrative and the external chaos, and enter reality creation mode.

Poke The Brain

Think of the last time you felt torn between an internal experience and an external event. How could accessing the Middle World have changed the outcome?

Your Next Power Move

Practical Exercise: Embrace the Magic of the Middle World.

Engage in this exercise to explore the Magical Middle World, where your Inner World and external experiences converge. By finding a non-disruptive space and getting creative, you can harness your energy for new profitable endeavors.

Instructions

Create a Tranquil Space: find a quiet and non-disruptive space where you can sit comfortably for the duration of this exercise. This could be a cozy corner, a serene park bench, or any spot where you won't be easily distracted.

Reflect on the Three Worlds: take a few moments to reflect on the concept of the three worlds: Inner, Outer, and the Magical Middle World. Consider how you experience these worlds in your daily life and how they influence your actions and emotions.

Harness Your Creative Energy: armed with a notebook, sketchbook, or digital device, prepare to channel your creative energy. This could be through writing, drawing, or any creative expression that resonates with you.

Enter the Middle World: as you sit in your chosen space, let your focus settle. Imagine yourself stepping into the Magical Middle World. This is where your inner thoughts and external experiences find harmony. Feel the balance and potential in this space.

Creative Exploration: in this Middle World state, engage in your chosen creative activity. Let your thoughts flow and ideas take shape. This isn't about perfection; it's about capturing the essence of this magical realm through your creative expression.

Observe the Tugs: as you immerse yourself in your creative activity, notice if your mind tries to pull you towards your inner dialog (Inner World) or concerns about your external environment (Outer World). Acknowledge these tugs and gently guide your focus back to your creative endeavor.

Reflect on Possibilities: once you feel satisfied with your creative exploration, take a moment to reflect. How did spending time in the Magical Middle World impact your creative process? Did you notice any shifts in your energy or mindset?

Future Focus: consider how you can apply this exercise's concept to your future endeavors. How might embracing the Magical Middle World enhance your ability to channel energy into profitable ventures? Jot down your thoughts on how this practice can become a tool for success.

End Note

By embracing the Magic of the Middle World through creative expression, you're tapping into a realm of balance and potential. This exercise isn't just about capturing a moment; it's about training yourself to navigate the inner and outer currents with intention and creativity. As you master this art, you'll discover new avenues for harnessing your energy and bringing profitable ideas to life.

Lesson 70

Superskill

Now we're cooking with gas! You're getting all the heavy-hitting mystical, metaphysical powerhouse concepts, so you can roundhouse kick your old, distracted self right through the door of the Middle realm. Ok, maybe I'm getting a little too carried away, but you know what? This stuff excites me, and I hope it gets you going too. You're learning to take back control of your thoughts, your energy, and with this lesson, an even deeper dive into taking back control of your attention. It's right here, my friend, the chance to change it all. You are immensely powerful, but you must see the power in your resources, and right now? Well, attention is the hottest commodity. Every powerful Matrix entity knows it, and if you stand strong, know your attention's worth, and keep that resource for your own evolution, well, you've hacked the Matrix. Let's dive in.

Ever felt like you're a little piece in the grand board game of life, being played by an invisible hand? Well, Quantum Capitalist, it's time for a rude awakening, and trust me, you'll thank me for this one.

"If your attention is not your own, your soul is not your own."

—Vadim Zeland

What a kick to the gut that is, isn't it? But it's the truth serum we need. Slumbering in the stupor of The Matrix, we're confined to scripted roles, with no ad-libs allowed.

Play along with me here: where was your attention just a minute ago? On my words? Or off on a trip to Mars? More often than not, it's stolen away by the Script of life, turning us into lifeless puppets. A dream is just like reality and vice versa if you're in zombie mode. But, if you choose to own your attention, you become the master puppeteer, the magician, the captain, and the ruler of your reality.

But here's the catch: most of us are so engrossed in the alluring theatrics of the Inner and Outer Worlds that we overlook the Middle World—the power seat of self-control. This shift isn't just about stirring from your sleep, but about setting an alarm to the "awake" mode. And not just once, but over and over again.

As you stride through the grand adventure of life, whisper this mantra to yourself, "I am awake." Put this thought on lock, or else it will slip away into oblivion. Don't let the comfort of lethargy and forgetfulness wrap you in its deceptive cloak. If you do, you're signing up for a masterclass in nothingness.

During your journey, you're bound to trip over your own shoelaces and drift off into the labyrinth of zombie land. Instead of wallowing in distress over it all, gather your wits, and pull your attention back into the driver's seat. Make it your personal mission to shadow your attention with your attention. It's a bit like a game of tag.

It's not about gluing your attention at the center without a breather. That's a ticket to burnout town. Instead, the real magic trick lies in your ability to react and respond to the dance unfolding around you.

Usually, even a random leaf fluttering in the wind can yank you into the swirling vortex of the Outer World or tangle you in the cobwebs of inner ruminations. It's like a sly hypnotist putting you into a slumber. Your task? Flip the Script. Don't surrender to sleep, instead, rouse yourself from it. Treat each whisper of your surroundings as a call to arms. Let every action you perform be a trigger to reorient your attention.

Remember, you've got two bullets in your chamber.

The Outer Bullet—The moment anything occurs, jolt awake.

The Inner Bullet—Before you make any move, power up.

Take these examples: bumped into a friend? Overheard a conversation? Did a bird just poop on your car? Irrelevant what it is, any flutter in your environment should put your senses on high alert. Focus on it, but like a seasoned tightrope walker, maintain your balance—keep your attention anchored in the Middle World.

Getting ready for a trip? About to fire off an email? Prepping for a chat with a client? Before you hit the launch button on any action, pull your attention back to the Middle World. Remember, the key is "before," because if it's "after," you'll find yourself waking up from a slumber, lamenting about your snoozefest.

The secret sauce here is repetition—it's your best bud. Like a martial artist refining their moves, the art of controlling your attention demands relentless practice. And when you master this, your once trivial life blossoms into a riveting saga of self-control and self-direction.

Here's a golden nugget for you: just because you've woken up, flexed your mental muscles, and are prancing around in the arena of awareness, doesn't mean you're the king of the world. Resist the temptation to perch on a high horse. Others may still be snoozing, but don't sneer at them. This is your journey towards personal evolution and the higher Sectors of existence. March forward, Quantum Capitalist, but let the slumberers slumber.

Let's emphasize the gravity of the situation. This is a hardcore mystical practice. Seriously. This is really for those seasoned and ready for this next level of advancement. Also, you might be wondering, why so much drama around this concept and why such a serious tone? Well, there are two reasons. First, it is serious. This is like going toe to toe with the big boss on the final level of a video game. Once you've beaten this level, you're in. You've unlocked the game. The second thing is, most people reading this need to hear it with a strong emphasizing tone because The Matrix has become increasingly cunning in getting you to part ways with your

attention. If you don't have what you want in life right now, yet struggle to get ahold of your attention, well, remember what I said about evolution and degradation? It's one or the other, and this is the line in the sand. If your attention is captivated more often than not, well, good luck with that. If you let it, The Matrix will consume you. This is serious business.

The Money Shot: Cashing In On Consciousness

When you're the master of your attention, you're also the master of your destiny, that includes your wealth too. Here's a secret worth its weight in gold: true wealth isn't just the jingle of coins in your pocket—it's about investing your time, energy, and focus wisely. And if these investments are being manipulated by an unseen puppeteer, you're left with the crumbs. But when you're the puppeteer and your attention dances to your tunes, you hit the jackpot! The world turns into a land of opportunities, secret pathways to riches reveal themselves, and voila—you're part of the elite club of Quantum Capitalists.

The Recap

The currency of this game? Your attention. Get a firm grip on it, and not only do you elevate your existence, but you also unlock the vault to quantum capital and opportunities.

Poke The Brain

Think about your day. When were you lost in a daydream and when were you tussling with your world? Now, imagine living each moment with your attention in the Middle World more and more. How might that reshape your reality?

Your Next Power Move

Practical Exercise: Attention Audit.

Objective: embark on this exercise to enhance your awareness of where your attention is directed throughout the day. By setting hourly alarms and performing quick check-ins, you'll gain insight into whether you're dwelling in the Inner, Outer, or Middle World. This practice empowers you to take charge of your attention and orchestrate your focus more effectively.

Instructions

Preparation: set hourly alarms during waking hours on your device for the next 24 hours. Each alarm will serve as a reminder to pause and check where your attention currently resides.

Hourly Check-in: when the alarm rings, stop whatever you're doing and take a moment to reflect.

Inner, Outer, or Middle: during the check-in, ask yourself: "Am I in the Inner World, Outer World, or Middle World, right now?" Pay attention to your thoughts, emotions, and surroundings to determine your current state of attention.

Mindful Analysis: take a few deep breaths and observe the quality of your attention. Are you lost in daydreams (Inner World)? Are you engrossed in external stimuli (Outer World)? Or are you present, aware, balanced, and creative (Middle World)?

Redirecting Focus: depending on your observation, gently redirect your attention as needed. If you find yourself drifting into unproductive thoughts or distractions, bring your focus back to the present moment.

Quick Note: after each check-in, jot down a brief note about your findings. You can use keywords like "Inner," "Outer," or "Middle" to indicate your state of attention.

Progress Review: at the end of the 24 hours, review your notes. Notice any patterns or trends in your attention's flow. Are there specific times of day or activities that tend to pull you into certain worlds more than others?

Reflection: reflect on how this exercise affected your awareness of your attention's movement. Did you catch yourself more often in a specific world? How did redirecting your focus impact your overall presence and engagement?

End Note

By setting regular check-ins and redirecting your focus as needed, you'll enhance your ability to stay grounded in the Middle World. As you continue practicing this exercise, you'll cultivate a deeper sense of presence and empowerment over where you choose to invest your attention. Get ready to witness the magic of mindful engagement with the world around you.

Lesson 71

Ending the Battle

You're doing it! Can you sense the surge of energy building within you? With this newfound knowledge, you are not only reclaiming your power but also transforming into a dauntless navigator of The Quantum Field. Your awareness is sharp, your attention is focused, and everything is aligning perfectly. And the best part? This unlocks the gateway to the most magnificent quantum treasure of all—FREEDOM. Much like the enigmatic secrets of the Emerald Tablets, the key to emancipation is surprisingly straightforward—stop resisting! It may seem as though you are caught in an incessant boxing match, contending with yourself, the world, and all its puppeteers. However, once you recognize that this struggle is nothing more than a complex illusion and you step out of the ring, the world becomes a boundless playground, no strings attached!

Listen closely, the Blackholes have been manipulating your reality since the day you were born, constructing your worldview like an intricate house of cards, imprisoning you in a mental cage, and teasing the mirage of freedom just beyond your grasp. They'll assure you, "Friend, you have a choice. Here, take control of the puppet strings, desire anything, achieve everything, but always remember, you're playing by my rules!"

Your so-called "freedom" here is just the liberty to bash your head against the wall of their rigged game. Now, here's a groundbreaking revelation—you can't outfight a Blackhole. Few might snatch a prize or two, but most just keep flailing till they're spent. You want a shot at genuine freedom? Shed that excessive Importance, the overvalued meaning you ascribe to everything.

Let's rip the band-aid off, shall we? You've been playing a never-ending game of tug-of-war with battles that are as pointless as they are exhausting. It's time for, yet another, reality check.

The Tug-of-War You Can't Win: Common Battles and Why You're Losing

Needing to be Right or Valued: craving to be right or have your views cherished? It's like playing a never-ending game of emotional Battleship. When you're hell-bent on proving a point or basking in the glow of others' admiration, you're essentially handcuffing your creative mojo. Each battle for recognition is a drain on your energy—resources better spent on forging your path, not justifying it.

Approval Seeking: the relentless pursuit of approval is a quantum quicksand. It's as if you're standing on a stage, performing for an audience that keeps shifting their preferences. Seeking validation is an exhausting, unending performance that leaves little room for authenticity. Remember, the most potent approval comes from within, not from the ever-changing whims of the gallery.

Paralysis by Perfectionism: perfectionism is a sly foe disguised as a friend. It whispers sweet nothings about flawless execution but binds you in chains of hesitation and doubt. It's like trying to paint a masterpiece with a color palette limited to shades of gray. You end up tiptoeing around your potential, too scared to splash the canvas with the vibrant colors of risk and innovation.

Comparing to the Point of Insanity: the comparison game is a mind-bending maze with no exit. You're running in circles, measuring your journey against someone else's GPS coordinates. It's a race with no finish line, where the only prize is frustration and a distorted view of your unique path.

Worrying and Over-Planning: trying to script every aspect of your life in advance is like playing chess with The Universe—a futile endeavor. You're so entangled in the web of "what ifs" that you miss the magic unfolding right in front of you. Life isn't a problem to be solved but a mystery to be lived. Embrace the unpredictability; it's where the magic happens.

Battling Self and Others: engaging in constant battles, either with yourself or those around you, is like waging an endless war where the only casualty is your peace of mind. You're locked in a perpetual struggle, trying to sculpt your reality to match an idealized version. But here's the kicker: the more you fight, the more you lose touch with the very essence of your being and the potential of your world.

Letting Go of the Battles: it's time to lay down your arms. Release the need to control, to be right, or to have the last word. When you relinquish these draining conflicts, you're not just liberating your mind; you're setting the stage for a life where opportunities, connections, and experiences come to you not by force, but by flow. It's like swapping a seat on a dilapidated bus for a first-class ticket aboard a spaceship bound for "Planet Fuck Yes."

Are you ready to kick it up a notch? To let go of the needless conflicts and step into a realm of endless possibilities? It's a choice between staying stuck in the quagmire of battles or soaring into The Quantum Field where an improved reality is just a thought away. Your Quantum Self is asking: are you in, or are you out?

The Money Shot: Break On Through

By ending the battle once and for all, you are tuning your frequency to the vibration of wealth and opportunity. No longer will you be bashing your head against the wall of the rigged game. Instead, you'll be in the driver's seat, steering your life towards a horizon of endless possibilities. This is not just about money in the bank (although that's a nice perk), it's about unlocking a wealth of opportunities, experiences, and connections. It's about creating a life that is rich in every sense of the word. The problems of yesteryears won't evaporate in a day, but armed with these potent techniques to shape your destiny, you'll find that over time, they'll look more like speed bumps, less like impenetrable walls.

The Recap

This lesson highlights that true freedom, along with a life of wealth and opportunity, is achieved by recognizing the struggles as a complex illusion, and stepping out of the self-imposed mental cage.

Poke The Brain

Are you ready to end your battles once and for all?

Your Next Power Move

Thought Exercise: Check Yourself Before You Wreck Yourself.

The Matrix wants us entangled in a fight. Remember, when your attention isn't your own, neither is your soul. If The Matrix can keep you captivated by the Outer Screen, it owns you. Political battles, social justice causes—these preoccupy millions worldwide, with Importance levels through the fucking roof. But you have a choice. You don't have to engage in these battles. Exiting the boxing ring allows you to reclaim your energetic resources and channel them into endeavors that foster your evolution.

Here is a simple exercise... Think of a single battle you've been engaged in that you could drop right now. Have you been overly involved in a cause or a heated debate? Are you battling someone in your life over a difference in perspective? Identifying the battle is easy... But do you have the nuts to let it go?

Do it and thrive!

After the simple exercise, take a moment to reflect on how you feel. Notice any shifts in your perception of battles, struggles, and the Importance you've given to certain aspects of life. Remember that this is a reminder of your power to choose your battles and to let go of the unnecessary fight against external and internal pressures. As you continue this practice, you'll find yourself experiencing greater inner peace and a truer sense of freedom.

Lesson 72

Dividing Your Time

With all this newfound mental and energetic freedom, you've probably got some energy to spare—and it's crucial to channel it in the right direction. If you've hit the jackpot and identified a goal that truly resonates with the Quantum You, mastering the art of time and energy balancing is crucial. Also, after exiting a battle or two, you may be in need of a little recovery time. Let this lesson be the green light for you to luxuriate a bit more starting today. You do deserve it, you know?

Perhaps it's also time for a spring cleaning and reorganization of your life. Say goodbye to doom-scrolling, Netflix marathons, and relationships that weigh you down like a ton of bricks. It's time to categorize your life into a pie chart of essentials (mmm pie), and get brutally honest about your schedule. Elevate self-love and self-care to the top of your priority list—they've earned their VIP status.

Here's a sneak peek at my pie chart—it's pretty hard-core.

I cater to the must-haves in my life—my home, my romantic partner, my dogs. I uphold my roles and duties, pouring love and care into the people and things that make my world spin. The rest? It's divided between my professional creative zone in the Magical Middle World and some quality "me" time. A healthy exercise regimen, steamy baths, massages, meditation, journaling, and a nutritious diet are my go-to self-love and self-care activities. Making this a daily ritual ensures I have enough fuel to power through my days, not just surviving, but thriving.

If self-care skips out, my productivity nose-dives, and everything feels like a chore. Self-care isn't just a gust of wind in my sails; it's the whole damn breeze.

Start The Engine, Baby!

Alright, let's get this self-care party started! You're not a machine programmed to keep grinding until you break down. You're a fabulous, living, breathing masterpiece, and it's high time you started treating yourself like one. Now, although some of these items on the list are as basic as can be, it's a pertinent reminder. When was the last time you laid in bed past your bedtime with a fully lit screen telling your brain it's not time for sleep when it absolutely was? Exactly.

Now, let's get one thing straight—self-care isn't about being self-centered. It's about self-preservation, baby! So, repeat after me: taking care of myself isn't selfish; it's essential. And just like you wouldn't build a skyscraper on a foundation of quicksand, you can't build a kick-ass life on a worn-out, stressed-out, undernourished version of yourself. Meet Caleb.

Version 1: The Fractured Pie Chart

Caleb, a man of ambition and drive, found himself in a whirlwind of chaos. His days were a blur, his nights sleepless, his mind constantly racing. Each morning, he would dive headfirst into a sea of emails, meetings, and deadlines, his life resembling a disjointed pie chart, each slice too thin to taste any semblance of fulfillment.

His social media feeds were an endless scroll of others' lives, and his evenings were lost to the glow of his television screen, binging on shows he barely remembered. Relationships felt like obligations, and his hobbies were long forgotten. Caleb's self-care was non-existent, his exercise routine a distant memory. He was a man being pulled in a million directions, yet going nowhere.

One night, lying awake, he realized he was living life in a daze, a spectator in his own story. The realization hit him hard. He was losing himself in the cacophony of the world, his pie chart a muddled mess of misplaced priorities and neglected passions.

Version 2: The Aligned Pie Chart

Fast forward, and we find a different Caleb. He had taken control, realigning his pie chart with purpose and balance. Mornings now began with a jog, the rhythm of his footsteps a meditation in motion. Work was no longer a frantic race but a focused pursuit, with clear boundaries to protect his time and energy.

His evenings were a blend of creativity and connection. Caleb rediscovered his love for painting, the strokes of his brush a dance of self-expression. He rekindled relationships, now spending quality time with those who mattered most, their laughter and stories a balm to his soul.

His diet transformed, his body now fueled with nourishment that energized rather than drained. Meditation and journaling became his sanctuaries of reflection, tools that grounded him in the present. His pie chart was no longer fractured, but a harmonious blend of work, passion, and rest.

Caleb's journey from chaos to clarity was a testament to the transformative power of self-care and mindful living. He learned that by caring for himself, he could engage with life more fully, his time and energy balanced in a dance of productivity and peace. He was no longer just surviving; he was thriving, a man aligned, whole, and undeniably alive.

The Money Shot: Give Yourself The Ol' Razzle-Dazzle

And here's the zinger. With better self-care, you're not just going to get good at balancing your energy. You're gearing up to become a productivity powerhouse. And guess what follows? The ability to run on opportunities. Wealth. Success. Self-care isn't just the wind in your sails; it's the fuel taking you to Treasure Island.

The Recap

In this transformative ride towards Quantum You, maintaining your energy is the fuel and self-care is the pit stop. Shed the unnecessary, streamline your priorities, and infuse your routine with a deep love and respect for yourself. Ensuring your sails are always billowing with the wind of self-care allows you to navigate the vast ocean of responsibilities and creativity with unerring prowess and resilience. Remember, a well-cared-for you is an unstoppable you.

Poke The Brain

What's that one thing you need to change about your self-care routine today? Is your sail flapping listlessly in the wind?

Your Next Power Move

Creative & Juggernaut Journal Exercise: The Quantum Pie Chart.

The objective of the Quantum Pie Chart exercise is to visually assess how you currently allocate your time and energy in your daily life, and then redesign the chart to reflect the distribution of time that nurtures your Quantum Self through self-love and self-care.

Instructions

1. Draw Your Current Pie Chart:

   - Grab your Juggernaut Journal.
   - Draw a circle to prepare your pie chart. Now section it out. Each section represents a category of activities in your daily life.
   - Label each section with a category, such as work, sleep, socializing, entertainment, chores, etc.
   - Use your best estimate to determine the proportion of time you spend on each category in a typical day.

2. Reflect on Your Current Pie Chart:

   - Take a moment to observe your current pie chart. Notice how your time and energy are distributed among various activities.
   - Reflect on how much time you allocate to activities that nurture your well-being and self-care.

3. Design Your Quantum Self Pie Chart:

   - On a new piece of paper, create another pie chart.

- This time, redesign the chart to reflect how you would ideally distribute your time to nurture your Quantum Self.
- Prioritize self-love and self-care categories like exercise, meditation, reading, creative activities, quality time with loved ones, relaxation, etc.
- Adjust the proportions of each section to reflect the time you want to dedicate to each activity.

4. Embrace the Change:

- Compare your current pie chart with your Quantum Self Pie Chart.
- Notice the differences between the two charts and how they represent your current state and your desired state.
- Embrace the intention behind your Quantum Self Pie Chart and recognize the value of self-care in your journey.

5. Create a Plan:

- From your Quantum Self Pie Chart, identify one or two self-care activities that you can incorporate into your daily routine.
- Create a simple plan to integrate these activities into your day. Set specific times for these activities and commit to them.

6. Regular Check-Ins:

- Make it a habit to regularly check in with yourself and your Pie Chart. Are you aligning with your Quantum Self goals?
- Adjust your Chart and activities as needed to accommodate changes and maintain balance.

Reflection

After completing the Quantum Pie Chart exercise, take a moment to reflect on the insights you've gained. Consider how reallocating your time to prioritize self-love and self-care can impact your energy levels, productivity, and overall well-being. Remember that your Quantum Self Pie Chart is a visual representation of your commitment to nurturing yourself and living in alignment with your true priorities.

Lesson 73

Anomalous Action Ascension

Alright, you are free as a bird, self-care on fleek. You are feeling reality and you know what? Reality is feeling you too. Are you ready to exit the old Reality? I mean, lots of self-love and self-care can make things feel pretty comfy and cozy, but don't forget you're on a mission. So, are you soldiering on in your comfort zone? That warm, fuzzy, predictable Reality Rut? Remember, it can also be a trap, a life-force-sucking Blackhole. But don't worry, I've got a radical secret weapon for you—Anomalous Action! Let's ride!

Anomalous Action is that rebellious streak you need. It's taking the road less traveled on your daily commute, devouring a book from an alien genre, or finally saying "yes" to that salsa class you always dodge. It's the pin to your comfort bubble, and while it might sound simple, it's a potent weapon against your Reality Rut.

Here's why you need to initiate your Anomalous Action protocol:

Monotony Massacre: anomalous Action is a bull in the china shop of your repetitive life. It busts up the old, boring patterns, creating space for the new and exciting.

Opportunity Unleashed: being a little daring opens up untapped avenues and unexplored territories. You might just find your next big thing in untouched corners of your current Sector.

Adaptability Amplifier: Anomalous Action conditions you for change, the only constant in life.

Embrace change, and watch your life turn into a thrilling ride.

Awareness Ignited: step out of your comfort zone and your senses go on high alert. It's like switching on your opportunity radar, and suddenly, you see chances where you saw walls.

Meet Zara

Zara was caught in the quicksand of monotony. Same old, same old. Everything was as exciting as watching paint dry. Zara was craving change, something more exhilarating than picking a new cereal at the grocery store. Remembering a life hack about Anomalous Action, she decided it was high time to shake things up a bit.

Day 1: adios, boring black coffee! Zara went wild and ordered a matcha latte. Crazy, right? She even chatted up a stranger, also drinking a matcha latte. Woah. Plot twist: both were hiking enthusiasts and planned a weekend romp in the woods.

Day 5: Zara ditched the train and biked to work, feeling the wind in her hair like a protagonist in a movie montage. The exercise sparked a brainwave tsunami at work.

Day 10: Zara, the infamous party-pooper, said "yes" to salsa dancing. She tripped over her feet, but the laughter shared with a new dance partner made it a fun night. Zara was beginning to feel alive again.

Day 15: bye-bye, self-help snoozefest! Zara ditched the self-help book she'd been pretending to read and picked up a sci-fi novel that lit up her imagination like a fireworks factory in a four-alarm blaze. Who knew fictional aliens could teach you more about life than a self-help guru? The plot was thicker than her grandma's gravy, and by the end, she was so inspired that she started a creative writing side hustle. Her first story? "The Intergalactic Guide to Getting Your Sh*t Together"—a hilarious self-help manual for humans, written by aliens.

Day 20: instead of a doom-scroll coma, Zara volunteered at a shelter. The warm fuzzies from helping out lifted her spirits higher than a kite. When she got home, Zara looked in the mirror and saw color returning to her face. Hot damn.

Day 25: sayonara, couch potato weekends! Zara decided it was high time to give her couch a break from the dent her butt was making. So, she hit the road for an impromptu adventure to a neighboring city. The change of scenery was as exciting as finding a $100 bill in an old pair of jeans. She ended up at a random pie-eating contest and won second place. Score!

Day 30: Zara, the conflict avoider, finally tackled an issue head-on with a colleague. Armed with nothing but her newly found courage and a white flag just in case, she approached her coworker. Instead of the office brawl she had feared (and prepared for by watching a marathon of kung fu movies the night before), they ended up having a heart-to-heart conversation that strengthened their bond. Who knew honesty could be more effective than a roundhouse kick? Not only did they clear the air, but they discovered a shared love for cat memes and a mutual disdain for the office coffee. A friendship was born, all thanks to Zara's newfound bravery and her decision to face the music.

After a month of living on the wild side, Zara's world was turned upside down—in a good way. The yawn-inducing routine was history, new opportunities popped up like daisies, adaptability skyrocketed, and her opportunity radar was on fire. The Reality Rut was toast, and a shiny new Script full of possibilities replaced the same old, same old. Zara realized that stepping out of the comfort zone, taking risks, and embracing change were the golden tickets to a thrilling new reality.

The Money Shot: The Great Escape

Picture this: you step out of your daily routine, venture into the unknown, and suddenly, you strike gold! That's what Anomalous Action can do for your finances. Maybe it's an untapped investment opportunity, a breakthrough business idea, or a wealthy network connection—they're all out there, just waiting for you to break out of your rut.

The Recap

Anomalous Action is your secret weapon to break the chains of monotony. It is the lifejacket that can pull you out of your Reality Rut and push you into the uncharted waters of opportunities and higher Sectors.

Poke The Brain

Take a long, hard look at your daily routine. Is it your golden path or your prison?

What Anomalous Action can you take right now to rock your reality boat?

Your Next Power Move

30-Day Anomalous Action Challenge: Exiting the Reality Rut.

Objective: over the next 30 days, engage in Anomalous Actions to break free from your routine, ignite creativity, and invite new opportunities into your life.

1. Understanding Anomalous Action:

    - Begin by reading and understanding the concept of Anomalous Action from the lesson.
    - Internalize the idea that stepping out of your comfort zone can lead to exciting shifts in your life.

2. Create Your Anomalous Action List:

    - Spend some time brainstorming a variety of Anomalous Actions you can take throughout the 30 days.
    - Consider different categories like random actions, self-care, organizing, and cleaning, professional, and creative actions. Your world or other people may suggest Anomalous Action to take, too. Consider everything.

3. Plan Your Anomalous Actions:

    - Organize your list by assigning one Anomalous Action to each day of the challenge.
    - Keep your list easily accessible, such as in your Juggernaut Journal or mobile.

4. Execute Daily Anomalous Actions:

    - Each day, commit to completing the Anomalous Action scheduled for that day.
    - Embrace the experience fully, even if it feels uncomfortable or unfamiliar.

5. Reflect and Document:

    - After each Anomalous Action, take a few moments to reflect on your experience.
    - Record your thoughts, feelings, and any insights gained from each Action.

6. Share and Engage:

    - If you're comfortable, share your journey with a friend, family member, or our online community.
    - Encourage others to join you in the challenge and share their experiences.

7. Adapt and Explore:

    - Throughout the challenge, stay open to adapting your Anomalous Actions based on your evolving interests and experiences.
    - Don't hesitate to explore new categories or try more daring actions.

8. Final Reflection:
    - At the end of the 30 days, take time to reflect on the entire challenge.
    - Review your reflections and note any patterns or changes in your mindset, energy, or opportunities.

Conclusion

Completing the 30-day Anomalous Action Challenge will likely provide you with valuable insights into your capacity for change, creativity, and adaptability. Remember that breaking free from your routine can lead to new perspectives and exciting possibilities. Continue incorporating Anomalous Actions into your life beyond the challenge, using them as a tool to maintain a dynamic and ever-evolving approach to your evolving reality.

Lesson 74

Human Ego Sacrifice

Note: this is a repeat lesson because, let's face it, sometimes we need to be hit over the head with the truth multiple times before it sinks in. And then one more time for good measure. Let's roll.

Are you geared up to bid adieu to that Reality Rut, but Matrix You is still talking smack? Is your ego hogging the mic more than it's supposed to? Remember when you flirted with the idea of kick-starting your own podcast, but that internal party pooper chimed in, "Who'd tune in to your ramblings?" Time to put Debbie Downer in their place.

If you're making moves, there's most likely an ongoing battle ensuing in your mind, a relentless tug-of-war between your ego, your internal naysayer, and your Quantum Voice—the authentic, vibrant you. We all have these voices, but here's the kicker: you're the commander-in-chief, and you get to decide who takes the lead.

Your ego, oh that clever imposter, loves to pretend it's got your back. But let's face it, it's just a drama queen thriving on fear, feeding you a steady diet of self-doubt and playing it safe. On the other side, there's the naysayer, always ready with a bucket of cold water to douse your fiery dreams. But what about your Quantum Voice? That's your authentic, intuitive guide, waiting patiently for you to hit the mute button on the other bozos and tune into its open mic.

So, imagine this. You've got this spicy idea, a next-gen app set to light a fire under the gig economy's backside. Your Quantum Voice, the one with the backstage pass to your potential, is already setting off fireworks, seeing the ripples of impact you're about to make. But here comes your ego and your internal naysayer, those uninvited party poopers, whispering "What if you faceplant?" and "You're out of your depth here."

But wait, you've got your Quantum Voice on the megaphone, drowning out the downers, calling you to jump head-first into the mosh pit of opportunities. You rally, raise funds, gather a dream team. Your app goes live, and like an overnight SoundCloud sensation, it's blowing up the charts, raining prosperity like confetti. That's your Quantum Voice in action, your own personal hype-man.

Here's the cheat: How to Crank up the Volume of the Quantum You and Mute the Ego

Spot the Buzzkill: be sharp, identify when your ego or internal naysayer gatecrashes your brain party. They're the ones sowing doubts and fears, bringing down the vibe.

Hit Pause: when the unwanted guests start making noise, give them a time-out. This could be a cleansing breath, a walk around the block, or a mantra you belt out, "I'm DJ-ing this show; Quantum Voice is the headliner!"

Embrace the Silence: make room for mindfulness practices to pump up the Quantum Voice. This could be meditation, journaling, or reinforcing self-talk. The more you spin the

Quantum beats, the more they'll drown out the noise, guiding you to your headline act.

The Money Shot: Duct Taping Your Ego's Mouth Shut

Understanding and navigating these voices isn't just a spiritual jaunt, it's a key to unlocking your financial prosperity. By hushing the ego and the naysayer, and amplifying your Quantum Voice, you empower yourself to take calculated risks, seize opportunities, and materialize prosperity.

Imagine being able to confidently invest in that innovative startup, or kick-start your own venture without the constant second-guessing. That's the power of the Quantum Voice.

The Recap

Navigating and neutralizing the ego and the internal naysayer is crucial in accessing your true potential. It's about recognizing these voices, understanding their tricks, and choosing to tune into the Quantum Voice—your inner guide who leads you toward growth and prosperity.

Poke The Brain

What if that podcast idea you shelved could've been the next big thing in the industry? How many more opportunities will you let slip because of the naysayer and the ego?

Your Next Power Move

Juggernaut Journal Exercise: Amplify Your Quantum Voice.

Objective: strengthen your authentic voice and diminish the impact of negative thoughts and self-doubt through mindful reflection and positive reframing.

Step 1: Recognize and Label

Start your journal entry by acknowledging moments when self-doubt or negative thoughts emerge. These might include times when you've hesitated to pursue a goal or felt uncertain about your abilities.

Write down instances when you noticed these negative thoughts.

Give each negative thought a label, such as "Matrix Me," "ego," or "naysayer."

Step 2: Pause and Reframe

When you encounter these labeled thoughts, practice taking a mindful pause before reacting.

In your journal, describe the moment when the negative thought surfaced.

Note how you felt when you recognized the thought.

Breathe deeply and mentally label the thought as the "ego" or "naysayer."

Reframe the negative thought into a positive affirmation or statement.

Example: if the thought is "I'm not good enough," reframe it as "I have the skills and determination to succeed."

Step 3: Amplify Your Quantum Voice

Now, shift your focus towards nurturing your authentic, confident Quantum Voice:

Write about your strengths, achievements, and qualities that define your Quantum Voice.

Practice positive self-talk that aligns with your Quantum Voice.

Visualize scenarios where you confidently take action and achieve your goals.

Reflect on how embracing your Quantum Voice can influence your decisions and actions positively.

Conclusion

Completing this Juggernaut Journal exercise empowers you to recognize and redirect negative thoughts, ultimately amplifying your Quantum Voice. Over time, you'll develop a habit of reframing self-doubt and embracing your authentic self, leading to increased self-confidence and a more positive mindset. By nurturing your Quantum Voice, you'll be better equipped to pursue opportunities and achieve your aspirations.

Lesson 75
Monkey Brain, Rice Desires & Coconut Conundrums

You've cornered "Matrix You," and they know it. Quantum You has taken the reins and is starting to call the shots. But wait, there's a hiccup. You've been chasing something—a job, a relationship, a significant change, and you've been at it in the only way you know, probably for longer than you care to acknowledge. You're holding onto your burning desire and a method that's been your lifeline. But what if that lifeline is morphing into a noose? What if your tenacious grip is actually your shackles?

Let's take a detour to East India, where they have a cunning trick to catch pesky monkeys invading their homes for food. This scenario might shed some insight.

The villagers devise a trap—a coconut, drilled with a perfectly measured hole, and filled with yummy, aromatic rice. This coconut is then fastened with a chain to a stake.

Enter hungry monkey.

Attracted by the irresistible aroma of rice, the monkey slips its paw into the coconut and seizes the grains. But, oh, the surprise! Its fistful of rice can't slip back through the hole. Suddenly, the monkey finds itself a prisoner, trapped by its own desires and refusal to let go. Little does it know, beyond the village huts, lie vast unprotected rice fields—an endless feast, if only it would release its hold.

In life, we often mimic the monkey, held captive by our obstinacy and our failure to envision beyond the strategies we've sworn would yield results. Our inability to recognize and adjust our course leaves us trapped, potentially losing it all. Frustration and discontent mount as we repeatedly, albeit fruitlessly, fight with ourselves and our circumstances. Despite the glaring lack of desired results, we cling obstinately to our old ways. Yet, our hope, our salvation, lies in our capacity to broaden our perspective, to willingly let go, and to transcend into The Quantum Field. It is here that we connect with superior methods of achievement, satisfying the cravings of our humanness with those sweet results. Are you ready to make that leap?

Meet Emma

Emma had always dreamed of being a renowned chef. From a young age, she was enchanted by the magic that happened in the kitchen. After culinary school, she worked tirelessly in top restaurants, honing her skills and developing her unique style. She spent years perfecting her signature dish, a fusion of flavors from her multicultural background.

Determined to make a name for herself, Emma entered every prestigious cooking competition she could find. Yet, despite her best efforts, victory always seemed to elude her. She was either too experimental for the traditionalists or too conventional for the innovators.

Frustrated and disheartened, Emma decided to take a break from the competitive world and volunteered at a local community center, teaching healthy eating classes to underprivileged kids. It was a humbling experience, and she found joy in sharing her passion and knowledge with others.

One day, a local TV producer visited the community center and was impressed by Emma's ability to connect with the kids and make healthy eating fun and accessible. He offered her a spot on a local morning show, demonstrating easy and affordable recipes for families. Emma hesitated at first, as it was a far cry from the Michelin-starred aspirations she had held for so long. However, remembering the monkey and the rice story, she decided to let go of her previous ambitions and embrace this new opportunity.

Emma's segments quickly gained popularity, and she became a beloved figure in the community. Her approachable style and focus on affordable, healthy meals resonated with many viewers. Soon, she was offered her own cooking show, which became a hit. Emma had finally achieved her dream of being a renowned chef, but not in the way she had originally imagined.

Life often has a way of surprising us. Sometimes, the path to our goals is not what we expect, and we must be willing to let go of our preconceived notions and embrace new opportunities. Like the monkey, we can find ourselves trapped by our desires and our refusal to let go of a specific outcome. By releasing our grip and being open to new possibilities, we can find success in the most unexpected places.

The Money Shot: Breaking Chains

Imagine this: you're watching a suspense-filled movie, you spot the lurking danger before the protagonist does, and you're practically yelling, "Watch out!" That's me, right now, hollering, "Let go of the rice, you genius!" Your rigid adherence to old methods, your refusal to release your grip, has left you shackled. But here's the plot twist—your liberator is closer than you think. It surrounds you—The Quantum Field. It whispers sweet nothings of prosperity, prodding you to realize that the key to genuine comfort, security, and freedom lies not in grabbing, but in releasing. Loosen your grip, alter your strategy, let go, and witness Quantum Capitalism blow you away.

The Recap

What's the moral of our monkey saga? It's simple—if your plan isn't working, your ego is the monkey, keeping you from realizing it. The Quantum Field together with Quantum You is the liberator, leading you towards adaptation, higher opportunities, and true success.

Poke The Brain

How are you the monkey in the trap today?

Your Next Power Move

Juggernaut Journal Writing Exercise: Breaking Free from the Coconut Trap.

Objective: challenge your attachment to old methods and perspectives that might be hindering your progress. Explore the concept of letting go to embrace new opportunities and The Quantum Field.

Step 1: Identify Your "Rice"

Write down an aspect of your life or a method you've been holding onto stubbornly, despite lack of results or satisfaction. This could be related to a goal, a strategy, a habit, or a mindset.

Step 2: Monkey Mind Reflection

Imagine yourself as the monkey in the coconut trap. Reflect on how your attachment to the identified aspect is similar to the monkey's grip on the rice-filled coconut.

- Describe the parallels between your situation and the monkey's predicament.
- Note the frustration or dissatisfaction you've experienced while clinging to the old approach.

Step 3: Embrace the Quantum Leap

Shift your perspective towards embracing change and The Quantum Field as your liberator.

- Write about a scenario where you release your grip on the "rice" and step into The Quantum Field.
- Envision the opportunities, possibilities, and successes that await you once you let go.
- Describe the feelings of freedom and empowerment as you transcend old limitations.

Step 4: Your Quantum Sculptor Identity

Conclude your exercise by reflecting on your role as the Quantum Sculptor of your life.

- Describe the concept of embracing change and releasing attachment in your own words.
- Write a declaration of your commitment to letting go, adapting, and embracing new opportunities.
- Reflect on how adopting this mindset can lead to a more fulfilling and successful life journey.

Conclusion

This writing exercise prompts you to examine your attachment to old methods and perspectives, encouraging you to let go and embrace change. By envisioning yourself breaking free from the coconut trap and stepping into The Quantum Field, you open yourself up to new possibilities and opportunities for growth and success. Remember, you have the power to sculpt your own reality by choosing to release what no longer serves you.

Lesson 76

Trust

So, you've had the light bulb moment that you've been the monkey way too long. You know your fist is stuck in the proverbial coconut and you're dying trying to hang on, but trusting the unknown? Really? Yep, it's a thing, and guess what, it works. But first, you need to get that we're all programmed to think the opposite. The Matrix adores you in monkey mode; it literally thrives off it. It wraps you up in a snug blanket, whispering sweet nothings about trusting only yourself and your own Inner Force. Sounds badass, right? Wrong. It's a narrative dripping with sly manipulation, a crafty ploy designed to make you crumble under pressure, resign yourself to a life of consumerism, and trap you in an endless cycle of doom-scrolling and generating ad dollars. Time to flip that stale-ass old Script.

Trust in yourself, trust in your world, trust in The Quantum Field that vibrates with possibilities. The Matrix has fooled you into believing it's all up to you, that you need to grit your teeth and bear the entire world on your shoulders. But let me tell you, that's a lie.

I speak from experience, from a personal journey marred by battles with anxiety and depression, using raw Inner Force in every corner of my life. The results? Absolute depletion, out of sync with my Soul's Code, hanging on by a thread. Until I discovered a new path—trusting my world and The Quantum Field. Embracing this trust has been a game-changer, transforming not just every detail of my Sector, but also every inch of my being.

My mantra, my lighthouse in the stormy seas became:

"My world is taking care of me. Everything is going according to plan. Things are working out beautifully and will continue to do so with ease."

This mantra has been my saving grace, connecting me to my higher power, The Quantum Field, and my Quantum Self. By adopting this mantra, you too can experience a radical life transformation, a complete metamorphosis of reality right before your eyes.

Think of it this way—your world has never really let you down, has it? Sure, there were times when you didn't get what you wanted, or you felt you had to go without, or maybe a traumatic event turned your world upside down, leaving you picking up the pieces of your life. But all of that has brought you here, hasn't it? You're still going, you've still got it in you, and you still have the strength to evolve. Money is not solely where it's at, folks. It's the energy that circulates within every aspect of our world and is directly connected to our feelings of survival. Yes, it provides comfort and security, things we so desperately yearn for as humans, but that's all it really is. What truly matters is within you right now—that compelling fire in your belly to grow, experience new things, and squeeze every last drop out of life. If you've made it this far through the book, congratulations. My fire greets your fire. Moving forward with Quantum You engaged, looking to materialize those higher Sectors of Reality, this mantra, this mindset that I'm offering here, now, in this chapter, will serve you well. I promise you that.

The Money Shot: Exiting The Matrix

When you trust that your world is taking care of you, and that everything playing out externally is going according to plan, The Matrix releases its grip on you, and you can begin to transform some of your faulty financial narratives. When you believe that things are working out beautifully, and will continue to do so with ease regardless of the circumstances, you are greasing the wheels of personal evolution and prosperity. Exiting scarcity mindset and poverty mentality is all about trust. When you operate from a place of lack, you are essentially telling your world that you do not trust it. Believing that it all comes down to you and your sole abilities in this world will break you, as it has broken many throughout the human experience. Trusting your world is an art, and it pays off handsomely. Separating yourself from the emotional intensity of wondering if it will all work out is nothing short of a miracle. Trusting that your world will deliver is the ultimate tool for the evolving Quantum Capitalist. I compel you to sharpen this tool.

The Recap

The leap from Inner Force to trusting your world is a monumental shift, a revolution of the self. By loosening your grip on control and entrusting your world, you can instigate a transformation beyond words. Whatever it is that you desire for yourself, it is achievable. Tune out the false, Matrix version of you and tune in to the real, Quantum You, trusting your world knows the exact way, because it does. Let it show you.

Your Next Power Move

Embrace the Mantra

Objective: turn the empowering trust mantra into visual reminders and place them around your daily environment.

"My world is taking care of me. Everything is going according to plan. Things are working out beautifully and will continue to do so with ease."

Step 1: Mantra Integration

Read and absorb the trust mantra. Understand its shift from Inner Force to trusting your world and The Quantum Field.

Step 2: Visual Transformation

Stickers: create stickers featuring the mantra. Place them on your mirror, laptop, notebook and anywhere else in your home, office, or car where you will see them frequently.

Screensavers: make a screensaver with the mantra. Set it on your devices to reinforce the message.

Step 3: Daily Reinforcement

- When you see the visuals, take a moment to recite the mantra.
- Repeat it during your morning routine, throughout your day and before sleep. Step 4: Reflect and Integrate

Observe any changes over a few weeks:

- Note mindset shifts and positive experiences.
- Embrace the trust mantra as a guiding force in your decisions and actions. Conclusion:

By incorporating the trust mantra into your surroundings, you actively cultivate trust in your world and The Quantum Field. Visual reminders enhance your daily practice, promoting a mindset of empowerment and positive transformation.

Fun Fact—Ripple Effect: placing this mantra around your home and office where others can see it will exert a positive influence on them, often subconsciously. Observe for yourself and witness the impact.

Lesson 77

Sovereign Self

There's no shying away from it, you're royalty. Maybe not the kind that wears a physical crown, mind you, but the one who sits at the helm of your own reality. Your home, your castle. Your community, your kingdom. This isn't about lording over others; it's about embracing the true power that's innately yours.

Every thought, every word, every action—they're your royal decrees, shaping the world around you. You are a force to be reckoned with. An artisan carefully crafting every facet of your reality. Every interaction, every encounter, it's an opportunity for you to exert your influence, to radiate your wisdom and ability.

Every monarch has a council, a group of trusted advisors to guide them. But you're no ordinary monarch, are you? So, your council, your companions, should be nothing less than extraordinary. Surround yourself with those who fan your flames, those who believe in you as much as you do.

Beware the Blackholes, the ones who drain your power. They're crafty, promising comfort while leeching away your magic. Do not give them your resources. Protect your kingdom, guard your reality.

From this moment forward, declare yourself the royalty of your own reality. No longer leave things up to chance or circumstance. You are divine and possess all the power you need to materialize the Sectors you choose. Never again doubt this power.

The Quantum Field basks in your sovereignty. It sees you shining, unhindered, and tuned to your Soul Code. Should you choose the Quantum Capitalist journey, reality will begin to take on a dream-like quality, opening paths and doorways you never even knew were available to you. This is where The Matrix You and Quantum You diverge and go their separate ways.

Have you ever witnessed a miracle? Not a minor serendipitous event, but a genuine, life-changing miracle? I have, and it is my life. All worldly logic would point to one simple fact: I don't belong in the reality I have chosen for myself. I should have been another statistic, a young child or teenager succumbing to an unfortunate set of circumstances, but I'm not. This miracle I have encountered, the miracle that is my life, is available to you too. You can be a miracle. You are a miracle. Keep that close to your Heart as you explore distant Sectors of Reality. Keep that close to your Heart as you evolve into a person you perhaps never thought you could be. Keep that close to your Heart as you take command of your reality.

The Money Shot: Sovereignty or Bust

True sovereignty is the name of the game. Once you have declared a meaningful reason to obtain higher wealth, it comes to you. This reason should be sovereignty. Achieving higher wealth through meaningful endeavors, which is then used in

Sovereign Self

meaningful ways, allows us to sever many energetic cords that connect us to The Matrix. The one truly meaningful goal I have set for myself in my life is to be financially sovereign. In my previous sectors of reality, the external variables were crushed with debt, under-earning, and toxic Matrix laden programming. These tools, this system, have helped me to extract myself from those fates and take the reins of my reality. I now sit in a kingdom of my own design, financially comfortable and free from all the encumbrances that suffocated the generations before me. This freedom is available to us all, but you must wake up and initiate the shift. This knowledge is here for you, but to become sovereign, you must utilize it.

The Recap

You create your experiences, define your interactions, and build your kingdom.

You are not a serf in the field of your reality but the regent on the throne. Dismiss any scarcity mentality—do not live with the mindset of a destitute peasant. Never relinquish your power to The Matrix and Blackholes that sow doubt, fear, or insecurity.

Poke The Brain

Think about this: if you could change the laws of your reality right now, what would you change?

Your Next Power Move

Meditation: Sovereignty of Self.

Claim Your Throne: find a quiet space and sit or lie down comfortably. Close your eyes and take a deep breath. Visualize yourself in a majestic castle, sitting on a regal throne. Feel the power and authority within you.

Golden Decrees: imagine your thoughts as golden orbs of light. With each inhale, envision positive, empowering thoughts radiating from your Heart and filling the room. As you exhale, imagine these thoughts shaping your reality, bringing positivity and abundance.

Circle of Allies and Shield: envision a circle of trusted advisors around you, supporting and uplifting you. Feel their positive energy. Imagine a protective shield forming around you, repelling doubts and negativity. This shield keeps your power intact and your reality aligned with your desires.

Declaration: "I am the ruler of my reality. My thoughts create my kingdom of positivity and plenty."

Take a few more deep breaths, and when you're ready, open your eyes, carrying the sense of empowerment and sovereignty with you throughout your day.

I Decree the Quantum Me

We've journeyed far and wide together, you and I. We've swam in the depths of self-awareness, climbed the mountains of understanding, and dared to dance in the tempest of our own vulnerabilities. Today, we find ourselves at the edge of the precipice, facing the final leap. This is where the rubber meets the road, where the theory transforms into life-altering action.

We've challenged the status quo. We've shaken the very foundation of your belief system, and in doing so, unlocked a power within you that rivals the mightiest of forces. Nearing the end of these lessons, I hope you see that you have everything within you, right now, to become a creator.

Reflect on everything you've learned so far. Your perception isn't just a lens; it's a veritable paintbrush, capable of creating vast landscapes of reality. But here's your golden key: you're not just the artist, but also the canvas and the very essence of the painting.

Your life is a masterpiece of your own making, and your perspective is the brush strokes defining your existence. It's all you, baby. You are the force behind every decision, every feeling, every thought. And that power, that raw energy coursing through you, is your birthright.

You Are the Power!

Ever watched a superhero movie where the hero discovers they've had the power all along? It's the moment when Spider-Man realized he didn't need the suit, or when Wonder Woman understood that she is the God Killer. It's thrilling, exhilarating, empowering.

And you, my friend, are about to have that same epiphany. You've journeyed with me through these lessons, and now it's time for you to take the wheel, to decide that you are the power. No more sideline spectating. This is your game. You make the rules. You are the hero, the power, the driving force.

Are you ready for your next Sector?

Let me leave you with this: if you have the power to shape your reality, what's stopping you from creating the life you've always dreamed of? What's your next move? How will you harness your power? Where will this knowledge take you?

Your Next Power Move

Power Exercise: Declare Your Verdict.

Set the Stage: find a quiet and comfortable space where you won't be disturbed. Take a few deep breaths to center yourself.

Write Your Verdict: grab your Juggernaut Journal and paper or open a digital notepad. Write down the following declaration in bold letters:

"I am the power. I shape my reality. I am Quantum Me."

Speak Your Truth: stand up or sit up straight. Read your written declaration out loud with conviction. Feel the words resonate within you. Say it multiple times if you need to, letting the power of the words sink in.

Visualize and Embrace: close your eyes and take a moment to visualize yourself standing strong, surrounded by an aura of confidence and calm control. Imagine your reality bending to your intention, as you shape it according to your desires.

Affirm and Believe: open your eyes and repeat the declaration once again, looking at the words as you say them. Believe every word you utter. This is your truth, your affirmation of your power.

Anchor Your Verdict: keep your written declaration somewhere visible, like a mirror, a vision board, or as your phone wallpaper. Whenever self-doubt creeps in, return to your verdict, reaffirming your power.

CONCLUSION

Well, here we are. If you've made it this far, you're no longer the person you were at the start. If you've felt provoked, unsettled, or even had a couple of laugh-out-loud moments, then this book has done its job.

We've covered a lot of ground together. We've explored the vast expanse of your potential, confronted the coconuts of your life, learned the power in letting go of the "rice," and tuned into your Quantum Voice. If your mind is whirling, that's a good sign—it means you're processing, challenging your narrative, and evolving.

Remember, change doesn't happen overnight. It's like tending a garden; it requires constant nurturing. The seeds have been sown in your subconscious. Now it's up to you to water them with introspection, bask them in the sunlight of action, and weed out the remnants of resistance.

And as you move forward, remember that you are the quantum architect of your life. You have the power to sculpt your reality, not through rigid control, but through the art of letting go and allowing The Quantum Field to show you the way.

In closing, we're handing you back the reins. Your life is a masterpiece in the making. Paint it with broad strokes of bravery, speckles of spontaneity, and don't be afraid to color outside the lines. Embrace the process, celebrate the progress, and remember—you're not just surviving; you're thriving.

Thank you for embarking on this journey with us. Here's to breaking chains, shaking things up, and living your life on your own terms. Cheers to you, the quantum architect, the brave explorer, the forever learner—the change maker.

The Extras

The Burning Ritual

This powerful ritual signifies moving on from limiting beliefs and thoughts that are no longer serving you. It involves acknowledging these beliefs, saying goodbye to them, and then physically burning them as a symbolic act of release.

Step-by-Step Guide:

1. **Identify Limiting Beliefs:** write down all the limiting beliefs, thoughts, and anything else that is holding you back, each on a separate piece of paper.
2. **Prepare Your Space:** find a safe place to burn the papers, like a fireplace or a fire pit outside.
3. **Acknowledge and Say Goodbye:** take each piece of paper, one at a time, look at the belief written on it, acknowledge it, say goodbye to it, and then throw it into the fire.
4. **Watch the Belief Incinerating:** watch the paper burn and take a mental snapshot of the belief incinerating.
5. **Repeat:** move through each of the beliefs until they are all burned.
6. **Acknowledge the Release:** once all the papers are burned, acknowledge that you are leaving these beliefs as ashes.

Remember:

- The power of this ritual lies in the visual act of seeing your limiting beliefs burn. If these beliefs resurface later,

you can recall the image of them incinerating and remind yourself that you have moved on and no longer need to carry them with you.
- While this ritual can be particularly impactful at the start of a new year, it can be done at any time you feel the need to release limiting beliefs and start afresh.

Final Note

Letting go of limiting beliefs is crucial for personal growth and transformation. This burning ritual is a powerful way to symbolically release these beliefs and make room for new, empowering ones. Remember, it's not just about the act of burning the beliefs, but also about consciously choosing to move on and not carry them with you any longer.

THE MONEY MAGNET

I'm about to drop a cheat code for opening up energetic financial channels. Imagine if you could throw out a fishing line and instead of pulling in a bunch of seaweed and an old boot, you reel in money, connections, and opportunities. Sound woo-woo? Not in your reality, not when you've got the power of Quantum Capitalism at your fingertips. This meditation has served me and countless others well. Seriously, try it for yourself and see.

Magnetize Cash, Connections, and Cosmic "Coincidence"

Instructions

1. Get Real About Your Financial Fantasies:

The Quantum Field can't give you what you don't admit you want. No half-measures. We're talking money, opportunities, connections, serendipitous events—anything that pushes you up the wealth ladder.

2. Pick Your Quantum Anchor:

Grab an object—could be a quartz stone, a casino chip, or a paperweight. But listen, this object needs to be as neutral as Switzerland in a world war. No sentimental trinkets, got it? Also, it's best to choose an object that signifies wealth for you.

3. Zone Out to Tune In:

Find a spot quieter than a mouse in a library and sit in a Zen-like pose. You're the Buddha contemplating Wall Street here. Go into meditation mode. Deep breaths in and out. You know the routine.

4. The Power Grip:

Clasp that Money Magnet in your hands like it's your personal Holy Grail. Got it? Good.

5. Whip It, Whip It Real Good:

Imagine a whip unspooling from the crown of your head. At the end of this whip is a magnetized claw. Now, with your eyes still closed, envision throwing your whip out into the world. Throw it as far as you can envision, then returning, only to be thrown again.

As you launch this claw out into the world, repeat, "All the money, opportunities, and means to achieve, I call you closer to me now."

6. Reel in the Riches:

Draw it back and pull all that goodness into your object. Feel that claw latch onto every bit of money energy, the energy of every golden opportunity, and even the right people who can skyrocket your wealth game. Feel that energy connect with and move through your energetic whip, through the top of your head, into your body, through your arms, and into your object.

7. All Charged Up:

Keep doing it. Over and over. Until you feel your object humming with the energy of a Tesla coil.

Throw the energetic whip in all directions, imagining it going further and further with each throw.

Eventually, envision your whip traveling around the world.

8. Carry Your Money Magnet:

Keep this electrified object with you at all times. Every time you touch it, remember it's not just a piece of metal or a rock—it's a magnet attracting your future empire.

So, what are you waiting for? Wealth is for anyone daring enough to believe they deserve it. You do. Now go prove it.

REALITY REEL-IN RITUAL

A Tale and a Task

There are unmaterialized Sectors of Reality behind the Dual Mirror World, including the version of reality you are looking to materialize. You are going to create an anchor in your physical world that essentially acts as a connection between this version of reality and the version of reality you are looking to materialize behind the Dual Mirror World.

The Tale

Once upon a time, in a land far away, I stumbled upon a little white ceramic house while wandering the streets of Tbilisi. The homemade piece, crafted by a street artist, screamed out to me, "HERE I AM!" I knew instantly that it was my Object of Intention, the very thing that would connect my current reality to the unmaterialized Sector I longed to bring into existence.

Back home in the USA, I placed the ceramic house on my dining table, a humble abode for a tiny LED light that I could turn on and off, its glow illuminating the house from within. Each morning and each night, I lit up the house, cementing my intention within my mind and linking it to the house. Seeing it throughout the day reinforced my intention in the present moment.

I created a line of communication from my Object of Intention to behind the Mirror World. Focusing on it opened up the line, triggering a series of events. These events led to the information, opportunities, and means required to materialize my intention in the physical world. Acting on them methodically and rapidly, I began to pull that version of reality from behind the Mirror into my world.

The Object of Intention I selected was perfect for my goal, resulting in the rapid materialization of the Tbilisi house variation of reality. The ceramic house was not only a symbol of my goal but also beautiful proof of my power to materialize my dreams.

The Task

Now, it's your turn to materialize your desired version of reality. Follow these steps:

1. Choose Your Object of Intention: select an object that symbolizes the unmaterialized Sector of Reality you wish to materialize. Make sure it resonates with your intention and is free from any existing associations.
2. Create Your Connection: place your Object of Intention somewhere you will see it frequently. Each morning and night, spend 30 seconds to a minute focusing on your intention and connecting it to your Object. Use this time to reinforce your intention in your current space and time.
3. Activate Your Object of Intention: visualize a line of communication extending from your object to behind the Dual Mirror World. When you focus on your object, imagine that this line of communication opens, initiating events behind the Mirror that will lead to the realization of your intention in the physical world.
4. Take Action: as opportunities arise in your physical world that align with your intention, act on them quickly and methodically. This will help you to pull your desired version of reality from behind the Mirror into your physical world.
5. Renew Your Intention: once you have realized your goal, release your Object of Intention and select a new object

for your next goal. Your Objects of Intention should always be representative of your current goal.

Remember, the object you choose will virtually scream out to you, "HERE I AM!" Trust your instincts, stay committed to your intention, and watch as your desired reality materializes before your eyes.

THE POWER OBJECT

A Power Object is an object that resonates deeply with your personal strength and connects you to the powers of your Quantum Self that you might not have connected with yet. It symbolizes your unique set of skills, characteristics, and personal attributes that empower you to materialize your goals, intentions, and dreams.

In this exercise, you will identify and infuse an object with your power, thus creating a visual reminder to help you remain connected to your Quantum Self. This object will serve as a physical reminder of your Soul Code, personal power and the intentions you've set for yourself.

Steps

1. Choose Your Object: this should be an object that you can carry with you all the time, such as a piece of jewelry or something small enough to keep in your pocket. It can be anything—a gold chain, a coin, a leather bracelet—just make sure that when you see it, you feel an expansion of your personal power within.
2. Infuse Your Object: hold your chosen object in your hands and close your eyes. Feel your Soul Code, and imagine that energy flowing from your heart, down your arms, and into the object. Feel the object absorbing this energy.
3. Carry Your Object: keep your Power Object with you as much as possible. Look at it often and connect with it when you need power to move through your day rapidly and with ease.

Notes

- Your Power Object is a tool to remind you of your Soul Code and to keep you connected to your personal power.
- You can transfer power from one object to another if you want to upgrade or change your Object for any reason.

THE GOALS AND DOORS BOOK

The secret to achieving big things is to keep track of the smaller things. This is an easy-to-implement system that I've been using and recommending for a while, and trust me, it works wonders. Say goodbye to lost thoughts, procrastination, and underachievement. Say hello to focus, efficiency, and surprising yourself with your own power.

Step-by-Step Guide

1. **Select Your Journal:** grab a binder or a journal. This is going to be your Goals and Doors Book. This is where you'll capture all your steps, ideas, and actions towards your goal.
2. **Define Your Goal:** write your goal on a piece of paper and tape it to the front of your journal. And hey, don't be shy. If you think your goal is $25k, write down $50k. Aim high and you'll find yourself stretching to reach and surpass your own expectations.
3. **Record Your Thoughts:** anytime a thought, idea, or action aligned with your goal crosses your mind, write it down in the book. It could be a step you need to take, someone you need to talk to, or any move that will get you closer to your goal.
4. **Magical Middle World Time:** tune out of all distractions and go through the lists within the book, crossing off and completing as many items as you can. This will help you to feel empowered as you see you are moving through the items at rapid speed.
5. **Stay Organized:** organize your thoughts and steps efficiently. This system is not just for recording but for guiding your actions. By keeping track of your thoughts and planned actions, you'll complete tasks at a pace that will astonish your past self.

6. **Reflect on Your Power:** as you fill your book and achieve your goals, take time to reflect on your journey. Look back at your past Goals and Doors Pages and acknowledge your achievements. You've done all this stuff. Yes, you are killing it.

Remember

- Your mind is not built to remember every fleeting thought amidst the chaos of daily life. Put your thoughts on paper and keep your mind clear for action.
- Don't aim for easily achievable goals. Aim higher. The challenge will energize you, and even if you don't hit your target, you'll achieve more than you would have with a lower goal.
- This book will become a record of your power. Use it to fuel your confidence for future goals.

Final Note

This system is more than a tool; it's a backbone. It's the support that will help you achieve everything with ease. Start your Goals and Doors Book today and unlock a level of achievement and self-awareness that will leave you amazed at your own power.

THE LIVE STROLL

Walking is not just good for your body; it's also a powerful tool for manifesting your intentions. This exercise, The Live Stroll, combines physical activity with focused intention to generate ideas, steps, and information that will help you materialize your goals. By pairing this exercise with the Goals and Doors Book, you'll create a powerful system that guarantees progress and prevents stagnation.

Step-by-Step Guide

1. **Declare Your Awareness:** before starting your walk, declare to yourself that you see yourself and your reality. Feel your feet firmly planted on the ground and remind yourself of your powers.
2. **Start Walking:** begin your walk and focus on getting your blood circulating. After about 15 minutes of brisk walking and getting your heart rate up, you can start the next step.
3. **Project Your Intention:** imagine your intention being projected onto a film reel hovering in the sky. The intention of your walk is to attract ideas, steps, or any information that will assist in the materialization of your goal.
4. **Record Insights:** as you walk, make a mental note or record a voice note on your phone of anything that comes to mind that can help you realize your goal. After your walk, add these insights to your Goals and Doors Book.
5. **Visualize Your Progress:** with every step you take, imagine yourself getting closer to the version of reality you are intending.

Remember

- The purpose of the Live Stroll is to generate what you need to fulfill your goal. Combine it with the Goals and Doors Book to stay organized and on track.
- This exercise is not just about physical exercise but opening yourself up to information that you will use during your day.
- With every step, you are not only improving your health but also getting closer to your intended reality.

Final Note

The Live Stroll, combined with the Goals and Doors Book, is a powerful method for rapid materialization of your goals. Whether you are starting from scratch or looking to advance to the next level, these tools will help you progress with ease. Remember, the key to success is not just setting intentions but taking actionable steps towards them. Get started today and watch your reality transform.

MONEY ENERGY TRANSFORMATION

Money is not just a physical entity; it is a flow of energy. Your beliefs, thoughts, and actions all play a significant role in attracting or repelling money. It is, therefore, crucial to be mindful of your attitude and behavior towards money. This exercise will help you identify and understand the actions that attract and repel money in your life. By recognizing and altering your behavior, you can change your money energy and create a more prosperous life.

Instructions:

1. Take a few deep breaths and clear your mind. Center yourself and focus on the task at hand.
2. Carefully read through the lists of Money Attracting Actions and Money Repelling Actions.
3. As you read each action, take a moment to reflect on your own behavior and identify any areas where you could improve.
4. Make a commitment to yourself to focus on the Money Attracting Actions and limit the Money Repelling Actions.
5. Read through these lists daily for a week. Make it a part of your morning routine to set a positive tone for the day.
6. Throughout the week, be mindful of your actions and thoughts related to money. Make a conscious effort to change any negative behaviors.
7. At the end of the week, reflect on any changes you have noticed in your attitude and behavior towards money.

Remember, it is not just about the money you have in your bank account; it is about the energy you bring to it. By shifting your mindset and focusing on positive actions, you can attract more abundance into your life. Give yourself permission to succeed and create the prosperity you deserve.

Money Attracting Actions:

- Honoring your worth and time
- Giving and receiving freely
- Thinking of how you will create money
- Expecting the best to happen
- Coming from your Heart
- Doing your best
- Wanting everyone to succeed, cooperating
- Focusing on how you can serve others
- Telling yourself why you can succeed
- Coming from your integrity
- Being aware and paying attention
- Applauding others' success
- Embracing your challenges
- Releasing things easily
- Believing it's never too late
- Taking action on your intentions
- Believing your path is valuable
- Giving yourself permission to be and do what you want
- Doing what you love for your livelihood
- Detaching, surrendering to your higher good
- Giving to others' prosperity
- Doing your highest purpose activities first
- Seeing yourself as the source of your abundance
- Believing in abundance
- Believing in yourself, self-confidence, self-love
- Clear intentions
- Following your joy
- Expressing gratitude and thanks
- Trusting in your ability to create abundance
- Listening to your Quantum Self
- Looking for a winning solution for everyone
- Becoming your own authority

- Measuring abundance as fulfilling your purpose and happiness
- Enjoying the process as much as the goal
- Clear agreements
- Thinking how far you have come
- Speaking of abundance
- Remembering past successes
- Thinking in expanded, unlimited ways
- Focusing on what you love and want
- Allowing yourself to have

Money Repelling Actions:

- Not honoring your worth and time
- Not giving or being open to receive
- Focusing on how you need money
- Worrying that the worst will happen
- Getting into power struggles
- Cutting corners
- Competing
- Thinking only of what others will give you
- Telling yourself why you can't succeed
- Compromising your values and ideas
- Operating on automatic
- Feeling threatened by others' success
- Choosing safety and comfort over growth
- Hanging on to things
- Thinking it's too late, giving up
- Not believing in your path
- Waiting for others to give you permission
- Working only for the money
- Feeling needy or that you must have something
- Giving to others' need

- Putting off higher purpose activities until you have more time
- Viewing others as the source of your abundance
- Believing in scarcity
- Worrying, fears, doubts, self-criticism
- Vague or undefined goals
- Forcing yourself, creating "have tos" and "shoulds"
- Feeling the world owes you
- Worrying over finances
- Ignoring your Quantum Self
- Not caring if the other person wins
- Not believing in your inner wisdom
- Measuring abundance only by how much money you have
- Doing things only for the goal
- Unspoken or vague expectations
- Focusing on how far you have to go
- Talking about problems and lack
- Remembering past failures
- Thinking in limited ways
- Focusing only on what you don't want
- Feeling as though you don't deserve

REALITY RESCRIPTING

Hey, you! Yeah, I'm talking to you. You know that life you've been dreaming about? It's time to make it your reality. Don't roll your eyes; I'm dead serious. You have the power to reshape your narrative, and I'm here to guide you through it. Buckle up!

1. **Mindset Reset:** first things first, clear that beautiful mind of yours. Close your eyes, inhale the good stuff, exhale the bullshit. Let go of the stress and negativity. You don't need it.
2. **Set Your Sights:** what do you want, really want? Get clear on your intentions. This could be anything from gaining clarity on your goals to aligning your actions with your desires. Dream big, darling.
3. **Pick Your Preference:** are you old school and prefer pen and paper, or are you more tech-inclined and prefer digital? Decide where you're going to write your Script.
4. **Craft Your Tale:** time to write your Script. Describe your life as you want it to be, right now, in the present tense. Cover all bases—personal, professional, health, relationships, the whole shebang. And don't just focus on the external; the internal changes are just as crucial.
5. **Visualize, Visualize, Visualize:** as you write, picture the scenes in your mind. Engage all your senses. Smell the roses, feel the wind in your hair.
6. **Review and Refine:** read your Script. Tweak it, change it, add to it. Make it perfectish.
7. **Make It Stick:** read your Script daily, morning and night. Feel the emotions associated with your new reality. This isn't just a Script, it's your life.

8. **Action Time:** use your Script as a guide for your daily actions. Align your 4 Qualifiers with your new narrative. Walk the talk.

Example:

"Hey, I'm [Your Name]. I'm crushing it in my career as [Your Desired Profession], and I feel fulfilled and satisfied every single day. I have a loving, supportive relationship with my partner, and we communicate openly and honestly. I take care of my body by exercising regularly and eating nourishing foods. I feel confident and comfortable in my own skin. I have a strong, supportive network of friends and family who encourage me to be my best self. I make time for activities that bring me joy and relaxation. I manage my finances wisely and have a solid plan for my financial future. I am grateful for the abundance in my life, and I approach each day with a positive attitude and a sense of purpose."

Remember, this isn't a one-and-done deal. Be kind to yourself and allow for flexibility and change as you progress. You're not carving your Script in stone; it's more like molding clay.

MATRIX VS. QUANTUM BELIEF PURGE

The purpose of this exercise is to challenge and reframe your limiting beliefs. Remember, your Matrix Self is the version of you that's held back by limiting beliefs, while your Quantum Self is the version of you that's empowered, positive, and boundless.

Step 1: write down a limiting belief that your Matrix Self is currently struggling with.

Step 2: now, let your Quantum Self play devil's advocate. Challenge this belief with a positive and empowering reframe.

Formula:

Matrix Self: [Limiting Belief]
Quantum Self: [Positive and Empowering Reframe]

Examples:

1. I'm not good enough.
   Oh, please! You are more than enough just as you are, and you're getting better every day. Remember, even a diamond starts as coal.

2. I'll never be successful.
   Newsflash! Success isn't a destination, it's a journey. Every step you take is a step towards your own personal success story.

3. I don't deserve happiness.
   Hold on a second! You deserve happiness and fulfillment as much as anyone else on this planet.

4. I can't do it.
   Reality check! You are capable and strong. You've handled tough situations before, and you can handle this too.

5. It's too late for me.
   Time out! It's never too late to start. You can create change at any age. Remember, Colonel Sanders started KFC at 65!

6. I'm not smart enough.
   Excuse me! You are intelligent and capable. Plus, intelligence is not just about what you know, it's about your eagerness to learn and grow.

7. I'm not attractive enough.
   Seriously? You are beautiful inside and out. Your worth isn't determined by your appearance.

8. I'm not worthy of love.
   Let's get this straight! You are lovable and absolutely worthy of giving and receiving love.

9. I have to be perfect to be accepted.
   News alert! Perfection is overrated. You are accepted and valued for who you are, imperfections and all.

10. I'm not as good as others.
    Reality check! You are unique and valuable. You bring your own special qualities to the table.

11. I don't have enough time.
    Hold up! Time is what you make of it. Prioritize, organize, and make time for what matters most.

12. I'm too old to change.
    Oh, come on! Age is just a number. It's never too late to grow and evolve.

13. I'll always be broke.
    Newsflash! Money is energy, and you have the power to attract it into your life. Focus on abundance, not lack.

14. I'm not talented enough.
    Excuse me! Talent is overrated. Hard work, persistence, and a positive mindset are where it's at.

15. I'm too shy or introverted.
    Time out! Being shy or introverted is not a limitation, it's a superpower. Embrace who you are and let your light shine.... and so on.

Remember to challenge your beliefs and preconceptions in a way that is fun, clarifying, and convincing. You have the power to rewrite your limiting beliefs, so go ahead and let your Quantum Self shine!

GOODBYE MATRIX ME LETTER

Alright, it's time for some real talk. You're going to pen a letter from your Quantum Self to your Matrix Self. Yeah, that's right—you're about to have a heart-to-heart with yourself. But this isn't your typical, "Dear diary, here's how my day went..." kind of letter. Nope. This is a "Hey, things are changing, and you need to get on board or get left behind" letter. Because let's face it, your Matrix Self has been running the show for far too long, and it's time for Quantum You to take the reins.

Steps

1. Reflect on Your New Routine: before you dive into writing, take a hot minute to think about the changes you're making. What's in? What's out? Get clear on that.
2. Write the Letter: alright, here's where you get down to business. Start by acknowledging the good times with Matrix You. A little gratitude goes a long way. Then, lay down the law. Make it crystal clear that certain behaviors (I'm looking at you, doom-scrolling) are no longer on the menu. And don't forget to invite Matrix You to join the party. It's a new and improved shindig, and everyone's invited—as long as they play by the new rules.

Example Letter

Dear Matrix Me,

Sup? I hope this letter finds you somewhere between Netflix binging and scrolling through TikTok. I'm writing to say thanks for the ride so far. It's been real. But here's the thing—we've got some changes coming down the pike.

First of all, the doom-scrolling? It's gotta stop. I know it's like a train wreck and it's hard to look away, but it's doing us no favors. Also, the excuse-making and time-wasting? Those are out too. We've got big things to do, and we don't have time for that nonsense.

Now, don't get it twisted—I'm not kicking you to the curb. I'm inviting you to join me in this new routine. It's all about self-care, setting intentions, and doing things that light us up. I know it's a bit of a departure from our usual M.O., but trust me—it's gonna be epic.

If you're not ready to hop on this train, I get it. But I'm moving forward with or without you. I hope you'll join me when you're ready.

Catch ya on the flip side,

Quantum Me

Conclusion

Boom! You just laid down the law. But remember, it's all love. This exercise is all about setting boundaries with a side of humor and a whole lot of compassion. Change is tough, but it's how we grow. And let's be honest—it's about time.

Glossary

The Matrix

The Matrix refers to the conventional, often restrictive framework of reality as perceived by the collective consciousness. It's a metaphorical construct representing the societal norms, beliefs, and systems that shape our understanding of the world and dictate our behaviors. The Matrix is like the default setting of reality, often unnoticed yet powerfully influential, keeping individuals tethered to traditional ways of thinking and living. Stepping out of The Matrix implies a conscious shift towards a more liberated, self-directed approach to life, where one challenges and transcends these ingrained perceptions and norms to explore and create a more authentic, fulfilling reality.

Getting Played by The Matrix

This phrase symbolizes being unwittingly manipulated or controlled by the conventional societal norms, beliefs, and systems that comprise The Matrix. It refers to the scenario where an individual unknowingly conforms to the expectations and limitations set by societal standards, often at the expense of their own aspirations, creativity, or individuality. Being played by The Matrix means being caught up in the status quo, often living life reactively rather than proactively, and letting external influences dictate one's choices and path in life without questioning or challenging them. It's akin to being a passive participant in one's life journey, where the ingrained norms and societal constructs are the puppeteers.

The Quantum Field

This term refers to a conceptual energy field where all possibilities, potentialities, and paths of reality exist simultaneously. It embodies the idea that at a fundamental level, everything in The Universe is interconnected and influenced by energetic vibrations and frequencies. The Quantum Field is not bound by linear time or physical space, and it's where thoughts, intentions, and actions can influence and manifest reality. Engaging with The Quantum Field implies tapping into this sea of potential, aligning one's thoughts and energy with desired outcomes, and understanding that reality is fluid and moldable. It's where the principles of quantum mechanics meet the concepts of consciousness and manifestation, suggesting that our conscious and subconscious minds have the power to shape our experiences and realities.

Quantum Capitalist

A Quantum Capitalist is an individual who harnesses the principles of quantum mechanics and the concepts of energy, vibration, and consciousness to navigate and influence their reality. This person understands that their thoughts, beliefs, and actions are interconnected with The Universe's fabric— The Quantum Field. They skillfully use this knowledge to manifest desired outcomes, be it in personal growth, wealth creation, or other life aspects. A Quantum Capitalist doesn't just react to life circumstances; they actively create their reality by aligning their mental and emotional energies with their goals. This approach is a blend of metaphysical understanding, practical life skills, and a deep belief in one's power to influence and direct the course of their life through focused intention and mindful action.

Sectors of Reality

Sectors of Reality refer to the different levels or dimensions of existence and experience that a person can navigate and inhabit. These Sectors are not physical places but are conceptualized as varying states of being, awareness, or life circumstances. Each Sector represents a distinct frequency or vibrational state, reflecting the individual's thoughts, emotions, and overall consciousness. Moving through these Sectors involves shifting one's internal state, which in turn transforms their external reality. A higher Sector might represent a state of greater abundance, peace, and fulfillment, while a lower Sector could signify struggle, scarcity, or discord. The idea is that by consciously altering one's vibration through thoughts, beliefs, and actions, one can "travel" to different Sectors of reality, experiencing life in alignment with their desired state of being.

Guiding Theory

The concept of a Guiding Theory refers to the underlying set of beliefs and assumptions that shape an individual's perception of reality and drive their actions and decisions. It acts as an invisible framework or lens through which one views and interacts with the world. This theory encompasses personal philosophies, deep-seated beliefs about oneself and The Universe, and the narrative one tells themselves about their place and purpose in life. The Guiding Theory influences how an individual interprets experiences, reacts to challenges, and pursues goals. It is often shaped by a mix of past experiences, societal norms, and individual aspirations. Recognizing and consciously shaping one's Guiding Theory is crucial in Quantum Capitalism, as it directly impacts the ability to manifest desired outcomes and navigate different Sectors of Reality effectively.

By refining and aligning their Guiding Theory with their aspirations, an individual can more effectively harness the power of The Quantum Field to create a desired reality.

The 4 Qualifiers

In Quantum Capitalism, the 4 Qualifiers are integral elements shaping an individual's reality.

They include:

1. Guiding Theory: the core beliefs and narratives shaping one's worldview.
2. Thoughts: habitual thinking patterns influencing emotions and behaviors.
3. Actions: the tangible steps and efforts made towards goals.
4. Frequency: the energy or vibe emitted, influenced by emotional states and consciousness.

The alignment of these Qualifiers determines the effectiveness of personal growth and success within The Quantum Field. They emphasize a holistic approach to transformation and achievement in Quantum Capitalism.

Blackhole

Blackholes are energy vortexes that captivate and consume significant amounts of your time, energy, money, and emotional bandwidth. These are often created by external influences like media, social media, cultural norms, family dynamics, consumerism, and workplace environments. They manipulate emotions and thinking, pulling you away from more ideal Sectors of Reality. Blackholes can lead to misalignment with your goals and aspirations, as they divert attention and resources from more constructive and fulfilling pursuits. Recognizing and navigating away from these Blackholes is crucial for maintaining focus, balance, and progression towards desired realities.

Importance

Importance refers to the weight or significance we assign to our thoughts, actions, desires, or external circumstances. It's about how much mental and emotional energy we invest in specific aspects of our lives. Elevated levels of Importance can create imbalances, leading to stress, anxiety, and a skewed perception of reality. This can manifest as overthinking, fear of failure, or an exaggerated sense of urgency and consequence. Reducing and managing the level of Importance we assign helps in maintaining clarity, reducing stress, and making more balanced, rational decisions. It encourages a focus on flow and alignment with The Quantum Field, rather than getting caught up in the turbulence of overvalued thoughts or events.

Disproportionate Energy

This term in Quantum Capitalism refers to the scenario where the energy expended on a task, thought, emotion, or situation significantly outweighs its actual relevance or value in the broader context of one's life. It's like using a sledgehammer to crack a nut. Disproportionate Energy often arises from elevated levels of Importance, leading to unnecessary stress, anxiety, and resource depletion. It manifests when one fixates on minor details, overanalyzes situations, or obsesses over outcomes, thereby draining energy that could be more productively or enjoyably used elsewhere. Recognizing and redirecting Disproportionate Energy is key to maintaining balance, enhancing productivity, and aligning more effectively with one's true intentions and the flow of The Quantum Field.

Gravity

Gravity signifies the inevitable pull or consequence that follows when we give undue Importance to something, leading to Disproportionate Energy. This concept is akin to the physical law of gravity where every action has an equal and opposite reaction. In personal development, it manifests as the counterproductive outcomes that occur when we become overly fixated or obsessed with a particular aspect of our lives, whether it's a goal, fear, problem, or desire. This intense focus often creates a negative spiral, pulling us further away from our desired state or outcome, much like being caught in a gravitational pull. Understanding and managing Gravity involves recognizing where we are exerting too much force or attention, thus allowing us to release unnecessary burdens and realign with a more balanced and efficient path towards our goals within The Quantum Field.

The Downward Spiral

The Downward Spiral refers to a negative, self-perpetuating cycle that ensues when an individual becomes ensnared in counterproductive thoughts, emotions, or behaviors. This concept encapsulates how a single negative event or mindset can trigger a cascade of further negative experiences, emotions, or reactions, leading to a progressive decline in personal well-being, effectiveness, or happiness.

The Downward Spiral is often characterized by escalating negativity, where one adverse situation or mindset leads to another, creating a vortex of declining mental and emotional states. Breaking free from this spiral involves conscious effort to shift focus, employ positive coping strategies, and realign with constructive patterns and energies that promote upward movement towards more desirable Sectors of Reality.

The Upward Spiral

The Upward Spiral refers to a positive, self-reinforcing cycle of thoughts, emotions, and actions that lead to progressively better outcomes and an enhanced state of being. It's the antithesis of the Downward Spiral. This concept highlights how a single positive action or mindset can initiate a series of further beneficial experiences and states, creating a momentum of positivity and growth. The Upward Spiral is characterized by escalating positivity, where one favorable situation or mindset catalyzes another, fostering a cycle of increasing well-being, success, and fulfillment. To sustain and amplify this Spiral, individuals focus on nurturing positive thoughts, engaging in uplifting activities, and fostering constructive relationships, which cumulatively contribute to upward movement towards more desirable and fulfilling Sectors of Reality.

The Cosmic Comet of Fortune

The Cosmic Comet of Fortune is a metaphorical concept representing a rare, swift, and potentially transformative opportunity that suddenly appears in one's life. It symbolizes a moment of serendipity or a stroke of luck that, if seized, can lead to significant positive changes or advancements. Much like a comet that briefly lights up the sky, these opportunities are often fleeting and require quick, decisive action to capitalize on them. The Cosmic Comet of Fortune encourages individuals to be alert and prepared so they can recognize and grab these rare chances. It's about being in the right state of mind and readiness to ride the wave of an unexpected but favorable turn of events, leading to a rapid ascent in one's personal or professional life. This concept underscores the importance of agility, awareness, and the ability to harness sporadic opportunities in the journey of quantum growth and success.

The Quantum Flow

The Quantum Flow refers to a state of being where an individual is perfectly aligned with the rhythm and energy of The Quantum Field. It is characterized by effortless action, synchronicity, and a harmonious connection with The Universe. When someone is in the Quantum Flow, they experience a seamless integration of their intentions, thoughts, and actions with the opportunities and possibilities presented by The Universe. This state allows for the optimal utilization of personal energy and resources, leading to increased efficiency, productivity, and success. It's akin to catching the perfect wave in surfing; everything feels natural, timely, and in sync. The Quantum Flow emphasizes the importance of being attuned to one's environment and inner self, facilitating a smooth journey through various Sectors of Reality. It's about being in the "zone" where challenges are met with intuition and ease, leading to peak performance and fulfillment.

The Anti-Flow

The Anti-Flow symbolizes a state of resistance, struggle, and misalignment with The Quantum Field. It's like swimming against a relentless current; efforts feel laborious, progress seems stagnant, and every move is fraught with friction and frustration. When someone is caught in the Anti-Flow, they encounter continuous obstacles, setbacks, and a sense of disharmony with their environment and goals. This state is often marked by forced actions, contrived efforts, and a general feeling of being out of sync with The Universe's natural rhythm. It's akin to trying to force puzzle pieces into places where they don't fit—the more force applied, the less progress made. The Anti-Flow highlights the importance of recognizing when efforts are counterproductive, urging a reevaluation of strategies and attitudes. It serves as a reminder that sometimes, the best course of action is to realign one's approach, reassess goals, and attune more closely to the intuitive guidance of The Quantum Field. In essence, it's about recognizing when to stop pushing against the tide and instead find a more harmonious path forward.

Guiding Signs

Guiding Signs are subtle cues from The Quantum Field that aid in navigating life's journey. They appear as synchronicities, recurring themes, or intuitive nudges, acting like a cosmic GPS to guide you through various Sectors of Reality. These signs can affirm your current path, suggest a course correction, or encourage exploration of new possibilities. Recognizing and interpreting these signs enhances your connection with The Quantum Field and aids in making choices aligned with your goals and desires. Paying attention to Guiding Signs helps a Quantum Capitalist make informed decisions and progress towards a fulfilling life.

The Mirror World

The Mirror World is a concept symbolizing how our external reality is a reflection of our internal state, encompassing thoughts, emotions, and beliefs. It posits that our internal dialogue, attitudes, and perceptions are mirrored in our experiences and interactions. Beyond this reflection, the Mirror World holds different variations of reality, existing as potential outcomes. Our actions in the tangible, physical realm act as catalysts, pulling these variations into existence. This concept underscores the interconnectedness of the inner self and the outer reality, emphasizing the power of mindset and perspective in shaping life experiences. By understanding and engaging with the Mirror World, Quantum Capitalists can align their internal state with desired outcomes, navigating through various Sectors of Reality to actualize potential versions of their life, thus making the intangible tangible.

Inner Force

Inner Force refers to the intense, often strenuous personal effort and energy exerted to achieve goals or drive change. It's characterized by a strong sense of determination and a willingness to push through challenges. However, Inner Force often involves a battle against existing circumstances, requiring substantial mental or physical exertion. While it can lead to progress, it may also result in exhaustion or burnout due to its forceful nature. Inner Force is contrasted with the concept of Outer Power, where instead of using intense personal effort, one aligns with the flow of The Quantum Field to achieve goals more effortlessly and intuitively. Understanding and managing Inner Force is crucial for Quantum Capitalists to maintain balance and avoid the pitfalls of overexertion while pursuing their objectives.

Outer Power

Outer Power is a concept representing the effortless, almost magical alignment with The Quantum Field to achieve goals and manifest desires. Unlike Inner Force, which involves intense personal effort and struggle, Outer Power is about tapping into the natural flow of opportunities and synchronicities in The Universe. It's the ability to attract resources, connections, and circumstances that align with one's intentions, often with minimal direct effort. This concept suggests that when individuals align their intentions, beliefs, and energy with The Quantum Field, they open themselves to a smoother, more harmonious path towards their goals. Outer Power is about harnessing the supportive forces of The Universe, allowing a person to navigate through life's challenges with grace and ease, and manifesting desired realities by being in tune with the natural rhythms and cues of the world around them.

Soul Code

The Soul Code represents the unique essence of an individual, encapsulating their deepest desires, intrinsic talents, and fundamental truths. It serves as a personal blueprint, steering passions and purposes that echo one's genuine self.

The Soul Code is crucial for aligning your energy with The Quantum Field, thereby attracting experiences and opportunities that are a true reflection of your innermost being. It involves delving into what truly fulfills you, transcending societal conditioning and superficial yearnings.

By attuning to your Soul Code, you resonate with a frequency that aligns with an ideal Sector of reality, specifically tailored for you. This attunement ensures that your external reality mirrors not only your innermost nature but also guides you to a realm of existence where your true potential can flourish.

Heart and Mind Synchronization

Heart and Mind Synchronization refers to the powerful alignment of one's emotional intuition (Heart) with rational thought and reasoning (Mind). It's about creating a harmonious balance between your feelings and thoughts, ensuring they work in tandem rather than in opposition. This synchronization is crucial for making decisions that are not only logically sound but also resonate deeply on an emotional level. When your Heart and Mind are in sync, your actions and choices are more aligned with your true self and The Universe, leading to a more authentic and fulfilling life. This state of alignment facilitates a smoother navigation through the Sectors of Reality, as it ensures that your actions are driven by a blend of intuitive wisdom and rational understanding, opening pathways to greater success and contentment.

Goals and Doors

Goals and Doors symbolize the objectives we set for ourselves and the opportunities or pathways that open as a result of our actions and mindset. Goals represent our desired outcomes, aspirations, or states of being that we strive to achieve. They are the targets we set in our journey of personal and professional growth. Doors, on the other hand, symbolize the opportunities or possibilities that emerge as we pursue our goals. These can be unexpected chances, new connections, insights, or shifts in our environment that align with our intentions and efforts. The concept emphasizes that while setting goals is essential, being open and responsive to the Doors that appear is equally important. This approach encourages a dynamic interaction with The Quantum Field, where setting clear goals and staying attuned to arising opportunities creates a powerful synergy, leading to the realization of these goals in often surprising and serendipitous ways. It highlights the importance of both intention and flexibility in navigating one's path to success and fulfillment in the desired Sectors of Reality.

The Script

The Script refers to the predetermined narrative or set of expectations that society, culture, or individuals impose upon themselves. It's like a pre-written storyline that dictates how one should think, act, and live. The Script often includes societal norms, cultural beliefs, family expectations, and personal limitations based on past experiences. Following The Script can lead to a life lived on autopilot, where decisions are made based on external pressures rather than personal desires or authenticity. Breaking free from The Script involves questioning these ingrained beliefs and societal norms, and consciously choosing to write your own narrative. It's about embracing your unique path and making choices that align with your true self, rather than adhering to a predetermined plot. In doing so, you open yourself to new possibilities, greater freedom, and a more authentic expression of who you are, paving the way for a reality that resonates more deeply with your individual aspirations and values.

The Mindfilm

The Mindfilm refers to the mental imagery or scenarios that individuals play in their minds, akin to a personal movie. This concept encapsulates the visualization process where you project your desires, goals, and aspirations as vivid, detailed mental scenes. It's akin to creating a film in your mind, complete with sensory details, emotions, and experiences that reflect the reality you wish to manifest. The Mindfilm is a powerful tool for shaping your reality because it aligns your subconscious mind with your conscious desires, reinforcing your intentions and goals. By regularly visualizing your desired outcomes in this detailed, immersive way, you effectively program your mind to recognize and align with opportunities that can make these scenarios a reality. It emphasizes the principle that the mind can't distinguish between what's vividly imagined and what's real, thereby attracting experiences that resonate with the imagery you've created. The practice of creating and revisiting your Mindfilm harnesses the power of visualization to reinforce your path towards desired Sectors of Reality, making it a critical aspect of transforming thoughts and aspirations into tangible outcomes.

SectorSyncing

SectorSyncing is the process of aligning your personal energy, intentions, and actions with the specific Sector of Reality that resonates with your desired outcomes. It involves fine-tuning your thoughts, emotions, and behaviors to be in harmony with the frequency of the Sector you aim to access or manifest in your life. This concept is akin to tuning into a specific radio frequency to catch a desired station; when you sync up with the right Sector, you unlock experiences, opportunities, and connections that are aligned with your goals and aspirations.

SectorSyncing requires a conscious effort to maintain a vibrational match with your target Sector. It's about embodying the mindset, emotional state, and actions consistent with the reality you wish to experience. For example, if you aim to thrive in a Sector characterized by abundance and success, your thoughts, feelings, and actions must reflect confidence, positivity, and proactive steps towards your goals. This synchronization is not just about wishful thinking but involves practical steps and consistent behavioral patterns that steer your life trajectory towards the chosen Sector.

By practicing SectorSyncing, you essentially navigate The Quantum Field with intention, steering your life's course towards Sectors that resonate with your highest aspirations. It's a strategic approach to reality creation, where you become an active participant in shaping your life's path, harmonizing your Inner World with the external Universe to manifest desired experiences and outcomes.

Negative Mindfilm

The Negative Mindfilm is a strategic mental exercise used to counterbalance overly optimistic expectations. It involves visualizing scenarios where goals don't materialize, serving as a grounding tool. This approach might seem counterproductive, but it helps in several ways:

1. Reducing Importance: by imagining the failure of your plans, you detach from the intense pressure and anxiety linked to specific outcomes. It's a mental rehearsal for disappointment, lessening its sting when reality diverges from expectations.
2. Neutralizing Disproportionate Energy: confronting potential failures head-on dissipates the emotional and mental overload often associated with personal goals. This process keeps your energy balanced and prevents emotional spirals.

3. Building Resilience Against Gravity: anticipating setbacks prepares you for the real thing. If setbacks do occur, their impact is less shocking, as you've already mentally navigated these scenarios.
4. Emotional and Mental Equilibrium: regularly engaging with the Negative Mindfilm keeps you adaptable and emotionally stable, ready to face life's uncertainties with clarity and confidence.

The Negative Mindfilm is not about nurturing pessimism or self-defeat. Instead, it's a tactical method to maintain emotional balance, ensuring you're prepared for any outcome in your quantum journey. It's about embracing potential disappointments in controlled bursts, not to dwell in negativity but to disarm its impact and continue your path with resilience and adaptability.

Transport Links

Transport Links symbolize the incremental steps or stages that lead to the realization of a goal. They are the successive milestones that bridge the gap between your current position and your ultimate objective. Imagine them as links in a chain connecting you to your goal. Instead of overwhelming yourself with the entire journey, you focus on one link at a time. Each link represents a significant phase in your journey, whether it's acquiring new knowledge, gaining experience, or achieving a smaller milestone. By concentrating on one link at a time, you move steadily towards your goal, ensuring that you are prepared for each subsequent stage. Transport Links emphasize the importance of progression and adaptation, allowing for flexibility and responsiveness as circumstances evolve. By utilizing Transport Links, you navigate your path with focus and clarity, aligning your actions and decisions with each step towards your ultimate goal. This approach ensures a structured yet adaptable journey, making the attainment of complex goals more manageable and systematic.

The Labyrinth

The Labyrinth is a metaphor for the complex, self-created maze within our minds, constructed from the walls of Importance, insecurities, self-doubt, and feelings of inadequacy. This mental Labyrinth becomes more constricting and intricate as we attribute greater Importance to our perceived negative traits and shortcomings. The walls of the Labyrinth symbolize the barriers we erect through our overemphasis on imperfections and fear of judgment, creating a sense of being trapped in a cycle of self-doubt. The key to navigating and ultimately exiting this Labyrinth is not found in the pursuit of perfecting these undesirable traits. Rather, it lies in taking action regardless of them. As we act despite our fears and perceived flaws, we diminish the Importance we place on them, causing the walls of the Labyrinth to dissolve. This act of moving forward, irrespective of self-imposed limitations, leads to a liberation from the mental maze, fostering personal growth, confidence, and the realization that we are not defined by our insecurities. It teaches us that progress and success are attainable, not by eradicating our flaws, but by courageously moving through them.

Cracks in The Matrix

Cracks In The Matrix symbolize those rare, unexpected moments that reveal opportunities for significant change or advancement. They are like brief glitches in the usual fabric of reality, offering glimpses into alternative paths or Sectors of

Reality. These Cracks represent deviations from the typical Scripts of life, where one can upgrade their version of reality. They might manifest as unusual occurrences, serendipitous encounters, or seemingly random opportunities that diverge from the norm. Engaging with these Cracks requires a keen sense of awareness and the courage to step into the unknown. It involves recognizing these moments as more than coincidences but as intentional invitations from The Quantum Field to explore new possibilities and pathways. Cracks in The Matrix are gateways to transformative experiences, leading to personal growth, unexpected successes, and a deeper alignment with one's Quantum journey. They are The Quantum Field's nudge towards greater Sectors, often laden with golden opportunities and are essential passageways to prosperity in both tangible and intangible forms.

The Candy Bridge

Candy Bridges refer to those serendipitous shortcuts or pathways that unexpectedly appear in your journey, accelerating your progress towards a goal or a desired state of being. They symbolize opportunities or connections that present themselves almost magically, offering a faster or more efficient route to your objectives. Candy Bridges can take various forms such as a piece of crucial advice, a sudden invitation, a chance meeting that opens new Doors, or even a stroke of luck that propels you forward unexpectedly. These Bridges are about recognizing and seizing opportunities that align perfectly with your intentions, allowing for swift and often surprising advancements. Engaging with Candy Bridges requires a keen awareness and readiness to act; they are about spotting these golden chances in your external environment and harnessing them effectively. By tuning into these opportunities and embracing them, you can move rapidly through The Quantum Field, navigating towards higher Sectors of reality with ease and grace. Candy Bridges are essential elements in Quantum Capitalism, representing The Universe's way of facilitating your journey towards success, fulfillment, and the realization of your aspirations.

The Law of Advantage

The Law of Advantage refers to the principle that in every situation, regardless of its apparent disadvantages or challenges, there exists an inherent advantage or opportunity. This Law emphasizes the concept that every circumstance, even those that seem unfavorable or problematic, can be leveraged for positive growth, learning, and advancement. The Law of Advantage encourages individuals to shift their perspective from seeing obstacles to recognizing opportunities. It's about understanding that every challenge is an opening for improvement, every setback a chance to refine strategies, and every failure a lesson in resilience and adaptation. This approach is crucial in Quantum Capitalism, as it promotes a mindset that consistently seeks out the silver lining or the hidden benefit in every scenario. By applying the Law of Advantage, Quantum Capitalists are able to transform potential losses into gains and turn what might seem like dead ends into new pathways. It's about harnessing the potential in every moment and using it to propel oneself towards greater success and fulfillment in their journey through The Quantum Field.

Anomalous Action

This is the practice of intentionally stepping outside of one's habitual routines and comfort zones to create new opportunities and pathways in life. It involves embracing change, exploring uncharted territories, and taking risks that may seem unconventional or counterintuitive. By engaging in actions that diverge from the norm, individuals can stimulate growth, discover hidden potentials, and align themselves with unique and rewarding opportunities in The Quantum Field. Anomalous Action is about challenging the status quo, nurturing adaptability, and fostering creativity, leading to personal and financial breakthroughs. It's a strategy for those who dare to experiment with the fabric of their reality, seeking to transform their life Script into a dynamic, evolving narrative.

Matrix Self

Matrix Self refers to the concept of one's identity and existence within the framework of The Matrix, a metaphorical representation of the conventional, routine, and often predictable aspects of daily life. It encompasses how individuals perceive themselves and their roles in the world, typically shaped by societal norms, expectations, and their own patterns of behavior.

The Matrix Self is the self-image or persona that individuals construct based on their interactions with the external world and the roles they play in society. It can be influenced by factors such as cultural norms, family dynamics, societal pressures, and personal experiences. This concept suggests that individuals may conform to certain patterns of behavior and thought, often remaining within their comfort zones and the confines of societal expectations.

In the context of personal development and Quantum Capitalism, breaking free from the limitations of the Matrix Self is essential. It involves exploring new possibilities, embracing change, and taking actions that go beyond one's comfort zone and preconceived identity. By doing so, individuals can tap into their true potential, discover hidden talents, and create a more fulfilling and dynamic reality that transcends the constraints of The Matrix.

In essence, Matrix Self represents the self-image and identity that can either confine individuals to a routine and predictable life or serve as a starting point for transformation and personal growth in the Quantum Capitalism framework.

Quantum Self

The Quantum Self refers to the concept of an individual's self-identity and existence in the context of Quantum Capitalism and personal development. Unlike the Matrix Self, which is limited by routine, societal norms, and predictable patterns, the Quantum Self represents a more expansive and dynamic sense of self.

In the framework of the Quantum Self:

1. **Expansive Identity:** individuals with a Quantum Self view themselves as limitless beings capable of continuous growth and transformation. They recognize that their identity is not fixed and can evolve over time.
2. **Open to Possibilities:** Quantum Selves are open to exploring new opportunities, taking risks, and embracing change. They see the world as full of possibilities and are willing to step out of their comfort zones.
3. **Alignment of Heart and Mind:** the Quantum Self is in harmony with both the emotional compass of the Heart and the analytical prowess of the Mind. This alignment

helps individuals make decisions that resonate with their true desires and values.
4. **Awareness and Synchronicity:** individuals with a Quantum Self are highly aware of their surroundings and experiences. They are attuned to synchronicities and opportunities that may lead to personal and professional growth.
5. **Continuous Learning:** Quantum Selves are lifelong learners who seek knowledge and personal development. They recognize that growth occurs through education and self-improvement.
6. **Courage and Resilience:** having a Quantum Self involves the courage to face challenges and the resilience to overcome obstacles. Individuals with this mindset are not deterred by setbacks but see them as opportunities for growth.
7. **Creative Expression:** the Quantum Self often involves creative expression and the pursuit of one's passions. Individuals may engage in creative endeavors as a means of self-discovery and personal fulfillment.

In summary, the Quantum Self represents a mindset and self-identity that transcends the limitations of the conventional Matrix Self. It is characterized by a willingness to explore, adapt, and evolve, leading to a more fulfilling and dynamic life experience. This concept aligns with the principles of Quantum Capitalism, where individuals harness their full potential to create a rich and transformative reality.

Printed in Great Britain
by Amazon